To Florence A. Browning and Jack Garriss
for their endurance and support

The owl **Hootus Climaticus Maximus** has been used by courtesy of Rainbow Touraine.

Past and Future History

A Planner's Guide

Iben Browning and Evelyn M. Garriss

Fraser Publishing Company

Past and Future History, A Planner's Guide

©1981 Iben Browning and Evelyn M. Garriss

Library of Congress Cataloging in Publication Data

Browning, Iben.
    Past and future history.

    (Contrary opinion library)
    Bibliography: p.
    1. Climatic changes— Popular works. I. Garriss, Evelyn M., 1949-   . II. Title.
III. Series.
QC981.8.C5B74   551.6   81-69751
ISBN 0-87034-063-8   AACR2

Book design by Mary Jaquier for The Couching Lion, Winooski, Vermont
Text typeset in Palatino by Northlight Studio Press
Titles typeset in Matt Antique by RW Roulston
Printed by Braun-Brumfield, Ann Arbor, Michigan

Contents

List of Figures

Introduction

This book is written for non-scientists — especially for business, farmers, and other professionals whose activities are affected by climate and weather.

Geologists, anthropologists, archeologists, palynologists, and indeed every kind of specialist will find his own subject short-changed and inadequately rigorous.

We expect that this book will be a bore to mystics, unless they like their mysteries very deep and remote, because the book deals with documented hard facts.

This book may offend scientists because it covers a wide range of subjects, and is not rigorous on any of them. The events considered were complex; there were no controls in the scientific sense; the complex events are not fully understood; and the reasoning is mostly *aposteriori*. To the end of fair warning, we quote a quote from Brier and Bradley (1964) :

> The authors cannot resist the temptation to borrow a remark from the classic by Fielding (1748), '...it is our province to relate facts, and we shall leave causes to persons of much higher genius. [1]

History as a discipline is not served, because the data tends to show that Man is not in control of his destiny; rather, his behavior in surprising detail is controlled by his environment.

To any of the above other than the business person, farmer, rancher, hunter, interested non-specialist and possibly the military or policy people — this is fair warning. This book is not your cup-of-tea.

For anyone who has to act, and whose situation is not absolutely secure, this book lays out a vignette of history and a justification for reasoning by analogy which may permit such person to infer the timing, character and gross geographical location of future events. This book is primarily for decision makers — who never have enough data.

For those who love and enjoy Mankind and marvel over his behavior; for those who enjoy rational analysis of past events; for those who are grateful for the past which made the present possible and who are not apologetic for the past which is obviously beyond control; this book is intended to be thought provoking, and hopefully, even entertaining.

Chapter I

Climatic Dominance of History

Introduction

It is obvious to the Naturalist and to the nature lover, alike, that the environment dominates everything you do.

Don't worry about it, and don't think that the assertion is profound. The statement is merely an example of circular reasoning.

The environment is everything except yourself. It is the air you breathe; the food you eat; the people around you; your pets; the Sun; the Moon; space; and even the very Laws of Nature. Since your everything constitutes your total environment, it defines a set of absolute limits of what you **can** do.

You, then, with your own mind, body, and abilities, determine what you **will** do from among the things you **can** do.

You see — there is no mystery about it.

History (and Prehistory) is the sum total of what was done; and lies within the limits of what could have been done — a rather narrow range of options.

Future history has the same narrow set of options.

It is the despair of all new administrations that they have such narrow sets of options. Most of them weren't expecting it.

Given this limiting perception of history, the task that is attempted by this book looks more nearly achievable.

Hammond (1971) points up Longacre's study of the Pueblo named Grass-hopper in Arizona — how behavior is forced by the environment:

'The study concerns the behavior of human populations under stress, especially environmental stress, a problem that Longacre thinks is at the root of the evolution of culture in the southwest (of the U.S.A.).'
'...Environmental conditions were apparently very rough during this period, which Longacre thinks was one of the selective factors leading to aggregation.' [2]

Nature works its will upon the constructs of Man, and as the Durants [3] say:

'...history is subject to geology. Every day the sea encroaches some-where upon the land, or the land upon the sea; cities disappear under the water, and sunken cathedrals ring their melancholy bells. Moun-tains rise and fall in the rhythm of emergence and erosion; rivers swell and flood, or dry up, or change their course; valleys become deserts and isthmuses become straits. To the geologic eye, all the surface of the earth is a fluid form, and man moves upon it as insecurely as Peter walking on the waves to Christ.' [3]

but

'...in the words of Pascal: 'When the universe has crushed him man will still be nobler than that which kills him, because he knows that he is dying, and of its victory the universe knows nothing." [3]

Before the grandeur and force of Nature, and the dignity of all life, and in particular — Man — one almost is seized with a convulsion of humility.

A. Prehistory

It is clear that advancing glaciers have displaced people. Failure of rain has been followed by expansion of deserts, and hunting, fishing and farming cultures have been killed or expelled by the shifting sands. Excessive rain and cold has destroyed crops and caused great famines to sweep whole pop-ulations into oblivion. Others have been hurt so badly that they lose their freedom, or are forced to abandon their ancestral homes and seek survival in the unknown with physical and intellectual tools that have already failed.

That man is found everywhere is less a monument to his explorations than to the inadequacy of every place that he has ever been because — in the words we apply to our 'Hypothesis of Equivalent Misery':

People will keep going from where they are to where they want to be until they believe that it would be as miserable where they would have gone to as where they would have come from.

The whole concept of violent resistance to invasion by residents is an effort to make a potential migrant believe that he would be unacceptably miserable where he would have to go.

In some instances, prehistoric migrations can be traced by diseases as was done by Suggs (1960). [4] Although the filaria parasite (elephantiasis) was known to the natives in Polynesia, Melanesia, and Papua in pre-contact times, it is not found prehistorically in the New World tropical areas, despite the fact that swarms of Culex or Aedes mosquitoes abound in the New World, and carry the disease in Polynesia.

Conversely, the work of Dr. Robert Proper, of Albuquerque, showed from prehistoric skeletons, that syphilis was endemic in various areas of North America, Mexico, the Caribbean and the Pacific coast of South America. Yet syphilis was unknown among the Polynesians until it was introduced by Europeans. Clearly, this very special human evidence indicates no significant New World/Polynesian traffic — at least after the origin of the diseases. (One writes off intuitively that the people could have mixed and not have transmitted venereal disease, especially in light of the attitude the Polynesian culture had (has) toward sex.)

Suggs sees the Polynesians as a Southeastern Asian mixture of preponderantly proto-Caucasoid with Mongoloid and Negroid. The latter dark-skinned (Negroid) people were reported on the South China coast by early Chinese historians, and these historical documents reveal remnants remaining there as late as the T'ang Dynasty (ca. A.D.700). The Polynesians migrated eastward from the Southeastern Asia area to the islands of the Pacific. Great population pressures occurring in severe climatic times have repeatedly forced movements on Southeastern Asian peoples.

At a still earlier time, judging by the anthropological work reviewed by Hawkes [5], man became *homo sapiens* in Africa, then migrated to the rest of the world. Davidson expresses the situation slightly differently. Pointing out that Leakey's finds of skeletons of Proconsul (25 million years — probable ancestor of man) and Zinjanthropus (2 million years — a kind of man):

'After that the story of Man's first faltering movement in the direction of civilization (see Appendix I) becomes a little less obscure, and merges into what is known as the Old Stone Age, a period of enormous length during which various types of Man appeared and disappeared, failed or

survived, found slightly better ways of living, and eventually, by selec-
tion through unnumbered generations, gave birth to our own ancestors, whether in Africa or elsewhere.' [6]

The way of life of people shifted with climate. As the climate changed, so
did the kind, quantity and amount of plant life. The herds moved with the
forage; the forage for the herds moved with the climate; and the hunters
followed the herds.

Meanwhile, a curious 'experiment' was being made by Nature. Very long
ago, the animals with backbones exhibited advantages over those with
none. The liver and muscles continued to give their possessors advantages,
and really—by now—must be considered successful. The brain as a large,
functional organ is still 'experimental' on the long-term scale. To be sure,
the opossum has had to grow a larger and larger brain through the millions
of years just to hold on to his niche as a lowly scavenger. Yet the use of the
brain by the 'possum' hardly constitutes an experiment in intelligence. The
possum still has as its ultimate defense a state of semi-shock which is equivalent to 'playing dead'—hardly an exercise in intelligence.

Man was the first species to really pit his intelligence against all aspects
of his own environment. His gains were glacially slow; but in fact, Man
finally gained control of his own development. We are today what our ancestors chose to be.

Some Environmentalists today convey the idea that, with their love of
Nature and hatred of Man and his societies, they would have chosen to be
something else—one wonders what they might have preferred to be.

B. Ancient History

It is a startling fact that Paleolithic and Neolithic men have taken up 99%
of Man's existence upon earth. [7]

Man's heritage when history came upon the scene contained almost all
of the Great Ideas of Mankind (see Appendix II). That is to say: When
history began, Man was completely Man. He had begun as proto-man, and
with his generally accepted ideas, he made the transition to Man as we know
him today. There is really very little about Man's activities that can surprise
a student of history.

Wheeler [8] pointed out that the thinkers '...in almost every century since
the time of Ancient Greece have recorded as their judgment that man is in
profound and sundry ways affected by the climatic characteristics of his
environment.' Wheeler agreed fully with the long line of his historian-

predecessors that climate makes the man. Thus:

'...the temperate zone with its seasonal changes is the best suited for human vitality, for the tropics offer too little stimulation while the heat will drain man's energies, and severely cold climates will absorb so much of his vitality that he has little left for anything else.'

This statement agrees precisely with McClelland [9] in his carefully **measured** 'need-of-Achievement' ethic.

According to Wheeler [8], Huntington (one of the early comprehensive researchers on climate and its effects on Man) identified the storm tracks as very significant. The particular track that he referred to is that zone raked by the scalloped edge of the Circumpolar Vortex*, from its lowest latitude reaches — poleward to the agricultural limit. In terms of the last 2000 years, this zone would range generally between about 30 and 55 degrees latitude; swinging further northward with the Gulf Stream.

It should be noted urgently that higher latitudes have both colder temperatures and greater variability; so temperature alone is not a simple determining factor.

The sort of climatic change that dominated Egyptian history according to Barbara Bell (1971) was drought [10]:

'...the two Dark Ages, and the numerous disasters in the periods c. 2200-2000 and c. 1200-900 B.C., can be given coherence and can all be explained at once by a single primary cause. The cause I postulate as 'historical reality' is drought — widespread, severe, and prolonged — lasting for several decades and occurring more or less simultaneously over the entire eastern Mediterranean and adjacent lands. This is not to deny the significance of contemporary political and social factors; it is, however, to assert that a climatic-economic deterioration of sufficient magnitude can set in motion forces beyond the strength of any society to withstand.'

As Bell indicated, Rhys Carpenter [11] had previously advanced the drought theory for the Second Dark Age** based on his study of the decline of Mycenaean Greece and the Hittites. Donley [12] in his doctoral dissertation done with Bryson in Wisconsin demonstrated meteorologically that, indeed, drought did occur and was indeed responsible for the decline of the Mycenaean Civilization.

---

*The volume of air over the pole which expands in winter and rotates majestically (west to east) with the pole as its axis.

** 1200-900 B.C.

During the 'revolt of nature' in which the Nile sank to and remained at a very low level, every kind of disorder swept the land. Widespread famine; hordes of invaders — from hungry wandering wretches to armed and fighting Asiatics; mutiny of the army; disintegration of the government; a peasant revolt; rise of local (i.e., feudal) lords; cannibalism; advance of the desert sand dunes into the Nile basin and across the farm land — all of these things and more tore Egypt asunder (the data include one inscription that mentioned plague).

A fast turnover of rulers occurred with as many as thirteen in a single adult lifetime. Between 31 and 40 kings ruled Egypt in a period now believed to have lasted only 60 years — from 2190-2130 B.C. Such extremities as the barrenness of peasant women (none conceived), and the murder of all children (their existence being taken as proof of immoral eating by the rich and powerful) swept the land.

A second period of disorder occurred with drought, sandstorms, invading sand dunes, low Nile, famine, invasion, civil violence and very fast turnover of kings. This period began in about 2000 and lasted about 10 years to 1990 B.C. It was about this time that the great wave of migrations occurred around the world [13], and it is almost certain that — as in the case of the Egyptians — climatic change was at the root of it.

Referring back to Donley's dissertation [12], we see that he identifies the decline of the Hittites as a drought phenomenon in which the persistent pattern was similar or identical to the five month (November 1954 - March 1955) drought period. Famine was the historical reason for the Hittite decline* about 1200 B.C.

Egypt, at the end of the 13th century, B.C., (i.e., 1200 B.C.) was plagued with land and sea invaders, drought and famine, and thus entered a Dark Age. The Libyans were among the invaders, and almost surely were precipitated into action by a severe drought — as little as 50% normal rainfall for a period of time. The Egyptians (i.e., Ramses III) had to hold off the Philistines in 1288 B.C.; but subsequently lost their freedom to the Syrian Kings who ruled from 1205 to 1197 B.C. [12] To understand the Egyptian situation, see Appendix III.

---

*Modern research has begun to throw considerable light upon events from the past which are known, but have heretofore not been understood.

Jorde and Harpending of the University of New Mexico showed mechanisms relating drought and birth decline. Dietary deficiencies lead to increased frequency of stillbirths, spontaneous abortions, and if severe, suppress menstruation. Prolonged nursing of babies also suppresses menstruation. Decreasing food supply will cause postponement of marriage. These factors and others lead to a high positive correlation between food supply (determined largely by rainfall) and birth rate. [17]

The return of the Israelites to Canaan is said to have been because of its greater productivity – the Negev being worse off than Canaan; yet the latter had a severe drought.* [12]

Donley pointed out that the flooding in the Hungarian plains probably was the cause of the hasty removal of the Phrygians into Asia Minor (Anatolia – or modern Turkey).** Soil moisture would have prevented proper seed germination, thus would have caused subsequent crop failure.

C. Modern History

It is clear from the following brief list of examples that man has not learned to manage his affairs independently of climate and changes of climate.

'General Winter' helped the Russians to withstand two colossal military invasions in recent times – Napoleon's Armies of 'twenty Nations' in 1812; and Hitler's inadequately equipped armies in 1941. Western Europeans seem unable to comprehend the severity and variability of Russian winters.

The great famine and migration in the Sahel area south of the Sahara was clearly the result of the disastrous drought. Every government in the area was overthrown during and immediately after the 1974 famine.

The battles in New Mexico (in which 10 or more people were killed) [14] is clearly associated with the tidal derivatives which have been shown elsewhere [15] to trigger volcanoes, and thereby induce weather variation. (see **Fig. 1**)

The great wheat crop failure in the Soviet Union, China and India in 1972 was the sequel of the extraordinarily cold winter of 1971-72 [16]; and the subsequent drain on world food reserves, and the 'detente' period among probable enemies derived from the cold winter. (See **Fig. 2**)

The drought in Western Europe and four extremely severe winters in the

---

*Holy Bible, Ruth 1: 1,2.

1. '...there was a famine in the land.'

2. Ruth was permitted to glean and gather after the reapers and even among the sheaves on the farm of a rich remote kinsman, Boaz. (Gleaning is picking up individual grains and heads of grain that have been dropped in the harvest. Though this practice was common in olden times, it is only in quite recent times that conditions have become so desperate that gleaning has begun again. The U.S.S.R. resorted to gleaning in the bad harvest of 1975).

**Note that the Hungarian anti-Communist revolution occurred in the year following Donley's five-month Mycenaean drought configuration (Nov. 1954 - March 1955). The shift in climate could well have triggered the dissatisfactions (revolutions) that led to the emigration of 10% of the Hungarian population in 1956.

Eastern U.S. have reminded people how small is the power of humans when pitted against the climate. In quiet and steady times, people quickly forget their limitations.

Bibliography

INTRODUCTION

[1] Brier, Glenn W. and Donald A. Bradley (1964) The Lunar Synodical Period and Precipitation in the United States. *Journal of the Atmospheric Sciences* 21 [4]: 386-395.

I. CLIMATIC DOMINANCE OF HISTORY

[2] Hammond, Allen L. (1971) Research Topics: The New Archaeology: Toward a Social Structure. *Science* 172: 1119-1120.
[3] Durant, Will and Ariel Durant (1968) *The Lessons of History*. Simon and Schuster; New York.

A. PREHISTORY

[4] Suggs, Robert C. (1960) *The Island Civilizations of Polynesia*. The New American Library; New York.
[5] Hawkes, Jacquetta (1963) *History of Mankind: Cultural and Scientific Development* Vol. I, Part 1, Prehistory. The New American Library; New York.
[6] Davidson, Basil (1964) *The African Past*. Little, Brown and Company; Boston, Toronto.

B. ANCIENT HISTORY

[7] Bone, Robert G. (1964) *Ancient History*. Littlefield, Adams & Co.; Paterson, N.J.
[8] Wheeler, Raymond Holder (1943) The Effect of Climate on Human Behavior in History. Transactions of the Kansas Academy of Science: 46.
[9] McClelland, David C. (1961) *The Achieving Society*. D. Van Nostrand and Company.
[10] Bell, Barbara (1971) The Dark Ages in Ancient History: The First Dark Age in Egypt. *AJA* 75: 1-26.
[11] Carpenter, Rhys (1966) *Discontinuity in Greek Civilization*. Cambridge University Press.
[12] Donley, David Lee (1971) Analysis of the Winter Climatic Pattern at the Time of the Mycenaean Decline. A thesis submitted in partial fulfill-

ment of the requirements for the degree of Doctor of Philosophy (Meteorology) at the University of Wisconsin.

[13] Winkless, Nels III and Iben Browning (1975) *Climate and the Affairs of Men.* Harper's Magazine Press; New York.

C. MODERN HISTORY

[14] *Browning Newsletter* Vol. 1, No. 5, (June 21, 1977) Migrations, Raids, Tribute, Taxes and Transfer Payments.

[15] Roosen, Robert G., Robert S. Harrington, James Giles and Iben Browning (1976) Earth Tides, Volcanoes and Climatic Change. *Nature* 261: 680-682 (24 June 1976).

[16] Kukla, G. J. and H. J. Kukla (1974) Increased Surface Albedo in the Northern Hemisphere. *Science* 183: 709-714. *Note:* Other like data using the Kuklas' format is added by way of updating, sucMOSAIC, Sept-Oct. 1978.

[17] Jorde, L.B., and H.C. Harpending (1976) Cross-spectral Analysis of Rainfall and Human Birth Rate: An Empirical Test of a Linear Model. *Journal of Human Evolution* 5: 129-138 (1976).

Foreword to
Chapters II, III and IV

We seek the reader's indulgence for having the audacity to attempt to bring together, hopefully in readable language, the major factors which produce the Earth's climatic changes.

Perhaps the problem has never been better stated than by Gordon Manley (1961) in his report on a symposium titled:

Solar Variations, Climatic Change and Related Geophysical Problems*
His concluding paragraph follows:

It became abundantly clear how large a number of investigators are patiently accumulating evidence of the amplitude, character, effects and especially the dating of climatic fluctuations all over the world. Speculations regarding the causes abound; supporters of each of the popular theories — solar variation, atmospheric turbidity, carbon dioxide, ozone, variations in the Earth's orbital elements — find their several gods alternately set up and cast down. Workers in one field find themselves unable to judge the validity of the evidence from other disciplines; in this regard, the sessions and the informal discussion resulting from personal encounters between different kinds of specialists are for many a real help. A great deal of enjoyment is had by all, and those who are tempted to advocate simple explanations are repeatedly reminded of the complexity of the problems they so hopefully seek to solve. It now seems almost certain that no one simple panacea is in any way adequate to explain the intriguing patterns of climatic fluctuation to which the evidence points. Almost all the many processes involved seem likely to play some essential part, small or large. The forthcoming volume of papers will provide welcome reading.

GORDON MANLEY

* from *Nature* 190: 967-968.

Chapter II

Mechanics of Climate — Very Long Term

Introduction

There are theories all over the place concerning what causes climates to vary.

An outstanding piece of intellectual health is that what people are arguing about is WHAT causes climate to vary; not WHETHER it does.

As a first approach to wisdom, let it be pointed out also, that climatologists agree that the last few decades have been uncommonly warm in the Northern Hemisphere.

Now for the first question — given that:

(1) It has been unusually warm* [18]; and

(2) It is changing** [18 and 19].

What is happening to climate?

---

*Quoted from reference [18]: 'The present pattern of world civilization has developed during our present interglacial period. If the past is any guide to the future, we must expect that this balmy period in the earth's history will eventually end, with a return to the predominantly glacial conditions prevailing during the bulk of the last two million years.'

'...There is a growing volume of evidence that the extraordinary warmth of the early 20th Century is drawing to a close...'

**'...and that we are entering a period of less favorable climate worldwide. Snow and pack ice boundaries have been advancing in northern latitudes. Warmth-loving animals in Europe and North America are shifting their ranges southward...'

The reason this is important is that if you know what factors are causing the change; and if those factors are analyzable in physical terms, then projections of the future can be made.

There are three factors which occur in nature that have been widely discussed in the literature as individual facts, and these appear to account for the lion's share of climatic change. The people who claim that PEOPLE are changing the climate are probably just overwhelmed by Man's seeming importance; and have no appreciation of Man's truly trivial position.

If you want to impress yourself with the smallness of Man's presence on this globe, do this experiment: Imagine, if you will, what would happen to you, if you could rent an airplane; fill its tank with gasoline; fly it in a randomly chosen straight line until it runs out of gas. Look around for a place to land.

If you survive the landing, look around for gasoline. Ninety-nine times out of a hundred, you will be many miles from available gasoline. The point is:

Man occupies a mighty small part of the land; and even so, most of the world is water. When you do find people, you find very few of them with gasoline, smokestacks, big machinery, etc., or anything else that would permit them, even theoretically, to affect the world.

The problem is that environmentalists and others who think Man is altering the world live in cities. If they earned their way by living and working in the country, they wouldn't be environmentalists. In the country, the 'varmints' kill your chickens and steal your eggs; coyotes, wolves and wild dogs kill your sheep, and the wooly-worms kill your crops and pastures. On farms, your goslings drown in the rain, snakes bite the turkeys, and rabbits eat your carrots. Then you have a drought or flood. You are constantly and severely humbled so that you never get the impression that humans can influence the world very much, if at all. The only life forms that seem to be threatened from the country vantage point is your own and everything you need for survival. The environmentalists and the bureaucrats are on the side of the damned 'varmints'.

The point of these observations is that warm climate gives rise to easy overhead, and a lot of ideas that utilize overhead. All such ideas go away in severe climatic times like those before us. Any investments in those sorts of things will be lost as they are abandoned.

It's a true statement that people have done so little to the planet that in the world as a whole, you have to have a sensitive instrument tuned to particular things to detect Man's effect.

As far as Man's effect on climate is concerned, it is a good first approximation to ignore Man entirely. He has had no appreciable effect.

But if not Man, then what?

Following is a table of physical factors which have been documented in the following text, except that the very longest periods are not to be addressed in detail. It is not supposed here that the literature search has been completely exhaustive; but it has been quite thorough.

The student who pursues the subject through the references will find that each reference has a sizeable number of references, etc.

Documented Periodicities of Climate

	TIME (YRS)	REFERENCES
Geological Ages from Bolide (Large Meteorite) Strikes	10-40 MIL.	[20,21,22]
Unknown Cause	c.9.5 MIL.	[23]
Variation in orbital ellipticity	c.100,000	[24]
Variation in Earth tilt in orbit	c.42,000	[24,25]
Polar precession period	c.26,000	[24]
Polar precession half-period	c.13,000	[25]
Geomagnetic period	c.8,600	[26,27]
Magnetic pole precession (Dipole field)	c.7,200	[27]
Magnetic pole precession (Non-dipole field)	c.1,600	[28,29,31]
Tidal cycle (small)	1,682	[32]
Magnetic intensity period (precession of ellipse — semi-period)	c.800	[31,33]
Tidal Beat (very large)	353	(op.cit. I.C. [14])
Tidal beat (large)	179	[32]
Sunspot cycle	178	[34]
Sunspot cycle/Tidal cycle: BEAT	44.5	[35]
'Double sunspot cycle'; sunspot/tidal: BEAT	22	[36,37]
Tidal beat	19	[38]
Tidal beat	18.6	[38]
Sunspot cycle	11.125	[39,40]
Tidal cycle	8.85	[38]
Chandler Wobble (energized by earthquakes) according to Mullan	c.428 days	[41,42]
Annual cycle (common knowledge)	365.2422 days	
Anomalistic tidal cycle	27.5545 days	[38]
Lunar declinational (tropical) tidal cycle-twice	27.2122 days	[38]
Fortnightly synodic tidal wave	14.7653 days	[38]
Polar vortex peripheral oscillations	6.6486 days	[43]

A. Bolide Strikes

Mullan (1973) [44] proposed that earthquake waves energize the geomagnetic dynamo. He calculated that fluid motion in the iron core may be sufficiently energized by earthquakes that it has enough energy to be in equipartition with magnetic fields as large as 100 gauss — an extremely impressive amount of magnetic energy. He further states that seismic waves from meteoritic impacts have sufficient energy to reverse the earth's magnetic field every 170,000 years.

Urey [20] showed that geologic eras lasting about ten million years could be, and probably are terminated by the impacts of billion-metric-tons-mass meteorites. Alvarez [22] and his co-workers showed that the species extinctions (dinosaurs, etc.) and the end of the Cretaceous Era were brought about by the collision of an asteroid (bolide) with the Earth. The size of the object was ten plus or minus four kilometers (6.25 plus or minus 2.5 miles) in diameter. This event, 65 million years ago put into the Earth the energy that subsequently raised the Rocky Mountains. It is estimated that the explosion blew 15,000 cubic miles of rock — ground up to powder — into the near space around the Earth. The midday sun would have been no brighter than 10% of ordinary moonlight. Things died in the 2 to 3 years of darkness that followed the explosion.

The frequency of such massive events, which have shaped the geological and biological history of the Earth, is known to be compatible with the density and size of asteroids that are available in the solar system. The great round scars on all the planets and moons are the price of Solar System membership.

Among the kinds of evidence for such events is the magnetic field switch that occurs. The impact stirs up the liquid iron core, which shifts the magnetic field [21].

Öpik showed in 1963 [45] that the supply of asteroids (bolides) in the Solar System is great enough to continue the bombardment of the Earth and the other planets and moons for many, many millions of years into the future. Thus far, such explosion marks have been shown on the Earth, Moon, Mars, Venus, both of Mars' moons — Phobos and Diemos, the moons of both Jupiter and Saturn, and the planet Saturn. In short — every Solar System body that we have been able to examine has had the marks.

Geomagnetic reversals — theoretically caused by these massive collisions — have been shown by Cox [26] to be on the average of about every 230,000 years, with about twenty intensity fluctuations per reversal.

The lines of evidence all converge upon one concept:

(1) There are large objects in the Solar System, and some among their number have collided with the Earth and the other members of the system.

(2) The supply of such objects is still large. The 'bullets left in the shooting gallery' remain in the tens of thousands.

(3) The energy of collisions is demonstrably great enough to explain the following mysteries:

A. Species 'kill-offs';

B. Magnetic field switching;

C. Tektite splashes;

D. Mountain building;

E. Continental drift; and

F. The energy — though not the mechanism of the Ice Ages.

The energies of these colossal explosions are astounding. The crescent southeastern shore of Hudson Bay implies a crater some 275 miles in diameter. In South Africa, the 'Vredefort structure' — circular in shape, and some 75 miles across — has been demonstrated to be of bolide-strike origin.

The fabulous explosive power blows chunks of material back into space where they orbit the Sun, intersecting Earth's orbit again and again until some day, they too collide in the fiery display of a rock returning to its Earthly home as a meteorite.

These great Earth energies; the movements of continents poleward or equatorward; the upthrust of great mountain chains which interfere with airflow; the enshrouding of the Earth with sunlight-blocking dust; — these things, and more, clearly modify the Earth's climate. These ideas, once conceived, are so obvious that it is almost impossible to recall why it was not obvious before.

These events are not confined to the obscure geological past. One historic event may have had a real bearing on our recent past, and may have contributed to the immediate past so specifically as to be a major cause of today's geopolitics.

The following quote from Calame and Mulholland (1978) [46] sets the scene: '...the chronicles of Gervase of Canterbury include a striking eyewitness description that may be interpreted as being of the scattering of debris from a major (bolide) impact on the lunar surface. This was viewed by several 'reliable' persons on the evening of 18 June 1178, Julian calendar (25 June 1178 Gregorian calendar). Apparently, the lunar crescent, which was very thin, was partly obscured by several successive events cutting the horns apart. It is clear that these witnesses were convinced that this remarkable sequence of events was truly of lunar origin...'

Calame and Mulholland found that lunar data taken with presently available techniques and instruments is compatible with the bolide-strike hypothesis, which was originally advanced by J. B. Hartung. The Moon is still resonating from some cause as it should be from the Giordano Bruno event.

The crater is not visible from Earth, but with a diameter of 20 kilometers (12.5 miles), it would have lost some 4.5 cubic miles of dust and debris TO THE EARTH. Such an amount is grossly equivalent to the eruption of the volcano Tamboro on April 5, 1815, on the island Sumbawa (Java), with the ejection of some 36 cubic miles of material; a part of it into the stratosphere, where it spread to cover the world. Following Tamboro, a blizzard in Connecticut on June 6, 1816, with two feet of snow, typified the grossly unusual weather and caused 'the-Year-Without-a-Summer'. Famines swept the world; 737,000 people died in Ireland, and the following two years, Egypt's greatest floods occurred.

So it must have been following the bolide strike on the backside of the Moon as witnessed in Canterbury in 1178. It is interesting that the climate turned dramatically worse as indicated by Bryson, et al. [47]. He found that the artifacts which showed the migration of the Athapascans (Navajo, Apache, and Comanche) from the drought-stricken areas of Iowa and Nebraska to the Panhandle of Texas and Oklahoma began abruptly at about that time. Of this he says:

'...With considerable statistical certainty one can say that the people were **Not** there between A.D. 1180 and 1200 and that they **Were** there by A.D. 1220. Evidently the sudden climatic change was followed by a rapid immigration of sedentary* peoples into the Panhandle — probably not as rapid as the 'Boomers' of 1889, but also not a slow drift from site to site that finally dribbled into the Panhandle.'

Tradition among the Elders of Oraibi (a very ancient Hopi Pueblo in Northeastern Arizona) is that the first Navajos who trickled into the area were unkempt, starving, wild, and so ignorant that **They Had To Be Taught How To Farm Corn.**

This was a unique time in history. The leaders of the world's peoples at that instant were of such magnitude that they stand out in bold contrast from all other times. Following is a brief description of the better known ones:

GENGHIS KHAN, Lord of the Earth, Founder of the Mongol Empire, b.1162, inherited the Leadership in 1176, ruled until his death in 1227. Con-

---

*The Iowa people had been corn farmers.

quered from Budapest to the Pacific; from Persia to the Arctic. History's **Greatest Conquerer**.

SALADIN, Leader of Islam; b.1138, (1173-1193); led the Jihad (Holy War) against, and conquered the Crusaders. He united Islam, beat the Crusaders, signed a truce with Richard the Lion Hearted giving access to Holy Places to unarmed Christians. He was an absolutely honorable enemy who kept his word to Christendom.

PHILIP II AUGUSTUS, b.1165, (Assoc.King 1179;K.1180-1223) — '...perhaps the outstanding figure of his time...' He consolidated territory for France from Normandy to Barcelona; and from the Atlantic to the Rhone River. He initiated Modern France.

WALDEMAR I THE GREAT, b.1131 (1147-81), Founder of the Waldemarian Dynasty of Denmark; led a great expansion of his Empire eastward; established Copenhagen as his capital. Stopped piracy in the Baltic.

HENRY II of England, b.1133 (1154-1189), established English hegemony over both Ireland and Scotland; established a central court; and by the Assize of Arms, made freemen responsible for the defense of England. His incompetent son, John, was forced to sign the MAGNA CARTA in 1215.

FREDERICK I (BARBAROSA), b.1123 (1152-1190), Holy Roman Emperor, presided over the dissolution of the Empire. King of Germany. Led the Third Crusade to the Holy Land, and died there.

YORITOMO, THE FIRST SHOGUN (1185-1199), gained his power in a war which lasted from 1180 to 1184, when the Taira and Fujiwara clans were destroyed by the Minamoto clan. He was the Minamoto leader, and was made by the Emperor — 'a Sei-i-tai-shogun' ('barbarian-subjugating generalissimo') or general-in-chief. The Shogunate lasted until 1867.

GHIYAS-UD-DIN OF GHOR (1173-1203) conquered Afghanistan. He assigned his brother, Mohammed of Ghor, to be Governor of Ghazne, and to expand the Empire. Mohammed of Ghor conquered Northern India for the Afghanistan Empire.

PARAKRAM BAHU, KING OF CEYLON (1164-1197) took his country '...to the Zenith of Sinhalese glory...'

BALDWIN IV, the Frankish King of Jerusalem, b.1160 (1174-1185) the 'Leper King'; admired even by his enemies for his incredible courage; and without hands, feet, face or sight (leprosy) he defeated Saladin a second time. He had first led his army to victory over the great Saladin at age 16.

Could these momentous events have been precipitated by a great bolide strike on the Moon?

The timing is right, and the dust was undoubtedly enough to change the weather for years. The occurrence was at the very time that the tidal forces (30 North Latitude) began to go up very sharply until a little after 1200 A.D.

B. Mountain-Building and Erosion

It has been said that there have been fourteen major mountain-building periods in the geological history of Earth.

It is clearly true that the strike of a huge bolide which cranks up the geological dynamo (i.e., the liquid iron core) inserts enough mechanical energy into the liquid core to build mountains. (Urey calculated that a 'cometary collision'—10E 18 grams at 45 km. per second—would yield 10E 31 ergs.) (*op.cit.* II. Intro. [20]) This incredible mass of liquid obviously rubs its mechanical motion against the walls of its container—the mantle. Motions in the mantle are known—such as the motions in the 'plumes'. (*op.cit.* II. Intro. [26]) These vertical circulating columns [48] come up from the Earth's core, and approach the crust in such places as the Hawaiian chain, Iceland and Yellowstone National Park, there to heat up the crust and supply the energy for volcanoes. Perhaps the midocean volcanic island chains all have plumes as their energy sources.

The reason the islands would occur as chains, of course, is that the crust is floating steadily by. The plume, however, stays put within the mantle, and supplies the heat for volcanoes to the crust as it passes over.

Creeping of the mantle [49] consequent to motions in the core could account for the motion of the plates (continents, etc.) which constitute the earth's crust. The writers are not aware of any hard proof of this model, however; and much geological research is required to prove such points.

This suggests a fascinating feed-back model. Plate motion can cause earthquakes either by side-slipping, or by subduction (underthrusting margins) [50]; earthquakes can stir-up the geomagnetic dynamo; and movement of this iron core may supply the motion to the plates. If this were the case, one would expect the forces and motions to converge over a period of time, and thus help to account for regularities of crustal behavior.

When collision between plates causes one to underthrust the other, several things occur:

1. Deep earthquakes [50];
2. Thickening of the crust, hence mountain building [49];
3. Generation of great heat, hence melting of crust to lava which, due to subsequent upward flotation force of the underthrust rock, pops out as a volcanic eruption; and
4. Constitute an 'oceanic deep' at the point where the underthrust contacts

the overriding plate [51].

5. Secondary folding, slipping and compressing occurs within the bodies of the plates. Wherever thickening occurs due to any of these processes, the flotation of the lighter crust to a position of equilibrium (i.e., 'isostasy') builds mountains, raises continents, raises islands from the ocean, and all of those uplifting sorts of things. [51]

As a matter of curiosity, the reader may be interested in the fact that — when the ice cap that covered Scandanavia melted, the land began to rise. Since then, "...the area has raised 500 meters(1640feet)and isostatic readjustment has not yet been achieved. There still remain some 210 meters (689 feet) of height to regain, which threatens to leave a good number of Baltic ports high and dry, although it is true that it takes a long time for all this to happen". ([49] p. 93)

Once a plate projects above the level of the oceans, it begins to modify climate.

The absorption of sunlight by land and water is different. If the land mass is large and high, it physically lifts the air over it, and on occasion drops out its moisture. The Himalayas are an almost total barrier to the south-to-north passage of moisture in the winds, thus producing the great central Asian deserts.

Coolness of high altitude mountains determines that the moisture remains as a solid (ice or snow). If the mountain's height and the climate combine to prevent the ice from melting, a glacier forms; and under its own pressure, it flows.

On the Earth, the water and wind make common cause in weathering away the mountains; and removing them ultimately to the sea from which they originally emerged. ([49] pp.94-5) The richness of life which gets a free ride on all of these magnificent astronomical and geological processes is a by-product of the energies available from sunlight, and the shifting elements of wind, water and earth.

For life survives on negative entropy — sapping up the energies which Nature uncaringly supplies.

"I exist."
Said the Man
To the Universe.
"Even so,"
Replied the Universe —
"I feel no sense of obligation."
Anonymous

C. Orbital Mechanics

Enormous amounts of work have been done in solar-system astronomy, surely the MOST precise science.

Vernekar [52] calculated both orbital and insolation factors. The change in amount of sunlight arriving on the earth — a function of 1) solar intensity, 2) mean solar distance, 3) and position of the earth — is a determinant of climate.

Hays, Imbrie and Shackleton (*op.cit.* II Intro. [24]) and Kerr [53] showed that the orbital mechanical periods were indeed the periods shown by test as temperature periodicity in sea-bottom cores. The mechanism may not be as simple as this insolation, or input sunlight-model, suggests, however.

We believe that the change in orbit produces its effect — not by the effect of the earth's position on sunlight reaching the earth — but rather by the change in tidal forces which trigger volcanoes; then these, in turn modify incoming sunlight with volcanic dust in the stratosphere, and increase cloud cover due to seeding the volcanic debris.

Quoting Kerr in his extraordinarily concise specification of the problem:

"While most researchers now believe that the influence of orbital variations on climate is real enough, many still hold strong reservations about the ability of orbital variations to actually control major climate cycles. One problem is the unexplained dominance of the 100,000-year cycle. This cycle has been seen in many geological records, but its only connection with orbital variations is through the supposedly insignificant effect of variations in the eccentricity of the earth's orbit. The eccentricity cycle causes at most a 0.1 percent change in the total sunlight, or insolation, falling on the earth. The problem is to demonstrate a physical mechanism that can link the small eccentricity effect on insolation to the large changes in climate represented by the 100,000-year cycle. In any case, even the magnitude of the shorter cycles needs to be explained by some amplifying effect within the climate system."

The mechanism may well be known; but it remains for someone to make a cohesive study and tie it all together.

Hamilton (II. Intro. [38]) discussed and demonstrated tidal triggering of volcanoes extensively. His concluding remark was:

"One naturally wonders if the Milankovitch theory of causation of periodic continental glaciation (van Woerkom, 1953) may be correct but for the wrong reason. If volcanic activity can help induce glacial episodes, rapid climate warming might be attributed to quiescence following the decrease in tidal stresses related to lowering of sea level (and perhaps reduction in length of day) resulting from the accumulation of large amounts of ice in polar regions."

In fact, the volcanism mechanism can be demonstrated as is shown in the following section, and it is to be hoped that someone will do a definitive, quantitatively complete study to resolve the issue.

One is tempted to want such a study done right away; but considering that the subject is "What really is the mechanism of the Ice Ages?" the subject isn't really all that pressing.

Some people will tell you that we might have an Ice Age within one-to-two thousand years.

Don't worry about it — they are just trying to frighten you into giving them money.

The preponderance of evidence points to an Ice Age 25-35,000 years from now. The problem cannot be regarded as more urgent than any other kind of ignorance that we suffer from.

You should suspect the motives of anyone who claims that it is urgent.

Bibliography

II. MECHANICS OF CLIMATE — Very long term

INTRODUCTION

[18] Interdepartmental Committee for Atmospheric Sciences (1974) Report of the Ad Hoc Panel on The Present Interglacial, Federal Council for Science and Technology, Science and Technology Policy Office, National Science Foundation, ICAS 188-FY75, August 1974.

[19] Dansgaard, W.K., S.J. Johnson, H.B. ·Clausen and C.C. Langway, Jr. (1971) 3. Climatic Record Revealed by the Camp Century Ice Core. *Late Cenozoic Glacial Ages*; K.K. Turekian, Ed.

[20] Urey, Harold C. (1973) Cometary Collisions and Geological Periods. *Nature* 242: 32-3 (2 March 1973)

[21] Glass, Billy P. and Bruce C. Heezen (1967) Tektites and Geomagnetic Reversals. *Scientific American* 217 (1): 32-38 July 1967.

[22] Alvarez, Luis W., Walter Alvarez, Frank Asaro, and Helen V. Michel (1980) Extraterrestrial Cause for the Cretaceous-Tertiary Extinction. *Science* 208 (4448): 1095-1108 (6 June 1980)

[23] Wolfe, J.A. (1971) Tertiary Climatic Fluctuations and Methods of

Analysis of Tertiary Floras. *Paleogeography, Paleoclimatology, Paleoecology* 9: 27-57.

[24] Hays, J.D., John Imbrie and N.J. Shackleton (1976) Variations in the Earth's Orbit: Pacemaker of the Ice Ages. *Science* 194: 1121-32 (10 Dec. 1976)

[25] Van Den Heuvel, E.P.J. (1966) On the Precession as a Cause of Pleistocene Variations of the Atlantic Ocean Water Temperatures. *Geophys. J.R.Astr. Soc.* 11: 323-36 (1966)

[26] Cox, Allan (1969) Geomagnetic Reversals. *Science* 163 (3864): 237-245 (17 Jan. 1969)

[27] Nagata, Takesi (1965) Main Characteristics of Recent Geomagnetic Secular Variation. *Jour. Geomagnetism and Geoelectricity* 17 (3-4): 263-76 (1965)

[28] Bucha, V., R.E. Taylor, Rainer Berger and E.W. Haury (1970) Geomagnetic Intensity: Changes during the Past 3000 Years in the Western Hemisphere. *Science* 168: 111-4 (3 April 1970)

[29] Malin, S.R.C., and I. Saunders (1973) Rotation of the Earth's Magnetic Field. *Nature* 245: 25-6 (7 September 1973)

[30] Lowes, F.J. with answer by S.R.C. Malin and I. Saunders (1974) Rotation of the Magnetic Field. *Nature* 248: 402-5 (29 March 1974)

[31] Riketake, Tsuneji (1966) *Electromagnetism and the Earth's Interior.* Elsevier Publishing Company; Amsterdam, London, New York.

[32] Browning, Iben (1978) The 350-Year and the Approximate 800-Year Tidal Cycles — I've Finally Found Them. *The Browning Newsletter* 2(1): 1-2 (21 Feb. 1978)

[33] King, J.W., and D.M. Willis (1974) Magnetometeorology: Relationships between the Weather and Earth's Magnetic Field. FROM: Bandeen, W.R. and S.P. Maran, Editors (1974) Possible Relationships Between Solar Activity and Meteorological Phenomena *Proc. Symp.* 7-8 (Nov. 1973) NASA-Goddard X-901-74-156 (Preprint)

[34] Wolff, Charles L. (1976) Timing of Solar Cycles by Rigid Internal Rotations. Laboratory for Solar Physics and Astrophysics, NASA-Goddard Space Flight Center, Greenbelt, Md. (Preprint)

[35] Kullmer, G.J. (1943) A Remarkable Reversal in the Distribution of Storm Frequency in the United States in Double Hale Solar Cycles, of Interest in Long-Range Forecasting. *Smithsonian Miscellaneous Coll.* 103 (10): 1-20 (5 April 1943)

[36] Abbot, C.G. (1955) Periodic Solar Variation. *Smithsonian Miscellaneous Coll.* 128 (4): 1-20 (14 June 1955)

[37] Roberts, Walter Orr (1974) Relationships between Solar Activity and

Climatic Change. FROM: Bandeen, W.R. and S.P. Maran, Editors (1974) Possible Relationships Between Solar Activity and Meteorological Phenomena. *Proc. Symp.* 7-8 (Nov. 1973) NASA-Goddard X-901-74-156: pp 3-23.

[38] Hamilton, Wayne L. (1973) Tidal Cycles of Volcanic Eruptions; Fortnightly to 19-Yearly Periods. *Journal of Geophys. Research* 78 (17): 1-3 (10 June 1973)

[39] Abbot, C.G. (1952) Important Interferences with Normals in Weather Records, Associated with Sunspot Frequency. *Smithsonian Miscellaneous Coll.* 117 (11): 1-3 (20 May 1952)

[40] Abbot, C.G. (1935) Solar Variation, a Leading Weather Element. *Smithsonian Miscellaneous Coll.* 122 (4): 1-15 (4 August 1953)

[41] Hughes, David W. (1975) Earth Wobble, Day Length and Continental Drift. *Nature* 253: 591-2 (20 February 1975)

[42] O'Connell, R.J. and Adam M. Dziewonski (1976) Excitation of the Chandler Wobble by Large Earthquakes. *Nature* 262: 259-262 (22 July 1976)

[43] Abbot, C.G. (1949) Short Periodic Solar Variations and the Temperatures of Washington and New York. *Smithsonian Miscellaneous Coll.* 111 (13): 1-8 (4 October 1949)

A. BOLIDE STRIKES

[44] Mullan, Dermott J. (1973) Earthquake Waves and the Geomagnetic Dynamo. *Science* 181: 553-4 (10 August 1973)

[45] Öpik, Ernst J. (1963) The Stray Bodies in the Solar System Part I. Survival of Cometary Nuclei and the Asteroids. *Advances in Astronomy and Astrophysics* 2: 219-62. Academic Press; New York.

B. MOUNTAIN BUILDING AND EROSION

[46] Calame, Odile and J. Derral Mulholland (1978) Lunar Crater Giordano Bruno: A.D. 1178 Impact Observations Consistent with Laser Results. *Science* 199 (4331): 875-77 (24 February 1970)

[47] Bryson, Reid A., David E. Baerreis and Wayne M. Wenland (1970) The Character of Late-Glacial and Post-Glacial Climatic Changes. FROM: Pleistocene and Recent Environments of the Central Great Plains, Dept. of Geology, Univ. of Kansas, Special Publ. 3.

[48] Vogt, Peter R. (1977) Hot Spots. *Natural History*: 36-44 (April 1977)

[49] Calleux, Andre (1968) Trans. by J. Moody Stuart. Anatomy of the Earth. *World University Library*. McGraw Hill Book Company; New York, Toronto.

[50] Chappell, J. (1973) Astronomical Theory of Climatic Change: Status

and Problem. *Quarternary Research* 3: 221-36 (1973)
[51] Wyllie, Peter J. (1976) *The Way the Earth Works: An Introduction to the New Global Geology and Its Revolutionary Development.* John Wiley & Sons, Inc.; New York, London, Sydney, Toronto.

C. ORBITAL MECHANICS

[52] Vernekar, Anadu D. (1972) Long-Period Global Variations of Incoming Solar Radiation. *Meteorological Monographs* 12 (34): Publ. by Amer. Meteor. Soc., 45 Beacon St., Boston, Mass. 02108
[53] Kerr, Richard A. (1978) Research News: Climate Control: How Large a Role for Orbital Variations? *Science* 201 (4351): 144-46 (14 July 1978)

Chapter III

Mechanics of Climate — Intermediate Long Term

Introduction

In fact, there are three things that seem to have a big effect on long term climate. These are:

1. Volcanism;
2. Solar activity; and
3. Position of the Earth's magnetic field.

In none of these cases do we know in detail how the effect occurs. The linkage is complex. There is almost nothing in Nature that's simple. Everything is a system or part of a system. An example will make the point that natural things are inherently complex.

As an example of a system situation, consider the fact that there have been enormous efforts to put out forest fires. Yet critical studies are now showing that forests are doomed if they are not permitted to burn out from time to time. If Man stops every fire he is capable of stopping, then when the inevitable drought comes that renders the forest so flammable that Man cannot control the fire; the result is that a fire will ensue that sweeps the whole forest. The situation is that forests burn in Nature, and all of the great forest fires occur during droughts. Some forestry people now have a program of putting out man-made fires only. Which fires, if any, should be extinguished by Man depends solely on your frame of reference.

At any rate, let's circle back and admit that nothing in Nature is really simple. Keep in mind, also, that Man has no science of complexity — science is that branch of human endeavour which seeks understanding. Its primary dogma is Occam's Razor* which proposes the working principle that the SIMPLEST explanation is the most likely one to be correct. Acceptance of this hypothesis makes science a glorious tool for understanding simple things; but eliminates it as an appropriate tool for studying either Natural systems, or Nature in its entirety — which are complex.

To rule **out** normal scientific methods is not to rule IN mysticism. Just because I can't completely understand a human, a puppy, a lily, a virus or a volcano does not — for an instant — validate the supposition that any one of these has an aura, or any super-natural force or property. To rule out one thing does not inherently rule in any alternative. **Ignorance doesn't produce nor constitute knowledge.**

The fact is that some physical phenomena have been shown to relate to climate through statistical tools like correlation, chi square, T-test and multiple regression. It has been found that the mechanical distortions in the earth's orbit and position of the earth with respect to the sun occur with a timing that corresponds to the timing of the Ice Ages. It is very clear that ice on the earth is not changing the orbit; so it follows that cause-and-effect flows in the opposite direction. Orbital warp, then, is somehow a cause; temperature is somehow an effect.

A. Volcanism

Getting closer to home and the present than orbital warps or Ice Ages, Hamilton (II. Intro. [38]) took a list of volcanoes that had been prepared by someone else, and he compared the timing of their eruptions with the times of high tidal forces. Since high tidal forces are produced by certain well known astronomical configurations of earth, moon and sun, the quantitative and timing aspects are calculable to very precise tolerances.

Of course, he found that there is a relationship. There are several very precise periodicities of tidal forces, and volcanic eruptions vary at these

---

*William of Occam (1300-1349)

"Essentia non sunt multiplicanda praeter necessitatem."

"The number of entities should not be increased unnecessarily." This quote is now known as "Occam's Razor".

same periodicities; clearly cause and effect. The volcano marches to the tidal-force drummer's beat.

Since volcanoes get their driving forces from geological sources (heat and pressure); and the tidal forces, whose drum the volcano marches to, are extremely small* — it follows that the force is a trigger, somehow. An engineer would refer to a triggered process as — among other things — non-linear. The explosive gas (i.e., gas with an increasing pressure) doesn't get to expand until it ruptures its container, then it expands sharply. The question of the immediate source of energy for enough volcanism to produce the Ice Age is a fundamental question — which is at least partially explained in Appendix IV.

Any tidal force — however close it may be to a rupturing force — does not cause the volcano to rupture if it falls short of the required force; but does cause the volcano to rupture if it (plus the volcanic internal pressure) exceeds the required force by any margin, however small. This describes a trigger (indeed, a "hair-trigger") and shows that it is highly non-linear.

There are different tidal force sources — the direction and distance of both sun and moon. The planets and stars "don't amount to a hill of beans". Planetary, stellar and galactic tidal forces are calculable of course, but are too small to be measurable. Any process which responds linearly to such forces can be analyzed and the frequencies of the inputs identified.

But if there are non-linear processes such as volcanic triggering to be analyzed, one will find that the input cyclical forces have **mixed****. Beat frequencies appear. Frequency interactions occur.

This is the point at which people who "believe in cycles" go astray.

If one does a frequency analysis of a complex systems' behavior, and if there are non-linear processes taking place, he will find all sorts of harmonic and beat frequencies present. As far as linear physical causes are concerned, many of these cycles will be spurious. As far as effects are concerned, the cycles will come and go as the mixing periodicities exceed or fall below the non-linear response zones of whatever it is in the system that is responding to them.

In short, beware of **cycles**. If you don't know what is causing them; you may find that they disappear just when you have decided to count on them.

---

*The maximum differential of tidal forces compares roughly as follows: a 200-pound weight on a spring scale would decrease the measured weight at high tide by an amount equal to the weight of a single drop of water.

** The term **mixed** is used here exactly as it is used in electronics.

We can review the relationship of climate to volcanism by referring to **Figures 3** through **16.**

Figure 3. The Earth is one of the inner, small planets among a small family of planets that revolve around a perfectly ordinary star. This star — our Sun — is one of a couple of billion stars in our galaxy which is one of some one hundred-million galaxies in our Universe. (We express it this way so that you can get a grasp of the fraction of the action that you control. It's good for the humility.)

Figure 4. The Earth is layered — probably with a solid ball in the middle. This ball might be a thousand to fifteen hundred miles in diameter — it's hard to get information from down there.

The layer surrounding the ball is probably a solution of molten nickel-iron — under very high temperature and pressure. This is the liquid iron core we will refer to later.

On top of the core lies the mantle which at its high temperature and pressure acts like a squishy solid. Shear waves will pass through it — so it's solid. It creeps and flows, so it's liquid. [54 and 55]

(Physicists used to have an identity problem like that about light. They knew it was a wave, and they knew it was a particle. So the story grew that it was particulate on Mondays, Wednesdays and Fridays; and wavelike on Tuesdays, Thursdays and Saturdays.)

The part of the Earth that we take the most seriously is the scum that is floating around on the top. North America is currently floating westward at about an inch-and-a-half a year. That's why it is wrinkled on the leading edge. [56]

Figure 5. Once in a while (170,000 years on the average?) a bolide (a giant meteorite) strikes the Earth (*op. cit.* II. Intro [20]).

Think of it as a one-mile diameter bullet that comes ripping in at about 40-miles a second. It pushes a plug of atmosphere in front of it and jams a hole in the crust, finally coming to a highly compressed and completely dissatisfied stop. It proceeds to blow up with an energy of about one-and-a-half million megatons of T.N.T.

This energy blasts a hole maybe fifty miles across [57] and blows thousands of cubic miles of rock — ground up into dust and pebbles — into space*. [58]

---

*Dr. Stanislaw M. Ulam — then at Los Alamos — (co-father with Edw. Teller) of the hydrogen bomb, made a calculation at the request of Browning. His calculated rule of thumb: the Earth recovers one ton of mass (Moon dust) for every ton of T.N.T. explosion on the Moon.

Figure 6. The incredible shock waves from a two-mile diameter bolide hitting Eastern Kentucky would knock down every man-made structure east of the Mississippi River. If a one-mile diameter bolide hit an ocean deep, it would make four-mile-high tidal wave.

The shock waves of such an event would be — as are earthquake waves — both in pressure and shear (P and S). The reason geologists know that the iron core of the Earth is liquid is that shear waves are absorbed by it. It follows that the enormously energetic shear waves would be absorbed-by and would stir-up the liquid-iron core. Such a great bolide strike would produce three effects simultaneously — magnetic field reversal due to the stirred-up liquid-iron "dynamo"; tektites (splashed rock) (*op. cit.* II. Intro. [21]); and the initiation of a new geological age (*op. cit.* II. Intro. [20]).

If you stir coffee in a cup, then let it set, it will eventually quit moving. The liquid will have rubbed its mechanical energy off onto its container. Similarly, the liquid-iron core rubs its mechanical energy off onto its container which is the mantle. The mantle creeps as a result, and causes cracks that form oceans, continental drift, etc.

We postulate that the long warm ages such as the dinosaur age — when volcanism and mountain building were minimal; when continents eroded away to shallow oceans; when temperature was very warm; and which were ended by a great bolide strike (*op.cit.* II. Intro. [20]) — were periods when the liquid iron core had run down and come to rest. Probably magnetic fields were minimal at such times.

Figure 7. The new scum (i.e., crust) that wells up to the surface and pours out onto the surface of the Earth finds it already occupied, of course. Crust is consequently underthrust (a process called subduction); and, not being very well lubricated, goes jumping and crunching down producing earthquakes — which is how we discovered it was there. The heat of the Earth and the heat of friction (*op.cit.* II.B. [50]) of this process ([about 3 x 10E19] ergs/second) melts puddles of material, and the crust itself finally melts completely after having been mechanically injected (subducted) about 300 miles deep.

This is half-enough energy required to explain the amount of volcanism that would produce the Ice Ages. The other half is explained by Appendix IV as a feedback energy system resulting from water evaporating from the oceans and ice settling on the continents — primarily Northern Hemispheric, although temperatures in both the northern and southern hemispheres vary together in an Ice Age [59, 60, 61, 62, 63 and 64]. The consequence of huge water mass leaving the equator, and settling as a solid around the poles is an enormous change in angular momentum of the rotating Earth.

Figure 8. The best known great volcano was Krakatoa, both because it was so interesting, and because the Royal Society of London (which was in its heyday) made an extraordinarily complete report.

The spectacular aspects of the Explosion were:

- 36,380 were killed by tidal waves.
- Sounds of the explosion were heard 3,080 miles away on Rodriquez Island.
- Pressure waves went several times around the globe, and were repeatedly measured in Berlin.
- All vessels near the shore were stranded.
- Tremendous quantities of dust were injected 40-50 miles high into the stratosphere, resulting in extended red twilights. The main mass of ejecta went over 20 miles high.

There are whole books about this event [65], and for sheer fascination, the reader would find them hard to beat for real world excitement.

A part of the excitement is to realize that Krakatoa is only one of some 100 great volcanoes to have erupted since 1500, and is considered nominal.

There is, in other words, a running average of about one great volcano every five years during the present period of history.

And how do Man's activities compare with Nature's?

If we were to take all of the **garbage** produced by 220,000,000 Americans for a year (at 3-pounds per day), grind it into dust in a giant blender, and dump it into the stratosphere; we would have inserted only 1% as much dust as Krakatoa put up in one shot. And Krakatoa was **nominal.**

Man's effects are truly trivial.

Figure 9. The charts after which this figure was drawn were styled after charted data in a series of references [66, 67, 68, 69 and 70). Many kinds of data show the type of temperature variations of the last hundred thousand years, or so, and a variety of data also shows that such variation accompanied volcanic activity, both theoretical [71 and 72] and measured observations [73, 74, 75 and 76].

Specifically, every time there is increased volcanism, the climate gets cooler and vice versa.

Figure 10. By far the best known and understood science is Astronomy (perhaps because it comes the nearest to fitting the philosophical constraints of Occam's Razor). Workers have calculated ellipticity of the Earth's orbit back as far as 4,000,000-years, and forward for 100,000-years.

The plot of ellipticity shown in this figure turns out to correspond in a highly non-random way with change in temperature of the Earth's atmosphere as shown by change of oxygen-18 isotope concentration in microscopic sea-shells taken from cores drilled in ocean bottoms.

Every time the ellipticity of the Earth's orbit increased, the temperature plunged, with the result that an Ice Age occurred as the ellipticity was increasing.

The Ice Age **did not occur when maximum ellipticity occurred** — which one might have expected from the diminished amount of sunlight reaching the Earth.

Öpik (1965) said:

> 'The 'astronomical' (i.e., input sunlight-'insolation') theory of Quaternary climatic change is thus inadequate quantitatively as well as unconvincing chronologically."

But increasing volcanicity from rising tidal triggering forces **could** account for the Ice Age (Appendix IV).

Figure 11. Using the exceptionally well-known figures for the solar system, one of our associates calculated the vector sum tidal force envelopes (*op.cit.* I. B. [15]) and found a strong 8.85-year and somewhat weaker 179.33-year tidal force beat.

The tidal envelopes of these two periods show the variation in tidal-force maxima.

Figure 12. Interestingly, the tidal-forces in the Northern and Southern Hemispheres beat out of phase. When tidal forces are rising in one hemisphere, they are falling in the other.

Curiously, also, the equator has a 4.425-year tidal-force beat as the tilt of the earth with respect to the solar direction rocks the equator back-then-forth for each full 8.85-year tidal-force cycle.

Figure 13. The 179.33-year tidal force envelope can be examined further for a step-by-step rate of tidal force increase or decrease. This "derivative" curve is a measure of how rapidly the stress forces are changing on the crust.

Assume that you want to study large explosions. There is an easy way. Put water in a boiler, fasten the valves down tight, and build a roaring fire under it. You have arranged for a large explosion.

Now, go by it every five minutes or so, and tap it with a hammer.

You have now arranged to be there when it happens.

Similarly, volcanoes are going to go off for sure. The tidal force tap determines when, by adding a triggering strain on top of all of the strain caused by the pressure inside. The crustal retainer material finally gets a little more than it can "stand", and gives way.

Plotting these tidal derivatives against temperature as shown by Dansgaard's Greenland Ice data, we showed a very significant degree of correlation.

Why Greenland Ice?

Because Camp Century is contained year-around in the Polar Air Mass (Polar Vortex); hence the mixing of tropical air surges does not reach it. The data is pure Polar, hence it contains the oxygen-18 isotope data that, in a few years, reflects the world averages.

Figure 14. The effect of tidal forces on temperature is shown dramatically in this figure. The thirty-year running averages of English winter temperatures [78] is put on the same scale as the calculated vector-sum-high-tidal-forces at 60-degrees North Latitude. The correlation is non-random; and, of course, the temperature lags the tidal forces. The probable mechanism of relationship is tidal forces and small volcanic eruptions — as opposed to the episodic great volcanoes which a 30-year running average would suppress.

Note in particular that winter temperatures average **warmer** as tidal forces rise. This is in apparent opposition to **Figure 13** which shows temperatures **cooler** as tidal derivatives rise.

The explanation is that increased volcanism puts more debris (including sulfuric acid and ammonium sulfate) into the stratosphere; and the trickle-down into the trophosphere increases nucleation of clouds, and thereby increases cloud-cover. The result is that heat is held in in winter, and sunshine is kept out all around the year. The **winters are warmer** at high tidal forces; the **years are cooler** at the time of rising tidal forces.

Figure 15. The calculated tidal envelope (see also **Figure 13**) is plotted here relative to earthquake energy released. The earthquake data is from D.L. Anderson's paper [79]. It is easily seen from this figure that the great family of earthquakes shown by Anderson, immediately followed the highest tidal force in 1097-years (see Appendix IV. A. 60-degrees North Latitude).

These data are exceptionally reliable.

The same institution (Cal. Tech.) produced definitive proof of the relationship between tidal forces and earthquakes (Heaton [80]) in showing a specific case. His data

"...strongly suggests that shallow (less than 30 kilometers) larger magnitude oblique—slip and dip earthquakes—are triggered by tidal stress."

It comes as no surprise that earthquakes are triggered by tidal stress; because Moonquakes have been known for sometime now to be triggered by tidal stresses. For a review of this information, see reference [81]. The Moon has a clean seismic situation (no oceans, no atmosphere, and nobody stomping around). The "families" of tidal-stress triggered quakes are to be expected.

To come full-circle, note that earthquakes immediately precede, and almost surely assist, in triggering volcanoes within their areas by insulting the crustal material that contains the volcanoes' pressure [82], at least at convergent plate margins. [82]

After a general discussion of the relationship of earthquakes and volcanoes (or—in some areas—an apparent lack of relationship) Carr states (in his only remark about great volcanoes):

"In the past the two largest eruptions in Central American history (Coseguina in 1835 and Santa Maria in 1902) occurred within months after nearby great earthquakes."

Figure 16. A compilation of 568 volcanic eruptions* between 1774 and 1974 was segregated into Northern and Southern Hemisphere events. All of the volcanoes were tabulated by decade, and a running 30-year ratio of Northern Hemispheric volcanoes divided by all volcanoes—decade by decade—was calculated and plotted.

The figure shows that northern hemisphere volcanoes were "exhausted—or purged", and a period of relative geological quiet ensued after the earthquake activity shown in Figure 13, beginning around the turn of the twentieth century.

It has been in this Northern Hemisphere "volcanically exhausted" period that the climate has been so warm. The air has been extraordinarily clear.

This "volcanic exhaustion" phenomenon occurs at the end of each Ice Age (Hamilton II. Intro. [38]), despite a general increase in volcanism during the last 2-million years (the Quaternary, worldwide [83]). Hamilton believes that this accounts for the rapid warming at the end of the Ice Ages.

A recent survey of material settling to the bottoms of the oceans (about

---

*It is not supposed that 568 volcanic eruptions by latitude and date is comprehensive. It is simply all that we could readily locate. We did not select them in any way. A complete listing is contained in Tom Simkin *et al*, *Volcanoes of the World*, Hutchinson Ross Publ. Co., Stroudsberg, PA, 1981 (10,000 years through 1980).

40 years to settle from surface to the bottom of a deep) shows that volcanic ash is much greater in the Northern Hemisphere than in the Southern Hemisphere at present [84].

We can look forward with some confidence (thanks most to the work of the Russians, who lead in volcanic prediction as they did in earthquake prediction) to the accurate forecasting of volcanic eruption timing and magnitude of the eruption [85]. This is a useful thing to know.

Volcanism changes the climate, as shown above, but it does not stand alone as effector. Solar variation plays an approximately equal role.

B. Solar Activity

"Thou risest beautifully in the horizon
   of heaven
Oh living Aten who creates Life!
When thou risest in the eastern horizon
Thou fillest every land with thy beauty.
Thou art beautiful, great, gleaming and
   high over every land.
Thy rays, they embrace the lands to the
   limits of all thou hast made.
Thou art Re and bringest them all,
Thou bendest them (for) thy beloved son.
Thou art afar off, yet thy rays are on
   the earth;
Thou art in the faces (of men) yet thy
   ways are not known."

This emphasis on the omnipresence of the sun, whose rays "...embrace the lands to the limits of all thou hast made,..." suggests an attempt to introduce the worship of a Universal God acceptable not only to the Egyptians but to the foreign peoples over whom they now ruled. This is brought out very strikingly in the further passage from the reference already quoted.

"All the distant lands, thou makest
   their life.
Thou settest a Nile in Heaven that it
   may descend for them
And make floods on the mountain like the
   sea,

In order to water their fields in their
    towns."

These fragments of a hymn — perhaps written by Akhnaten himself in the
14th Century B.C. — sang the praise of Aten alone — perhaps not merely to
the physical disc, but also to its life-giving power [86].

It has been suggested that the symbol (the 'ankh):

was the Sun's disk immediately on the horizon; the horizon itself; and the
Sun's reflection on the Nile.

Inasmuch as most worship has been aimed at the female (the fertility
figure), and "life-giving" is common to both Aten and the female, it is but a
short step to the symbol for female:

Whether or not these conjectures truly happened in that order, they
clearly might have.

Not only has the Sun been worshipped as the Giver-of-Life by untold
generations; it has also been studied with the utmost scientific appreciation
by a brilliant few in every generation.

To all of these we are indebted for an enormous lore, knowledge and
understanding of the Sun. Indeed, if it is possible to point to one thing in
our universe that is most important to Mankind, it is the Sun.* A few
Men have lived, however tenuously, on the Moon for awhile outside the
absolute domination of Earth; but no Man has ever lived outside the
domination of the Sun.

There is not even any prospect for existence of any human outside the
domination of the sun, although such fictional programs as Star Trek
clearly envision it.

The stage is set by the centuries in which the Sun has been regarded
as the ultimate constant. The religions, the superstitions, the very structures
which have housed every civilization and every philosophy upon which
civilizations are founded regard the Sun as constant. People who do not
understand about eclipses are very upset when the Sun is not constant.

---

*It's logically impossible to rank the importance of essentials.

Small surprise — scientists being human — that the literature is flooded with papers about the solar constant.

Detrich Labs and Heinz Neckel published a paper titled "The Solar Constant" in *Solar Physics* 19: 3-15 (1971) and their abstract follows:

"Abstract. A detailed compilation of the most recent values of the solar constant is given (13 values published from 1967 to 1970). The most probable value seems to be 1.95 cal cm min or 1.36 kWm with a formal rms error of + or − 0.3%. The corresponding effective temperature is 5770K.

Systematic errors of the order of + or − 1%, but also a possible variability of the same order cannot be excluded."

One percent, indeed. Plus a possible variability of the same order — a total of 2% —

A 2% change downward could cool off the Earth by about 5.5 degrees Centigrade which is just barely short of an Ice Age.

It is within this error in the solar constant that all of the solar variability will be found. That's what makes it such a difficult subject — small differences in very large values — which is about the most difficult sort of thing that you can try to measure.

Theories concerning solar variability and instability "rage hotly" in current scientific literature.

An outsider wading into the literature has a very hard time attempting to interpret the state of knowledge for the interested, but uninvolved, public.

Assuming, for the moment, that solar variability affects climate on Earth, one looks to see if there is any way to project future solar variability in order to project future climate.

Throughout nature, the observer sees persistence in form and behavior. However poorly trends established in the past can be projected to reveal the future; the fact is that the past is all we have; and it is viewed through limited records of limited observations.

With this generic apology out of the way, let us proceed.

Consider the variables;

1. Of sunspots:
   a. Number;
   b. Size;
   c. Direction of rotation;
   d. Location on the Sun; and
   e. Umbral to penumbral ratio.

2. Length of sunspot cycle(s);
3. Magnetic effects:
    a. Directly upon Earth; and
    b. Modulation of the galactic nucleonic flux.
4. Flares;
5. Faculae;
6. Ultra-violet radiation emission;
7. Solar winds;
8. Temperature; and
9. Rate of rotation.

Since the sun is one object, it is a matter of physical faith that the entire ball-of-worms is interrelated. Don't expect to see one formula, however elaborate, anytime soon, however.

The physical facts about many of the sun's characteristics can be readily reviewed. Making something of it is more difficult.

The following quotation [87] is a fair measure of what the public wants to know about the sun's status. (One must believe that with a century of success, the World Almanac editors can accurately judge what the public wants to know.)

"The sun, the controlling body of our solar system, is a star whose dimensions cause it to be classified among stars as average in size, temperature, and brightness. Its proximity to the earth makes it appear to use as tremendously large and bright. A series of thermo-nuclear reactions involving the atoms of the elements of which it is composed produces the heat and light that make life possible on the earth.

"The sun has a diameter of 864,000 miles and is distant, on the average, 92,900,000 miles from the earth. It is 1.41 times as dense as water. The light of the sun reaches the earth in 499.012 seconds or slightly more than 8 minutes. The average solar surface temperature has been measured by several indirect methods which agree closely on a value of 6,000 degrees Kelvin, or about 10,000 degrees Farenheit. The interior temperature of the sun is about 35,000,000 degrees Farenheit.

"When sunlight is analyzed with a spectroscope, it is found to consist of a continuous spectrum composed of all the colors of the rainbow in order, crossed by many dark lines. The "absorption lines" are produced by gaseous materials in the atmosphere of the sun. More than 60 of the natural terrestrial elements have been identified in the sun, all in gaseous form because of the intense heat of the sun."

So much for the status; but what about the variations?

1. Sunspots:
   a. As clean a set of numbers as one can find in most libraries is shown in **Figure 17**, and the world's standard — the Zurich Relative Sunspot Numbers — is to be found in references [88] and [89], which list the sunspots month by month.

   We are in possession of a copy of "Zurich Final Daily Sunspot Numbers 1818-1973" which is detailed with most days back to 8 January 1818. This was information supplied for a fee by the World Data Center A for Solar-Terrestrial Physics, National Oceanic and Atmospheric Administration, Boulder, Colorado 80302 U.S.A. There is also in the literature some sunspot data going back to 1610 [90].
   b. The sizes of sunspots vary through the entire range from barely visible (the size of the Earth) up to almost 60,000 miles in diameter at maximum. To normalize sunspots is a gross oversimplification of their enormous variability. The simple count fails to convey the sense of variability.
   c. Many sunspots are paired:
   "A bipolar sunspot group usually has its joining axis in an east-west direction. During one nominal 11-year cycle the eastern spot of the group in the northern solar hemisphere will be north-pole-seeking, and in the southern hemisphere south-pole-seeking. During the alternate 11-year cycle the eastern spot will be south-seeking in the northern hemisphere and north-seeking in the southern hemisphere. This polarity change indicating the 22-year or "sunspot-magnetism" cycle was first noted at the 1913 minimum." [91]

   It is the number of spots that people refer to as the 11-year cycle; but with the alternate magnetic orientation, it is the magnetic orientation that people refer to as the 22-year cycle (see **Figure 18**) [92].

   There is no generally accepted theory on how this magnetic effect might change climate, but the correlation with weather seems to pass statistical significance tests.
   d. Sunspots vary in their location on the sun. At the beginning of each 11-year cycle, their location is at high latitude, and during the cycle, the mean latitude moves toward the solar equator (see **Figure 19** [93]).
   e. A beautiful piece of work done by Douglas V. Hoyt [94] has

such a striking result that it deserves special attention.
Hoyt postulates:

"...that the umbral/penumbral ratio is proportional to the solar luminosity and that long-term variations in the luminosity lead to corresponding changes in the climate of Earth." [94]

A sunspot is composed of two kinds of areas, as distinguished by luminosity. The umbra is about one quarter as luminous as the sun's average surface; and the penumbra is at an intermediate brightness (i.e., about three-quarters as bright as the average surface). Both of these "shadow" regions have sharply defined areas which can be measured.

The measure does not depend upon the number nor size of spots; rather it seems to reflect some internal condition that pervades the entire sun. It therefore might turn out to be a much better measure than the number of the problematical spots.

In his treatment of the data, Hoyt finds that he must disregard the data for those years in which the areas of the penumbras total less than one-hundred-millionth of the area of the solar disc.

The plotted umbral/penumbral ratio superimposed on a plot of northern hemisphere mean temperatures from 1874 to 1970 shows that the two correlate significantly at the 1% level; and that the cross-correlation coefficient of .56 could explain 31% of the climatic variance with this mechanism.

Hoyt's review of the literature suggests that "...the umbral/penumbral ratio may be a measure of the convective energy transport in the photosphere of the sun..."; that is "...it is an index of global property of the sun..."

His data implies that when the rotation rate of the sun is high, the umbral/penumbral ratio is low and the Earth's climate is cool. The reverse situation is warm.

The angular momentum of the sun (according to Hoyt's model) is related to its luminosity negatively, and to the eighth power of the total angular momentum. The effect would be caused by energy shifting back-and-forth between the rotational energy reservoir and "the radiative-convective flux in the sun" of which the umbral/penumbral ratio would be a measurable monitor.

The conservation of angular momentum remains to be satisfied; but it is well documented that the rate of rotation of the sun's visible surface varies [95 and 96] and is currently increasing [94].

Hoyt found two autocorrelation periods that are of interest and may be of some importance — peaks at both 11- and 20-years (which, because of error tolerance he suggests, might turn out to be the much-talked-about 22-year period). This is an umbral / penumbral significant auto-correlate — and may be the first really important clue as to what the heretofore anomalous 22-year period is all about. This could turn out to be a 22-year luminosity period in the sun.

Of considerable related interest as a correlation, but with no obvious mechanism, is the fact that the umbral / penumbral maximum occurred when **sunspot activity** peaked in phase with **Jupiter's tidal maximum** on the sun. Further, the phase shift cycle of these two factors is very approximately 178-years; Wolff's predicted periodicity.

Finally, the solar tidal forces exerted by Jupiter, Earth and Venus beats about the 22-year period reported.

2. The subject: "length of sunspot cycle(s)" would surely make strong experts quail, and weak ones run for cover. The advantage that we — as "lay observers" have — is that we can propose, knowing full well that experts will dispose.

So here are the facts revealed by — or hypothesized by — experts, and our proposals follow.

Wolff (*op.cit.* II. Intro. [34]) reviewed the sunspot literature with exhaustive thoroughness. He lists 25 periodicities greater than three years which have been reported in sunspot data:

Cohen and Lintz [97] analyzed and projected sunspot data on the assumption that there is a major 179-year periodicity.

From their spectral analyses done under the 179-year assumption, they projected that there will be low solar activity for the next 30 years (beginning about mid-1970's). In fact, a moderately high peak occurred about 1979-80.

Wolff's very acute theory of sunspots used the suggestive form of past data as a theoretical take-off point to postulate inertial oscillation modes of the entire sun — that is, the dense inner mass of the sun is ringing like a gong.

The nearest thing to this phenomenon that effects the Earth happened in 1960 when the great earthquake happened in Chile. The Earth rang like a gong, with Washington, D.C., vibrating up-and-

Table I.
Period (years)
180 + / − 35
84 + / − 8
59 + / − 4
26 + / − .7
14.9 + / − .2
12.2 + / − .16
11.85 + / − .15
11.10
10.45
10.03
9.50
8.5
8.1
7.13
5.74
5.56
5.37
4.78
4.44
4.12
3.85
3.66
3.50
3.22
3.08

down an inch once every twenty minutes or so; and this vibration took over a month to die out.

The Sun, of course, is a very dense gas; so it goes on oscillating for centuries; and in fact may be getting some feedback from external sources. It is also rotating; so the result is that different vibration modes rotate at different speeds. Sometimes they are in phase, and at other times they are out of phase.

Dr. Wolff pursued this line of thought, and found that it explained the frequencies in the Sun so well, that there is no more than about one chance in a million that the agreement between theory and observation is an accident.

The longest term period identified by Wolff was 178-years, and he suggested that 1957 and 1779 were the last two years of modal beat — based upon those years having the highest sunspot numbers. These two years were the two most active 11-year sunspot cycle peaks ever recorded.

These oscillations contribute to high solar activity, according to Wolff.

What, then, suppresses solar activity? Why isn't it high all of the time?

There is a disagreement in the scientific literature about possible planetary influence on sunspots that — even in this carefully impersonal and formal exchange — leaks out almost passionately-held points of view. (Scientists are human, after all; and it's a darn good thing. They are even American, British, Russian, German, etc.; and loyal to their countries and ethics — and we think that's a good thing, too.)

Yet, though we must concur with careful workers that a tide of a millimeter or so on the sun from the planets seems ridiculously small to produce an effect; yet non-linear responses of systems makes us sensitive to **small triggering forces. This is especially true in the case of the chromosphere of the sun that some modellers hold to be metastable.**

Anything at all will upset a metastable situation. (ex., a glass marble at rest on a level glass-topped table. The least force will change its position.)

So we are not wholly discouraged by the relatively miniscule dimensions of the forces.

One of the careful pieces of work [98] seems to have been a rather direct rebuttal of another [99]. The latter paper by K.D. Wood related sunspots to tidal effects of planets upon the sun. The former paper denies such effects.

Yet the table of sunspot data from Okal and Anderson [98] **makes** a case for planetary effect; if it is combined with a column of Zurich Sunspot numbers. (see Table II.)

Of more significance is the fact that Hoyt's [94] umbral / penumbral ratio peaks in the early 1930's (see **Figure 20**) just when the planetary tidal peak is in phase with the sunspot cycle. The more out of phase these two things are, the lower the umbral / penumbral ratio. Our calculations show that the planetary tidal forces on the sun were at a maximum in 1939 (the highest in more than a 200-year period).

Wolff arrived at a 178-year sunspot period on theoretical

grounds; Okal and Anderson showed that the Jupiter period (11.862-years) is the dominant planetary tidal period; so one might expect to test the idea of a "forcing-function" of some sort if planetary tidal forces on the sun has any detectible effect on sunspots.

To this end, by beating the Jupiter period against the 178-year sunspot period, we can test:

$$\frac{1}{P} = \frac{1}{11.862} + \frac{1}{178}$$

P = 11.120898; which corresponds closely to the length of the sunspot cycle.

Since 178 / 11.862 = 15.0059; or conversely,

11.862 × 15 = 177.93; if we beat the Jupiter period with something 15 times as long, it follows that the beat produced is 16 in that period. The calculation has inserted it.

Nothing surprising so far.

Table II.

Tidal Peak	Sunspot Peak	Dts*	Sunspot Maximum
	FROM [98]		FROM [88]**
1809	1816	−7	45.8
1822	1830	−8	71.0
1833	1837	−4	138.3
1845	1848	−3	124.3
1857	1860	−3	95.7
1869	1871	−2	111.2
1881	1884	−3	54.3
1892	1894	−2	78.0
1905	1906	−1	53.8
1916	1918	−2	80.6
1927	1928	−1	77.8
	Phase Change		
1939	1939	+1	109.6
1951	1948	+3	136.2
1963	1958	+5	184.7
1974	1969	+5	105.5

*Dts is the difference between tidal and sunspot peaks in years.
**Zurich relative sunspot numbers.

The surprise is that the 11.12-year result of P is the average time of sunspot cycles.

And that there are 16 cycles of sunspots in 178-years, whether or not Jupiter tidal forces reinforce them.

And that the Hoyt maximum u / p ratio occurs at the time when the planetary tidal forces are in phase with the sunspot cycle. (1930's) (See **Figure 20**)

And the planetary tidal forces were at a 200-year maximum at that time.

And that the Dts correlates with sunspot maximum numbers at a significant level (.594 — which gives an r(test) figure of 98%; the "Confidence of Relationship).

These things certainly do not prove that Jupiter and other planets' tides have anything to do with sunspots; but they are extremely entertaining, and mighty suspicious.

A compilation of calculated curves based on various strength hypotheses is shown in **Figure 21**. The upper curve is a soundly-based calculation of the 60-degree North Latitude tidal-forces envelope on Earth. The second curve is taken in part from Eddy [90] (1050 to the present), and is combined with the change in Carbon-14 concentration data taken from several sources for the dates of about 450-1050 A.D. This curve should be regarded as data on the solar luminescence. The third is a generalized curve of suggested beat nature describing the theoretical solar output. It should not be taken too seriously.

3. The magnetic effects of the Sun upon the Earth are a major source of effect upon the Earth. The effects are twofold: directly upon the Earth, itself; and secondarily by modulating incoming ionized or other electrically charged particles from space.

   a. As to the direct effect upon Earth, the most direct and immediate was shown by Gribbin and Plagemann [100] as a change in the rate of rotation of the Earth for a few days following the great solar storm of August 1972.

   Most effects are slow compared with this, however.

   The flow of charged particles (solar winds) from the sun varies with degree of solar activity. This, in turn, constitutes a "sheet" of current flowing from the sun — which produces a very complex magnetic field (see **Figure 22**), from reference [101].

   b. This magnetic sector noise scatters particles that are approaching Earth from outer space, and causes a modulation of cosmic rays into the Earth's influence [101].

This supersonic current flow — or solar wind — confines the Earth's magnetic field to a cavity (called the Magnetosphere) which has a blunt forward end; has about 10 times the Earth's diameter; and has a long tail that extends beyond the Moon's orbit — away from the Sun. Our magnetic field shields us from more than 99% of the solar winds; but the Moon (having a very low rotation rate, hence a very low magnetic field, as well as virtually no atmosphere) takes the full blast. [102]

One of the things that Moon-rocks are good for is to study the Sun.

4. Flares are great storms that rage off the surface of the Sun. No systematization of note is known to us.

Certainly the magnetic, earth-rotation, solar wind and heat (i.e., radiance) effects change the Earth's weather. Since we do not know of a periodicity of flares, we regard them as more appropriate to the study of **weather** than to **climate**.

5. Another aspect of the Sun is called faculae.

These hot "plaques" are thought to be gas descending back toward the Sun from the ascending "solar-prominences".

Solar faculae vary with sunspots, and the solar constant (i.e., the energy given off by the sun) is reported to vary with the faculae.

6. Measurement of ultra-violet and X-ray emission by the Sun has been greatly facilitated by the space program. Measurements must be made above the atmosphere, because of a high-percentage absorption by the atmosphere.

These highly energetic wavelengths comprise less than 2% of total solar energy; but their importance lies in the fact that radiation of this energy promotes chemical reactions in the upper atmosphere — such as the production of ozone.

Such information is highly systematized, and is obtainable from a standard handbook [104].

7. Solar winds are being studied intensively in the space program, and copious data is available in the scientific literature. [105]

Perhaps of greatest importance to one interested in climate is the solar wind **after** it enters the upper atmosphere. Here it appears as aurorae (see **Figure 23**). The ions in the solar wind are very energetic, and they react in the upper atmosphere to make ozone, for example — as judged by the fact that the greatest concentrations of ozone are in the vicinity of the magnetic poles [104], where the charged particles are guided into the atmosphere by the Earth's magnetic field.

Ozone has been much talked about by environmentalists, ecologists, and other political activists in recent years. Their position appears to have been consistent that: since they don't know everything about the subject; the world must do two things:

a. Fund their studies, and
b. Wait until they say they are satisfied.

On that philosophical basis, Man would not yet be permitted by his intellectual guardians to use fire.

A paper in the literature which takes the opposite approach is reference [53]. These authors studied the priceless Smithsonian data (spectroscopic plates photographed at several solar observatories around the world for over half a century under the rigorous supervision of C.G. Abbot) and extracted ozone data from these plates. In their own words:

"Stratospheric total ozone values have been obtained for the period 1912-50 from analysis of Smithsonian data. Naturally-caused variations of 25% or more are common over time scales ranging from months to decades. We suggest that the ozone layer acts as a shutter on the incoming solar energy, providing one of the long-sought trigger mechanisms between solar activity and climatic change. The present state of knowledge of ozone climatology is not sufficient to support popular speculations about man's effects on the ozone layer."

Note in particular that ozone **absorbs light in the visible spectrum.**

The meaning of this phenomenon is that when ozone increases in concentration, the atmosphere absorbs more light energy, hence it heats up. Upper air temperature depends in part upon ozone concentration.

When solar activity maximizes, the hot faculae give off more ultra-violet light, and the sunspots give off more solar winds. These produce ozone, especially over the poles, and make a greater temperature inversion over the poles.

Since the highly energetic solar emissions produce ions in the air (see the quote from Humbold's "Cosmos" later in this chapter), clouds are nucleated and hover in the inversion.

Now note: the maximum umbral/penumbral ratio (i.e., solar turbulence) occurred in about 1932; but the successive three sun-

spot cycles (30-years) went UP numerically while Hoyt's umbral /
penumbral ratio went down.

More sunspots — more polar ozone.

More ultraviolet (i.e., higher u / p ratio) — **more global ozone.**

This can be checked out by seeing whether such a change of **relative**
ozone concentration occurred.

According to Angione, Medeiros and Roosen [106] the observed change
of about 15% in Chappuis (pronounced sha-pwee') band in the spectrum
represents a **change** of 0.5% of the total solar flux at mid-latitudes.
Because of the slant at which sunlight passes through high latitude atmosphere, much **more** is absorbed there.

With decreasing u / p ratio and increasing sunspot activity, the polar
air cloud cover rapidly increased, and the northern polar air mass has been
expanding. Now, both u / p ratio and sunspot activity are generally declining, so the size of the polar air mass is continuing to stay large.

The phase relationship is such that the polar air mass should continue
to grow slowly until between 2000 and 2010 A.D. from this cause.
(Other calculations suggest that this period of polar air mass growth should
extend to 2030 A.D.)

Meanwhile, harking back to the section on volcanoes — the **northern**
hemisphere is in a phase of rising tidal forces (the 179.33-year cycle).
Rising volcanicity during the period up to about 2060; especially in
the first half of that period to about 2020, will make for sharply declining
temperatures during this period.

How firm are these suggestions?

Abbot [107] comments on this particular factor in the introduction of
his paper entitled "Solar Variations, a Leading Weather Element", and
inasmuch as the publication has imprinted on it the Smithsonian seal
which says:

"FOR . THE . INCREASE . AND . DIFFUSION . OF . KNOW-
LEDGE . AMONG . MEN";

the following extended quote is intended to comply with their avowed
purpose:

"On January 28, 1953, the American Meteorological Society devoted
the day to consideration of the influence of solar variation on weather.
An early speaker said he acknowledged the results of conscientious
studies of total variation, which had been made, as probably sound.
But the variations found appeared to be of the order of 1 percent,

or much less. No reasonable theory could show that these might have important weather influences. He distrusted statistical conclusions, unless grounded on sound theory. Statistics might show that it is dangerous to go to bed, for the great majority of decedents died in bed. The remainder of the panel appeared to agree with him that, because percentage solar-constant variations are small, it is needless to consider the possibility that variations of total solar radiation affect weather importantly. The discussion was mostly confined to matters relating to the high atmosphere, in the stratosphere and beyond. Suggestions were discussed as to whether the large effects of solar changes known to exist in the high atmosphere could be connected with weather changes in the troposphere. No positive result was reached.

One gathered the impression that meteorologists are so firmly convinced that variations of total solar radiation are of negligible weather influence, and that statistical methods of proof are to be ignored, that they probably do not read attentively any publications of the contrary tendency. I do not agree that the last word has been said. I submit several propositions.

1. Statistically derived results may be accepted, if well supported by observation, without supporting theory. Kepler's laws were accepted statistically for many years before there was any supporting theory.

2. A conclusion may be accepted as a valuable working hypothesis, without being proved in the rigid sense, e.g., that the square of the hypotenuse of a right-angle triangle equals the sum of the squares of the other two sides.

3. In lieu of theoretical support, to be supplied later, a statistically derived proposition, A, may be adequately supported as a working hypothesis, if accepted phenomena, B, C, D, E, — which stem from a related source — are harmonious with proposition A. I propose to show that the proposition that the variations of solar radiation are important weather elements is thus adequately supported. Further support comes when forecasts with high correlation compared to probable error result from such hypotheses. **I depend strongly on this paragraph in what follows."***

---

*The authors of this book agree with Abbot that consistent statistical relationships must not be ignored. They constitute knowledge—which is a basis for proceeding carefully. They do not constitute positive understanding—which is the only basis for proceeding at "full-blast".

Items 8 and 9 — temperature and rate of rotation of the sun — have been covered in the preceding discussion.

For the relationships of volcanism and sunspots to weather or climate, one can find various reviews. Perhaps the most dispassionate, objective, and thorough reviews are papers by J. Murray Mitchell, Jr., of the U.S. Weather Bureau.

In summary of sunspots:

Sunspots are beginning to be understood, and various periodicities of sunspots and climatic variation have been correlated. Such correlation does not address the subject of mechanism.

Mechanisms are little understood.

The alignments of planets as related to effects on sunspots are not now ciritically proven; and no mechanism is understood, given that there are some correlations.

The umbral to penumbral ratios of sunspots correlate very significantly with climate and it may very well be that the u / p ratio varies in a 178-year cycle — maybe 102 years going up, and 76 years going down. This appears consistent with other data.

One other fact of interest is that Gribbin and Plagemann [47] have shown that the Earth changed its rate of rotation for a few days after a great solar flare.

Unfortunately, solar flare occurrence has not become a very well-defined science, so we don't know how to make anything of this interesting fact at the present.

Long term projections based upon III. a. (volcanism) and III. b. (solar activity) point to continually generally declining temperatures in the northern hemisphere, whereas diminishing solar activity and diminishing volcanism in the southern hemisphere have contradictory effects. The southern hemisphere should stay close to level.

Climate for the Next 30 Years
1980 - 2010

	Hemisphere	
	Northern	Southern
Solar Effect	Cooler	Cooler
Tidal Effect	Cooler	Warmer
Net Effect	Much Cooler	Steady

C. Magnetic Field

The volcanic, solar and magnetic field effects range from relatively simple to relatively complex.

Please try to keep your sense of humor while reading about magnetism. Cherish the people who like to work on this subject. They are, intellectually speaking, kind-of martyrs. Every cause needs people to work on the infinitely difficult things, but most people would rather see than be one.

The literature abounds in information leading to the conclusion that the magnetic field influences weather — especially in connection with the solar winds. An outstanding feature of this field is the breathless beauty of its fundamental phenomenon — the Aurora (see **Figure 23**). One would look far to find a more lyrical scientific discussion of the subject than appears in the rare old book by Humboldt, "Cosmos", Volume I, published in 1870. We quote at length here from this rare book, rather than referencing it; because so few libraries would have it.

"The luminous arch remains sometimes for hours together flashing and kindling in ever-varying undulations, before rays and streamers emanate from it, and shoot up to the zenith. The more intense the discharges of the northern light, the more bright is the play of colors, through all the varying gradations from violet and bluish white to green and crimson. Even in ordinary electricity excited by friction, the sparks are only colored in cases where the explosion is very violent after great tension. The magnetic columns of flame rise either singly from the luminous arch, blended with black rays similar to thick smoke, or simultaneously in many opposite points of the horizon, uniting together to form a flickering sea of flame, whose brilliant beauty admits of no adequate description, as the luminous waves are every moment assuming new and varying forms. The intensity of this light is at times so great, that Lowenorn (on the 29th of June, 1786) recognized the coruscation of the polar light in bright sunshine. Motion renders the phenomenon more visible. Round the point in the vault of heaven which corresponds to the direction of the inclination of the needle, the beams unite together to form the so-called corona, the crown of the northern light, which encircles the summit of the heavenly canopy with a milder radiance and unflickering emanations of light. It is only in rare instances that a perfect crown or circle is formed, but on its completion the phenomenon has invariably reached its maximum, and the radiations become less frequent, shorter, and more colorless. The crown and the luminous arches break up, and the whole vault of heaven becomes covered with irregularly-scattered, broad, faint, almost ashy-gray luminous immovable patches, which in their turn disappear, leaving nothing but a trace of the dark, smoke-like segment on the horizon. There often remains nothing of the whole spectacle but a white, delicate cloud with feathery edges, or divided at equal distances into small roundish troups like cirrocumuli.

"This connection of the polar light with the most delicate cirrous clouds deserves special attention, because it shows that the electromagnetic evolution of light is a part of a meteorological process. Terrestrial magnetism here manifests its influence on the atmosphere and on the condensation of aquaeous vapor. The fleecy clouds seen in Iceland by Thienemann, and which he considered to be the northern light, have been seen in recent times by Franklin and Richardson near the American north pole, and by Admiral Wrangel on the Siberian coast of the Polar Sea. All remarked "that the Aurora flashed forth in the most vivid beams when masses of cirrous strata were hovering in the upper regions of the air, and when these were so thin that their presence could only be recognized by the formation of a halo round the moon." These clouds sometimes range themselves, even by day, in a similar manner to the beams of the Aurora, and then disturb the course of the magnetic needle in the same manner as the latter. On the morning after every distinct nocturnal Aurora, the same superimposed strata of clouds have still been observed that had previously been luminous. The apparently converging polar zones (streaks of clouds in the direction of the magnetic meridian), which constantly occupied my attention during my journeys on the elevated plateaux of Mexico and in Northern Asia, belong probably to the same group of diurnal phenomena.*

---

* "On my return from my American travels, I described the delicate cirro-cumulus cloud, which appears uniformly divided, as if by the action of repulsive forces, under the name of polar bands *(landes polaires)*, because their perspective point of convergence is mostly at first in the magnetic pole, so that the parallel rows of fleecy clouds follow the magnetic meridian. One peculiarity of this mysterious phenomenon is the oscillation, or occasionally the gradually progressive motion, of the point of convergence. It is usually observed that the bands are only fully developed in one region of the heavens, and they are seen to move first from south to north, and then gradually from east to west. I could not trace any connection between the advancing motion of the bands and alterations of the currents of air in the higher regions of the atmosphere. They occur when the air is extremely calm and the heavens are quite serene, and are much more common under the tropics than in the temperate and frigid zones. I have seen this phenomenon on the Andes, almost under the equator, at an elevation of 15,920 feet, and in Northern Asia, in the plains of Krasnojarski, south of Buchtarminsk, so similarly developed, that we must regard the influences producing it as very widely distributed, and as depending on general natural forces."

"Southern lights have often been seen in England by the intelligent and indefatigable observer Dalton, and northern lights have been observed in the southern hemisphere as far as 45° latitude (as on the 14th of January, 1831). On occasions that are by no means of rare occurrence, the equilibrium at both poles has been simultaneously disturbed. I have discovered with certainty that northern polar lights have been seen within the tropics in Mexico and Peru."

If the uninitiated now accepts the idea that magnetism is related to **weather**, the next idea to gag-down is the idea that the magnetic field, itself, changes not only from day-to-day and month-to-month, but also from year-to-year, and millenium-to-millenium. These deliberate, long-term periods constitute a force leading to a change in climate.

The field even reverses, and does so in a relatively systematic way.

The curve shown in **Figure 24** shows that the magnetic field reverses at different rates through time—with the principle periods of nominal or reversed polarity being flipped by great bolide strikes. The short reversals seem to result from instability of flow of liquid iron in the core [108].

This reference lists a series of average times of magnetic field variations, some of which are obviously periodic, and some that appear to be random.

Effect	Years	Cause
Period	700,000,000	Cause unknown.
Period	250,000,000	Galactic rotation?
Period	75,000,000	Solar vibration perpendicular to the galactic plane?
Reversals	30,000 to 30,000,000	Bolide strikes, and perhaps other causes.

Nagata's (*op.cit.* II. Intro. [27]) abstract briefly reviewed the main long-term data revelations:

"The secular variation in the geomagnetic field revealed from geomagnetic data during the latest Century may be characterized by the following five major characters; i.e., (a) decrease of the moment of geomagnetic dipole* with rate of 0.05% / year, (b) westward precessional rotation of the dipole with speed of 0.05 degree / year, (c) north-

---

*A magnet has two poles—North-seeking and South-seeking. One magnet (such as a bar magnet) is called a dipole. A magnet could have a concentrated North-seeking pole with a diffused opposite pole. This might be caused by a whirling vortex of magnetic material which would have such a magnetic field to be called a "non-dipole".

ward shifting of the dipole with speed of 2 km / year, (d) westward drift of the non-dipole field with speed of 0.2 degree / year, and (e) growth and decay of the non-dipole field with annual rate of 10r / year (a very small amount) in the order of magnitude."

Bullard [109] originally calculated the westward drift of the non-dipole magnetic field, and found it to be westward at 0.18° / year which gives a period of: $P = 360 / 0.18 = 2000$ years.

Nagata's number of 0.2° / year gives: $P = 360 / 0.2 = 1800$ years.

Bullard quotes from Halley's 1692 determination of 0.5° / year and his remark:

"the nice Determination of this and of several other particulars in the Magnetick System is reserved for remote Posterity".

Nagata says of (a) and (b) (quoted above: these "...characteristics are hardly possible to be quantitatively interpreted at present..."; or, in his words about all of these factors:

"Based on the concept of the hydromagnetic dynamo of the earth's core, a possibility of theoretical interpretations of the five main characteristics is discussed. (a) and (b) characteristics are hardly possible to be quantitatively interpreted at present, (c) characteristic may be interpreted as due to a simple harmonic oscillation of $S°_2$ component, (d) characteristic has been interpreted by Gullard *et al* as due to the electromagnetic coupling between the conductive liquid core and the less conductive solid mantle, (e) characteristic may be interpreted as due to growth of magnetic fields caused by upwelling of the strong toroidal field $(T°_2)$ by local convection motions and their decay."

Even for computers, the question of magnetic fields is virtually as complex as meteorology — except that we can't get to the core or mantle to measure temperature, movements, permeability, hysteresis and the like.

Analogously, how much would we know about biology if the only information you had available was the sounds you can hear through walls at a zoo?

Clearly, "...remote Posterity..." has a lot left to do.

The dipole field — the one the compass points to — has its pole off of the geographic north and south poles by about 11° and 22° respectively. Its westward drift of about 0.05° / year gives a period:

$$P(\text{dipole cycle}) = 360 / 0.05 = 7200 \text{ years.}$$

Various kinds of data verify this approximate period such as shown in **Figure 25**.

The resultant beat of the magnetic field is a combination of the dipole /
non-dipole fields, thus:

$$\frac{1}{P} = \frac{1}{2000} + \frac{1}{7200} = 1565$$

Measurements have shown at the latitude of Central America an approximately 1600-year magnetic cycle of intensity, and in Czechslovakia, the
same with a probable overtone (i.e., $\sim$ 800 years).

This 1600-year magnetic cycle with its influence on climate shows up
very strongly in the stability / instability of Egyptian history (see Appendix
III).

Shorter term relationships have been found between climate and magnetic
intensity of the earth's field [110] and between the field in space resulting
from solar activity and terrestrial weather [111] — and both appear statistically significant.

An article bearing on the westward precession of the Earth's non-dipole
is quoted in full from *The Browning Newsletter* 1[3]: 21 April 1977 (see
Appendix VI).

A partial verification is contained in an article in a magazine called
Modern Maturity [112]. The article is based on an interview with and the
work of Dr. Hurd C. Willett, Professor of Meteorology Emeritus of MIT.

He stated that, from 1880 to 1920, with the exception of the East Coast,
it was "prevailingly wet across the United States in lower middle latitudes...
The only drought of consequence...occurred in the Mexican border states
in the 1880's".

We take this to mean that it was relatively dry on the East Coast
from 1880 to 1920.

The article further states: from 1910 to 1940, dry weather prevailed.
"The outstanding features of the 1925 to 1960 period as a whole," he
adds, "are recurrent and severe droughts in the Midwest coincident with
extreme wetness on the East Coast (including Northeasters in winter and
spring, and hurricanes in summer and autumn)."

As of the current period (1970's and 1980's), western Kansas and Nebraska
and Eastern Colorado have had blowing dust and grasshopper plagues.
This is clearly uncommonly dry for these states.

Inasmuch as the period of extreme wetness follows hard on the drought,
it is clear that the Colorado River Basin faces a period by about 2050
of extreme flooding like it had in the 1300's (see Appendix VI).

Even before that, an area of interest is the Great Lakes region. On the basis of a decadal running average, lake levels of Michigan and Huron minimized about 1930. The maximum drought condition in the Colorado was followed in the 1200's by maximum flooding in about 70 years. This phenomenon should have moved gradually westward across the entire width of the U.S.-Canada land-mass; and appears to be in the process of repeating the performance.

Upon examination of the map, one can assign the following rough values:

East $\cong$ 78° W Longitude

Midwest $\approx$ 90° W Longitude

High Plains $\cong$ 102° W Longitude

West Coast $\cong$ 123° W Longitude

Starting in 1880, progression of the Earth's non-dipole field should have been (at 1600 yrs / 360°, or .225° / yr):

East Coast - 78° - 1880
Midwest   - 90° - 1933.3
High Plains - 102° - 1986.7
West Coast - 123° - 2080

By implication, by the year 2000 A.D., there will be general flooding conditions in Lakes Huron and Michigan. They should reach levels 4 to 5 feet **above** the 1974 high level. This upward surge should be of interest to people along the lakes. They need not bother to check with authorities. They will be reassured that not an ounce of government data backs up this projection.

Maybe you should ignore this warning — it might be wrong.

These events associated with the westward precession of the non-dipole magnetic field are of great significance to Canada, Mexico and the U.S. for the next hundred years.

Of course, the similar set of events are precessing westward from China, and will be of importance.

Europe has recently reversed its magnetic intensity trends, and can reasonably be expected to get gradually cooler for the next 400 years.

How incredibly interesting it all is.

The magnetic field operation can be visualized by using **Figures 26** and **29.**

Figure 26. Visualize the earth's magnetic field as a sort of a "donut-shaped" magnetic bottle. Solar winds and other charged particles from space get captured in the magnetic field and oscillate in it. When the particles lose enough energy, they leak out of the bottle into the polar air over the magnetic poles below.

The persistent high concentration of ozone over the magnetic poles implies that these high-velocity ions react to produce ozone.

Of course, ozone absorbs visible light; and between the energetic solar winds and energy absorption of the ozone — combined with the persistent cold of the ground below — a persistent inversion can be expected.

Figure 27: The mean 500 millibar chart of the Januaries of the 1950's [113]* shows a pattern of atmospheric pressure over the magnetic pole which can be seen from:

Figure 28: to be closely related to magnetic inclination around the north magnetic pole. If you will keep in mind that the dipole field precesses around in about 7200 years, and the non-dipole field precesses around in about 1600 years — so that you do not have too simple a picture of the revolving ellipse, then examine:

Figure 29: This is intended to represent both the magnetic inclination in Paris and the average temperature in England (King and Willis, *op. cit.,* II. Intro. [33]). Archaeologists seek out fossil camp-fire sites where people have baked wet clay with their camp-fires. The charcoal preserves the date of the fire; the baked clay preserves the magnetic inclination data.

The pattern of inclination would occur with precession of the magnetic field, and is compatible with today's status as seen in **Figure 28**.

The implication is that western Europe has just entered a period of slow temperature decline from this mechanism — that should be expected to continue for about 400 years.

From Hoyt's umbral to penumbral ratio, temperatures should decline for a period of about 30 years.

From rising tidal forces, temperatures should decline ([179.33 / 2] + 1972) − 1979 $\doteqdot$ 83 years — especially sharply at the beginning of the period following 1972.

This is an interesting time, indeed, for Western Europe.

It can be seen from **Figure 28** that the ellipse, precessing westward at 360° per 1600 years would cause the westward drift of weather indicated by Willett and documented by Gribbin [114 — Chapter 7]; thus the scheduled completion of the drought's trip across the U.S. (see above).

---

*H.H. Lamb is perhaps the most distinguished climatologist in the world.

Europe's future is especially frigid; with volcanic action increasing to a crescendo around 2008; with the solar turbulence minimizing by 2010; with the Magnetic intensity increasing, and the temperature correspondingly decreasing. A sharp decrease in the average growing season is to be expected in Europe for the next 30 to 50 years.

Bibliography

III. MECHANICS OF CLIMATE - Intermediate Long Term

A. VOLCANISM

[54] Press, Frank (1968) Density Distribution in Earth. *Science* 160: 1218-1221.

[55] Konpoff, L. (1969) The Upper Mantle of the Earth. *Science* 163 (3873): 1277-1287.

[56] Hammond, Allen L. (1971) *Research Topics* — Plate Tectonics: The Geophysics of the Earth's Surface. *Science* 173: 40-41.

[57] Gay, N.C. (1976) Spherules on Shatter Cone Surfaces from the Vredefort Structure, South Africa. *Science* 194: 724-724 (12 Nov. 1976)

[58] O'Keefe, John D. and Thomas J. Ahrens (1977) Meteorite Impact Ejecta: Dependence of Mass and Energy Lost on Planetary Escape Velocity. *Science* 198 (4323): 1249-1251 (23 Dec. 1977)

[59] Fairbridge, Rhodes W. (1977) Global Climate Change During the 12,500-b.p. Gothenburg Geomagnetic Excursion. *Nature* 265: 430-431 (3 Feb. 1977)

[60] van Zinderen Bakker, E.M. (1962) A Late-Glacial and Post-Glacial Climatic Correlation between East Africa and Europe. *Nature* 194 (4824): 201-203 (14 April 1962)

[61] Street, F. Alayne and A.T. Grove (1976) Environmental and Climatic Implications of Late Quaternary Lake-Level Fluctuations in Africa. *Nature* 261: 385-390 (3 June 1976)

[62] Mercer, J.H. (1972) Chilean Glacial Chronology 20,000 to 11,000 Carbon-14 Years Ago: Some Global Comparisons. *Science* 176: 1118-1120 (9 June 1972)

[63] Vuilleumier, Beryl Simpson (1971) Pleistocene Changes in the Fauna and Flora of South America. *Science* 173 (3999): 771-780 (27 Aug. 1971)

"Pollen studies of lacustrine sediments of one of these lakes, which covers the Sabana de Bogata...One of the few pieces of evidence that definitely supports the contention that glaciations in South America were synchronous with those in North America..."

[64] Epstein, Samuel, R.P. Sharp and A.J. Gow (1970) Antarctic Ice Sheet: Stable Isotope Analysis of Byrd Station Cores and Interhemispheric Climatic Changes. *Science* 168: 1570-1572 (26 June 1970)

[65] Report of the Krakatoa Committee of the Royal Society (1888) The Eruption of Krakatoa and Subsequent Phenomena. Printed by Harrison and Sons, St. Martin's Lane, W.C. and Published by Trubner & Co., 57 and 59, Ludgate Hill, London 1888. Royal Society of London, Krakatoa Committee, 1888, pp. 1-56.

[66] Emiliani, Cesare and Nicholas J. Shackleton (1974) The Brunhes Epoch: Isotopic Paleotemperatures and Geochronology. *Science* 183: 511-514 (8 Feb. 1974)

[67] Milliman, John D. and K.O. Emergy (1968) Sea Levels during the Past 35,000 Years. *Science* 162: 1121-1123 (6 Dec. 1968)

[68] Johnsen, S.J., W. Dansgaard, H.B. Clausen and C.C. Langway, Jr. (1972) Oxygen Isotope Profiles through the Antarctic and Greenland Ice Sheets. *Nature* 235: 429-434 (25 Feb. 1972)

[69] Stuiver, Minze, Calvin J. Heusser, and In Che Yang (1978) North American Glacial History Extended to 75,000 Years Ago. *Science* 200: (4337): 16-21 (7 April 1978)

[70] Chappell, J. (1974) Relationships between Sea Levels, 0-18 Variations and Orbital Perturbations, during the Past 250,000 Years. *Nature* 252: 199-202 (15 Nov. 1974)

[71] Batten, E.S. (1974) The Atmospheric Response to a Stratospheric Dust Cloud as Simulated by a General Circulation Model. Dept. of Defense Advanced Research Projects Agency R-132-ARPA (March 1974)

[72] Pollack, James B., B. Toon, Carl Sagan, Audrey Summers, Betty Baldwin and Warren Van Camp (1976) Volcanic Explosions and Climatic Change: A Theoretical Assessment. *J. Geophys. Res.* 81 (6): 1071-1083 (20 Feb. 1976)

[73] Eruptions and Climate: Proof from an Icy Pudding. *New Scientist*: 367 (17 Feb. 1972)

[74] Hamilton, Wayne L. and Thomas A. Seliga (1972) Atmospheric Turbidity and Surface Temperature on the Polar Ice Sheets. *Nature* 235: 320-322 (11 Feb. 1972)

[75] Bray, J.R. (1974) Volcanism and Glaciation during the Past 40 Millennia. *Nature* 252: 679-680 (20 / 27 Dec. 1974)

[76] Bray, J.R. (1974) Glacial Advance Relative to Volcanic Activity Since 1500 A.D. *Nature* 248: 42-43 (1 Mar. 1974)

[77] Öpik, E.J. (1965) Climatic Change in Cosmic Perspective. *Icarus* 4: 289-307 (1965)

[78] Libby, Leona M., Lovis J. Pandolfl, Partrick H. Payton, John Marshall, III, Bernd Becker and V. Giertz-Sienbenlist (1976) Isotopic Tree Thermometers. *Nature* 261: 284-288 (27 May 1976)

[79] Anderson, Don L. (1974) Earthquakes and the Rotation of the Earth. *Science* 186: 49-50 (4 Oct. 1974)

[80] Heaton, Thomas H. (1975) Tidal Triggering of Earthquakes. *Geophys. J.R. Astr. Soc.* 43: 307-326 (1975)

[81] Toksöz, M. Nafi, Neal R. Goins, and C.H. Cheng (1977) Moonquakes: Mechanisms and Relation to Tidal Stresses. *Science* 196: 979-981 (27 May 1977)

[82] Carr, Michael J. (1977) Volcanic Activity and Great Earthquakes at Convergent Plate Margins. *Science* 197: 655-657 (12 August 1977)

[83] Kennett, James P. and Robert C. Thunell (1975) Global Increase in Quaternary Explosive Volcanism. *Science* 187 (4176): 497-503 (14 Feb. 1975)

[84] Lal, D. (1977) The Oceanic Microcosm of Particles. *Science* 198 (4321): 997-1009 (9 Dec. 1977)

[85] Tokarev, P.I. (1971) Forecasting Volcanic Eruptions from Seismic Data. *Bulletin Volcanologique* 35 (1): 243-250 (1971)

B. SOLAR ACTIVITY

[86] Cottrell, Leonard (1957) *The Anvil of Civilization*. Mentor: Ancient Civilizations. Publ. by The New American Library.

[87] *The World Almanac & Book of Facts* (1978) Publ. Annually by Newspaper Enterprise Assn., Inc.; New York, N.Y.

[88] Shirk, G. (Ed.) (1973) *Data:* Zurich Relative Sunspot Numbers. *Cycles* XXIV (10): 237-239 (October 1973)

[89] Shirk, G. (Ed.) (1977) The Recent Sunspot Numbers. *Cycles* XXVII (1): 14 (January 1977)

[90] Eddy, John A. (1976) The Maunder Minimum. *Science* 192: 1189-1202 (18 June 1976)

[91] Chernosky, Edwin J. (1966) Double Sunspot-Cycle Variation in Terrestrial Magnetic Activity, 1884-1963. *J. Geophys. Res.* 71 (3): 965-974 (1 Feb. 1966)

[92] King, J.W. (1975) Sun-Weather Relationships. *Astronautics and Aeronautics* 13 (4): 10-19 (Apr. 1973)

[93] Douglass, A.E. (1936) Climatic Cycles and Tree Growth — Volume III. A Study of Cycles. Publ. by Carnegie Inst. of Washington (1936) Publ. No. 289, Vol. III. 171 pages.

[94] Hoyt, Douglas V. (1978) Variations in Sunspot Structure and Climate. Prepublication — National Oceanic and Atmospheric Administration,

Boulder, Colorado 80303 (1978)

[95] Eddy, John A., Peter A. Gilman and Dorothy E. Trotter (1977) Anomalous Solar Rotation in the Early 17th Century. *Science* 198 (4319): 824-829 (25 Nov. 1977)

[96] Herr, Richard B. (1978) Solar Rotation Determined from Thomas Harriot's Sunspot Observations of 1611 to 1613. *Science* 202 (4372): 1079-1081 (8 Dec. 1978)

[97] Cohen, Theodore J. and Paul R. Lintz (1974) Long-Term Periodicities in the Sunspot Cycle. *Nature* 250: 398-400 (2 August 1974)

[98] Okal, Emile and Don L. Anderson (1975) On the Planetary Theory of Sunspots. *Nature* 253: 511-513 (13 Feb. 1975)

[99] Wood, K.D. (1972) Sunspots and Planets. *Nature* 240: 91-93 (10 Nov. 1972)

[100] Gribbin, John and Stephen Plagemann (1973) Discontinuous Change in Earth's Spin Rate following Great Solar Storm of August 1972. *Nature* 243: 26-27 (4 May 1973)

[101] Sualgaard, Lief and John M. Wilcox (1976) Structure of the Extended Solar Magnetic Field and the Sunspot Cycle Variation in Cosmic Ray Intensity. *Nature* 262: 766-768 (26 Aug. 1976)

[102] Burton, R.K., R.L. McPherron and C.T. Russell (1975) The Terrestrial Magnetosphere: A Half-Wave Rectifier of the Interplanetary Electric Field. *Science* 189: 717-718 (29 August 1975)

[103] Arctowski, Henryk (1940) On Solar Faculae and Solar Constant Variations. *Proc. N.A.S.* 26: 406-411.

[104] Valley, Shea L. (Scientific Ed.) (1965) Handbook of Geophysics and Space Environments, Air Force Cambridge Research Laboratory, Office of Aerospace Research, United States Air Force (1965)

[105] Neugebauer, Marcia (1975) Large-Scale and Solar-Cycle Variations of the Solar Wind. *Space Science Reviews* 17: 221-254 (1975)

[106] Angione, Ronald J., Edward J. Medeiros and Robert G. Roosen (1976) Stratospheric Ozone as Viewed from the Chappuis Band. *Nature* 261: 289-290 (27 May 1976)

[107] Abbot, C.G. (1958) Solar Variation, A Leading Weather Element. (Publ. 4135) *Smithsonian Misc. Coll.* 122 (4): 1-35. Published by the Smithsonian Inst.; City of Washington (4 August 1953)

C. MAGNETIC FIELD

[108] Jacobs, J.A. (1975) *The Earth's Core*. Academic Press; London, New York, San Francisco.

[109] Bullard, E.C., F.R.S., Cynthia Freedman, H. Gellaman and Jo

Nixon (1950) The Westward Drift of the Earth's Magnetic Field. *Royal Society of London* 243 (A. 859): 67-92.

[110] Wollin, Goesta, George J. Kukla, David B. Ericson, William B.F. Ryan and Janet Wollin (1973) Magnetic Intensity and Climatic Changes 1925-1970. *Nature* 242: 34-37 (2 March 1973)

[111] Knight, J.W. and P.A. Sturrock (1976) Solar Activity Geomagnetic Field and Terrestrial Weather. *Nature* 264: 239-240 (18 Nov. 1976)

[112] Moskow, Shirley (1979) Is Our Weather Crazy? *Modern Maturity*, April-May 1979: 7-9.

[113] Lamb, H.H., R.P.W. Lewis and A. Woodroffe (1966) Atmospheric Circulation and the Main Climate Variables Between 8000 and 0 B.C.: Meteorological Evidence. World Climate From 8000 to 0 B.C. Royal Met. Soc. Special Publ. (1966): 174-217.

[114] Gribbin, John (1976) *Forecasts, Famines and Freezes: Climate and Man's Future*. Walker and Company; New York, N.Y. (Especially Chapter 7)

Chapter IV

Mechanics of Climate — Short Term

Introduction

In the short term, individual volcanoes; short tidal oscillations (4.425-Yr. equatorial; 8.85-Yr. high latitude); sunspot cycles; a 22-year cycle of umbral to penumbral (sunspot) ratios; and lesser mechanisms affect the climate.

There is a gap between meteorology and climatology.

The numerical formulae and calculations of meteorological events require detailed knowledge of atmospheric measurements. The forecasts decay with time, that is, the further forward the forecast is aimed, the lower the probability it will be accurate. A one-month forecast by standard meteorological methods is very chancy; and a seasonal forecast is seldom attempted.

Annual forecasts can be much more accurate, provided the forecaster is adequately general:

"We expect the weather in Minneapolis to get colder toward the middle of winter; but have great confidence that May will be warmer."

In California with its Mediterranean climate, one earnestly expects less rain in June than in December — indeed, virtually no rain in June.

Between these long-range generalities and the confident short-term forecasts, there is a gap of desperate uncertainty between three weeks and one year that makes the difference of what crop to plant where, and when. Other things like drainage, irrigation, fertilization, or application of herbicides and pesticides, etc. depend on rainfall quantity and timing.

Choice of strain of crop will depend upon growing degree days.

This intermediate period forecast is the subject of the maximum dissent.

Things that affect this intermediate period may be divided into two categories for purposes of discussion: Natural, and Man-made.

A. Natural

The weather appears to be driven by even shorter duration forces.

As examples of measures of weather, one can take the derivative (i.e., the rate and direction of change) of Lakes Michigan / Huron levels, and compare them with the driving forces.

Figure 30 shows three curves: The uppermost is an actual plot of sunspot numbers (Zurich); the middle plot is derivatives of 60° N. Latitude tidal forces; and the lower curve is lake level derivatives (i.e., rate of change of 12-month running average of lake levels).

Lakes Michigan / Huron have a novel characteristic: their level tends to reflect the **rate of rainfall** in the drainage basin — because they drain almost entirely through the Detroit River which is essentially a constant-sized spigot. Thus, when rainfall is low in the "Corn Belt", the drainage into the lakes diminishes and the lake level declines.

Figure 31 shows the curves superimposed. When the two driving forces (sunspots and tidal derivatives) are in synchronism, there is a significant tendency for the drought (as signified by the solid area of the lake level curve) in the drainage area of the lake. Rain in the lake drainage basin depends, of course, on where the storm track is located.

Studies have shown that storm tracks can be figured on a long-term basis with tree-ring data, or tree-pollen data. An example of this is shown in **Figure 32.**

In an article by Schoenwetter (IV. A. [115]), pollen is studied with respect to both the modern pollen-rain, and pollen in dateable archaeological sites.

At each site, a 200-pollen grain (of wild-pollens) sample was taken from the surface (modern), and from the occupied level — from which datable ceramic fragments were taken.

The pollen was characterized into three classes — arboreal (wild) pollen; non-arboreal wild pollen; and domesticated-type pollens. The domestic pollens were set aside, and the percent of arboreal pollen (AP) was calculated against total wild pollens.

The archaeological sites in the Chusca Valley area in Northwestern New Mexico were dated by recognizable ceramic groups as follows:

Ceramic Group	Time Range
1	A.D. 500 - 725
2	725 - 800
3	800 - 875
4	875 - 950
5	950 - 1,000
6	1,000 - 1,075
7	1,075 - 1,125
8	1,125 - 1,200
9	1,200 - 1,325
10	1,700 - Present

Schoenwetter found that typically sandy areas had higher arboreal pollen (AP) percentages; because less grass and weeds grow on sand, and if pollen has to blow in, arboreal pollen can blow as well as other pollens. In the case of silty locations, the non-arboreal plant pollens could be produced by plants growing right there; so they deposited more local pollen.

Two samples of the report are quoted here:

"LA 7052 (Skunk Springs Locality, below 5900 feet)
(See **Fig. 38**) (of the reference)

"A modern surface sample and subsurface one were collected at this site. Though the AP frequency of the surface sample (12.5 per cent) is not quite half that of the subsurface record (26.0 per cent), the two are recognized as indicative of the same vegetation pattern: a fairly dry grassland below the savanna border. The site is assigned to either Ceramic Group 3 or Group 4. When the sample was deposited a vegetation pattern like that of the present seems to have prevailed, but precisely when that deposition occurred within the A.D. 800 to 950 range is unknown."

"LA 7215 (Crumbled House Locality, below 5900 feet)
(See **Fig. 50**) (of the reference)

"Both the surface and the floor samples from this site gave results. The former yielded an AP frequency of 17.0 per cent, the latter one of 29.5 per cent. Both are typical of the present vegetation pattern for this elevation. This site may be assigned to the Ceramic Group 4 horizon and the pollen data indicates conditions like those now prevailing. The only other site (LS 7013) definitely assigned to Ceramic Group 4 indicated conditions somewhat moister than on the prehistoric horizon. Thus environmental conditions on the Group 4 horizon may have fluctuated."

To summarize:

(1) Sample Ident.	(2) Arch. Sample (% AP)	(3) Modern Sample (% AP)	(4)* (2)-(3) ($\triangle$% AP)	(5) Date of Arch. Sample
LA 7052	26.0	12.5	+13.5	A.D. 800 to 950
LA 7215	29.5	17.0	+12.5	A.D. 875 to 950

These two sites showed higher tree-pollen (AP) percentages in the past time than at the present. One can get a fairly good grasp of the range of climates that the past has provided, and better project what is ahead with this understanding.

Figure 32 shows the pollen data where each horizontal bar is the range of dates of the Ceramic Group, and each vertical bar is the standard error of the pollen sample differences.

The solid curve is oxygen-18 isotope (temperatures) as taken from Dansgaard's Camp Century, Greenland ice data.

It will be seen that when northern hemisphere temperatures got cooler (up on the chart), the tree-pollens at these sites increased. This meant that the forest was advancing down the low slope of the Chuska Valley (which is in the far northwest corner of New Mexico).

At these cool times, rainfall had given way from monsoonal summer thunderstorms with great erosive degradation to winter drizzle or snow with consequent aggradation.

Erosion occurred during warm times; deep arroyos lowered ground-water, and trees died. In cool periods, the drizzle caused slow drainage; arroyos filled up and the ground-water table rose. Forests advanced, springs flowed and corn could be grown anywhere without irrigation.

Such a time is upon us as the Northern Hemisphere will be getting cooler for the next few decades.

One thing to keep in mind about this chart is that an effect by the

---

*Column (4) shows that 13.5 and 12.5% more of the pollen was aboreal or tree pollens at the earlier times than at present.

precessing non-dipole magnetic field is implied by the pollen data; but cannot show in the Greenland Ice data because Camp Century is contained entirely within the Polar Vortex. The magnetic field drought effect would show up on the pollen data in the late 1200's when the Chuska area was affected by the passing magnetic field inclination.

Another relatively short-term climatic effect is the 26-year drought-and-flood cycle at the equator observed at Ceara, Brazil, for example.

The apparent origin of this periodicity is as follows:

Dansgaard showed a strong 78 ± 5-year periodicity in the oxygen-18 (i.e., temperature) deposition in Greenland Ice.

The highest tidal alignment occurring with respect to Earth-Sun-Moon positioning is called the Saros cycle of eclipses

Lunar Period   29.530589 days × 223 = 6585.3213 days
Anomalistic Period 29.554551 days × 239 = 6585.5377 days
Nodal Period   27.212220 days × 242 = 6585.3572 days
           6585.3213 / 365.2422 = 18.030012 years
           18.30012 years × 3 = 54.090037 years

Since there is almost exactly one-third day above 6585 days (i.e., 6585.3213 days), the eclipse progresses almost exactly around the earth every three Saros eclipses.

Since the basic period of high latitude tidal beat is ∼179.33 years, then the beat of the 3 Saros cycle tidal-force with the ∼179.33 year beat is:

$$\frac{1}{P} = \frac{9}{54.090037} - \frac{1}{179.33}$$

$$P = 77.451048$$

which gives three periods of heightened volcanicity of 25.817 years (∼26 years) each. Of course, volcanicity interferes indirectly with the monsoons by cooling the air over the equator; so this could very well be the ultimate timer for the 26-year climatic cycle at the equator.

Considering the fact that Hamilton and others have proved beyond reasonable doubt that volcanoes are triggered by tidal forces, and these can so readily be calculated; and, finally, Bray and others have shown climate attuned to volcanoes; one can "wade-in" and calculate climatic variation with some confidence.

B. Man's Effects on Climate and the Gross Environment

Except for the political effects resulting from the efforts of simplistic scientists with preposterous extrapolations, an intellectually vacuous press, and affluent environmentalists who seem to believe that their esthetic judgments constitute some sort of a natural law, Man's effects on climate may safely be ignored by practical people.

By far the most popular doom-theory is the carbon dioxide-greenhouse effect; yet Öpik (*op. cit.* III. A. [77] p. 301) — an extremely careful worker with high qualifications in both astronomy and cosmology — says:

"...its greenhouse effect, a favorite idea in the past, must be definitely rejected..."

The aforementioned fraction of the intellectual community, along with its opportunistic political support is well along on the way to discrediting itself. The climate is getting more harsh, and people always change with it, consequently, most of these free lunches have been served. The bibliographic information is astronomical in quantity; but half of it denies the other half; so the environmentalist movement — as far as reality is concerned — should be ignored, except for its political aspect.

As reality of bad weather negates the environmentalist attitudes toward energy; famines are to be credited to their attitudes towards pesticides; depression is to be credited to their waste of capital in "air and water purification"; and scores of deaths must be charged against the requirement to contain explosive grain dust in elevators — people will carve this intellectual cancer from the body politic and leave it exposing its horror in the historic pickling jar. Charge another disaster to the tyrannical elitists.

Bibliography

IV. MECHANICS OF CLIMATE - Short Term

A. NATURAL

[115] Schoenwetter, James (1967) Chapter III. *Pollen Survey of the Chuska Valley. An Archaeological Survey of The Chuska Valley and the Chaco Plateau, New Mexico.* Part I. Natural Science Studies. Number 4. Museum of New Mexico Research Records. Museum of New Mexico Press; Santa Fe.

Chapter V

Man

Introduction

Man is an animal in that he eats what animals eat, bleeds like animals bleed, reproduces like animals reproduce, and a myriad of other descriptors like animals.

Man cannot demonstrate the general ability to do anything that some other animals cannot also do. His difference is only one of degree. In competition, he wins some and loses some. In combat, he wins some and loses some. Generally, he wins.

But the real world is great when compared to Man. He cannot win against the world.

This chapter examines Man as to his nature and behavior, and then briefly reviews his actions as related to climatic change.

A. MAN—Human Nature [121]

In the United States, the height of soldiers in war after war has been shown by Army records to increase. This has been attributed to shifting diet over the decades; but might be related in part to increasing genetic heterosis.

Following World War II, there was a similar increase in body size of Japanese who, under American influence, altered traditional diets.* The average

---

*Of course, some U.S. soldiers did all they could to increase Japanese heterosis.

granddaughter was taller than her grandfather. Small shoe sizes and school desk sizes were finally obsolete and abandoned.

Not only can body size be influenced in humans; but brains, in test animals, can also be increased in size. Stimulating environments cause rats' brains to increase in weight over non-stimulated controls. This implies that such an effect might be true in human brains, also. Such inference is strengthened by the fact that acetylcholine and also glial ribonucleic acid increased in enriched learning circumstances [116]. Rats raised in stimulating environments had an average increase of 4.6% brain weight over control rats.

An increase in brain size would be a gratifying, and expected result of the Head Start program; i.e., a stimulating environment for the preschool child.

Among humans, it has been found that high uric acid content in the blood correlated with "drive", "leadership", "achievement", "pushing self", and "range of activities" [117].

Tentative results obtained by experimentalists at MIT showed that neurones develop **after** birth, and that the number formed depend upon environment [118]. This is a surprising result, because it was heretofore held that only interconnections developed after birth.

More specifically, the effects of heredity and environment on I.Q. were reported in a 400-page study [119] to be:

Agent	Percent
Genetics	45%
Environment	35%
Unknown	20%

The characteristics of the mammals that typifies "intellectual level" are:

$$E = kp^c$$

Where E = brain weight,
p = body weight,
k = a constant that has a very narrow range for each species, and
c is about ⅔

A way to think about this formula is as follows:

The body weight of animals is mostly a function of volume, because most animals are about the same density as water. Most animals just will — or just won't — float.

Assuming density about that of water, then the cube root of the body weight represents the height, breadth, or depth of the body.

Since the most important thing to the survival of an animal is to detect anything that might be biting or eating it; then it follows that the **main function** of the nervous system is to report on anything that is **touching** — and especially **biting** the surface.

The surface is, of course, an area; and the area is a squared function. Thus:

Area is proportional to Body Weight, which is the square of the cube root of the body weight which is also expressed as: $p^{2/3}$

This, in turn, tells us about the size of the surface of the body. Now, the brain weight is a function of the surface area $E = f(p^{2/3})$

so the function $f(\ )$ tells how well nerves in the skin are serviced by the brain. There is such an earnest need to know whether something is biting you that your nerves literally report in on every place with the size of a grain of talcum powder.

Every hair has a nerve at its root that reports in every time the hair is disturbed. Now that is a lot more information than we can consider point by point.

We have a very cleverly designed system.

We don't have to consider every part of our hide twenty or thirty times a second. We do not say to ourselves: "nothing is biting that spot". Instead, the inrush of a faster signal from a localized nerve tells us something positive: "something **is** biting that spot". Never mind where you aren't being bitten. Pay attention to the place that **is** being bitten.

The mosquito defeats this clever system by injecting a pain killer before she bites. Unfortunately, she doesn't sterilize the system, hence malaria and yellow fever.

The sociological equivalent of a bad body design is the insane stupidity of the consumerists and the EPA which reports in from a billion places "twenty to thirty times a second" "HEY! NOTHING IS BITING MY SPOT". All proforma reporting is an expensive, and useless harassment.

The only report that living things ever need is "HEY! SOMETHING **IS** BITING MY SPOT!"

Then, and only then, can one spare the energy to scratch. It keeps the overhead down to survival levels.

Now, back to the formula.

$$E = kp^c$$

The c in the formula is not exactly ⅔ because organisms aren't really ball-shaped. But because animals are a lot closer to a ball than to a string, or a cluster of grapes, the ⅔ is a darn good approximation.

Finally, the k tells how much each kind of animal makes of the information it gets. This can be called logic.

For example, a human has about 500 brain cells for every channel (axon) that comes in from the outside to the brain; a rat has about 18 brain cells; and an ant has only 1.

In addition, since waiting until something is actually biting you is a little late; we have systems that work at giving a little advance information — namely sight, smell and hearing. One can use such information to prepare to bite back — or maybe to avoid the scene entirely.

Thus, eyes can use available light to see things moving at a distance. They really reach out there, because with them we can see the sun and moon "moving" (especially at rise and set). The eyes are mounted high up on the body so as to see over the grass; and are close to the brain so as to give priority information to the brain promptly.

Of course, tigers have stripes that camouflage, and they are really sneaky; but people who didn't pay attention didn't have descendants. The survivors, who were our ancestors, passed on to us a real sensitivity to movement. (That is how TV traps us. The image moves, and we **must** look at anything that moves; because only people who looked at **everything that moved** lived to become ancestors. We are hooked by that part of our heredity.)

Then there is the sense of smell.

The authors have a part-Cherokee ancestry. Grandpaw Browning hunted squirrels by sniffing. When he smelled one, we stopped dead still, and pretty soon it moved. Its curiosity overcame its discretion; and it didn't live to become an ancestor.

He could identify snakes by smell — a really important skill.

Human smell is as sensitive as a hound-dog's. The human is just tuned to different things. There is strong evidence that the sense of smell plays a large role in sexuality.

The third remote sensing mechanism is hearing.

The sense of hearing actually works at the same energy level as sight; but it gets its information from the mechanical motion of air within the frequency ranges that we call sound.

There was the story of a Country Cousin who was visiting the City Cousin in Chicago. While viewing the loop area, Country Cousin said — "listen to the bird singing". City Cousin said "How can you hear a bird singing in all this noise?"

Country Cousin said: "It's all in what you are trained to hear. Watch this." Whereupon he took a dime out of his pocket and dropped it on the sidewalk.

Everybody nearby looked around.....

A baby human is born with very little of its nervous system complete; and has to learn almost everything. The inherent capacity is modified severely by diet and degree of stimulus of the environment. The period of imprinting (essentially to age 7) determines **what** is accepted as the working definitions; and then the degree of education determines the specific information assimilated.

Alteration of performance (as measured by society's score-keeping method — income) is not achieved by school education.

Quoting from reference (V. A. [119]):

"...Anything we now know how to do to elementary and secondary schools, including spending money on them, integrating them or re-segregating them, grouping according to ability within them or not, adding preschool and kindergartens to them, will have trivial effects on the eventual incomes of the children in the schools."

The report winds up by concluding:

"...if one wants to equalize incomes, give the poor money, not education."

That is to say: the die is cast by age 7.

Thinking in analytical terms, there are several characteristics of mind and body which typify the human. Following is the set of descriptors of the human mind and body; although each is a descriptor, the characteristics are not independent of each other*.

1. Intellectual
    A. Having to do with places in the brain:
        a. **Knowledge** is structural (not chemical), and there are two types:
            1) **Intrinsic or hereditary connections** between sensory input and "effectors" — or action output. The sympathetic nervous system has a lot of structural knowledge.
            2) **Learned connections** (modifications of acetylcholinesterase at synaptic connections). The learning relates directly with sensory experience. The sensory and motor cortex areas hold the "conscious knowledge".
        b. **Wisdom** — The prefrontal lobes are found experimentally to be the site at which people decide **what to do** about **what**

---

*For the technically inclined, these can be considered a quasiorthogonal set.

they know. What people do about what they know is
their wisdom.

c. **Understanding** is located in the left temporal lobe in the case
of right-handed people (with too little information on left-
handed people to draw conclusions). The mechanics of
understanding appears to be, neurologically speaking, find-
ing the common denominator of different facts. This,
mechanically, is "relating observed facts". Appreciation of
the relationships between things is called understanding.

B. Having to do with states of the Mind:

a. **Flexibility** — There is an enormous variation in flexibility
of people.

A flexible person can act like he or she is inflexible; but an
inflexible person can never act flexible.

Flexibility probably has to do with a high rate of learning;
but it is also almost certainly true that brains that learn fast
also forget fast.

Inflexible brains learn slowly, and forget slowly (that is —
something once learned is remembered tenaciously). There
is no absolute value judgement that inherently can be
applied to flexible compared to inflexible minds. Each does
its possessor maximum good under optimum circumstances.

Flexible people tend to thrive most under conditions of
change, whereas inflexible people tend to thrive most under
conditions of stability. We are now going into a climatically
caused period of change.

b. **Irritability** — This is a physiological concept; and it is a condition which an individual can choose to alter. Another
term that might be considered the equivalent of irritability
is stimulability — or the capacity to be stimulated. This characteristic is probably dependent primarily upon the permeability of the nerve cells. A person may inherit physiological conditions that make the nerves excessively easy to
stimulate, and could become easily susceptible to epilepsy —
the state of being stimulated continuously so that the signal
can't be cut off.

Learning depends upon "successful" firing of one nerve cell
by another — via a synaptic connection; and **knowledge** is

the pattern of these "successfully fired" synaptic circuits which have been modified as a result, so that they may fire again more easily. **Forgetting** is the breaking and / or disablement of these circuits.

The brain's permeability, hence stimulability, is increased by (in plain English: the brain and nerves are stimulated by:)

1) Nicotine, caffeine, and the like;

2) Fat solvents such as alcohol, ether, chloroform; and

3) Anything that takes calcium out of the system; such as "Accent" (sodium glutamate), pregnancy, magnesium (such as epsom salts [Magnesium sulfate]), and a wide variety of such antagonistic or combinatorial things.

Oxalic acid is an example of a compound (used in bleaching), which is very toxic in large doses, but is a cellular stimulant in low concentrations. The oxalic acid combines with calcium which is thereby removed from the cell membranes (i.e., cortical gel). This leaves the cell increasingly permeable, and brings about a toxic and non-recoverable stimulability analogous to toxic levels of anaesthetics.

Calcium oxalate is somewhat less soluble than cement, so calcium is irreversibly removed from biological availability by oxalic acid "poisoning".

Stimulability is decreased systematically by:

a) Aspirin (Bufferin, etc.);

b) "Biologically available" calcium such as calcium pills for a person with cramps; the calcium in warm milk which puts a baby to sleep (i.e., the baby ceases to be "irritable"); removal of salt from a diet which removes the "antagonism" of the sodium in the salt, and permits calcium to accumulate in the cortical gel of the nerve cells, which decreases the permeability, hence the "irritability" of the nervous system;

c) Certain drugs like opium, heroin, and the barbituates.

If one turns his attention to a sequence of sought stimuli, he might see a dinner this way:

For those whose ethics, religion or morality controls their diet, this sequence would be different:

A "before-dinner" light-dry alcoholic drink which "sets up" the taste buds by leaving them more "alert" (or "stimulable");

Hors d'oeuvres — tasty tid-bits that exercise the taste buds in a variety of intensities and kinds of taste;

Salad — which is minimally nutritious — is bulky with lots of fiber, and is used to begin to lessen the appetite — and with salad dressings, and tid-bits (croutons, bacon bits, grated cheese, or a variety of bits of other things with flavors, garnishes, or textures; thus again achieving a variety of taste, texture, visual and even crunchy sound sensations.

Meat course(s) — if more than one, beginning with something like fish (with low-profile taste) consumed over highly sensitized taste buds. Bolder tasting courses come later, and are consumed over taste buds which are accumulating fatigue.

Dessert — a tasty preparation typically sweet with sucrose sugar. The physiological-neurological function of the sucrose is to constitute a very high osmotic pressure environment for the taste buds. The resulting osmotic-pressure dehydration of the taste buds render them insensitive, hence there is no "aftertaste".

After-Dinner-Drink — typically a liqueur — usually sweetened, with a syrupy viscosity and consequent high osmotic pressure. This has the effect of a dessert: to close down the taste buds thus to prevent "after-taste".

There is infinite variety of this theme; but in deference to the senses of taste, smell, touch (texture), and the aesthetics of appearance, the senses are tuned-up, titillated, satiated and shut-off.

A surprising fraction of Man's total effort is directed toward satisfying the senses.

Beyond the fundamental level of barest essential calories; peppers, herbs, spices, and nerve modifiers take a large part of human attention.

The athlete "psychs" himself.

The thinker is apt to tune himself up with stimulant; etc.

The human is what he is born to be, combined with what his diet makes him be, and this is superimposed on what he has been imprinted and trained to be.

B. MAN — Human Behavior

The rules of human behavior are straightforward, and are based upon his physical possibilities. No man can do those things that require fifteen fingers, or five legs.

No human capability exists for living at a temperature of over 800° C (Venus) or in a vacuum (Moon). He can take a capsule with him to such lethal environments; but its proper function is essential to his survival.

Man **requires** the environment offered by the Earth. Man sees best at the wavelength of light that is supplied in greatest quantity by the sun through the atmosphere of the Earth.

The most valid branch of medicine for man is surgery; because he has had plenty of time to develop the inheritance to cope with the problem of "cut-off" or "bit-off" parts.

Races whose ancestry had plenty of time to become adjusted to particular and differing environments are different from each other; and each is uniquely qualified to survive in the environment their ancestors survived in.

It is not just bigotry to assert that there is no difference among races — it is pure stupidity.

Along with their differences — all mainstream humans have certain features in common. Those things that make us uniquely human are:

- Opposing thumbs;
- Legs superior to all other animals;
- Brains superior to all other animals;
- The brain-speech complex (parrots can talk, chimpanzees can think sentences, man can do both);
- Accumulated recorded heritage (birds teach each other by example; dogs and wolves record their property claims; baboons have a complex-taught social heritage; man has it all including complex art);
- Manufacturing (i.e., things made with hands) (chimpanzees strip leaves to constitute sponges for gathering and handling water; grab sticks and hit with them. Spiders set traps and so do ant-lions. Some birds use thorns to gouge for grubs. Man, alone, manufactures complex items.); and
- Control of fire.

Nature supplies examples of about everything else:

artificial flight (spiders on webs, maple seeds);
beauty (peacock);
clothing (hermit crabs);

domesticated animals (ants);

education (training to hunt — big cats);

family (baboons, porpoises, etc.);

gurus (Young chimps defer to greybeards in strange situations.);

health care ("auntie" midwife elephants);

idiots (typically killed [chickens, turkeys] or abandoned [cats, dogs]);

joy (dogs, etc.);

killing one's own species (many species resort to cannibalism);

love (love birds);

medium of exchange (chimps — tokens for sex — Yerkes Primate Lab.)
   (males performed all tricks to earn tokens from visitors;
      females bought bananas; tokens changed hands in "red light" district.);

nuclear energy (chain reaction in uranium — remains in an African river basin), (fusion energizes the sun);

opiates (bears eat pine needles; obtain magnesium, a "sedative" for their hibernation);

parachutes (dandelion seed);

quotas (birds count their young sometimes);

rulers (boss monkey);

sex (animals);

territorial imperative (cardinals, etc.);

ultra-violet light (from the sun and stars);

value judgments (monkeys spank their babies);

war (ants, frogs);

xylophones (skeletal rib cages);

Yesterday (some dogs lie on the grave of their deceased master — clearly remembering their yesterdays); and

zoning (trees live only in their own zones).

This alphabetical listing is intended to imply an infinity of examples.

One could go on-and-on listing things that Man has or does that he does not have or do exclusively.

Humans are born with a minimal nervous system — not as rudimentary as the baby kangaroos — which doesn't even have hind legs; but with components which — except for the minimal essentials — are mere models of adult components.

The helplessness of human babies is a measure of how completely humans are shaped by the environment after birth.

Children apparently raised by wolves do not learn to walk or talk. Their mental development appears to be completely compatible with the life style of the wolves that taught them. They do not "act human" inherently; they must learn how to act human.

Children learn by mimicry. Those people who turn toward children for natural wisdom draw a blank, depending, of course on the age of the children. What they get is poorly understood knowledge based upon limited learning.

Children continue to learn; but some cultures play down understanding, and play up knowledge. In the tropics where the climate is almost constant, knowledge (taboos, customs, tribal memories) suffice for survival. At high latitude, those cultures which reinforce "understanding" (Nobel Award in Science, etc.) fare better because the environment is so fabulously complex that mere knowledge does not cover all of the cases, except in "the very best of times".*

The process of imprinting — which is the acquisition of knowledge at a very early age that becomes the ultimate "reality" filter — was first observed in birds.

Pigeons that hatch-out with a human hand in the nest in lieu of their mother, and which are associated with the human hand for their first thirty minutes, are said to attempt to mate *only* with the human hand.

Chickens that are given a colored ball with a bell in it to follow over an obstacle course for thirty minutes after hatching act as though the ball were "Mama".

Humans "imprint" by age seven:

"Give me a child until it is seven, and it will always be a Roman Catholic;" or

"People have to train their children how to behave in terms so simple that an Anthropologist should be able to understand them;" or

"Not one person in a hundred changes his mind about anything fundamental after he is seven."

Stable societies in equatorial climates are matriarchal; because women must keep control of the children as the condition of acceptance of new mates. If the society is patriarchal, and a new husband ejects the children of a previous marriage before the termination of their imprinting age, these "street-children" will not have had the knowledge required to maintain the culture (inasmuch as they **can** survive in benign climate).

At high latitudes, matriarchy is not essential to maintenance of the culture; because any young children that are ejected ("exposed") will not survive

---

*This is the reason that all education based solely on "learning by doing" fails when "times" get more difficult at higher latitudes.

to influence their culture with ignorance of the culture's requirements.

Matriarchal cultures need to discipline girls more than boys; patriarchal cultures — the reverse.

Since violence is a strong determinant of the nature of the culture, patriarchy wins at higher latitudes. Men are stronger, and do not have the physical limitations of pregnancy. Additionally, a man's death is a smaller hazard to offspring than a woman's death.

Thus, the fundamentals of individual behavior are fixed in the imprinting period by age seven.* Societies are groups of individuals, and are thus the sum total of all individuals plus their interactions.

"Brainwashing" (i.e., "late imprinting") at a later date can be accomplished by limiting the diet of an adult to a generally inadequate number of calories, with an extended severe protein deficiency. When metabolism is reabsorbing protein from the brain, the memory is gradually lost, and the individual sinks into a lethargic stupor.

A renewed protein supply, applied concurrently with intensive teaching, affects the brain similarly to imprinting. No human brain is immune to such chemical attack. **Anybody** could be converted from one behavior to another; such as from a law-abiding citizen to a bank robber by an adequate dietary and brainwashing attack.**

There is scattered data that indicates that a "lasting impression", or a "complete learning experience" can occur almost instantaneously under highly specific conditions.

Most Americans who were 20-years-old or more at the time, describe in minute detail their circumstances around the moment that they heard that the U.S. had been attacked at Pearl Harbor. Likewise, the scene before their eyes at the time of the Kennedy assassination can be recalled with clarity.

Most war veterans have one to a few scenes that come back with extreme clarity. The same phenomenon applies as with the Kennedy assassination.

This has to be a phenomenon related to the chemistry of extreme shock or trauma, with ordinary events learned extraordinarily well during the period of such chemical state. It does not persist for a long period of time; rather only for minutes — or at most, hours.

---

*Encyclopaedia Brit. 14: 130 (1943)
There was a young man who said "Damn!
It is borne upon me that I am
  An engine which moves
  In predestined grooves,
I'm not even a bus; I'm a tram!"

**Patty Hearst (?), P.O.W.'s in Korea and Vietnam (?), Vietnam boat people (?), Peoples Temple, Jonestown, Guyana (?).

One of the writers (Browning) was taken by his father to a survey stake in the edge of a large clearing on the farm and was told the following story:

"In Europe, in earlier times, when a boy reached twelve as you have, his father took him on the rounds of the estate to learn the location of the survey markers that mark the boundary.

"At each marker, the Father soundly whipped his son.

"Ever after, the recipient of the treatment could readily find the markers." End of story.

This writer (who had had some "sound whippings" from his father) was so shocked by the story that he remembers not only the survey stake (and can walk straight to it); but also the father, the story, the sound of the father's voice, color of his clothes and position of his hat, the texture and color of the grass, and where the cattle were standing at the time. And these memories are clear several decades later.

Continuing research establishes that — to a large extent — human behavior can be predetermined.

Such research can determine what people consistently do under particular circumstances, and either accurately forecast, or alternatively cause, such circumstances.

Political polls create an artificial sense of inaccuracy of the opinion-polling process. The break — in accuracy — around the number which constitutes a majority or a plurality, gives a 1:0 error with a shift from just to one side of such a majority or plurality to just beyond the other side.

Actually, any real (example: marketing) process would be almost equally pleased with either 49 or 52% of the market share. (The exceptions to this statement are those extremely stable and old markets like automobiles, and certain staple foods.)

Let us examine a list of human behavior determinants:

1. Sexuality is such a predictable more of human behavior as to be extremely notable in the exception — such as celibacy in the Roman Catholic priesthood. Even there, it is a major controversy. The Shakers were apparently celibate because they ceased to exist in one generation.
2. Violence is the human norm; so that pacifists are so exceptional as to be as often taken for cowards as for honest pacifists. Even so, they are considered strange, and barely tolerable. Indeed, societies do not tolerate pacifists under conditions of extreme peril. On occasion, Ireland drafted both priests and women; and many other sovereignties have done the equivalent.
3. Tribalism or ethnicity is a norm of human behavior.

4. Monolingualism is a norm. Bilingualism is historically transient.
5. A religion or "set of believed principles" is almost immutable.
   Belief is distinct from knowledge; for if one believes certain precepts that he does not know — then certainly he believes what he does know.

   "Strictly speaking, all knowledge is belief, though not all belief is knowledge." (*Encyc. Brit.*)

   One's beliefs act as a filter to perception; for one typically cannot even perceive what he does not believe can exist; without great repetition of the observation.
6. Real world perceptions acquired through one's sensory nerves take priority with frequent repetition over the much more "bland" neurological experiences related to reading, contemplation, understanding and the like.
7. Nutrition has a profound effect upon both the mind and body of a human.
8. Humans alter extremely little in their fundamental beliefs after they are seven years of age.
9. Skill in mind or body is acquired only by very extensive, self-disciplined repetition. Groundless inspiration is almost always ineffective.
10. Winners are typically very persistent, though not everyone who is persistent wins.
11. Humans can survive war, but cannot survive peace; because in peace, the unfit contribute almost equally to the gene pool, and breeds their own group down to the point of non-survival.
12. All humans react positively emotionally toward the following — or even some of the following characteristics:
    A. Faces with huge round foreheads;
    B . Big eyes;
    C . Big eye pupils;
    D. Small jaws.
    Examples: babies, Ike Eisenhower, Winston Churchill, poodle-cut dogs, etc.)
13. People react conversely to the opposites of the above. (Examples: snakes, Malibu storks, big-teethed dinosaurs, etc.).

One can use each of these sorts of truisms to lay a plan for human relationships — such as advertising campaigns, and the like.

There has been an enormous amount of measurement data published which concerned all of the kinds of things that humans do and are — books full of data.

The measurements are everything from finger length to head size; I.Q.

to acuity of hearing at different frequencies.

Given that behavior depends in part on physical characteristics, things for people depend upon a wide variety of factors including the physical. During the Vietnam war, the caliber of army rifles was greatly reduced to accomodate smaller soldiers—which our South Vietnamese allies were. Other reasons developed, but that's where it all started.

It appears from years of familiarity with the subject of "human engineering"; and years of effort to make sense of "soft sociological data" that human behavior is just as deterministic as shoe sizes.

One can list little vignettes of the human outlook under different subject headings:

Violence:
- People respond without intellectual rancor to **overwhelming** violence. They accept the new situation as real, and go from there.
- A person is much more likely to be murdered by someone he knows than by a stranger.
- All important issues are decided by violence. An alternative way of stating this corollary is: Any issue that is not worth defending violently is not considered to be important.
- The percent of a population killed in deciding an issue is a measure of the importance of the issue.

Change:
- People strongly resist change.
- People will accept change only when they fear the alternative more.
- The degree of resistance of a person to change depends upon his childhood imprinting.
- The mean resistance to change, and the statistical variability of the population with respect to attitude toward change is characteristically different for different ethics.
- The strength of an ethic varies highly positively as the ethic is flexible; i.e., willingness to change makes a society strong. (By the same rule— such institutions as the Environmental Protection Agency (The E.P.A.) which formalized resistance to change—makes a society weak.)

Communication:
- Communication influences people.
- People are much more eager to press their own views on others than to learn other peoples' views.
- Every reciprocal transmission is a communication.
- Body language is communication.

- The completeness and efficiency of communication depends upon the similarity of the people who are communicating.

Survival:
- A society cannot survive if risk-and-reward; or privilege-and-duty are disproportionate.
- The great inventions were made by barbarians, and were assimilated by civilizations (which otherwise are so inflexible that they refuse to change) only when they are conquered by the barbarians.
- Civilizations choose to be inflexible, hence they are always destroyed by barbarians in variable times.
- A society with strong leaders and weak people is easy to destroy. A society with weak leaders and strong people survives and survives and survives.
- The U.S. is basically barbarian — and usually has weak leadership. There is no fundamental relationship between the elective process and leadership ability. The situation is analogous to having a footrace to the Met — and the winner sings.
  Anybody that wants strong political leadership obviously wants a boss who will tell him what to do.

Commentary

It appears from these studies that civilization is the ultimate decadence to which humans can sink.* Order for its own sake renders any culture powerless to improve its own condition. On this basis, it would appear that the institution of law is the ultimate burden of Mankind.

Crime, war, famine, climatic change, pestilence, poverty, greed, and **jihad** (religious war) — all of these are transient. Only **law** goes on and on preserving the afflictions of Mankind by forbidding change.

Only law has made all afflictions of the human condition seem attractive by comparison from time to time. The evidence is that peoples launch into great revolutions which invite famine, pestilence, etc. in a frenzy of ridding themselves of law.

Throughout history, Man has gone from revolt to revolt attempting to thwart, escape or destroy the law.

No other concept in the **existence** (to say nothing of the **history**) of Man has evoked so many struggles — so much death and misery.

The great inventions all came from the Barbarians.

---

*This point is further expanded by Appendix I.

The great discoveries were made by the Barbarians.

The Renaissance occurred when Italy was broken into tiny Principalities — not in the times when Roman Law ruled the area.

Slavery was ended in the rough, brawling, barbaric era of the 1800's in crude places like the U.S. The great civilizations of Egypt, Greece and Rome carefully preserved slavery. Gladiators slew each other to amuse the operators of the Roman legal system; and Christians, men, women and children, were fed to the lions in the name of the law. History offers no hope that Man will ever rid himself of this aspect of his behavior.

As Chiang Kai-shek said of the Japanese and the Communists during the heat of World War II:

"The Japanese are a disease of the skin;
Communism is a disease of the soul."

So one might say of famine, pestilence, war, and other like afflictions of Man:

These afflictions are a disease of the skin;
Law (the imposition of one human's will upon others) is a disease of
the soul.

The great anomaly of human behavior is that — although all other behavioral traits are responses to sex, hunger, climate, competition, communication, etc., one characteristic at odds with all others is the will to law which attempts to stabilize control of humans over humans; to "civilize", stabilize and thus to forbid change of the human condition; to reduce all but a handful to docile compliance; and thereby to destroy the initiative which permits people to improve their condition.

Law is, indeed, the fifth and most terrible "horseman".

C. MAN — Human Action Related To Climatic Change

Climatic change occurs slowly. That is its very definition; for when change is rapid, we call it weather.

The major periods are:

178-year solar cycle: warmest time being (1932 - 178 x),
where x = a whole number ;
179.33-year solar-lunar-earth tidal beat where the warmest time may be
about 45 years after highest tidal-force; or about 45 years before lowest
tidal-force ; thus
(1972 - 179.33x) - 45, where x = a whole number.

Twice per 1600-year westward precession rate of the non-dipole magnetic
field (strength = Y).
(The pole precesses westward one revolution per 1600 years; the field is
elliptical.) (see **Figure 28**).
Twice per 7200-year westward precession rate of the dipole magnetic
field (strength 10Y).
Twice per 26,000-year precession rate of the earth's axis (wobbling like
a child's top) (see **Figure 43B**).
Once per ∿ 42,000-years wobble in the amplitude of the above axis
precession (see **Figure 43B**).
Once per ∿ 90 to 100,000-year warp of the ellipticity of the earth's orbit
under the influence of the other planets — particularly Jupiter. (see
Figure 10)

The last three periods are known to produce the Ice Ages, and resulted
in people's greatest migrations. People migrated from Asia to the Western
Hemisphere across the Bering Straits which was then land; from Asia to
Japan similarly; and during the warm period 7 to 4,000 years ago they
migrated from the Sahara to Western Europe and circum-Saharan lands.
These cycles of migration were all geared to the Ice Age Cycle conditions
(cold or hot).

Other human responses to climatic change are covered in Appendix III.
Briefly, they were; in the case of Lower Egypt, domestic dynastic over-
throws with respect to the timing of high and low tidal forces (wet versus
dry climatic conditions, respectively) 4 and 17 dynasties respectively. The
probability of this being a chance distribution of dynastic changes is less
than one in a hundred.

Taking all dynasties domestic and foreign in Lower Egypt for a period of
over 5000 years, and cutting them into 179.33-year periods, one obtains a
listing as seen in Appendix III (see also **Figure 33**). Then, by taking a running
sum of 5 such periods (about 900 years) (for the purpose of erasing any 800-
year cycle effects), one accumulates a set of data as shown in **Figure 33**.
The bar chart shows a cyclical change in number of dynasties per 900-year
period.

Taking information concerning the 1600-year period of magnetic intensity
change, and plotting it at the longitude of Lower Egypt, we obtain the
curve shown in **Figure 33**. Clearly, political stability was related to the magnetic field intensity — the greater the intensity, the less the stability; and
reasonably, the linkage is variation of climate with its influence on human
behavior.

Shifting to the world as a whole, data taken from a standard reference on all of the dynasties in history can be plotted on the 179.33-year tidal force cycle (see **Figures 34A** and **34B**). Even though the northern hemisphere is out of phase from the southern hemisphere; and though the 78-year cycle is dominant at the equator, there is a highly significant cycle of dynastic beginnings. When things get bad, people look around for somebody to tag. The government is a likely "fall-guy" when things get bad.

People have "tagged" the Jews also, throughout the last 3000 years of history. **Figure 35** is a bar graph showing the number of incidences of persecution — pogroms and other major events — covering the last two thousand years.* It is — as with dynasties — a significant tidal force (hence climatic) cycle correlated that other peoples persecute Jews. The current tidal-force correlates with **low** incidence of both dynastic overthrow and Jewish persecution.

Great Conquerers are born at high tide (i.e., the half of the 179.33-year period during which the high-tidal forces occur). The Great Conquerers were people like Hitler, Stalin, Napoleon, Tamarlane, Ghengiz Khan, Attila the Hun, etc.; i.e., people who really impressed their neighbors.

Figure 34A shows when the Great Conquerers were born. It's not that there is ever a shortage of people who **want** to be great conquerers. Edi Amin of Uganda just failed to conquer the world. Moamar Khadafi is working on it. It's only when a great people follows a leader that he becomes a Great Conquerer.

People follow "would-be-conquerers" when **they** are imprinted under conditions that make them believe that conquest is a valid and desirable goal.

A different point of view obtains between low and high tidal periods. Revelation-type religion-founders are essentially without exception born at low tide; reformers are born at high tide. (see **Figure 36**) During low-tidal times, which are good times in most populated areas, people tend to be more charitable. They come to believe the old dictum: "To each according to his need; from each according to his ability."

This tends to gain a lot of followers; especially among those who have needs, but little or no ability.

It is a curious fact that the papacy — which has lasted through ∼1900 years had its greatest stability at the times of the two highest tidal forces — 796 and 1893 (see **Figure 43C**).**

---

*Special thanks go to Dr. Albert Goodman, his Rabbi and such members of his synagogue who helped to accumulate the data on which this work was based.

**In 1870, the latest period of extreme stability, the Princes of the Church perceived and declared Infallibility!

During high-tidal-force times, the reformers arise. When people receive returns on belief (worship, demonstrations, election, etc.) at a sufficiently low gratification, the belief falls by the wayside. The people who produce actual products have the last word. If they don't produce, the show is over.

Words are cheap.

When it gets down to the "nitty-gritty", the people who produce have all of the power. They may or may not exercise it; but since no one can live without product, the producers have life and existence within their control. A society would be justified in limiting all social decision-making to people who produce products. This cannot be achieved by law, because since words are so cheap, laws would gradually make all sorts of pernicious claims of production by: politicians, lawyers, artists, philosophers, preachers, actors, etc. Revolutions would still have to to occur from time-to-time; but less often if only the producers of tangibles made policy.

We have tracked down battles in the history of New Mexico — throughout its history as pre-Spanish, Spanish, Mexican and U.S. The battles in which 10 or more people were killed (including hot pursuit as a continuing part of a battle) were the battles of interest. This elevates a given battle beyond a simple family fight or feud to chosen sides over larger issues (i.e., impersonal killings rather than murder).

There are two reasons for concentrating on such a narrow geographical area: one is that so little of historic interest has happened in New Mexico that killing 10 people seems like a "big deal". The other reason is that New Mexico has been literate longer than any other place currently in the United States; so the records are better.

Figure 1 shows a bar graph of the battles (103 in all) and the curve is the derivative of the solar-lunar-earth tidal-forces. When tidal-forces are rising, battles increase. Tidal-forces are now rising, and the authors live in New Mexico. We wait and watch with interest.

Indeed, all of the battles (of historic dimension) in the contiguous 48-state area of the U.S. follow roughly the same pattern (see **Figure 37**).* On a more limited time scale, the great volcanoes of 1783 were followed by the reports by Benjamin Franklin that the cold, miserable weather in France might be due to volcanic dust. The sun was not seen until it reached 17° above the horizon in Southern France.

In 1784, the snowstorm in August in the Mexico City valley killed the

---

*France, since 1500, has had high "aggressive" war casualties when volcanic dust concentration was high in the atmosphere; and high "defensive" war casualties when volcanic dust in the atmosphere was low (see **Figure 38**). This is cold-variable and warm-steady climate, respectively.

corn and 300,000 people starved to death.

The weather (reflected by wine crop records) stayed so bad that it almost surely triggered the French revolution of 1789.

The great volcano Tamboro in 1815 caused "the year without a summer" in 1816. This triggered a European demand for American farm staples. The profitable market resulted in a wave of land speculation. Collapse of the European commodities market in 1819 caused land values to sink rapidly, and "the first major banking crisis" in U.S. history caused a general severe business depression — brought on indirectly by the volcano.

Depressions in the United States are typically associated with dust-storm climate.

Some climatic changes that are associated with magnetic effectors can be shown to move waves of human behavior westward just as the magnetic field, itself precesses.

Measurements show that the non-dipole field precesses westward at about 0.225° per year (i.e., one full rotation in 1600 years). The field is roughly elliptical in shape; so it has a large and a small "effective end" — of which the larger end currently points toward the Midwestern U.S., the smaller toward Outer Mongolia.

The rotation of this field is almost surely what has produced a record of an 800-year modulation of climate in Western Europe (first one end of the ellipse, then the other); and has presumably similarly modulated the climate around the Earth along lines of latitude.

History has been influenced by the passage of this magnetic field effect as shown in **Figure 39**. Inasmuch as the non-dipole field precesses westward, the pole passed Moscow (about 1470 A.D.); and about 187 years later passed Madrid. The spectacular increase of the length of sovereign reigns occurred during the westward passage of the north magnetic pole.

In 1471, the Principality of Moscow (having abandoned the ancient appelation — Principality of Vladimir) conquered the Mother City of Russia, Novgorod. Ivan III absorbed for Moscow by purchase, conquest or marriage, in addition to Novgorod from 1471 to 1488: Yaroslvl in 1463, Rostov in 1474 and Tver in 1485. In 1480, he refused to pay the customary tribute to the Grand Khan Ahmed, ruler of the Golden Horde who had held the Rus in bondage since the earliest Mongol conquest of central Russia in 1239.

Ivan III married Zoe (in Russian: Sofia) the only niece of the last Byzantine Emperor, in 1472. Because Constantinople had fallen to the Turks in 1453 (which, coincidentally (?) was the very year that the British were driven out of France), the leadership of Orthodox Christianity was vacant. Ivan III constituted Moscow the "Third Rome" and made it the capitol of the

Orthodox Church.

Russia entered a new period as a World Power.

In Spain, the westward passage of the north magnetic pole was accompanied by the unfortunate death of John II, only son of Ferdinand and Isabella. The result was that after these Catholic monarchs had conquered the Moors, expelled the Jews, and established a major foothold in the New World; they were succeeded by "The Austrian House" in the person of Charles V. The subsequent involvement of Spain in the affairs of Europe led it to the pinnacle of its historic power and achievements; although intense bureaucratic regulation of its internal economy and huge human and economic outlays for military ventures eventually exhausted her.

A second interesting relationship on a much longer basis occurs between Lower Egypt and Spain and is related to the Earth's magnetic field.

In Lower Egypt, only 4 domestic dynastic changes occurred at "hightide" (climatic instability for 89 years) (with respect to the 179.33-year tidal period discussed elsewhere) and 17 occurred at "low-tide (climatic stability for 89 years) — a very significant relationship (probably related to the flooding of the Nile).

Memphis, Egypt, is about 31° E. Longitude.

Dynasties in Spain — if connected with climate which is related to the westward precession of the magnetic field — should begin to be affected when the magnetic pole is north of the eastern-most land ($\sim$ 3° E. Long.) of Spain. Certainly, it is conservative practice to regard the magnetic pole at 0° Longitude as having permitted sufficient time for the westward moving climatic change to have begun its political effect on a significant fraction of the Spanish land mass.

We can, on the basis of the length of time required for a magnetic field condition to precess from the Nile Delta to Spain, compare dynastic duration of the two areas.

The astounding result is a coefficient of correlation of 0.815 — such a high correlation that it gives a 99 + % "degree of certainty of the relationship"[*]

---

*31°-0° ÷ 0.226% / year = 137.77 years.

This is the time of westward precession of the magnetic field from Lower Egypt to Spain at 1 revolution in 1600 years.

History gives the years in which new dynasties were established; but the months are not recorded in most cases. For this calculation, and to minimize error, each dynastic date was taken as the half-year.

The formula used, then, was:

Spanish Dynasty ([years + 0.5] − 137.77) ÷ 179.33 = Period

The New Dynasties occurred in: 412, 711, 718, 756, 840, 860, 874, 914, 929, 1035, 1035,

A third interesting relationship relates to the westward precession of the dipole (as contrasted with the non-dipole field). The intensity of the dipole field is roughly 10x the intensity of the non-dipole field.

The period of rotation of the dipole field depends upon the rate of 0.05° / year westward precession. Thus, the dipole field pole would rotate

$$360° \div 0.05° / year = 7200 \text{ years / revolution.}$$

The pole appeared to be straight north in Chicago $\curlywedge$ 41.52° N, 87.38° W Longitude in 1950; and would have been at further east locations earlier (see **Figure 40**).

Thus, the dipole north has tended to be north of major power centers when they were **number one** in the world.

Since the north magnetic dipole is now at 98°, and the U.S. extends from grossly 74° to 122° W Longitude, the implication is that the U.S. could have a total of about 960 strong years (starting at about 1630) extending to about 2590 A.D. — or some 600 strong years yet; with the center of power moving westward gradually.

It would be a gross oversimplification to attribute power to the mere presence of the dipole north pole — but the effect of the pole on weather seems to have made success more likely. There appears to be a consistent effect of climate on human behavior that results in people influenced by proximity of the north magnetic pole becoming strong.

(Perhaps the effect is produced by extremely aggravating weather.)

There is another matter of interest, inasmuch as the magnetic field has been shown in Egyptian and Spanish history to be very relevant to political stability.

The dipole field precesses westward at about 0.05° Longitude per year, and the non-dipole field precesses similarly at 0.225° per year. Thus, the faster non-dipole field goes all the way around and overtakes the 10x stronger dipole field about every 2057 years.

1076, 1134, 1134, 1157, 1157, 1162, 1217, 1274, 1276, 1476, 1479, 1873, 1931, 1936 and 1975.

New Dynasties established in each 179.33-year period (staggered by the precession time of 137.77 years)

179.33-Year Periods	1	2	3	4	5	6	7	8	9	10
Spanish Dynasty	1	-	4	4	8	3	1	-	1	3
Lower Egypt Dynasty	1	-	2	2	3	2	1	1	-	3

r = 0.815 (r = coefficient of correlation)

degree of certainty = 99 + %**

Lower Egyptian Dynastic period is simply (Date A.D. ÷ 179.33);

Spanish Dynastic Period = ([Date A.D. + 0.5] − 137.77 ÷ 179.33).

**The statistical purist must take into account that this is *aposteriori* (i.e., after the fact) reasoning.

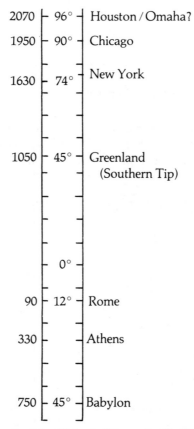

2070	96°	Houston / Omaha?
1950	90°	Chicago
1630	74°	New York
1050	45°	Greenland (Southern Tip)
	0°	
90	12°	Rome
330		Athens
750	45°	Babylon

Figure 40. Position (Longitude) of Dipole Magnetic North O Compared with National Power.

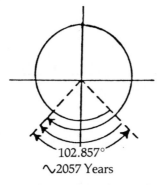

102.857°

∿2057 Years

Figure 41. Magnetic Dipole North and Non-dipole North Coincidence.

However the magnetic field relates to political affairs, it can be compared in increments of 2057 years; having been lined up only 3 times during the period of recorded history.

Date	Position of Pole, North of Location	Level of Power
1945 A.D.	Centroid of U.S. Population ~ 87° W. Long. (Centroid at 88°)	#1 in World — Post World War II: U.S.
113 B.C.	Roman Empire 3° L. East of Rome over Southern Italy ~ 15° E. Long. (Rome is at 12.4°)	#1 in World — Ruled Eastern Mediterranean, had beaten Carthage
2170 B.C.	North of Ancient Chinese Capitol Anyang ~ 118° E. Long. (Anyang at 114°)	Yü — The last of the Sage Kings — established the Hsia Dynasty (2206 - 1766 B.C.) in China. His Dynasty ruled 300 years. The Hsia Dynasty has only recently changed from Legend to Archaeological fact.

Centroid of U.S. ~ 1945 was 39° N. Lat.
Rome is at ~ 41.5° N. Lat.
Anyang, China was at ~ 36.5° N. Lat.

The conditions in Rome as described in the Encyclopedia of Military History* were as follows:

*Dupuy, R. Ernest and Trevor N. Dupuy (1977) *The Encyclopedia of Military History.* Harper & Row, Publishers; New York.

"The growth of large estates, operating with slave labor procured in overseas conquests, hastened the disappearance of the sturdy peasantry who had formed the Roman militia army. Those now pamperized peasants became the mobs of the city, or the permanent professional soldiery of the army. These soldiers lacked traditional Roman discipline. They owed allegiance only to generals, and were inspired by loot rather than patriotic ardor. The near-collapse of law and order was demonstrated in repeated uprisings of slaves, in the domination of the Mediterranean by pirates, and in recurrent civil strife. Yet, surprisingly, the essential vigor of Rome was demonstrated by a few military leaders of ability, like Scipio Aemilianus and Metellus, who inspired the degenerating army to fight worthily and to hold secure the far-flung Roman borders."

The similarity of these conditions to the U.S. are astounding.

In summary, the evidence, though merely correlations, is strongly persuasive that climate controls much of human behavior. Food, fuel requirements, transportation, and clothing requirements are strongly modified by climate. It is intuitively obvious that migrations, wars, revolutions, depressions and a myriad of social events are related to changes of climate. The subject will be further explored in subsequent chapters.

There is nothing that is done by Man which is not totally in compliance with his role as a functional part of a natural order. He is a part of it — not the Master of it.

He is smart enough to know that hundreds of thousands of species died-out as their final compliance with their role. Man may well be the first with enough intelligence to avoid the final act — or it may be that other organs (stomach, gonads) will exercise priority over the brain. We cannot know yet.

Bibliography

V. MAN

[116] Hyden, H. and E. Egyhazi (1963) Glial RNA Changes During a Learning Experiment In Rats. Institute of Neurobiology, University of Goteborg, Sweden. Communicated by Alfred E. Mirsky (March 13, 1963)

[117] San Jose Mercury - (Monday, February 21, 1966) From *The New York Times*. Uric Acid Level High In Leaders.

[118] Altman, Joseph, MIT Psycho-Physiologist (1967) Environment May Induce Formation Of Neurons After Birth. *Scientific Research*, October, 1967.

[119] Stinchcombe, Arthur L. (1972) The Social Determinants of Success. *Science*, Vol. 178: 603-604. Book Reviews (November 10, 1972)
[120] Jerison, Harry J. (1961) Quantitative Analysis of Evolution of the Brain in Mammals. *Science*; Vol. 133: 1012-14 (March 31, 1961)
[121] Pinto, William A. (Over Many Years) Personal Communication of an Extensive Review of neurological literature.

Chapter VI

Climate in Two Centuries around Two High Tidal Forces

Introduction

At 60° North Latitude, there have been two high tidal forces which were equal to each other and were higher than any other in this 10,250-year tidal half-cycle period (P)

$$\frac{1}{P} = \frac{1}{25,800} + \frac{1}{100,000}$$

$P = 10,250$ years

The two dates are 23 December 796 and 23 December 1893 (see **Figure 43A**).

On the theory that tidal forces trigger volcanoes; and that volcanoes influence climate [122], we have assembled data which can indicate climate through the period from 717 through 926. To put it mildly, the data is not very coherent. After all, this was the Dark Age in Europe and in Illinois; and there isn't much in the way of printed reports from the Americas (only three Maya Codices plus three more fragments); and during a part of this time, the Japanese and Chinese courts were out of touch with their countries. Where literacy resided in the Emperor's Court, and the country operated autonomously, written material has nothing to do with reality as seen by the citizenry.

These records are like trying to find out something about Iowa by reading the Washington Post during the Watergate hearings. The Capitol had disappeared into its own navel to be heard from nevermore. In China and Japan then, as in Washington in the early 1970's relevant and related government disappeared. Reinvention of relevancy in government was (is) necessary.

So learning about reality of climate in such times has been a widely dispersed and only moderately successful effort.

A. 1. Climate from 717 to 926 A.D.

A little bit of anticipation before the dates in question is constructive; therefore a few anticipatory dates are put in before the 717 A.D. era began.

Fair warning must be expressed that some of the data and inferences are very weak.

Date: A.D.

600   The brilliant death-centered Hopewell Culture in Ohio was abandoned [134]

600   Anasazi farmers arrived at Aztec, New Mexico, and farmed there until the mid-1100's. The site was then reoccupied in 1225 by Mesa Verde people, who in turn abandoned it in only 50 years [134].

Early   Severe climatic disturbances causing famines, wars, and a change
600's   of religion in Japan occurred, according to the Nihongi.

650   Anasazi pithouses (heat-conserving dwellings) were built in Chaco Canyon [134].

By 700   The Anasazi had learned enough about farming that they became Developmental Pueblo [134].

700   Middle Woodland* people settled near Nachez, Mississippi. They traded for flint from Ohio, marine shells from the Gulf of Mexico, greenstone from Alabama and copper from Lake Superior [134].

---

*The Woodland Culture ranged from eastern Canada down through New England to and included the Middle Atlantic States in the U.S. (New York, New Jersey, Pennsylvania). The Culture is usually divided into three developmental phases [134].

1000 B.C. to 500 B.C.   Early Woodland (Gardens in small clearings).

500 B.C. to 700 A.D.   Middle Woodland (Field crops plus gardens).

700 A.D. Onward   Late Woodland (Prosperous farmers / hunters / traders) [134].

After 700	Terra Ceia Island, Florida, became like Weeden Island, Florida [134].
After 700	Kolomoki mound village became like Weeden Island, Florida [134].
700	Late Woodland corn-planters settled at Cahokia*, Illinois [134].
Early 700's	A glacial maximum apparently occurred around the early 700's.
700's	In the 8th century, the canal connecting the Red Sea and the Mediterranean was abandoned for the fourth time; having been blocked for military reasons [123]. The present Suez Canal is the fifth in history to connect the seas.
400-750	In the Tyrol—Bunte Moor-South Central Europe—peat growth occurred during periods of withdrawal of the Fernau glacier.** Layers of morainic sand separates the layers of peat. There was a glacial maximum between 400 and 750 A.D. [124].
750	The Hopewell influence ended in Illinois [134].
750	The Patayan people called Cohonina was established on the South Rim of the Grand Canyon, and stayed there until 1100 [134].
Mid 700's	In the mid-700's, Germany and Bohemia suffered droughts [123].
764	The year 764 A.D. had one of the severest winters on record in England [123].
Late 700's	The late 700's was a cold phase in Europe [123].
790	In 790, Irish Monks reached Iceland [128].
790	If there were any substance to reports of an earlier occupation, the population must have died out in the probable intervening cold period. A party of Greenlanders reaching Norway in 1364 A.D. knew of the legend of King Arthur's expedition in 531 A.D., and claimed to be their descendents [123].
300-800	Disastrous drought had been occurring in Asia Minor—especially the Near East—since 300 A.D., and it continued until about 800 A.D. [123].

---

*Cahokia, Illinois, is near the Mississippi River across it from St. Louis, Missouri.

**Glaciers are a favorite source of climatic data because (a) they change very slowly; (b) they, in effect, integrate climate; and (c) they leave associated peat growth which can be Carbon-14 dated to establish their own calendar.

500-800   Within the 6th to 8th Century period, Irish Monks had encountered sea-ice, presumably in the Iceland area [123].

600-800   Mound-building stopped, and a "Dark Age" occurred in Illinois [134].

700-800   The Ballard Site Temple Mound was built and used in Arkansas [134].

800   An Anasazi pithouse was built near Window Rock, Arizona [134].

800   Mogollon pit houses were built in Grand Quivira, the dominant Pueblo in the Salinas Valley (now Estancia Valley) New Mexico [134].

805   In Ch'ang-an, the political capitol of China, 34° N., 109° E, in May, 805, towards evening when the sky grew clearer; in the South-east, the sky was still "...clothed in red..." [129]. The sky coloration must have been due to great volcanic activity, and ejecta in the stratosphere.

805
and / or
806   Much of Heligoland was lost; hundreds were lost, and there were floods in the Netherlands all winter [123].

806   The hill is covered with yellow grain—in Chou-chih near Ch'ang-an—and the harvest is bountiful.
The Secretary of a Deputy Assistant Magistrate got 300 tons of rice for a year's pay—the equivalent of U.S. $50,000 in the 1970's [129A.]. This is a tremendous salary for a 34-year-old very minor bureaucrat, and reflects extraordinarily good times, food-wise, for China.

768-814   The Sarthe River in France dried up once during Charlemagne's reign [123].

815   Hsün-yang, China (29° 45′ N. Lat., 116° 30′ E. Long.)
"Hour by hour bitter rain has poured.
On few days has the dark sky cleared;
In listless sleep I have spent much time.
The clouds sink till they touch the water's face.
Beyond my hedge I hear the boatman's talk;
At the street-end I hear the fisher's song.
Misty birds are lost in yellow air;
Windy sails kick the white waves.
In front of my gate the horse and carriage way
In a single night has turned into a river bed." [129A].

815   At Kiukiang (Ksün-yang) — in winter-heavy snow. The river-water covered with ice and the forests broken with their load (hence unusually heavy snow).

"Summer forgot to come." [129A].

816?   Hsün-yang, China. In April, the Sub-Prefect wandered in the spring winds (i.e., late spring at 30° N. Lat.) — and his friend Yüan-Chen served wine in the northern summer-house [129A].

818   Hsün-yang — The climate was somewhat cool, so that fevers and epidemics were rare. Snakes and mosquitos were few. River fish (Pen River) were remarkably fat. Local wine was good (Judgment made by a very cultured man — Po-Chü-i (implying that summers were *warm and dry*)); and for the most part, food is like that of the North Country [129A]. (This is at the latitude of — and in a geographical circumstance analogous to Houston, Texas, where summers are more typically *warm and wet*.)

819   Ssech'uan Province China — abundant crops [129A].

820   Ch'ang-an, China — Pine trees in the gales of autumn, suns of summer; and height of spring in the fine evening rain — at year's end the time of great snow — [129A]

820-823 The Emperor Saga of Japan (reigned 810-823) quoted from a poem composed by Po-Chü-i in 820 in Chung-chou, a remote place in Ssech'uan, China. This demonstrates that relatively prompt commerce existed [129A]

823 or   Hang-chow (30° 15' N., 120° 16' E.) Taxes were heavy, many
824   people were poor. Farmers were hungry, for often their fields were dry (a city which has a geographical location grossly equivalent to the geographical position of Savannah, Georgia, U.S.). This implies an extended period of drought, but would not have been related to magnetic field because of timing.

Po's dam was built on the Western Lake to help in a year when things were bad [129A]

829   There was ice on the Nile in Egypt [123].

838   There was a great flood on 26 December in Friesland, The Netherlands [123].

814-840 During this reign of Louis le Debonnaire, the Sarthe River in Northern France dried up once as it did once earlier in Charlemagne's reign [124].

800's   "...and at Aletseh the starting point of the Oberriederin (i.e., the early irrigation course) is still (1967) covered by the glacier."

[124]. (In other words, the (800's) irrigation canal was built where, in the 1900's warm period, a glacier still stands. The 800's were *warmer* than the 1900's.)

The preglacial (750-1200) trees which were eventually destroyed by the 1200 glacial offensive were at a site where no trees have grown in the interim [114], hence it was warmer then.

700-850   The 700's may have been drier in Italy, and this dryness may have continued up to about 850 A.D. [123].

860   The Rhine-Lek channel opened to the sea (presumably as a result of flooding) in the spring in the Netherlands [123].

860   Norse ships which were blown off course discovered Iceland, which was unpopulated [123].

864   Further devastation occurred in the Rhine-Lek area [123].

865   Ice filled one N.W. fjord "...and all the fjords on the northern side of the island..." (Iceland). There was a cold spring [123].

400-872   By using Bray's carbon-14 data [125], and by converting it to calendar dates with Suess' bristlecone-pine conversion chart [126], one can show that the periods of glacial advance were between 400 and 872 A.D. As of 872, the glaciers were in full retreat.

Early 700's   The glacial maximum could have been around the early 700's.

867-872   Adrian II — Pope of the Roman Catholic Church — was the last married Pope [130]. People are more tolerant in warm, easy times.

873   873 A.D. was a time of great famine, and plagues of locusts ranged from Germany to Spain [124].

874   In 874 A.D., the first Viking settlers arrived in Iceland [132].

879   879 is called the year of Universal Famine [131].

870-880   Reid Bryson, "prospecting west of Hudson's Bay, discovered on the shores of lakes Ennadai and Dimma the remains of a fossil forest, 25, 40 and even 100 kilometers north of the present forest limit. Four radiocarbon datings done for different sites showed that this forest was living about A.D. 880, 870, 1090, and 1140." [124]

600-900   Lamb quotes Wells who mentioned that the Anglo-Saxons in England were often crippled with arthritis, whereas the Bronze Age burials in Dorset show little sign of it. This may be a measure of cooler, damper climate of the 7th and 9th centuries as compared with the second millenium B.C. [123].

625-900 The earthquake data shown by Wilson in **Figure 42** is intended to imply a general cyclical periodicity of Chinese earthquake data.

If one assumes this data actually represents a cyclical periodicity of earthquakes, and extends it forward and back, one can see that toward the end of the 9th Century, the earthquakes (and presumably the volcanoes) were rising [127] (see **Figure 42**).

650-900 During the period 650 to 900 A.D., England, Wales and Scotland showed a standstill in peat growth (cool, moist climate) as compared with earlier and later times [123].

800-900 Lamb reported that there was greater sand dune activity in the Netherlands (either greater windiness or lowered water table). [123].

Floods were more frequent in Germany, Italy, England, France and the Alps [123].

~900 Eskimos first occupied Ellesmere Land (76° - 84° N. Lat., 63° - 89° W. Long.). [123]

900's Most prominent Vikings in Greenland sowed grain. [123]

Status In Ireland, peat grew slowly because the surface of the peat bog
717-926 was typically dry. Beginning about 1200, and up to the present, peat grows in Ireland, where it is cool and moist [123].

874-930 Viking settlement period in which sea-ice is practically never mentioned [123].

910-947 Oak tree-rings show droughts in Germany [124].

925-975 The 925 to 975 A.D. period was generally low-moisture in Italy [123].

900- Quite rapid growth of peat began in England, Wales and Scotland
1200 indicating the beginning of moist, cool climate [123].

700-1300 From the 8th to the 13th centuries, Empires flourished in the Mali area of Western Africa, implying a period of favorable climate [123] although favorable remains to be defined.

800-1600 Settlement of Cahokia — a large Mississippian population is well established on the basis of a large series of new radiocarbon dates as beginning about 800 A.D.

Population increases may be a reasonable factor producing migrations to the northern frontier [133].

Summary

In the early 700's, the Northern Hemisphere got very cold. A glacial maximum occurred, and sea-ice, presumably around Iceland, was encountered by Irish Monks. This cold period saw drier conditions at high latitudes (Europe) and in the Middle East; but improving conditions in the Maya area (18° - 20° North Latitude).

The highly-developed Hopewell Culture in Ohio had failed and was abandoned about 600 A.D. when the climate became cold and variable. This abandonment put Illinois into a Dark Age from 600 to 800, with Hopewellian influence ceasing altogether about 750 A.D., in association with the bitterly cold climate.

Woodland Culture farmers from the Northeastern coast spread westward to about East St. Louis, (Cahokia) Ill. about 700 A.D. Communities along the Southeast U.S. coast have a suddenly upgraded culture about 700 A.D. At this same time, the "Old Ones" — the Anasazi upgraded their farming and became Developmental Pueblo in the Southwest. The impression is strong that there was a "southwestward and sunbelt" migration of Northeastern cultures synchronous with the cold climate.

The Woodland Culture also spread to Wisconsin, and south to Nachez, Mississippi, where the people maintained extremely wide trading relations. This drive to get near rivers corresponds to the simultaneous century of droughts (700-800) in the Near East, Germany, Bohemia, France, and dry enough weather that the peat wouldn't grow in either Ireland, England, Wales or Scotland.

The Maya, French, and Arabs reached pinnacles of greatness by 800, and the Popes enjoyed the longest average tenure in their history up to that point in time (see **Figure 43C**).

After 800, the tree-rings of Mesa Verde show much warmer weather; the Maya, French and Arab Empires disintegrated; the Papal tenure became shorter; the Vikings and Saracens carried piracy to a new high; the pit-houses (heat economizing design of Southwestern U.S.) became apartment house complexes. The Irish died-off in Iceland and the Mississippian Culture moved north along the River and displaced the Woodland Culture at Cahokia, Illinois.

The reasons for these changes were all apparently climatic changes. The years were warmer, but clear skies led to bitter-cold winter nights.

According to Mesa Verde, Colorado, tree-ring data (see **Figure 48**) a "double-bump" occurred to temperature in the Northern Hemisphere in the 800's; the first centering about 815 and the second about 865.

The tree-rings (actually from Wetherill Mesa which is nearby the better-known Mesa Verde) are from atop a high mesa which is almost on the continental divide. Because of altitude, growth of tree-rings would typically be limited by low-temperatures. When the years get warm, the tree-rings grow rapidly.

One can fairly conservatively conclude, therefore, that the climate got warm early in the 800's and again, sharply, around 865 A.D.

Glaciers were in full retreat by 872 A.D. in the Northern Hemisphere; and it probably got a little warmer than in 1940. Vikings sowed grain in Iceland, and sea-ice rarely occurred.

Following this warm time, temperatures plunged again, and inhibited tree-ring growth to and beyond the end of the century. Peat began to grow rapidly in England, Scotland and Wales, and droughts occurred in Germany.

Feudalism replaced all great sovereignties in Western Europe, and China's revolutions became so severe that Chinese history ceased.

A. 2. Some Cultural Responses Around The High Tidal Force of 796 A.D.

The Maya culture is of major interest, but will be treated here only as it relates to events at 30° North Latitude or further north. The total range of the culture was from about 13° N. Lat. (El Salvador) to 22° N. Lat. (Yucatan, Mexico).

The Classic Maya culture is thought to have related critically to the placement of monuments (stela) every 20 years to commemorate the events of that "katun". (A buktun was 400 katuns [or 394.25 tropical years.])

The number of sites erecting monuments was a measure of the number of locations tightly ruled by the hierarchical organization of the Maya Culture; thus is a measure of the level of civilization. A peripheral fact that correlates with the number of monuments is the "quality" of the art ranging from grooved outlines; flat, then flat reliefs, then shallow and finally deep bas relief figures. To quote from Morley [135]:

"The Late period lasted from 9.8.0.0.0. (A.D. 593) to at least the end of the Maya Initial Series inscriptions at 10.3.0.0.0 – (A.D. 889). This period saw first an accelerated activity, and an increasing refinement in architecture and the arts, coupled with extensive religious construction in the eastern and western regions of the central Maya area. Both the architecture and sculpture of the central area reached their heights during the century preceding 9.18.0.0.0 (A.D. 790) in such eastern and western Maya centers as Copan, Piedras Negras, Yaxchilan, and Palenque. From this time on, the decline was rapid, with the Peten region in its van, until by A.D. 900, Long Count inscriptions were no longer written, and organized religious activities ceased." [135]

and

"By the end of Baktun 9 (A.D. 830), however, the crest had been passed and there followed an artistic recession from which the ancient Maya never recovered." [ibid]

By way of further clarification of "the stela cult":

"There may be a significant relationship between the stela cult and the successful agricultural enterprises at these large sites. The current understanding of the cult in the Maya lowlands is that the stelas recorded the inauguration, reign, military victories, death, and succession of rulers at specific sites where the inscribed stones were erected". ..."The organization of large numbers of people is required to bring an entire mountain valley or other large area into political unity and economic stability." [136]

The Maya civilization practiced severely disciplined land and water control. Various techniques include raised fields and terraces. "Water-control techniques, such as canals, wells, reservoirs, and cenotes (deep sinkholes with a pool at the bottom), were also used at many sites."

Dams, irrigation channels, walk-in-wells and springs were also important water sources. Large dams date from as early as 1600 B.C. (When Egypt was occupied by the Hyksos, and Europe was in a Dark Age; the Aryan Hindus had not yet arrived in India; and the hairy Caucasian Ainus of Japan (the mongoloid Japanese would not arrive for another thousand years) worshipped bears. The Shang Dynasty of China sought to know about drought and flood by writing questions on shoulder blades of the ox, and seeing where cracks occurred when the bone was roasted in a fire. The Hittites were ravaging the "cradle of civilization" — and at this time were presiding over chaos in the final throes of the Old Empire. Only in England, where Stonehenge was being erected as a superb astronomical observatory, and in Mexico and Central America, were there constructive centers of enlightenment in 1600 B.C.)

The Mayas controlled not only perennial water sources, (continuously flowing rivers and springs); but also ephemeral sources that dry up seasonally. Dam complexes controlled water levels and directed the water flow. [136]

Without detailing water control and land use, suffice it to point out that the Mayas had developed the most varied, extensive and comprehensive system of water control and land use that one can conceive short of the energy products (pumps, pipe, etc.) of the modern era. As an example, the walk-in well which they used required community-level participation in maintenance, and could not have functioned unless the siting of the ancient town and the location of the wells were planned together [136].

And what of the planners?

Folan *et al* [137] surveyed the kind and distribution of trees, soils, and Maya structures in Coba, Quintana Roo, Mexico. From the survey they determined that the lords and priests lived on the richest land—the poorer land being reserved to the lower-classes.

The ceremonially and economically important trees included those which produce fruit, fiber, bark and resin. Few would grow in the peripheral areas. The orchards of the lords were located around the wells, if there were only a few; and the improved fields were located nearby. Wealth, to the Maya, was extremely tangible. [137].

The Maya civilization rested on the control of planning, which, in turn, focussed its attention on water-control and land use, and skimmed off the cream for the planners. The similarity of the Maya civilization to the U.S.A. today is hair-raising. Really, it's not just the U.S.A. but all the world.

The classical civilization began in about 200 A.D. and collapsed by 900 A.D. [136]. Any society that lasts 700 years was obviously doing something right. It is just as obvious that the sudden collapse of such a society signals that whatever they were doing right before, quit working.

It is obvious, if one thinks about it, that with the lower-classes greatly outnumbering the upper-classes; revolution or abandonment of any society could wipe it out at any time. The lack of a fatal revolution at any time, therefore, should be taken as a measure that the society is serving the lower-classes' needs well enough that total destruction would not be worth it to them.

The needs of the Maya lower-classes were apparently being met through the 700's; and, judging from the sudden collapse of the society at its height; it suddenly and completely failed to meet their needs. (see **Figure 44**, Curve B).

What was their basic need?

Water! Because the entire civilization was based upon the control of water.

What happened?

A study of their calendar may tell us what happened.

Mayan philosophy is explained thus by Aveni [138]:

"The Maya priest felt a need to connect every aspect of human affairs —
war, politics, agriculture, climate, the environment — and the movements of celestial bodies."

Indeed, their astronomy has been called astrology; and in one critical
sense it was. Astrology contains those real world things that people know —
or believe that they know. Astronomy is not just knowledge — it is understanding.

Aveni says:

"The Maya calendar was a maze of day cycles, and most of the periods
seem to have been of astronomical origin, although some were not.
The important cycles were made to fit together like gears of a huge
machine, each meshing with another to click off the days one at a time,
like the odometer of an automobile."

They made excellent observatories. The astronomers dealt directly with
the people.

How does an astronomer — keeper of the calendar — do business with the
people?

Speaking of the Mayan reverence for Venus, and their acute knowledge
of its appearance, disappearance and position, Aveni points out that
"...its coming is frequently connected with the rainy season. In one passage
(in The Book of Chilam Balam of Chumayel [Roys 1933]) we are told
that there shall come "the Red Star, and in the wind-swollen sky there
shall be the House of Storms."

The Mayas apparently **used their calendar to predict the weather**. To
understand how, follow these details of the way their calendars worked.

Sacred year (*tzolkim*) of 260 days
   made up of numbers from 1 to 13 to one
  of 20 Maya day names:
     Example: 1 *Ik*, 2 *Akbal*, 3 *Kan.* etc.
   By the time each day name had had 13 number
   prefixes, 260 days had elapsed.
Civil year (*haab*) of 365* days
   made up of 18 months of 20 days each
   with a 19th month of 5 days.

---

*The Mayas did a correction similar to our leap-year, and defined the actual length of the
year within ½ hour per century.

Two cogwheels of 260 and 365 respectively, if rotated until the original teeth mesh, would have to turn the smaller wheel 73 times, the larger 52 times. Both numbers (i.e., 260 and 365) are divisible by 5, so only every 5th day could ever occupy the first day of *haab*.

The lowest common denominator is the same as the number of days for the full cycle of *tzolkim* and *haab*:

$5 \times 52 \times 73 = 18,980$ days —

which is, in fact 51.9655 of our tropical years; or 51.9634 sidereal years which was their concern.

Venus cycle 584* days:
The "magic number" combining the above is just two times the 52-year number; i.e.:

$2 \times 18,980 = 37,960$ days

Thus: $37,960 \div 260 = 146$ sacred years;
$37,960 \div 365 = 104$ civil years; and
$37,960 \div 584 = 65$ Venus cycles.

The Venus cycle is such that the planet returns, on the average, to the same position as a morning star or an evening star in the 584 days.

There was further elaboration of their numerical system; but the above numbers will suffice.

Dansgaard *et al* found that the two major periodicities in world atmospheric temperature as shown by his oxygen-isotope analysis of Greenland Ice were 181 and 78 ± 5% years.

The 181-year period is probably a combination (i.e., the "in phase" beat) of the 178-year solar period shown beyond reasonable doubt by Charles Wolff, and the 179.33-year beat period of solar-lunar tidal forces at high latitude.

The minimum level of the Nile River (Boda gage) since 622 A.D. has shown a 180-year "in phase" periodicity; which reflects rainfall at 10° N. Latitude in East Africa. The effect is shown strongly in Greenland at about 60° N. Lat.; and in Japanese tree-rings at about 35° N. Lat.; so one should expect a 180-year effect at Maya latitudes.

The 78-year period probably derives from the beat between 3 Saros

---

*The true period is 583.9211, and by means similar to the "leap-year" correction, the Mayas corrected down to an error of no more than ½ hour per century.

cycles and the above 179.33-year tidal beat.* This gives a 77.45-year beat.

Since the 77.45-year beat is made up of three subcycles, a 77.45/3 = 25.81-year volcano-activating tidal force is produced.

In fact, equatorial rainfall (in Ceara, Brazil) shows a 26-year cycle of drought and flood. The drought-phase lasts about 7 years.

Note: 78/3 = 26
          104/4 = 26

The basic period of the Venus calendar was 104 years which is exactly four weather cycles.

Note further that another "magic number" in the Maya calendar was 2,920.

Thus: 37,960 ÷ 2,920 = 13
          37,960 ÷   584 = 65 Venus cycles.
          37,960 ÷   365 = 104 Civil years.
          37,960 ÷   260 = 146 Sacred years.

and   2,960 ÷   584 = 5
          2,960 ÷   365 = 8

There were "exactly" 5 Venus cycles in exactly 8 years (rather, in 7.99329 sidereal years).

Further, there were exactly 13 × 8 = 104 years (65 Venus cycles) in the Venus table; and for tidal and volcanic reasons, there are exactly 104 ÷ 26 = 4 climate cycles in the Venus table; which the Mayas probably knew.

Thirteen was a very special number for them: they had thirteen heavens. The Maya lunar calendar is similarly cleverly made up.

"On pages 51 to 58 of the Codex Dresdensis, 405 consecutive lunations (about 32¾ years) are presented, arranged in 69 groups...

...These pages of the Codex Dresdensis are a solar eclipse table, since the closing days of each of these groups are days upon which, under certain conditions, a solar eclipse would be visible somewhere on earth." [135]

---

* $\dfrac{1}{P} = \dfrac{1}{(3 \times 6585.3213)} - \dfrac{1}{179.33 \times 365.2422}$

$P = 77.45$ years

$P/3 = 25.81$ years

This can quickly be seen as follows:
  lunar month $= 29.530589$ days, and
  eclipse month $= 27.212220$ days.
The average time (T) between solar eclipses would be:

$$\frac{1}{T} = \frac{1}{27.212220} - \frac{1}{29.530389}$$

$T = 173.30996$ days

But this is not an even number of lunar periods:

  $173.30996 / 29.530589 = 5.8688285$ Lunar periods.

An eclipse must occur in exactly five or six eclipse periods — averaging 147.65295 or 177.18353 days.

The length of the table — 405 consecutive lunar months is so chosen that: $405 \times 29.503589 = 11959.888545$ days; and

  $11959.888545 \div 173.309963 = 69.008662$ groups — or, effectively the 69 groups that they used.

They had an accounting of eclipses!

Of course, tidal forces are tightly related to eclipses; and tidal forces trigger volcanoes which change climate.

It would be astrology to determine the position of Venus and the Moon and specify expected drought or flood on that basis; because the positions of Venus and the Moon is coincidental; but Venus has nothing to do with the drought as a primary, secondary, or even tertiary effect. But it would be correct because of correlating periodicity.

Now, to tie all of this information into a package, consider the following:

Brooks [139] pointed out that since about 500 B.C., wet and dry climate has existed reciprocally between the Maya area and the Western U.S.A.

More specifically, current weather maps and satellite pictures show that monsoons in the Western U.S.A. have two joining sources. At a secondary level, clouds come into Arizona / New Mexico from a southwesterly direction. At a primary level, clouds swing in over the Yucatan and circle northward over Mexico entering Southwestern U.S.A. from almost straight south.

The high pressure cell over the Gulf of Mexico during the very active monsoon weather in Southwestern U.S.A. feeds the Yucatan. This is a **warm** weather phenomenon. As Morley [135] says — there is a long rainy season — from May through January. Matheny and Gurr [136] point out that the highland rainy season lasts from June to September — tapering off in December.

And Morley [135] said:

"Nor do the priests seem to have held an economically valuable monopoly of knowledge; weather forecasting, for example, is un-reliable even now in the Maya area."

But Morley wrote his book orginally in 1946 when the climate was exactly like the time when the Maya culture collapsed (equivalent to 830 A.D. climatically). Morley [135] was right that in 1946 weather forecasting was unreliable; but that statement is in no way equivalent to saying that weather could **not** be predicted by the Maya priests in 700's A.D.

Morley further points out that astronomy probably began to be known by the Mayas by 300 B.C.!

That the Mayas were deeply concerned with weather is heavily documented.

Ixchel was the Goddess of Floods, Pregnancy, Weaving and perhaps of the Moon.

Muluc years were supposed to be "good" years. If evil occurred, it would be the special evil of scarcity of water and an abundance of sprouts in the corn.

Ix years were supposed to be hot suns, drought, famine, thefts (especially heinous to the Mayas), discords, changes of rulers, wars, and plagues of locusts.

Cauac years were worse.

Kan years were good years.

The Classical Maya believed that there had been two previous worlds which ended by flood. The Codex Dresdensis last page predicted that their world would end by flood.

Again, quoting Morley [135]:

"In confirmation of this tradition, the end of the world by a deluge is graphically depicted on the last page of the Codex Dresdensis (**Fig. 9**). Across the sky stretches a serpent-like creature with symbols of constellations on its side and signs for solar and lunar eclipses hanging from its belly. From its jaws, as well as from the two eclipse signs, a flood of water pours earthward. Below the heavenly serpent, the Old Woman Goddess with long talon-like fingernails and toenails, the patroness of death and destruction, holds an inverted bowl from which also gushes a destroying flood. At the bottom stands Ek Chuah, the black God of War, the Moan bird of evil omen on his head. In his right hand he holds two javelins and in his left a long staff, all pointing downward."

The Modern Maya believes that their third world (classical Maya) was destroyed by flood; and that the present fourth world will be destroyed the same way. One of the theories that scientists have about the destruction and abandonment of the Classic Maya sites is based on the assumption that a much lower annual rainfall existed then; and that a shift of climate northward brought back the increased rainfall that they had in 1946 [135]; which would spoil agriculture.

That sort of shift is certainly implied by the tidal force sequence shown in **Figure 44** Curve C.

And what about the prediction in the Codex Dresdensis?

The very high tidal force of 23 December 796 was associated with an eclipse configuration — or something extremely close to it; because that is the only way such a high tidal force can occur.

A portent of great magnitude would have been that Venus transited the Sun in the June following the 796 high tidal forces. The Yaqui Indians say that (to put it in our terms) a transit of Venus across the face of the sun causes the appearance of a "tail" on the sun. (Of interest is the fact that Cortes' arrival in Mexico on 4 March 1519 which was 1-Reed (Ce Acatl) on the Aztec calendar followed a Venus transit in the preceding June. These calendric-portents destroyed morale.)

Their world did apparently end in a deluge due to eclipse-related tidal forces! Their prediction came true. Once again — the Maya gained autonomy in the 1840's but high tidal forces of 1893 changed the climate and they have been destroyed a fourth time. They are now in revolt and are trying to rise a fifth time.

But the winds that bore bad tidings for the Maya civilization bore good tidings to the Anasazi — the Old Ones of the Pueblo Culture as we can see below.

How the Bear Became a God: or the Classical Pueblo Period — a Lesson in History

An article in the Denver Post — dated 24 October 1976 — by Rich Mauer told a fascinating bear story:

"GRAND JUNCTION, COLO. — Along with the harvest and the first mountain frost, the change from summer to autumn has brought

an unprecendented invasion of high-country bears down into resi-
dential areas here."

The article reported that bears — mostly cubs — were streaming from the
mountains into orchards, farms, and even sub-divisions. The chief of the
wildlife division office said: "It's very unusual....In 30 years, this is the
first time I've seen such an invasion."

Investigation showed that "...a high-country freeze in mid-June that
wiped out most of this year's growth of oak brush and other shrubs...",
and made acorn and berry production very small, had caused the problem.
Bears hibernate, and they must eat berries and acorns to get fat enough
to make it through the winter.

The desperate, lean and hungry sows apparently abandoned their cubs.

The presence of the bears was a measure of a severe late frost,
which is followed by an early fall.

To understand the relationship of bears and the Classical Pueblo
Culture, keep in mind that the Pueblos lived in the "Four Corners"
area — among the same mountains from which the bears came. Further, the
Pueblos lived on the continental divide at about 6000 feet altitude.
One must believe that the bears came down to the Pueblo fields under the
same circumstances in those past times.

Let us now examine Man in this early time — Man so sophisticated that
his temple was also a celestial observatory with which he could determine
the equinox. He built elaborate irrigation complexes; built beautifully
planned and engineered towns; and built straight roadways — some cut
through hills — over which goods were transported.

All roads led to Chaco Canyon.

The time was a thousand years ago, when Western Europe was in the
Dark Age.

Chaco Canyon — Northwestern New Mexico, U.S.A.

37°12' North Latitude; 108°28' West Longitude.

The Chaco Canyon is 20 miles long; a half to three-quarters of a mile
wide; filled deeply with alluvium, and lies almost at the head of Chaco
Wash. The Wash drains about 4,500 square miles, beginning at the
continental divide, hence the Canyon is not subject to flooding from
upstream sources.

The Canyon area may be thought of as three separated areas, environ-
mentally: 1) the mesa tops; and within the Canyon: 2) the north side,
and 3) the south side.

The following regime constitutes the established dates of human occupancy (See **Figure 1**) in Chaco Canyon (CC) the nearby Navajo Reservoir District (NRD) only 50 miles northeast of (CC); and the Tsegi Phase [in general the Black Mesa area (BMA)] about 130 miles west-northwest of CC.

The area of the Classical Pueblo Culture was about the same as Belgium. All dates are A.D.:

Before 700 (BMA) Basketmaker II people lived by mixed hunting-gathering-horticulture; moving toward farming as time passed; and (CC) Pithouse settlements were common on the mesa-tops and in the rolling hills area south of CC.

700-800 (NRD) changed from winter-dominated to summer-dominated precipitation. Brief rise in effective moisture values.

After 750 (CC) aboveground structures were used in a population shift to the canyon bottomlands. No arroyos; shallow water-table on the flood-plain.

800-975 (NRD) Trend of decreasing total rainfall — minimum   1025.

850-1000 (Entire Area — Pueblo I Period) People built towns on the flood plains.

859-1150 (CC) This was the Classical Pueblo Period — "...a long but not uninterrupted period of aggradation..." Two community types occurred — beginning with Pueblo Bonito in 825. The smaller type was amorphous (i.e., unplanned) villages — almost certainly farm villages. The larger towns were planned and constructed carefully. There were tens of towns and hundreds of (200-400) villages.

(CC) evolved towards "...increased nucleation rather than fragmentation..." in the face of environmental change (p. 78). (Note well: every change led to bigger, more uniform towns, more planning — in fact, **more bureaucracy**.) After 1000 A.D. water control systems appeared in (CC) and all over the Anasazi area (now Southwestern U.S.A.). After 1025 (NRD) annual precipitation appears to have increased.

Before 350 to circa 1000 "...summer rainstorms were not so numerous, water tables were higher, dissection of flood plains (i.e., arroyo-cutting) was not so widespread and possibly, winter rainstorms were more numerous than they are now...(Schoenwetter 1926:198)." (Entire Four-Corners Area)

1000 to Present "...a pattern of numerous rainstorms (i.e., thunderstorms) contributed the majority of available water to plants in the eastern-Arizona-western-New Mexico area and initiated conditions of sediment disturbances and arroyo cutting...(*ibid*)". (Entire Four-Corners Area)

1130 to 1150 The entire Classical Pueblo area was abandoned. Southern

Paiutes (nomads) penetrated the area. This was the time of the end of alluviation, and the initiation of sheet erosion.

1150-1250 There was essentially no human occupation of the entire area.

1250 People moved back into the Pueblo areas. Populations peaked about 1285. By 1300, they were all gone again.

All of the above Pueblo information is from the superb book edited by [140] Longacre, William A. (1970) *Reconstructing Prehistoric Pueblo Societies*. A School of American Research Book, University of New Mexico Press: Albuquerque, N.M.

The authors can do a favor for anyone who is interested in migrations as a general phenomenon, by referring to Schwartz' paper in the above book: "The Postmigration Culture: A Base for Archaeological Inference," pp. 175-193. Schwartz discusses and classifies dozens of migrations — Puebloan and others — worldwide.

How does one tentatively interpret this remarkably independent birth and death of a civilization — for civilization it certainly was — in the light of causative climatic forces and events?

The utmost caution is required in the interpretation of the role of climate in the rise and fall of the Classical Pueblo Culture. The reader should refer to **Figure 45**.

The highest tidal forces gave rise to the highest tidal derivatives: i.e., the rate of change of tidal forces. These rates of changes and some other data are shown in **Figure 45**.

Curve A (**Fig. 45**) is composed of averages of three successive decades (by five-year steps) of tree-ring index deviations in standard deviation units (i.e., "sigmas") in tree-ring growth on Mesa Verde, Colo., as published by Fritts (1965) [141] of the University of Arizona Dendrochronology Laboratory.

Curve B (**Fig. 45**) is a synthesized curve done by Dansgaard *et al* in their classic paper on world atmospheric temperature as represented by the change in oxygen-isotope ratios.

Curve C (**Fig. 45**) is the actual measurement data which yielded the above frequencies by the process of Fourier (i.e., "frequency") analysis [142].

It has been stated that mean world atmospheric temperatures can be estimated to $\pm$ 0.2° Centigrade from such data. The synthesized curve is made up of the two primary frequencies found by Dansgaard and his team in the Camp Century, Greenland, ice core: Namely, 181- and 78-years plus or minus 5% [142]. Libby *et al* found these same frequencies in Japanese cedar tree-rings. [143 and 144].

Curve D (**Fig. 45**) is calculated from calculated tidal maxima. The increments of this curve are rate of change of tidal force:

$$- \frac{T_2 - T_1}{t_2 - t_1} = R$$

where T_1 and T_2 are successive tidal forces; t_1 and t_2 are the times when the tidal forces were calculated to occur; and R is the calculated rates shown in **Figure 45** Curve D in arbitrary units — and they are inverted.

The reason for inverting the curve is as follows:

When tidal forces are rising, they trigger volcanic eruptions of those volcanoes which "are ready" to erupt.

Volcanic debris in the upper atmosphere cools the climate, leading to larger per mille values of oxygen-isotope ratios (i.e., lower temperatures) and to lower tree-ring growth as shown in Curve A (i.e., downward on Charts A and D).

When tidal forces are falling, fewer volcanoes erupt, and the clearer air permits the sun to shine through and the temperature-sensitive Mesa Verde tree-rings grow more — (i.e., upward on Charts A and D).

In both of the above examples, inversion of the answer permits the plot to have the same "sense" as the tree-ring growth deviations: lower tidal derivatives — less volcanic debris, clearer air, warmer temperature, faster tree-ring growth.

Finally, Curve E (**Fig. 45**) (top) is sunspot (i.e., solar) activity as published by Jack Eddy (*op. cit.* III. B. [90]). Dr. Eddy used a composite of astronomical and historic data to arrive at this curve which represents solar activity for almost a thousand years.

Note that the periods with little activity (the Sporer and Maunder Minima) were especially carefully documented by Eddy.

Historic data proves that during these solar minima, the air got very cold. The period was known in Europe as the "Little Ice Age".

We know from the recent observations by Kukla and Kukla (*op. cit.* I.C. [16]) that in very cold winters, the 12-month-running-average snow-coverage of the glacial areas expands.

Further, the snow reflects sunlight which further reduces the amount of heat being absorbed by the earth. Thus, the temperature sank in the last half of the 1600's (see Curve C) and the tree-rings grew slowly (A) despite low tidal derivatives (D) with consequent low volcanic activity. The lack of solar activity had more net effect than its opponent — the low volcanic activity.

The pattern of causes which result in fast growth of tree-rings at Mesa Verde (**Figure 45** Curve A) is clear from the work of LaMarche (1974) [145]. He showed that upper tree-lines on mountains are growth-limited by temperature. They grow more at warm times. They grow less in cold times.

By comparing Charts A and C, one can see that there is a considerable degree of correspondence, excepting only the times of solar minima — which had greater effect on Greenland Ice than on Mesa Verde tree-rings.

Schoenwetter (*op.cit.* IX. A. [115]) studied alluvium and pollen extensively. He concluded that aggradation occurs in periods dominated by the gentle rain of winter storms. Degradation occurs with the powerful storms of summer. The water falls so fast that:

1. it drains-off rather than soaking-in; and
2. it causes severe arroyo-cutting.

Schoenwetter said the following:

"Aggradation was interpreted as occurring during wet periods and degradation during droughts. But palynological records from alluvium (Martin, 1963) have recently begun to indicate that this interpretation was somewhat gross. During some periods of degradation the pollen record appears to indicate that even more water is available for some kinds of plant growth than during periods of aggradation, so the drought theory seems discredited. However, during periods of degradation, though there may be more rainfall, it is almost entirely in the form of summer precipitation." (i.e., thunderstorms with violent rainfall compared with the gentle rain of winter)

In the light of the recent findings, the Classical Pueblo Period may be interpreted as follows; and we submit the following as an hypothesis:

To 750 A.D. Rising tidal forces triggered volcanoes and maintained cold climate with winter-dominated rainfall. Continuous aggradation, and hunting / gathering / farming was good everywhere on the rich alluvial flood plain — high-ground water table.

To 800 A.D. The high tidal forces (peaking in 796) purged the Northern Hemisphere of volcanoes, and introduced a period of clear air and summer warmth, including thunderstorms.

800 to 1100+ A.D. (from Schoenwetter: "Most of the pollen curve from the Chusca Valley is thus seen to occur during periods of summer-dominated rainfall." (*op. cit.* IV. A. [115])

By 850, the planned towns had become established **for the purpose of controlling water.** Irrigation is the basis on which most civilizations have been built; because in its traditional form, it is inherently a community effort. This was a time when farmers did better **with irrigation**, so they tolerated organization.

As the community authority over water intensifies, people accept a general loss of freedom, and gain a centralized authority; or, quoting R. Gwinn Vivian from Longacre: "Chaco towns seem to have their roots in an organizational system that became more complex through time, allowing for increased nucleation rather than fragmentation in the face of changed environmental conditions." also "...Irrigation agriculture of the eastern Pueblos required centralized control of communal labor..." (Farmers lost their freedom to bureaucrats.) [140]

1150 A.D. The summer dominance of rainfall ended (see **Figure 45** Curve A) and two things happened:

1. Irrigation systems designed to capture thunderstorm precipitation **ceased to function**, because no water fell in them; and

2. Winter drizzle and beginning aggradation made conditions favorable for the individual farmers.

Farmers found that if they walked away, two things happened by "magic": They regained their freedom and they ate better; because they were not sharing their products with the priests and planners.

We hypothesize that in the 800's, the weather deteriorated from a farmer's point of view. It got very warm; monsoonal summer-thunderstorms became the dominant form of precipitation. As a direct consequence of the climate change, farmers found that they did better if they pooled their efforts and irrigated. They adopted the forms of civilization because they did better with it.

About 1180, the weather got cooler and precipitation shifted to winter snow and drizzle. Irrigation systems — lacking thunderstorm water — ceased to function. Yet aggradation began again; hunting / gathering / farming on an individual basis improved. The forms of civilization became a liability rather than an asset.

The people walked away.

In other words, we hypothesize that the towns disintegrated — not because the climate got worse — but because it got better for the farmer. Civilizations represent loss of freedom by producers, and a continuous accumulation of burdensome overhead organizations; and people accept these things only as long as the bottom line shows a net gain. When the situation becomes favorable to abandonment by the producers (who have no worries — because **they are** the producers), the organization is left to crumble without products to live on; because the producers have gone away; and people, however skilled in ceremony or the arts, have nothing to eat.

The present century is comparable with the 800's climatologically, and the battles over communal labor, water, bureaucratic control, etc. are being fought again. The "Planners" want it all; and the producers have been abandoning the cities. "Tax evasion" is causing less and less product to go to the planners.

The "tax-rebellion" is intended to literally destroy the bureaucracy.

Given this understanding of the Classical Pueblo Culture, we can now go back to how the Bear became a God.

The Bears that came down into Grand Junction, Colorado, in October 1976 gave a three-month notice of colder years. In January / February of that winter, we had the worst winter in 200 years. It has been followed by two more "200-year" winters.

The Bears "delivered themselves to the people as a bearer (no pun intended) of terrible tidings — the horrible winter; and following summer drought with dust storms; and their bodies could have been taken for meat to help the people through the terrible times that their presence announced".

Isn't that Godlike?

But the Bear shares with the Eagle the mantle of enormous respect and even worship. Why the Eagle?

People who study the Pueblo Culture have known all along that it is exactly as honorable to sit in the shade as to work in the corn-field. There are probably two reasons. One is that the Pueblo People do not hasten to fasten value judgements onto everything. But maybe they learned that the hard way.

When the Wise Men of Old sat in the shade, they watched, they saw and they remembered.

Remember! The subject is water — or, more specifically thunderstorms. When you see Eagles soaring upwards, there is an updraft. Updrafts make thunderstorms.

The Eagle predicted rain!

Had you ever wondered why the Eagle is called a THUNDERBIRD?

Rain was life! Knowledge was life!

Setting in the shade was **valuable** and worth some respect.

Hats off to the pragmatic Pueblos.

B. Climate from 1814 to 1979 A.D.

Whereas the lack of data from the period from 717 to 926 A.D. makes a definitive statement regarding climate difficult; it is the **enormous** quantities of available data covering the 1814-1979 period that makes a definitive statement difficult.

For a precise statement of what the 1814-1979 A.D. climate was like, refer to **Figure 52**.

Increasing volcanic (A) dust-veil [123] was accompanied by a decrease in temperature to the first-half of the 19th century. The dust-veil disappeared, and permitted the warming trend of the period to the first-half of the 20th century. Beginning in about 1940, the northern hemisphere got cooler (the reciprocal happened in the southern hemisphere).

The per-mille variation in oxygen-18 / oxygen-16 ratio of isotope concentrations of Camp Century, Greenland, ice [142] shows the change from low world atmospheric temperature in 1820-1840 to high from about 1925-1938. The temperature has declined since then. (See also **Figure 13**.)

Curve **Figure 52** C is the much-used Budyko (1969) curve (updated by Asakura (1974) and further updated by Mitchell) of northern hemispheric annual means [146]. This curve is compared with solar umbral to penumbral ratios (see **Figure 20**).

Curve **Figure 52** D is after **Figure 1** in the publication concerning the deuterium study in tree-rings by Schiegl [147].

Local areas varied one way or another for the gross climatic change. For example, refer to **Figure 14** for the relationship of the tidal envelope at 60° Lat. north and English winter temperatures.

The rising tidal forces were undoubtedly triggering small volcanoes, which put dust and sulfur dioxide into the stratosphere. The SO_2 combines with H_2O or ammonia; and, along with dust, trickles down from the stratosphere into the troposphere. In the latter, nucleation of cloud formation enabled winter clouds to hold heat in the winter, and hold out sunlight the year-around. This leads to a time of warmer winters and cooler years.

The northern hemisphere has rising tidal forces since 1972 to about 2040, so this causative effect will make for net warmer winters until about that date.

Figure 48 shows Mesa Verde tree-ring growth which occurred between 717-926; then again 1813 to the present (30-year running average). Each upward surge of tree-ring growth was a warm period.

Bibliography

VI. CLIMATE IN TWO CENTURIES AROUND TWO HIGH TIDAL FORCES

INTRODUCTION

[122] Roosen, Robert G., Robert S. Harrington, James Giles and Iben Browning (1976) Earth Tides, Volcanoes and Climatic Change. *Nature* 261: 680-2 (24 June 1976)

A. 1. CLIMATE FROM 717 TO 926 A.D.

[123] Lamb, H.H. (1977) *Climate: Present, Past and Future.* Vol. 2. Climatic History and the Future. Methuen and Co. Ltd.: London. Barnes & Noble Books: New York.

[124] Ladurie, Emmanuel Leroy (1971) *Times of Feast and Times of Famine: A History of Climate Since the Year 1000 A.D.* Doubleday and Company, Inc.: Garden City, New York.

[125] Bray, J.R. (1972) Cyclic Temperature Oscillations from 0-20, 300 Yr. B.P. *Nature* 237: 277-9 (2 June 1972)

[126] Suess, H.E. Bristlecone-Pine Calibration of the Radiocarbon Time-scale 5200 B.C. to the Present. Reprint: 303-311. Department of Chemistry, University of California, San Diego, California.

[127] Wilson, J. Tuzo (1972) Mao's Almanac — 3,000 Years of Killer Earthquakes. *SR*: 60-4 (19 February 1972)

[128] Langer, William L. (1872) *An Encyclopedia of World History — Ancient, Medieval, and Modern — Chronologically Arranged.* Houghton Mifflin Company: Boston.

[129] Waley, Arthur (1941) *Translations from the Chinese.* A. Poetry of Po-Chü-i (A Government Official) Alfred A. Knopf: New York.

[130] McWhirter, Norris and Ross McWhirter (1973) *Guinness Book of World Records.* A Bantam Book, Sterling Publ. Co., Inc.: New York, N.Y.

[131] *Encyclopedia Brittannica* (1943)

[132] Paxton, John (Ed.) (1970-1) *The Statesman's Year Book.* Macmillan & Co., Ltd.

[133] Baerreis, David A. and Reid A. Bryson (1965) Climatic Episodes and the Dating of the Mississippian Cultures. *Wisconsin Archeologist,* 46 [4]: 203-220 (Dec. 1965)

[134] Folsom, Franklin (1974) *America's Ancient Treasures.* Rand McNally & Company: New York, Chicago, San Francisco.

A. 2. SOME CULTURAL RESPONSES AROUND THE HIGH TIDAL FORCE OF 796 A.D.

[135] Morley, S.G. (Revised by George W. Brainerd [1978]) [1056] *The Ancient Maya*. Stanford University Press: Stanford, Calif.

[136] Matheny, Ray T. and Deanne L. Gurr (1979) Ancient Hydraulic Techniques in the Chiapas Highlands. *American Scientist* 67 [4]: 441-449 (July-August 1979)

[137] Folan, William J. and Laraine A. Fletcher and Ellen R. Kintz (1979) Fruit, Fiber, Bark, and Resin: Social Organization of a Maya Urban Center. *Science* 204 [4394]: 679-701.

[138] Aveni, Anthony F. (1979) Venus and the Maya. *American Scientist* 67 [3]: 274-285 (May-June 1979)

[139] Brooks, C.E.P. (1926, 1949, 1970) *Climate Through the Ages*. Dover Publications, Inc.: New York.

HOW THE BEAR BECAME A GOD: OR THE CLASSICAL PUEBLO PERIOD – A LESSON IN HISTORY

[140] Longacre, William A. (Ed.) (1970) *Reconstructing Prehistoric Pueblo Societies*. U.N.M. Press: Albuquerque, New Mexico.

[141] Fritts, Harold C. (1965) Tree-Ring Evidence for Climatic Changes in Western North America. Reprinted from: *Monthly Weather Review* 93 [7] L: 421-443.

[142] Dansgaard, W., S.J. Johnsen, H.B. Clausen and C.C. Langway, Jr. (1971) 3. Climatic Record Revealed by the Camp Century Ice Core. *Late Cenozoic Glacial Ages*; K.K. Turekian (Ed.)

[143] Libby, Leona Marshall, Louis J. Pandolfi, Patrick H. Payton, John Marshall, III, Bernd Becker and V. Giertz - Sienbenlist (1976) Isotopic Tree Thermometers. *Nature* 261: 284-288 (27 May 1976)

[144] Libby, Leona Marshall and Louis J. Pandolfi (1977) Climate Periods in Tree, Ice and Tides. *Nature* 266: 415-417 (31 March 1977)

[145] La Marche, Valmore C., Jr. (1974) Paleoclimatic Inferences from Long Tree-Ring Records. *Science* 183 [4129]: 1043-1048 (15 March 1974)

[146] Mitchell, J. Murry, Jr. (Personal communication).

[147] Schiegl, W.E. (1974) Climatic significance of deuterium abundance in growth rings of *Picea*. *Nature* 251: 582-584.

Figures 1 through 52

(Authors' note: The following figures were originally created as slides for an illustrated lecture series. They graphically represent the flow of ideas and the history of events within the book.)

Figure 1. Battles in New Mexico.

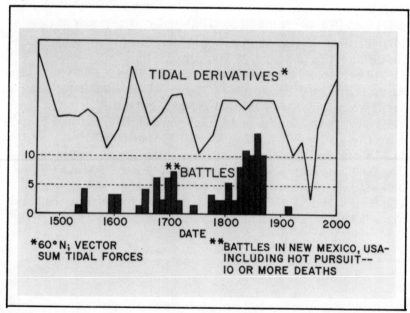

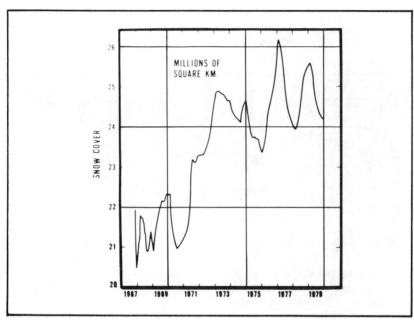

Figure 2. Earth's Ice and Snow Cover. (Northern Hemisphere)

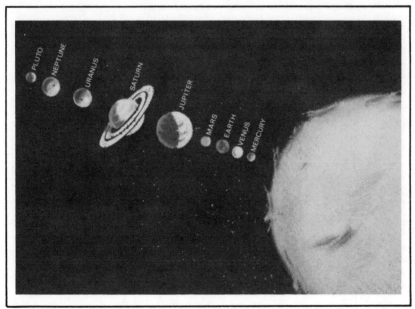

Figure 3. Solar System.

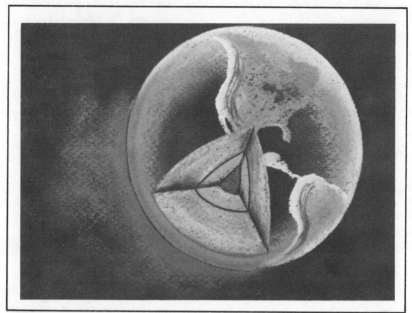

Figure 4. Major Earth Layers.

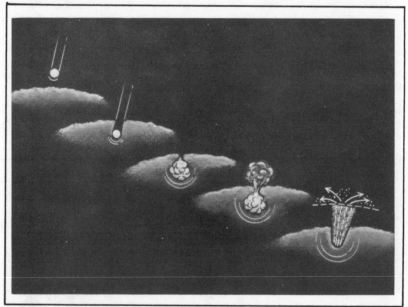

Figure 5. Bolide Strikes.

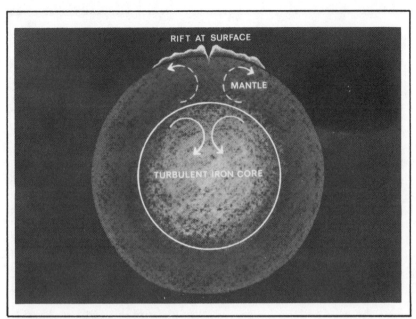

Figure 6. Turbulence in Earth's Core.

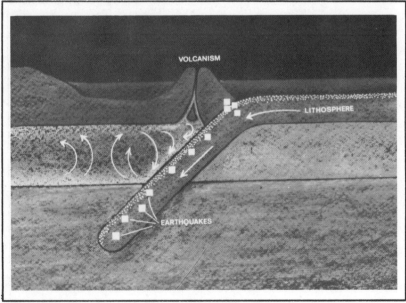

Figure 7. Subduction in Earth's Crust.

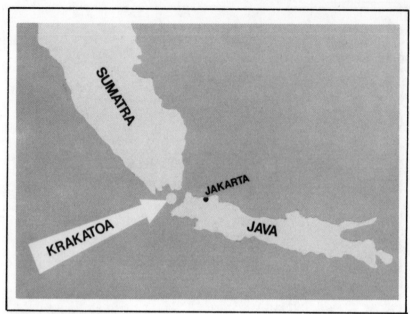

Figure 8. Krakatoa.

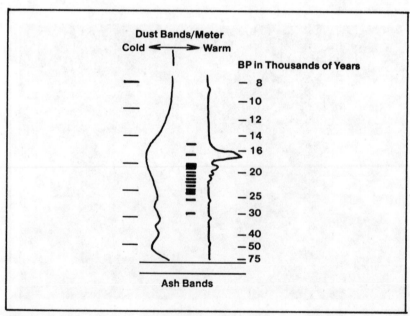

Figure 9. Volcanism vs. Temperature (Antarctic Ice Record).

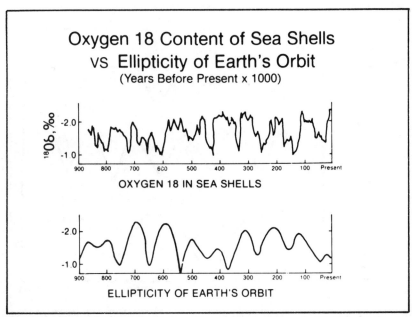

Figure 10. Orbital Ellipticity vs. Temperature (i.e., δ (O-18); in Ocean Bottom Cores).

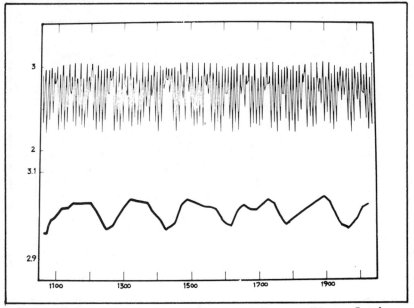

Figure 11. Calculated Envelope of High Tidal Forces (Vector Sum).

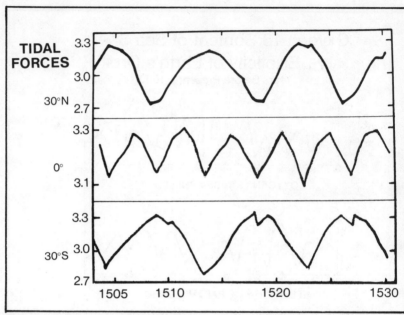

Figure 12. Calculated High Tidal Forces (30° N. Lat., 0°, and 30° S. Lat.) 1500-1531.

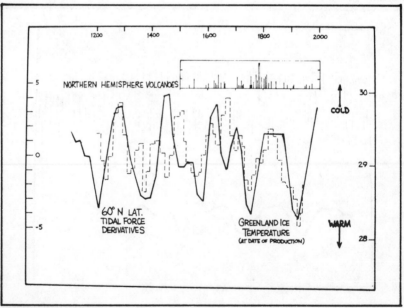

Figure 13. Tidal Derivatives — 60° N. Lat. vs. Temp. (i.e., δ {0-18}; Greenland Ice Core).

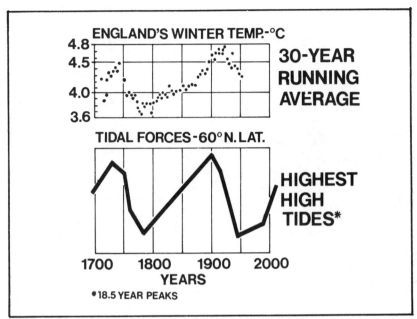

Figure 14. English Winter Temperatures vs. Tidal Forces.

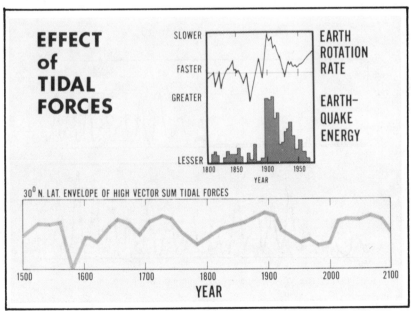

Figure 15. Tidal Forces vs. Earthquake Energy and Earth Rotation.

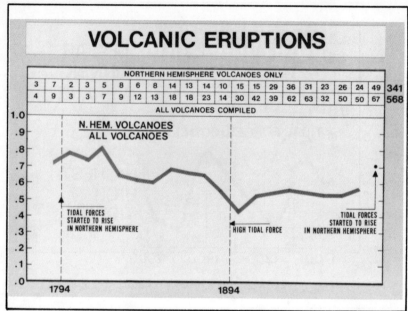

Figure 16. Northern Hemisphere/World Volcanoes 1794-1978.

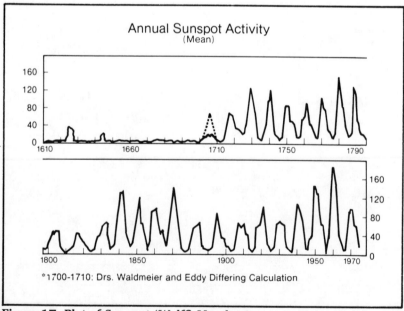

Figure 17. Plot of Sunspot (Wolff) Numbers.

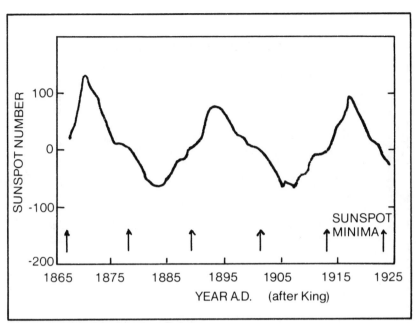

Figure 18. Double Sunspot Patterns.

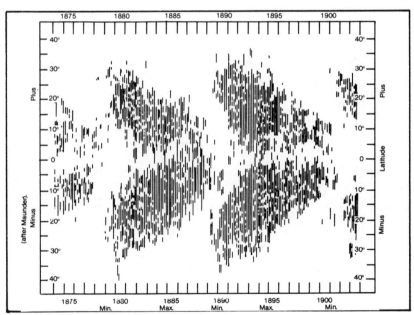

Figure 19. 'Butterfly' Sunspot Patterns.

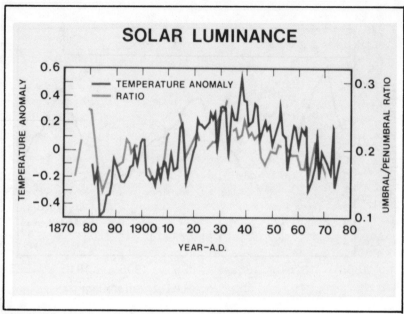

Figure 20. Solar Sunspot Umbral to Penumbral Ratio.

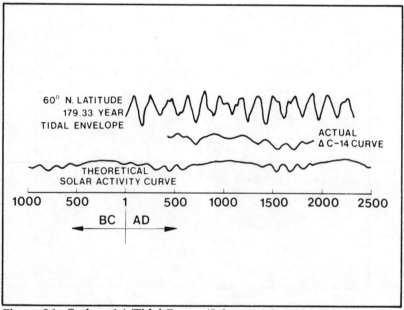

Figure 21. Carbon-14/Tidal Forces/Solar Activity (Calculated).

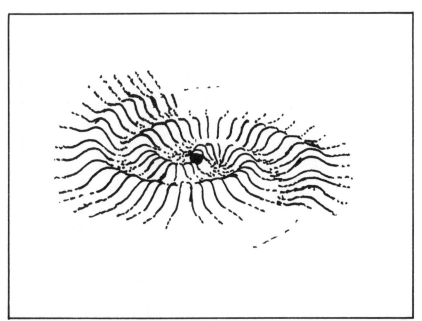

Figure 22. Warped Current Sheet Around Sun—Producing Magnetic Variations.

Figure 23. Aurorae (Solar Winds).

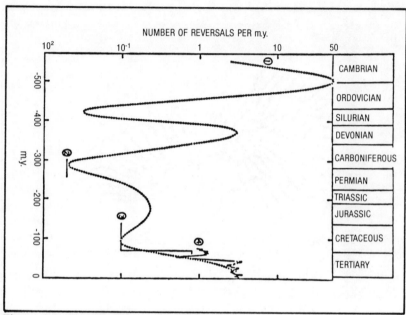

Figure 24. Reversal Rate of Earth's Magnetic Polarity.

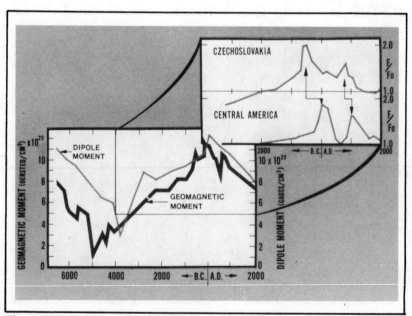

Figure 25. Geomagnetic Field Periods.

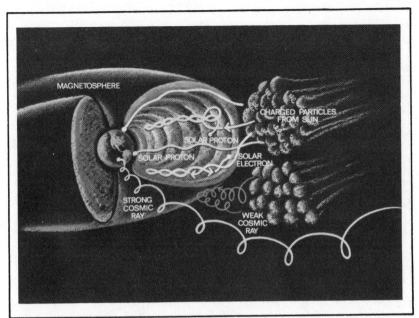

Figure 26. Earth's Magnetic Field in Space.

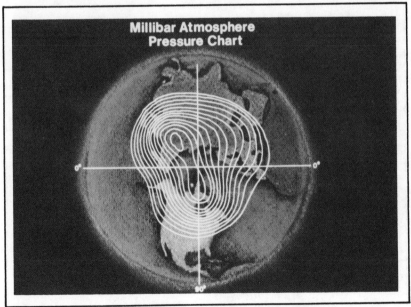

Figure 27. Mean January 1950's — 500-Millibar Chart.

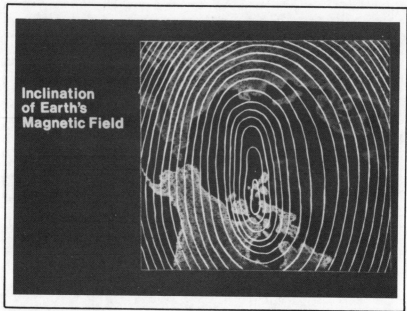

Figure 28. Northern Hemisphere Magnetic Inclination.

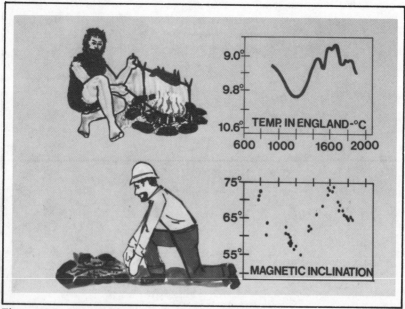

Figure 29. Temperature and Magnetic Inclination—Western Europe —700 A.D. to Present.

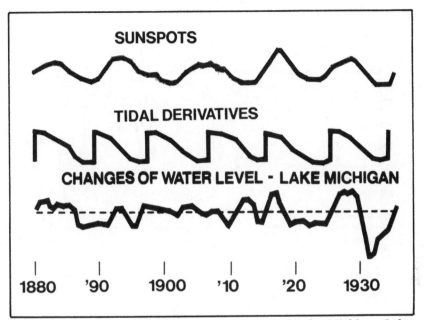

Figure 30. Sunspots, Tidal Force Derivatives and Lake Michigan Lake Level Derivatives.

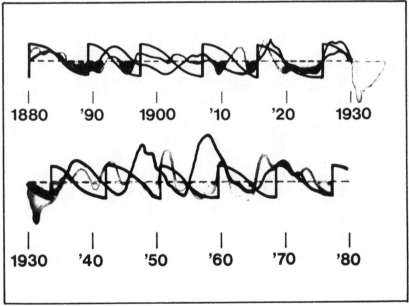

Figure 31. Above Curves Superimposed.

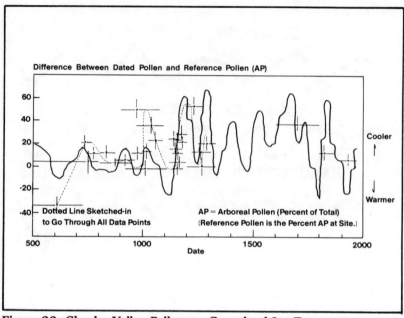

Figure 32. Chuska Valley Pollen vs. Greenland Ice Temperatures.

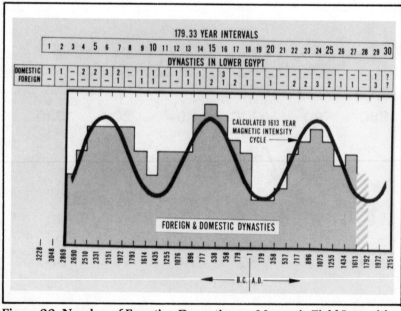

Figure 33. Number of Egyptian Dynasties vs. Magnetic Field Intensities.

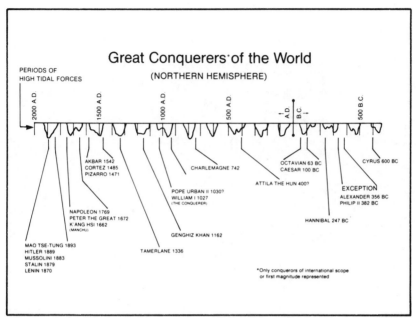

Figure 34. A. Birth of Conquerors at High-Tidal Times (re: the 179.33-Year Period); and

Conquerers and Dynasties of the Northern Latitudes

(GREATER THAN 10° NORTH)

	Great Conquerers	All Who Established Dynasties
.001-.10	0	23
.101-.20	3	30
.201-.30	3	46
.301-.40	3	59
.401-.50	11	69
.501-.60	8	57
.601-.70	5	34
.701-.80	6	43
.801-.90	3	48
.901-.00	1	30

*Data calculation: $\dfrac{1976 - \text{Date of Birth}}{179.33134} = K$

Plot based on mantissa of K

Figure 34. B. Table of Birth of Conquerors.

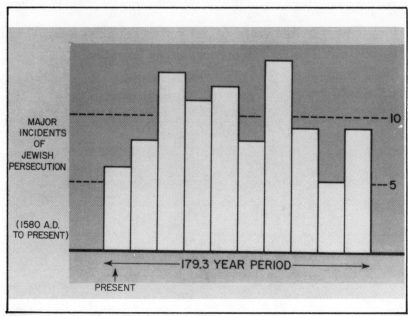

Figure 35. Incidences of Jewish 'Persecutions' by 179.33-Year Time Intervals.

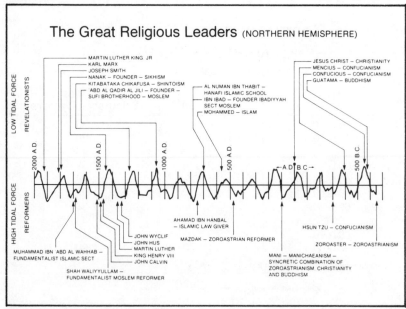

Figure 36. Birth Dates of Religion Founders (and Reformers).

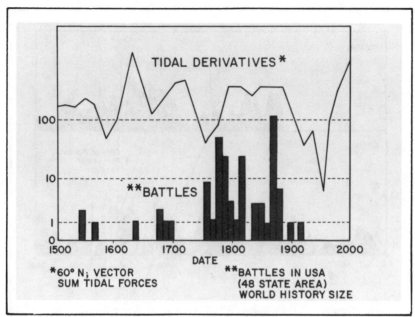

Figure 37. Battles in the U.S. vs. Tidal Derivatives.

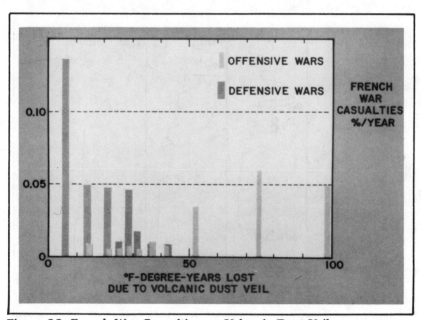

Figure 38. French War Casualties vs. Volcanic Dust Veil.

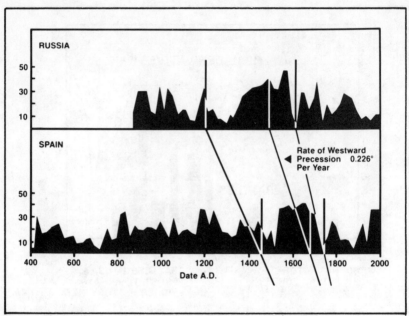

Figure 39. Effect of Magnetic Field on Tenure of Rulers.

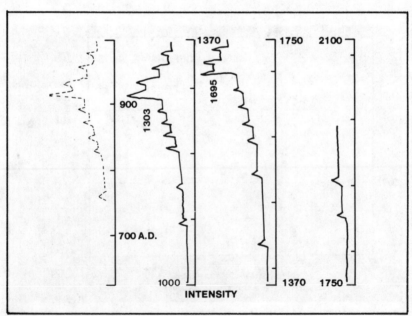

Figure 42. Historic Chinese Earthquakes.

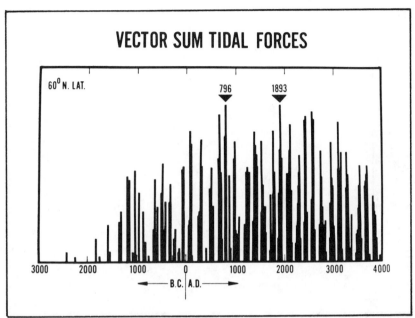

Figure 43. A. Highest Tidal Forces 60° N. Lat., 4000 B.C. to 4000 A.D.

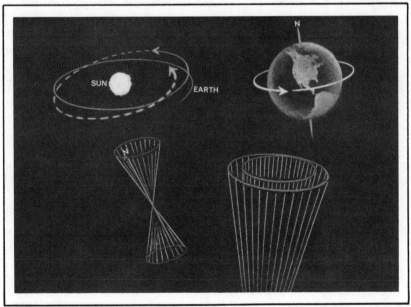

Figure 43. B. Mechanical Movements of Earth Affecting Tidal Forces.

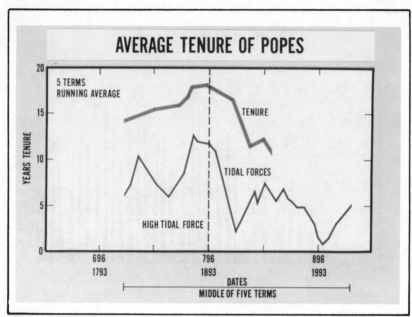

Figure 43. C. Tenure of Popes (Five-Term Running Averages).

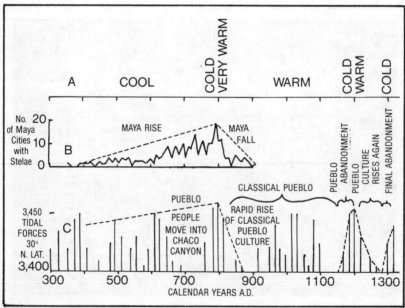

Figure 44. Climate, Maya; and Classical Pueblo Rise and Fall, and Tidal Forces; 300 to 1300 A.D. at 30° N. Lat.

E.
+10
A.
Mean
-10
B.
Rise and Fall of the
classical Pueblo Culture.
-28
Warmer
C.
-29
Cooler
-30
Tidal
Forces
D.
800
1000
1200
1400
1600
1800
2000

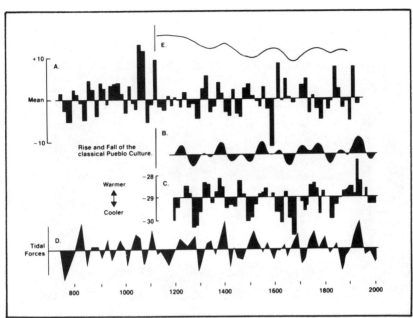

Figure 45. Solar Activity, Tree-Ring Growth, Temperatures (i.e., {O-18} Greenland Ice) and Tidal Derivatives at 30° N. Lat.; All with Respect to Rise and Fall of the Classical Pueblo Culture.

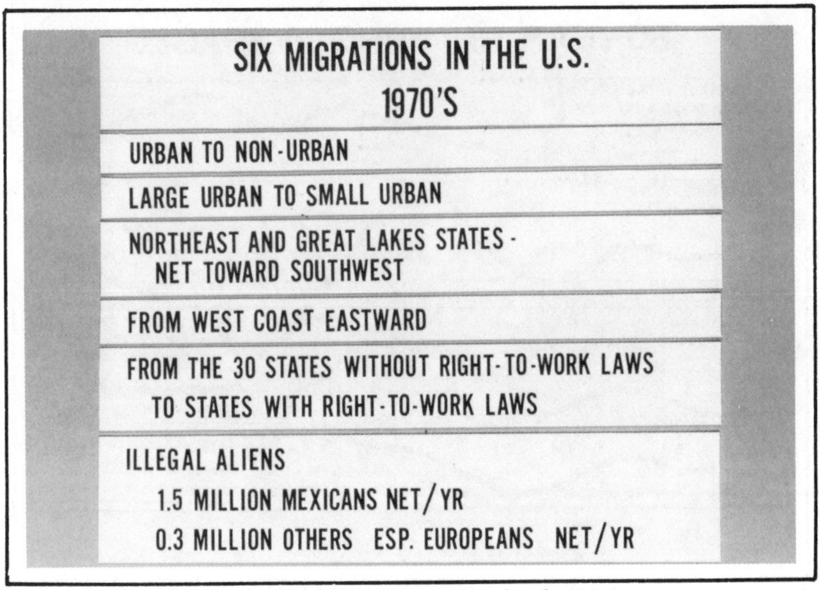

SIX MIGRATIONS IN THE U.S.
1970'S
URBAN TO NON-URBAN
LARGE URBAN TO SMALL URBAN
NORTHEAST AND GREAT LAKES STATES -
NET TOWARD SOUTHWEST
FROM WEST COAST EASTWARD
FROM THE 30 STATES WITHOUT RIGHT-TO-WORK LAWS
TO STATES WITH RIGHT-TO-WORK LAWS
ILLEGAL ALIENS
1.5 MILLION MEXICANS NET/YR
0.3 MILLION OTHERS ESP. EUROPEANS NET/YR

Figure 46. Migrations Currently Occurring in the U.S.

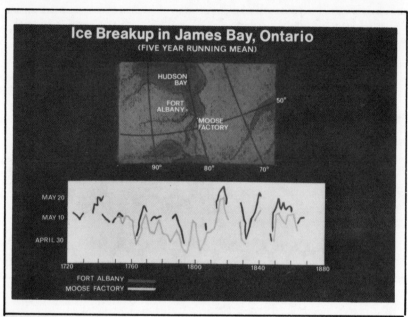

Figure 47. Time of Year Changes of Ice Breakup in Rivers Serving James Bay.

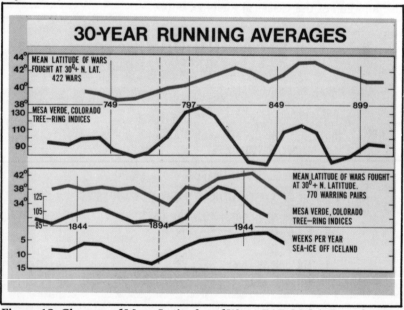

Figure 48. Changes of Mean Latitudes of Wars: 717-926 A.D. and 1814-1980 Compared with Climate Indices.

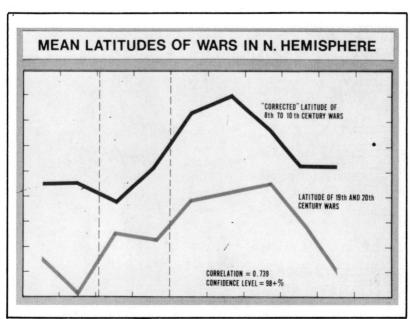

Figure 49. Latitude of Wars 'Corrected' for Climate.

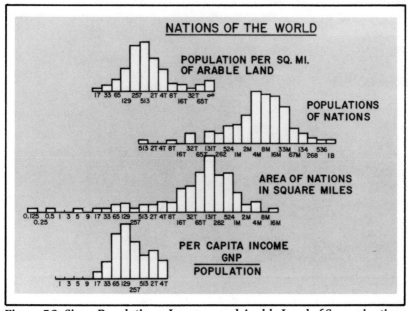

Figure 50. Sizes, Populations, Incomes and Arable Land of Sovereignties.

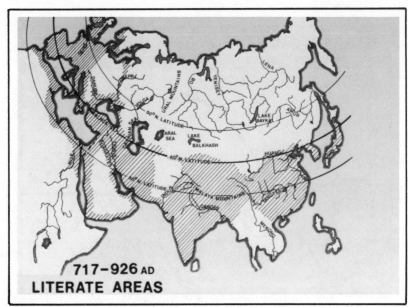

Figure 51. Maps of the Eurasian Land Mass: 717-926 A.D.

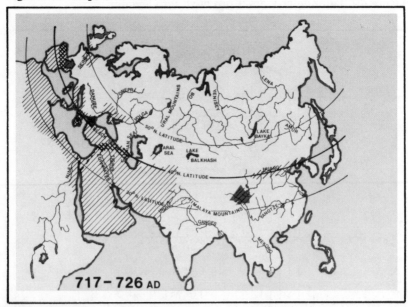

717-726 A.D.
Literate Areas. **Wars**— Simple Shading – 1 War During the Decade; — Cross Hatch – 2 Wars During the Decade; — Solid – 3 or More Separate Wars During the Decade. — **Migrations** — Arrows.

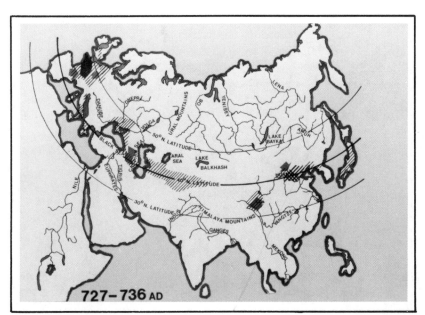

727-736 A.D.

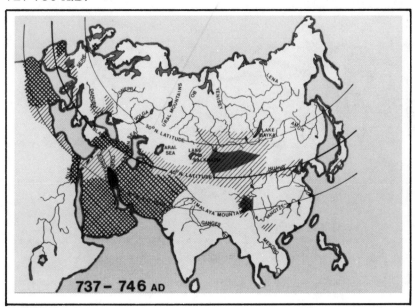

737-746 A.D.
Literate Areas. Wars— Simple Shading – 1 War During the Decade; — Cross Hatch – 2 Wars During the Decade; — Solid – 3 or More Separate Wars During the Decade. — **Migrations** — Arrows.

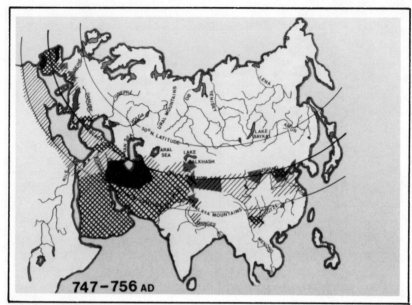

747-756 A.D.

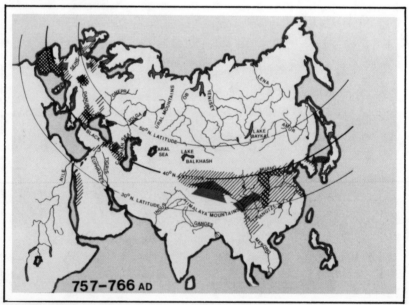

757-766 A.D.
Literate Areas. Wars— Simple Shading – 1 War During the Decade; — Cross Hatch – 2 Wars During the Decade; — Solid – 3 or More Separate Wars During the Decade. — **Migrations** — Arrows.

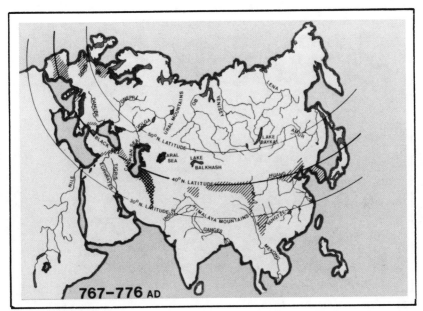

767-776 A.D.

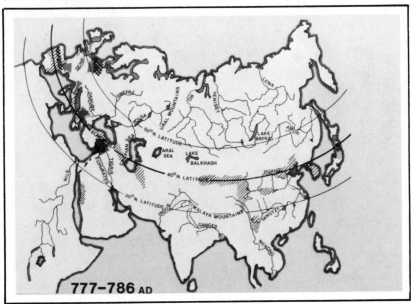

777-786 A.D.
Literate Areas. Wars— Simple Shading – 1 War During the Decade; — Cross Hatch – 2 Wars
During the Decade; — Solid – 3 or More Separate Wars During the Decade. — **Migrations**
— Arrows.

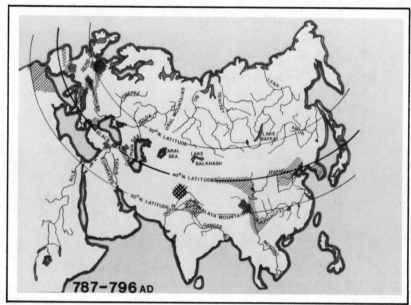

787-796 A.D.

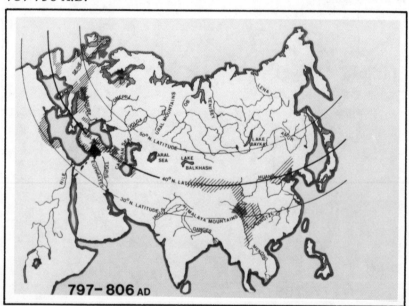

797-806 A.D.
Literate Areas. Wars— Simple Shading – 1 War During the Decade; — Cross Hatch – 2 Wars During the Decade; — Solid – 3 or More Separate Wars During the Decade. — **Migrations** — Arrows.

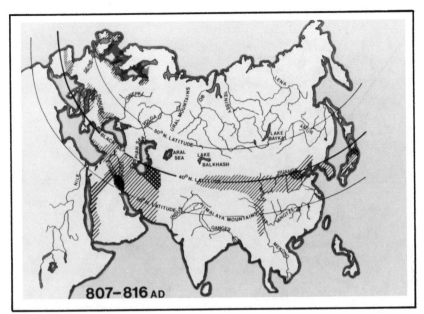

807-816 A.D.

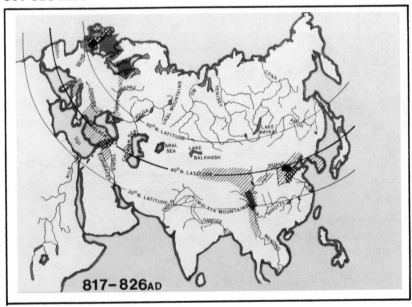

817-826 A.D.
Literate Areas. Wars— Simple Shading – 1 War During the Decade; — Cross Hatch – 2 Wars During the Decade; — Solid – 3 or More Separate Wars During the Decade. — **Migrations** — Arrows.

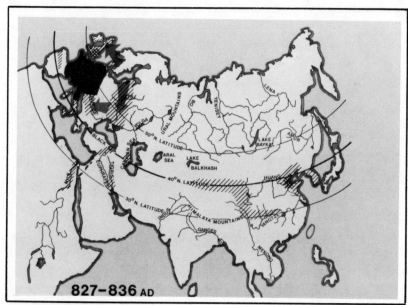

827-836 A.D.

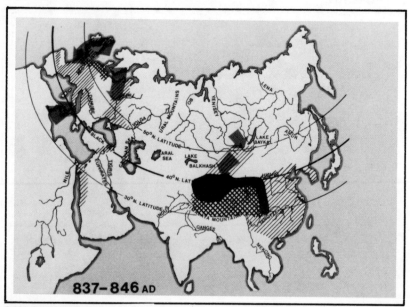

837-846 A.D.
Literate Areas. Wars— Simple Shading – 1 War During the Decade; — Cross Hatch – 2 Wars During the Decade; — Solid – 3 or More Separate Wars During the Decade. — **Migrations** — Arrows.

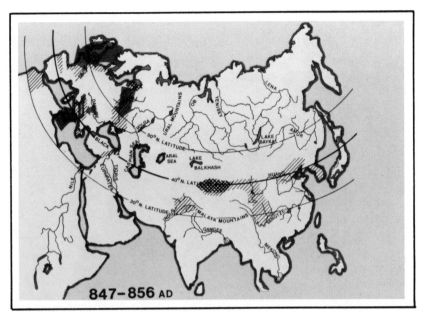

847-856 A.D.

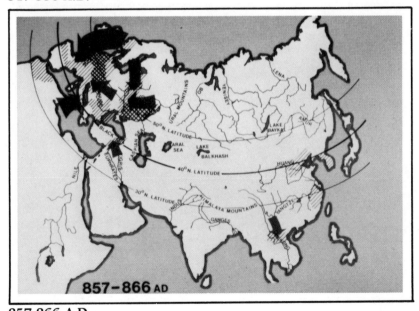

857-866 A.D.
Literate Areas. Wars— Simple Shading – 1 War During the Decade; — Cross Hatch – 2 Wars During the Decade; — Solid – 3 or More Separate Wars During the Decade. — **Migrations** — Arrows.

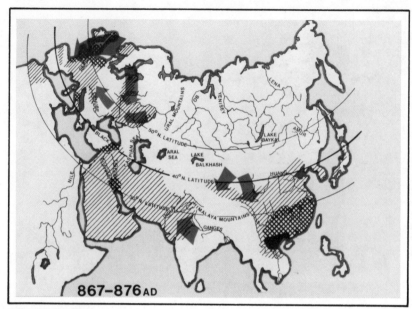

867-876 A.D.

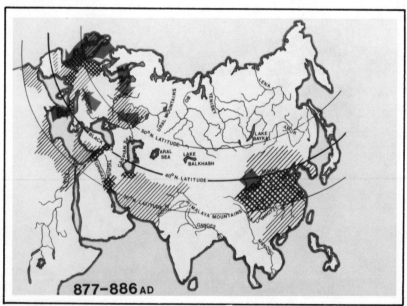

877-886 A.D.
Literate Areas. Wars— Simple Shading – 1 War During the Decade; — Cross Hatch – 2 Wars During the Decade; — Solid – 3 or More Separate Wars During the Decade. — **Migrations** — Arrows.

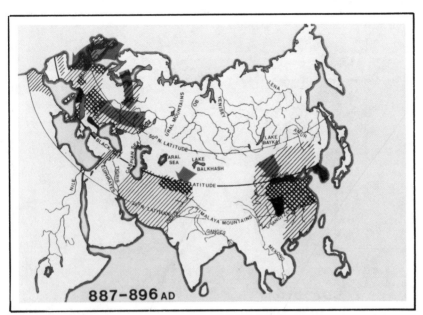

887-896 A.D.

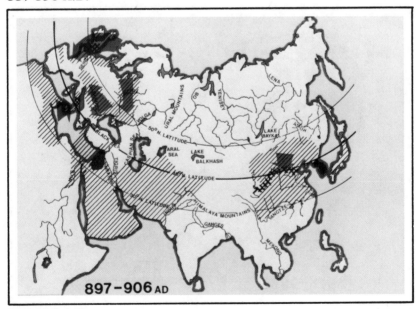

897-906 A.D.
Literate Areas. Wars— Simple Shading – 1 War During the Decade; — Cross Hatch – 2 Wars During the Decade; — Solid – 3 or More Separate Wars During the Decade. — **Migrations** — Arrows.

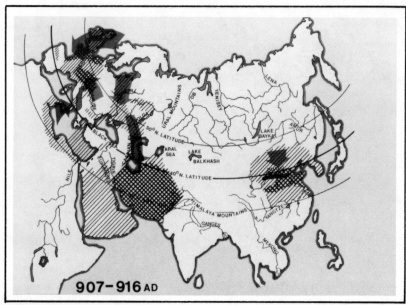

907-916 A.D.

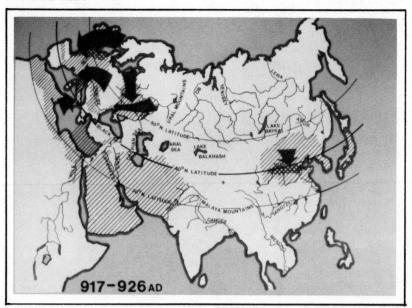

917-926 A.D.
Literate Areas. Wars— Simple Shading – 1 War During the Decade; — Cross Hatch – 2 Wars During the Decade; — Solid – 3 or More Separate Wars During the Decade. — **Migrations** — Arrows.

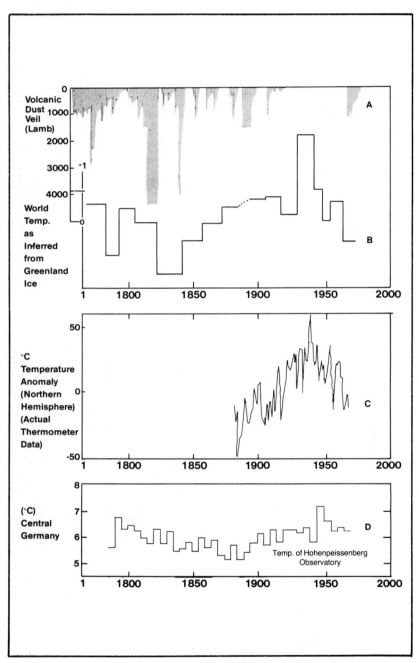

Figure 52. Volcanic Dust Veil and Climate in the Northern Hemisphere
        1814- 1979 A.D.

Chapter VII

The Stage Is Set by the High Tidal Forces of 796 and 1893 A.D.

A high tidal force does not just occur randomly. There are a series of rising high tidal forces leading up to it. The particular highest tidal forces occurred after several increasingly higher tidal forces, as shown in **Figure 11**.

With the ever greater and greater crustal strain, volcanoes that can be triggered are, and the hemisphere is purged of all of the volcanoes that are ready to erupt (see **Figure 16**). Typically, the big ones are not at the beginning of such a series — rather they erupt long after a trend has been established [148], and the tidal strain has built up and up and up. Thus, the great tidal force of 31.1 December 1986 will be the highest at 30° S. Lat. since 27.6 December 1818 — 168 years and 4 days.

The great tidal strain of 1818 was preceded by the eruption of Tamboro in Indonesia in 1815, and caused "the year without a summer" in the northern tier of states in the U.S.; famine in Ireland (737,000 dead); terrible floods in the Nile (Boda Island was completely flooded in 1817 and 1818). There was drought in the blacksoil regions of Russia in 1817 (which is not all that unusual); and altogether, the volcanic activity at the time was enormous (see **Figure 52**) and the climatic results generally much colder (∼2° C).

Following the 1986 high tidal force in the Southern Hemisphere, that hemisphere will be stripped of significant volcanoes for decades, as the Northern Hemisphere has been between the 1912 high tidal force, and the beginning volcanic resurgence in about 1950. In fact, the Northern Hemisphere tidal forces didn't begin their long-term build-up until 1972.

During the rising tidal forces of the 1800's (**Figure 14**) the annual temperature was very low, as it was during the early 700's. After 1900 and after 800 — roughly equivalent dates — with respect to the referenced extremely high tidal forces — the climate got warm.

After the warm period, the climate got cold again.

To the degree that human behavior is constrained by climate, the periods from 717 to 926 should have had the same sort of human behavior as the period from 1813 to the present — except we know how the earlier period turned out.

The way the previous period turned out is what can be inferred to be our immediate future.

The bases are simple; but they are only partly-proved assumptions:

1. Human behavior is constrained by climate;

2. Material means do not appreciably affect behavior; and

3. People haven't changed in 1100 years.

Bibliography

CHAPTER VII

[148] Rampino, Michael R., Stephen Self and Rhodes W. Fairbridge (1979) Can Rapid Climatic Change Cause Volcanic Eruptions? *Science* 206 [4420]: 826-9 (16 November 1979)

Chapter VIII

Historical Comparison of the Decades Around the Two Highest Tides — 796 and 1893 A.D.

Introduction

It is clear that much historical material can be found, and relatively easily, for eight decades before, and all of those since, 1893. But it takes two to make a comparison. What is the nature of the source material available for the period between eight decades before and twelve or thirteen decades after the high tidal force of 796 A.D.?

Although the term is loose, somewhat obsolete, and chronologically ill-defined; it is nonetheless valid to call the period from the end of the Roman Empire for the next six centuries the Dark Ages. Although this applies in particular to Western Europe, it extended across Europe, into North Africa and the Middle East.

Indeed, although the Roman Empire was in no known way involved, the period 600 - 800 A.D. is referred to as a Dark Age in Illinois after the end of influence by the Hopewell Culture.

The term Dark simply refers to the paucity of historical material that derived from a period so austere that the overhead represented by record-keeping was seldom afforded. Literacy was rare; and very few

163

people were secure, and not otherwise employed — thus available to keep records which were to become history.

Most records were kept by one of two sorts of organizations — governmental or religious — of the respective societies.

The Western World of Europe and the Middle East connected literacy with their religions. Both Christian and Moslem religious cultures supported enormous centers of scholarship and record-keeping. The records have little organization other than observations and hearsay by the recorder written in sequence as a chronicle. Comings and goings, sparrows falling, miraculous healings, and other happenings of interest to a cloistered Monk hardly gave an overview of society. In a Dark Age, most people live a day at a time. The luxury of perspective comes on a full stomach, and with a modicum of security.

Government records, such as those kept by the courts of China and earlier Japan give a marvellous overview of the workings of a society. These records are not ordinarily as detailed as records kept by religious recorders. The reason is obvious — governments contact their people on the very few facets of their lives; and ordinarily governments do not deal with people on nearly as personal a basis as do religions. Typically, governments look at facets like war, money (taxes) and crime. In other words, typically, governments exist and operate primarily, or solely, for their own sakes. The historical picture presented is the picture of the government — not the people; and ordinarily, the two are quite different.

A monk is as likely to record an unfortunate event as a fortunate one, since both reflect the will of God. God does not keep historical records; His subjects do. A bureaucrat, on the other hand, is much more likely to cover up all unpleasantness that makes him look bad. Governments are in the business of controlling things; and events that prove that the government is not in full control are apt to be glossed-over, ignored, or reinterpreted. In the latter case, it is the government keeping historical records — not its subjects. The points of view are thus different between the Monk who is a subject of God and the bureaucrat who plays God.

In China, for example, a war where hundreds of thousands of people were killed, an army destroyed, and a large fraction of the empire lost, was left totally unrecorded, presumably because it discredited the Imperial court.

Of course, a few societies managed to combine the worst of both worlds. The tiny states of Northern India, Tibet, and the Japanese court in later times, combined the provincial outlook of the elite centralized core of bureaucrats with the hazy mysticism of monks. Records left by these theocracies are almost useless, and give no clearer picture of what these societies were doing than do the neighboring illiterate societies.

Allowing for these limitations, the following is the picture that the historian perceives at the beginning of our period of study (717 A.D.):

A person could have crossed on land from the Atlantic to the Pacific Oceans over the territory of only two Empires. Most of the world that was known to literate peoples was dominated by the two Empires: the Moslem Empire and the T'ang Empire of China.

The Moslem Empire was founded in 630 A.D. by Mohammed and was spread by the military competence of a force which may have been the most zealous of all times. The Empire's primary growth was in the 600's, but there was still some growth during the early 700s. The Moors were in the process of overwhelming Spain, and were spreading northward in the French Riviera. To the east, they were continuing to conquer the oasis societies of Afghanistan and Central Asia. All of the land in between, Northern Africa and the Middle East, lay under its power.

The T'ang Empire confronted the Moslem Empire in Central Asia, and stretched eastward to the Pacific Ocean. It included Mongolia, Korea and North Vietnam. Like the Moslems, it had done most of its growing in the 600's. Beginning in 618 A.D. with the overthrow of the Sui Dynasty by Kao-tsu, it continued aggressively by Kao-tsu's son, T'ai Tsung, and fueled its drive by the aggressiveness of its nomadic Uighur tribesmen. By the 700s A.D., the main drive was gone; but slow expansion continued.

Both of these Empires lay primarily between 10° and 40° North Latitude. Empires to the north of them were generally in a state of decline. The Frankish Empire of France and the Byzantine Empire of Eastern Europe and Anatolia (now Turkey) were reeling from Moslem attacks and governmental chaos. The Jewish state of Khazaria of the Caucasus Mountains and Ukraine region were withstanding the assaults more successfully.

The smaller empires of the east were also faring poorly. Korea had to accept the suzerainty of the T'ang Empire, and Tibet was in the process of doing so. Only the Japanese Empire was expanding as the Mongoloid peoples from the Mainland (Korea) expanded their island holdings at the expense of the aboriginal Caucasoid Ainus.

Decade by decade, events of the Afro-Euro-Asian land mass unfolded as follows:*

---

*There is one map for each decade. Simple-hatching shows one war in the area in the decade. Cross-hatching shows two wars in the area in the decade. Solid areas show three or more wars in the area in the decade. Arrows show migrations.

A. Chronology — 717 to 926 A.D.

717-726 A.D.
BRUTALLY COLD, GLACIERS NEARING MAXIMUM

T'ang Empire Peace reigned in Central and Southern China. Northern China was subjected to Khitan raids. Two major migrations were occurring: 1) the Tu Yu Huns were settling in Western China after being driven eastward out of their homeland by the Tibetans; and thousands of Korean prisoners-of-war had taken advantage of the confusion in Northern China's border region to mix with the Khitans and Mongols; and had fled to Manchuria where they set up the Kingdom of Parhae.

Byzantium A successful revolt against the central government produced Leo III, who allied Byzantium with neighboring Bulgar tribesmen and successfully defeated and repelled the attacking Arabic Moslems.

Revolts occured in both Italy and Greece.

Moslem Empire Moslem successes included consolidation of their hold on most of Spain in the west; and takeover of Kasgaria (now Sinkiang Province, China). Their major military effort was their attempt to conquer Constantinople and the Byzantine Empire — in which they failed.

The first of a number of revolts arose among Southern Arabs.

Franks The southern Frank Empire along the Riviera was taken by the Moors. Charles Martel began to gain control of the central Frank Empire, and conquered parts of Germany.

Lombards The Lombards took advantage of Byzantine weakness and seized parts of Italy.

Japan The Mongoloid Japanese spread eastward and northward on Honshu, the main island. There were major campaigns of Caucasoid Ainus against this invasion of their homelands, but the Ainus failed.

Khazaria Border raids were exchanged with the Moslems. This Jewish nation was a bulwark of resistance to Moslem expansion.

Tibet The Tibetans — temporarily independent — raided in China.

Khitans Made raids on Northern China, and had numerous coups and revolutions.

727-736 A.D.
EXTREMELY COLD. PROBABLY GLACIAL MAXIMUM

T'ang Empire The Chinese and their Turkish subjects and allies expanded westward against the Arabs and Tibetans, but made no headway against the Jewish Khazars. These successes were balanced by a major defeat by the Khitans, and the inability of the Empire to stop nomads from raiding along the northern border. The T'ang Empire was forced to recognize the independence of Silla (Korea) because of its weakness in the north; but suppressed the bid for independence of Nan Chao by the Thais in the south. Tibet was made a vassal state.

Moslem Empire The northward expansion of the Moors in France was stopped by the Franks under Charles Martel at the battle of Tours (Poitiers). Raids on Sicily were rebuffed. The Chinese were eating away at the eastern end of the Empire.

Only in the north was conquest going well. A Khazarian campaign was repelled, and the Moslems took Georgia and the Ukraine up to the Caucasus Mountains. They also put down a revolt in the northeastern parts of Persia.

Franks The Franks under Charles Martel stopped the Moors and expanded his control to Aquitaine and further into Germany.

Lombards Continued their expansion in Italy against the weak Byzantines.

Byzantine Empire The Byzantines crushed a Greek revolt and beat off Arab raids on Sicily.

Japan Mongoloid Japanese increased their brigandage and expansion against the Caucasoid Ainus.

England Small kingdoms continue to battle each other for territory and power.

Tibet Lost its independence whereupon the king was forced to marry a Chinese Princess and accept the suzerainty of the T'ang Empire.

Khitans Same activities as previous decade.

Khazaria The major campaign by Khazaria into the Mesopotamian area triggered the Arab/Moslem retaliatory campaign which conquered and took all Khazar land south of the Caucasus.

737-746 A.D.
END OF GLACIAL MAXIMUM

T'ang Empire This decade was a period of enormous success and prosperity for China.

The Khitans raiding along the northern border were suppressed for a while by a major military campaign. The Min revolt in the south was successful. The Uighurs—who were allied with and related to the T'angs spread throughout the Mongolian area from Lake Balkash to Lake Baikal.

Success lay in all directions.

Moslems The Moslem Empire stopped growing everywhere but in the east; and began to shrink along some borders.

The Berber revolt weakened the Moors so much that the Christian kingdom of Asturias went on the offensive.

The Franks began their drive to remove the Moslems from the Riviera. The Byzantines pushed them out of Cyprus.

Berbers of the Kharijite sect revolted and won their independence from the remainder of the Moslem Empire.

The Copts in Egypt revolted, and such a large percent were slaughtered that whole areas were opened up for resettlement along the Nile; and whole tribes were sent in by the Moslems to settle there.

A widespread civil war between Northerners and Southerners among the ruling Umayyads split the fabric of the Empire apart; and various religious sects and ethnic groups seized the time of disarray to revolt.

Only in the East did the Empire grow with the completion of the conquest of Tukharistan.

Byzantium A successful campaign against the Arabs in Syria was interrupted by a two-year civil war in which the Christian icon worshippers attempted to seize the government.

England At about this time, Aethelbald established sovereignty over all of the island (i.e., England) south of the Humber.

Lombards Continued expansion in Italy against the Byzantines.

Franks Under Pepin III, the Franks began to drive the Moors out of the Riviera.

Khazars The Khazars began what would become a long-term border war against the Arabs with no major victories on either side.

Khitans This horde was pushed eastward by the Chinese.

Japan The Mongoloid people (hereinafter referred to as Japanese) continued to expand their Empire at the expense of the native Caucasoid Ainus.

A major revolt led by Fujiwara Oskikatsu forced the temporary abandonment of the capitol—Nara.

747-756 A.D.
NOT AS COLD AS BEFORE, BUT COLD.

T'ang Empire China was at perhaps the peak of its powers and glory at the beginning of this decade; but sank into a civil war which was one of the most disastrous in China's entire history.

At the beginning of the decade, a major part of the Chinese Army in combination with the Uighurs waged a successful campaign westward through Central Asia to Transoxania.

The T'ais (now the Thais of Thailand) took the opportunity presented by the absence and remoteness of T'ang armies to initiate a revolt in Nan Chao. The revolt was successful, and Nan Chao seized 32 provinces.

Tibet also revolted, and the Turks and Khitans chose this time to invade and raid China.

The Chinese Army under General An Lu Shan attempted to protect the empire; and was disastrously defeated by the Khitans; who then, in their proven military superiority, settled in the North Chinese plains.

In Central Asia (at Talas) in 751 A.D., in one of history's great decisive battles, the Arabs beat and turned back the Chinese / Turkish expansion.

The final disaster of the decade was a civil war in Northern China led by General An Lu Shan. Millions of people died: the Emperor was driven out of his capitol, and his favorites were killed. China was ruined.

Moslem Empire Fractional and religious revolts finally climaxed in a violent civil war. The Umayyads were overthrown by the Abbasids; in part because the Umayyad dynasty focussed power solely in Arab hands and taxed non-Arabic Moslems—despite the fact that Islamic traditions made all Moslems tax exempt. This was taxation without representation.

Entire cities were massacred, and the Umayyad clan was extirpated. A survivor—Abd al-Rahman—escaped, fled to Spain, and took it. Despite Abbasid efforts to take Spain from him, Al-Rahman remained in control of Spain and independent.

After the important battle of Talas in which the Arabs turned the Chinese / Turkish forces back from Central Asia, the two Empire governments reached such an accord that the Arabs sent mercenaries to assist the Chinese imperial court fight its own people during the great An Lu Shan Civil War.

Byzantium Despite a monastic pro-icon revolt, this decade was a period of expansion for the empire. After the revolt was suppressed, the government confiscated monastery properties.

During this decade of severe disorder in the Moslem Empire, Byzantium reconquered large parts of Armenia from the Arabs, and also expanded westward into Bulgaria and Thrace.

Franks The Franks had driven the Moors out of the Riviera by 759; then invaded Italy at the invitation of the Pope. Some of the land captured at that time formed the original "Donation of Pepin" which subsequently formed the basis of the Papal States.

England The Welsh Kingdom of Strathclyde was absorbed by an alliance of Northumbria and Picts.

Lombards The successful attacks on Rome forced the Pope to ally himself with the Franks. The alliance led to the Frankish invasion of Lombardy.

Khazaria The long-term border war with the Arabs continued to yield no major victories for either side.

Japan The Japanese continued to expand against the Ainus.

Tibet Eastern Kansu and Turkistan were lost to China. The Tibetans mounted an unsuccessful campaign to take the headwaters of the Indus from Kashmir; then won Tibetan independence from the T'ang Empire of China.

757-766 A.D.
STILL COOL, BUT NO LONGER EXTREMELY COLD.

T'ang Empire of China Dissention within An Lu Shan's forces led to his death and a weakening of the rebel cause. By 763, a combination of Chinese and Uighur troops crushed the rebels, and the Imperial court reentered the capitol.

Thousands of years of suppression or conquest by "foreign-devil" troops —with the government, itself, using such troops against the Chinese people—have contributed to the development of the Chinese attitudes seen today.

China remained weakened after the civil war—especially in the North.

The Tibetans took advantage of the diversion of troops in the civil war to invade the northwestern provinces of Sinkiang, Kansu and Szechwan; and ultimately the Imperial Capitol, itself—in the north central region. This is a tremendous region of perhaps three-quarters of a million square miles.

Nan Chao, the Khitans and the Uighur Turks also took advantage of China's weakness to plunder and take territory.

Moslem Empire The Empire accepted the loss of Spain and the French Riviera, and turned its attention inward. A Shi'ite rebellion of the Hajiz and Medina area was quelled, and a Byzantine invasion was repulsed.

A surviving leader of the rebellion — a descendant of Mohammed, escaped and set up an independent state in Morocco.

Byzantium The invasion of the Arab Empire was unsuccessful, but the Byzantines had more success along their western borders. They took Thrace and drove out the Slavs. To take eastern Thrace, they had to subdue the Bulgars; who thereafter had repeated coups and attempts to retake the land.

Franks Under Pepin the Third, the Franks quelled a revolt in Aquitaine, but failed to prevent Bavaria from winning independence. The Franks expanded their territory and forced Saxony to pay tribute.

England Aethelbald was murdered in 757, and within a year, another Mercian King — Offa — established his position as Bretwala (overlord) of England south of the Humber River. He proceeded to work on the absorption of his dependencies.

Spain Abd-er-Rahman consolidated his controls over Spain and established the Omayyad Dynasty. Christian expansion stopped.

Khazaria Same as last decade.

Tibet The Tibetans took advantage of the absence of Chinese (and Uighur) troops during the An Lu Shan revolt and invaded Northwestern China. They also plundered widely including the Imperial capitol of China.

Japan A clique of Shinto priests attempted to overthrow the Imperial family, but were unsuccessful. The Japanese made a massive naval invasion attempt against Korea with limited success.

767-776 A.D.
GETTING WARMER.

T'ang Empire The internal affairs of China quieted down. China was never to regain its former power. The warlords of Hopei retained their independence from the T'ang. Sporadic raiding along China's borders by her neighbors became a way of life.

Moslem Empire The mass of the Empire was quiet. Two small unsuccessful rebellions occurred in Khorasan (Parthia of earlier times; Northern Iran in Modern times) (this is the frontier between Shi'ite and Sunnite Moslems — Kurds and Persians — mountain, inland sea and desert). The usual border conflicts continued.

Byzantium The Byzantines quelled the revolts of the Bulgars.

Franks Charlemagne completed his conquest of Northern Italy with successful campaigns against Aquitaine, Saxony, Spoleto and Lombardy.
  He was crowned King of the Lombards.
  Charlemagne, in 772, launched against the Saxons and came up against the frontier of the Danes. The Danes were among the several Viking kingdoms.

Silla (Korea) Conservative aristocrats unsuccessfully tried to overthrow their Chinese authorities.

England Mercia continued to absorb its dependencies.

Spain Same as previous decade.

Khazaria Same as previous decade.

Tibet The Tibetans continued raiding across and expanding their borders at the expense of China's T'ang Empire.

Japan A major, though unsuccessful, Ainu campaign tried to oppose Mongoloid Japanese expansion.

777-786 A.D.
MODERATELY WARM.

T'ang Empire The Chinese began the decade by defeating and subjugating the Nan Chao (the T'ai people). Toward the end of the decade, China had a civil war which — though ultimately unsuccessful, forced the Imperial Court to temporarily abandon the Capitol.

Moslem Empire Aggression against the Byzantine Empire recommenced. Two of the invasions of Byzantium forced the payment of tribute. A rebellion in the Hajiz, led by a descendent of Mohammed, was crushed.

Byzantium Great military weakness lay across the land. Though a raid by Bulgars against Greece and Macedonia was repulsed militarily; Moslem attackers had to be **bought** off.

Franks The Franks, led by Charlemagne, made an unsuccessful campaign into Northern Spain. Though Charlemagne had captured Pamplona (778), he failed before Saragossa. At that point, news reached him of a Saxon revolt, and recalled him to the banks of the Rhine. In his withdrawal through the Pyrenees, the rearguard was massacred at Roncesvalles. This massacre of Franks by Basques resulted in the glorification epic in memory of Hruodland (i.e., "Roland"), "praefect of the Breton march". Thus: "The Song of Roland".

This was a small military action; but items of interest were hard to come by in those days.

A successful campaign to conquer Southern Italy was mounted.

A giant effort to subdue Saxony was only moderately successful. The Saxon King was baptized; but the truce kept coming unstuck, and revolts of Saxony were almost annual.

Charlemagne's forces quelled revolts in Thuringia, Britanny and Frisia.

Spain The Moors conquered the Basques, and repelled a Frankish invasion.

Khazaria Same as last decade.

England Mercia continued to expand at the expense of its neighbors. The Vikings first settled in the Shetland and Orkney Islands.

Tibet Same as last decade.

Japan The Ainu campaign against Mongoloid Japanese intensified. This decade saw the beginning of a trend wherein peasants turned to warlords rather than to the central government for protection. The province Ise-s'ming broke loose from the central government, and more were to follow.

The capitol was moved from Nara to Nagaoka, probably to escape the influence of the Buddhist priesthood.

An unsuccessful coup was attempted within the royal family.

The Emperor Kammu vigorously reestablished central authority and his General overcame.

Silla A civil war began between rival branches of the royal clan. It was to last over a hundred years and destroy the central government.

787-796 A.D.
GETTING WARM.

T'ang Empire This decade in Chinese history was quiet, but was characterized by rising piracy in the surrounding seas.

Moslem Empire Border conflicts with the Khazars and Byzantines. Maghrib (Morocco and Western Algeria) became totally independent.

Byzantium Weakness continued in the Empire, and its navy was defeated in Italy, leading to a coup which deposed Empress Irene and her pro-monkish party.

An unsuccessful invasion was mounted against the Arabs; and in the West, the Bulgars looted eastern Thrace.

Franks The Franks reconquered Bavaria, thus ended its fifteen years of independence. They quelled revolts in Southern Italy, Frisia and Saxony.

The Slavs and the Avars unsuccessfully attacked the Franks. The Avar attack led to retaliatory raids with eventual conquest. Other successful raids seized Byzantine ports in Italy. A "Spanish march" (i.e., border region) was established as a no-man's land between the Franks and Moors as retaliation for a devastating raid by the Moors against the French Riviera.

Spain The Moors' attempt to reconquer the French Riviera was not only unsuccessful — it provoked the Franks into massive retaliation. The Moors were driven below the Elbo River and the Spanish march was established south of the Pyrenees.

England In 787, England was subjected to its first Viking raid. The raids continued and grew in number, spreading to Wales, Ireland and Scotland.

Vikings The Vikings not only raided the British Isles; they also settled on Shetland and Orkney Islands, and along the East Baltic coast.

Khazaria Same as last decade.

Tibet Not only did Tibet continue intermittent border conflicts with China; it also initiated an indecisive war with Nan Chao which was to last for thirty years.

Tibet rebuffed an Uighur invasion.

Japan The Ainu campaign against the Mongoloid Japanese began to fade in 790. Captured Ainu were resettled throughout the island.

The Imperial Capitol was moved from Nagaoka to Kyoto.

This concludes the review of eight decades of the history of the Eurasian land mass in those sovereign entities which were — at least in part — north of the 30° North Latitude parallel.

On 23 December 796, the tidal vector sum tidal force at 60° North Latitude was the highest that it had been for several thousand years; and it has been equally high only once more 23 December 1893. It will not be that high again for many, many thousands of years.

At 30° North latitude, the tidal force was as high in 778 as in 796; and in 1912 as in 1893. This separation in years of successive high tidal force is by one Saros cycle — i.e., 223 lunar months (also 239 anomalistic months (from perigee to perigee) and 242 eclipse months — 6585.32 days or 18 years 11⅓ days). (Note that tidal forces depend upon latitude.)

Considering history near 30° North Latitude, it is probably most equivalent in studying charts of events to superimpose 1893 and 1912 over 778 and 796 respectively. This is done in the final comparison of wars (see **Figure 48**)

The following series relates to dates of historical events **after** the high tidal force of 796 A.D.:

THE POST HIGH-TIDAL PERIOD
797-806 A.D.
VERY WARM — WARMEST FOR 1100 YEARS,
ALONG WITH NEXT DECADE.

T'ang Empire The Empire remained fairly stable. Khitan and Tibetan raiding along the border continued, and the coast was harassed by pirates. The unsuccessful rebellion in Szechwan was the only internal disturbance.

Moslem Empire As with China, the Moslem Empire remained fairly stable except along its borders. The Khazars and the Byzantines attacked unsuccessfully. Arabs raided in Anatolia where the Byzantines had to buy them off; but further raiding and looting finally resulted in expansion due to the capture of some Byzantine cities.

The Arabs successfully raided some Mediterranean islands; but the Franks drove them out of Corsica.

Two rebellions flared up — one in Libya which the Empire crushed, and one in Khorasan which the Persians continued.

Algeria and Tunisia drifted into *de facto* independence around 800 A.D.

Byzantium The Byzantine Empire lost its power altogether, and received several severe shocks. Two coups in 797 and 802 overthrew the Emperor. Land and many cities were lost to or sacked by the Arab Moslems.

The Bulgars looted border territories freely.

Islands were sacked by the Moslems.

This decade was a Byzantine debacle.

Japan This was a decade of Japanese weakness. The Ainu conflict in the north continued, and near anarchy swept the land. Authority in remote provinces collapsed; and the trend of peasant attachment to warlords instead of the central government continued. This was a strong movement toward what the West was later to call feudalism.

Spain The Moors lost some of their northern territory to Christian Spaniards and Franks.

A revolt in Cordova was put down.

Franks The Franks, during the glorious reign of Charlemagne, continued to expand. They took more of Spain, and they took Dalmatia, Istria and Corsica. Rebellion in Brittany was put down.

A rebellion in Rome aroused Charlemagne's intervention.

When he reinstated the Pope, Charlemagne was crowned *Imperator* (Emperor) by Pope Leo on Christmas Day, 800 A.D. — despite his aversion. He told Einhard (his subsequent biographer) that he would not have set foot in the Church on that day, if he could have forseen the design of the Pope.

Since the Frankish armies and Empire henceforth consisted largely of a multitude of ethnic groups, this chronology will henceforth refer to the Empire by its new title — the Holy Roman Empire.

Tibet Same as last decade.

Silla Same as last decade.

England From 802 forward, the Vikings raided almost yearly. King Offa and his son had died by 796, and their deaths cost Mercia its overlordship of Southern England. Mercia continued to control the kingdoms it had incorporated; but it failed in the attempt to incorporate Wessex.

Vikings The Vikings continued to expand. They settled in the East Baltic, Orkney, and Shetland Islands. They repeatedly raided England, Scotland and Ireland. At this point in time, the Vikings refrained from raiding the Holy Roman Empire; but they raided the East Baltic Christian Slavs who were allied with Imperial Forces.

807-816 A.D.
100-YEAR HIGH. VERY WARM, BUT STARTING TO COOL.

T'ang Empire A severe revolt in this northeastern part of the Empire started in 809 and took over a decade to subdue. Another revolt occurred in Honan, south of the Yellow River.

Raiding by Tibetans in the West and Khitans in the North continued along the borders.

A major campaign of the T'ang forces against the Tatar raiders in Central Asia proved unsuccessful.

Moslem Empire The rebellion of Khorasan in Persia ended inconclusively with the death of the Caliph, Harun al-Rashid of Arabian Nights fame. This death marked the death of the Golden Age of the Moslem Empire, and the rise of fractionalism. The fraternal conflict between al-Rashid's two sons became an Arab-Persian Civil War which resulted in a Persian victory. The capital was removed to Mary (the Merv of antiquity which was believed to be the original site of Paradise).

These events sparked an Arab revolt in Iraq, and a Shi'ite revolt in the Arabian Peninsula. Neither of these revolts was settled in this decade. Border regions reflected the internal confusion of the Empire. The Byzantines regained all of their Anatolian territory that had been lost to the Moslems in Anatolia. The Khurramite religious sect along the northern border raided into the interior.

Byzantium The decade began well. The Byzantines regained all of the territory that they had lost to the Arabs in Anatolia. The Franks gave back most of the territory they had taken in Dalmatia. Two Byzantine expeditions captured the Bulgar capital of Pliska.

Then events turned sour. In 811, the Bulgars ambushed and killed the Emperor, and began a major campaign against the Byzantines. They sacked and ravished Thrace, then besieged Constantinople itself.

A successful coup was brought off; and in 815, the Byzantines defeated the Bulgars at Mesembria.

North Africa It is difficult to get records of these times for the independent states of Western North Africa. It is obvious, however, from other sources that the coasts of Italy and France, and other circum-Mediterranean areas, as well as Mediterranean islands, which were subjected to pirate raiding and plunder, that Western North Africa was the source of the pirates.

Barbary pirates have operated from this area for a very long time. In this period, plunder, tribute and Christian slaves were the objective.

Japan Triumphs and problems characterized this decade. An unsuccessful coup attempt occurred, and conditions around the capital were reported to be so disturbed that a "police action" was necessary. This implied unrest and confusion in the Empire.

The Imperial forces triumphed against the Caucasoid Ainus. The "final solution" of extermination was successfully applied to several tribes of Ainus; and the Ainu northern harassment generally ceased after 812.

Spain The Moors lost Tortosa, and the Franks completed the establishment of the Spanish March. The Moors stayed South of the Elbo River.

Mutual raids continued on the border that the Moors and Leon shared. Spanish raiders harassed the Mediterranean islands. An unsuccessful revolt occurred in Toledo.

Holy Roman Empire Expansion ended in this decade.

Recently-captured Byzantine territory was returned in exchange for official recognition of Charlemagne's status as Emperor of the West. Only Istria was retained.

Charlemagne spent his last years in unsuccessful attempts to conquer more of Moorish Spain and also Venice. He succeeded in conquering territory along the South Baltic coast, and in incorporating Slavs into the Empire.

In 810, the first Viking raid hit the Empire and was rebuffed. Unrest in Southern Italy was put down.

Charlemagne died in 814; and expansion ceased.

A campaign against Jutland was defeated by the Danes; and the Spanish / Basque revolt in Huesca achieved independence from the Empire. A second major — though unsuccessful — Viking raid was mounted.

England Viking raids continued.

Cornwall was conquered and incorporated into Wessex.

Tibet Same as before.

Silla Same as before.

Vikings Raiding continued — but expanded to the Holy Roman Empire — which retaliated with an unsuccessful attack on Jutland. The Abodrits (Slavs) were forced to pay tribute to Denmark. The Vikings took Limerik in Ireland, and made it their capital.

There was civil war in Denmark.

817-826 A.D.
WARM YEARS, COLD WINTERS. WEATHER COOLING RAPIDLY.

T'ang Empire The border wars continued, and unrest continued in the northern area. Both the thirteen-year long rebellion in the northeast and the Honan revolt which began in the last decade were finally quelled;

along with another rebellion that broke out in Hopei.

Moslem Empire After a five-year absence in Persia (Mary — east of the Caspian Sea) — the Caliph moved his capital back to Baghdad, thereby ending Iraqi unrest.*

The Arab / Persian split (along ethnic lines) continued. Persia remained technically a part of the Empire; but had its own hereditary governor, who governed independently.

The split sparked a revolt in northern Syria and Iraq against the Caliph's "pro-Persian" administration.

A similar revolt in Alexandria was sparked by arrival of Spanish refugees. Both revolts were quelled.

The Khurramite rebellion on the northern border — a holdover from the previous decade — dragged on without resolution.

Byzantium The decade began with the Bulgars returning all of the land that they had taken during the previous few years.

In 822, there was a civil war.

The island of Crete was lost to Moslem refugees from the Alexandrian revolt, and converted to a pirate base to prey on Byzantine shipping.

Japan Honshu was swept by a famine so severe that the Emperor was forced to fast and the Imperial Court was on short rations (imagine what it must have been like for peasants; because previous ghastly famines had not affected the court).

North Africa A rebellion is crushed in Qayrawan. Their piracy continued.

Spain Border wars continued between Christians and Moors. A major, though unsuccessful rebellion occurred in Cordova. The Moorish rebels that survived fled to Alexandria; sparked an unsuccessful revolt there; then fled to Crete and became pirates.

---

*History shows that many people like to have the capital of Empire close at hand. It "helps the economy".

For example, statistics show that — wherever the capital was in China — the nearby provinces got special consideration in famine relief, and the like.

Ghengiz Khan, Alexander and Charlemagne all practiced moving their capital. When the camp-followers became intolerable, they would start marching. They would continue until they lost all camp-followers; then pitch a new capital.

Being a capital-camp-follower is like having the rest of the citizens pay tribute. The risk is getting killed in a revolution when the overhead becomes intolerable to the productive citizenry.

Khazaria The first-known conflicts between the Khazars (Jews) and the Rus* (Vikings) occurred. The Vikings moved down from the Baltic, along the great rivers to the Ukraine and took the city of Tmutorokan, which challenged Khazar control of the Don to Constantinople trade routes.

Holy Roman Empire The Empire began to weaken. A large Danish (Viking) raid succeeded. The first family split occurred — which set the tone and method of disintegrating the Empire.

A nephew — leading Italy — revolted against a son, Louis the Pious, unsuccessfully.

Charlemagne's family was tearing the Empire apart. No one could dominate.**

England The direct line of the Mercian royal family ended, and with it, the supremacy of Mercia ended. In its place, Wessex rose — having succeeded in its decade-long struggle to conquer Cornwall. The king of Wessex, Egbert, had the last royal house that was descended from the Saxon chiefs.

The Mercian dependencies proclaimed Egbert 'bretwalda', and in 825 Wessex defeated Mercia at Ellandune and confirmed this overlordship.

The East Angles, who were under attack by Mercia, acknowledged Egbert as overlord in return for "protection".

Silla Conflict continued as before, but greatly increased in intensity.

Tibet The Tibetans ended their war with Nan Chao without resolution. They continued to raid the border of China.

Vikings This was a period of major expansion. The raids (largely Danish Vikings) were especially successful in Ireland; but also succeeded in Scotland and England.

The Swedish / Varangian / Russians were expanding into the Ukraine as well as the Baltic. They attacked the Holy Roman Empire successfully.***

827-835 A.D.
COOL AND GETTING COLDER.

T'ang Empire This was a quiet period by T'ang standards. True, the T'ang

---

*Russians (Varangians — i.e., Vikings — i.e., Swedes intermixed with Slavs).

**Alexander's, Ghengiz Khan's and Tamarlane's Empires suffered similar fates. That's the way the cookie crumbles if there is a really strong leader, followed by several weak ones.

***Calendar-wise, this was the warm period which gradually became even warmer than the 1930's and 1940's. This became the warmest time in the last 1100 years.

were so weak that the eunuchs were able to kill the Emperor in a coup attempt; but they could not replace him with their own candidate.

In 829, Nan Chao regained its independence from the Empire, and also seized part of the province of Szechwan.

Another sign of weakness was the inability of the Empire to prevent a merchant who, frustrated with Empire inaction against piracy, conquered Wando Island with 10,000 followers, and became "King of the Yellow Sea". He then eliminated piracy, and dominated all Yellow Sea shipping.

The ultimate demonstration of weakness of the Empire was achieved in 834, when the palace guards, led by the eunuchs, ran amuck, killing most of the central bureaucracy and plundering the capital city.*

Moslem Empire The central government was in severe decline. The Arab / Persian split led to an unsuccessful Persian coup attempt. In 836, the Caliph imported Turks (Mamluks — mercenaries) as a "disinterested" pro-Caliph force.**

There was a massive emigration of 17 to 27 thousand Gypsies from India. After a major revolution, they were deported into Byzantine territory.

A Coptic revolution on the Nile led to a massacre of the Christians and their replacement by Arab Moslems. This massacre and replacement accounts for the present ethnic balance in Egypt.

The Khurramite revolt continued.

Byzantium The border conflict with the Moslem Empire continued. The Moslems showed their relative strength by dumping many thousands of unwanted Gypsies across the Byzantine border*** (in Anatolia). These

---

*The most comparable event in modern times was the sack of Washington, D.C., to commemorate the assassination of Martin Luther King, Jr.

**It has always been considered "bad form" to use foreign mercenary troops against one's own people. It makes people mad.

The foreign legion versus Rome.

England's use of Hessians against American colonists.

Mao's use of nomads against China.

Neto's use of Cubans against Angolans.

Russian use of German mercenaries against the Bolsheviks.

Franco's use of the foreign legion, Germans and Italians against Spain.

Sandinista use of foreign Communists against Nicaragua.

***The nearest comparisons in modern time is Mexico dumping millions of peons into the U.S.; and the Communists dumping "boat people" into the U.S. The relative merits of acquiring Gypsies, peons or "boat people" is not addressed here.

refugees were funneled into Eastern Europe by the Byzantines.

At the same time, the Byzantines began to lose control of Sicily, to the North African Moslems (Saracens, Barbary pirates). The Saracens had taken the southeastern corner of Sicily by the end of the decade.

Japan In the Introduction to this chapter, the Japanese court was mentioned as an example of the type of monastic bureaucracy that completely lost contact with its people in the countryside.

In this decade, not a single, significant, dated event was chronicled for the whole of Japan. Nobody at all was minding the store.

North Africa The Barbary Pirates — Saracens — from Aghlabid (Tripoli and Tunisia) invaded Sicily and took at least three cities in the southeast.* By 836, they were raiding south and central Italy.

Spain The Christian / Moor border war continued. Spanish Moors raided, looted and pirated the Mediterranean.

Khazaria Conflict between the Khazarian Jews and the Rus Vikings continued.

Sillia Same as last decade.

Tibet Tibetan border conflicts with the Chinese T'ang Empire continued.

Holy Roman Empire The Viking (Norsemen) made at least two successful raids directly upon Frankish towns. The Empire's weakness was due to the internecine warfare among Charlemagne's heirs.

Three rebellions occurred; but Louis the Pious was ruling again at the end of the decade, even though he had been overthrown twice.

Bulgars Byzantine records show that the Bulgars raided from Croatia to Pannonia.

England Three civil wars within five years eliminated the last vestige of Mercian power. Egbert, King of Wessex, is finally acknowledged as overlord by all the land — except that which was controlled by Vikings.

The Viking raids intensified.

Vikings The Vikings had one internal war to determine who would control the Danish throne.

Raids were intensified in England and Scotland; and Thorgist began the

---

*The modern equivalent of this activity is the acquisition of Malta by Libya (Khadafi — who lives in Tripoli) for use as a military base. This acquisition is proceeding, step by step.

conquest of Ireland.

Viking raids against Holy Roman Empire trading centers were successful, and the different tribes continued to expand into the Baltic and the Ukraine.

837-846 A.D.
COOL.

T'ang Empire A major event in Central Asia had a profound effect on the Chinese Empire. The Uighurs were defeated by the Kirghiz. The Uighurs had been a great help to China, and after their defeat; not only did some of them go to the Tarim Basin to live; but another group tried to seize land from China. At a stroke, China's main military defense force became an enemy. This left the entire northern border open to invasion. Power had moved northward.

Similar problems in the South permitted Nan Chao to take Annam (northern third of Vietnam).

An internal revolution racked China, and hundreds of thousands who adhered to foreign religious creeds were massacred. The entire Manichean, Zoroastrian and Christian communities were wiped out.

The one sign of central government strength was the reduction of Wando Island and assassination of the "King of the Yellow Sea". To the T'ang, he had had too much influence.

Piracy returned to the Yellow Sea.

Civil War in Tibet ended the 85-year war between China and Tibet.

Moslem Empire The importation of Mamluk Turks as an army for the Caliph as a way to bypass the ethnic struggle between Arabs and Persians triggered a revolt in northern Persia by the Bedouin Arabs.

The Khurramite revolt was finally quelled; but the Byzantine war flared up with renewed vigor. The deep penetration of a Byzantine thrust into the Moslem Empire resulted in a major retaliatory invasion of Anatolia. A storm sank the Moslem navy that was laying a siege on Constantinople.

Byzantium The Gypsies finally filtered through the empire and out into Thrace and Eastern Europe.

A successful invasion of Syria triggered a greater retaliatory invasion, with massacres and sacking; but the threat to Byzantium was ended by the destruction of the Arab fleet by a storm.

Japan No significant event was chronicled in this decade.

North Africa The Saracens took central Sicily, and Naples and Rome were sacked. Bari was taken, and Naples finally held them in a sea battle off Licosa.

Spain Essentially the same as the last decade, except Toledo revolted. It is ironic that the Moors were practicing piracy in the Mediterranean, and the Vikings came and sacked Seville.

Khazaria Same as last decade.

Silla Conflicts continued and intensified even more.

Tibet Tibet fell apart. There was a major imperial campaign against Buddhism.

The last King died childless, and various nobles contended for different candidates for the throne.

Khotan seized this moment to declare its independence.

The Uighurs seized and occupied the Tarim Basin.

Holy Roman Empire The civil conflicts among Charlemagne's heirs became so intense that in 843, the Empire was formally divided into three Kingdoms. Saxony failed in its attempt to break away.

Vikings raided the Empire with impunity. They sacked such cities as Rouen, Antwerp and Nantes. They conquered and settled in Frisia (now part of the Netherlands) and the Loire River valley.

In Italy, the Saracens sacked major cities, and took and held territory.

Vikings ended this traumatic decade for the Holy Roman Empire with a three-pronged attack.*

Bulgars The Bulgars gradually spread to Macedonia and Serbia.

England Vikings ripped through England. Different kingdoms fared differently. Most of their power was used against Mercia and Northumbria.

---

*One of the problems that students have is the handling of data. It is the philosophical basis of this age that people work from data rather than from pure theory and thought.

Data tends to be gained in lumps. First you don't have any, then when you learn to get certain kinds of data; that's the kind you get. It is not representative. One can "drown" in data.

The political polls have pointed the way to use statistics meaningfully. They take what they call *randomly selected* data. You may say: "how can you use those two words together? If it is selected, it can't be random."

Well, it isn't easy or obvious; but it is a valid concept.

You take random samples of selected types. But the system crashes if you don't correctly distinguish the significant types of data.

This chronology, for example, deals exclusively with events recorded by *literate* people — with all their limitations; non-objectivity, affluence, etc.

Major cities like London were sacked. Only Wessex, facing mostly secondary armies, has victories.

Vikings The Vikings raided and plundered more than ever, and to a greater degree settled down and held territory. They began to settle in Scotland; and Thorgist became king of half of Ireland before his death.

These Viking outposts, themselves, spawned raids like the Irish raid on Nantes.*

Settlements of Vikings remain in the Holy Roman Empire in Frisia and the Loire Valley. Settlements continue in the east in "Russia". Where the men settled, they took local women to wife, and their children and children's children spoke French, Russian, English, etc. They forced their genetics upon local populations and forever altered them. (For better or worse will never be agreed upon.) The culture, however, was determined by the women.

The complexity of the raids continued to grow. The major three-pronged raid devastated the Holy Roman Empire.

One famous raiding force hit Spain, the Moors, Northern Africa (Vikings raiding Saracens) and finally Rome. Only the Spanish Christians rebuffed their attack.**

The Moors defeated them only after they had sacked Seville, and were so impressed with them that they sent the survivors home to negotiate a permanent trade treaty.

847-856 A.D.
GOT VERY WARM VERY FAST.

T'ang Empire More and more of China disappeared from mention in the Imperial chronicles. The northern border lay particularly open to inroads by Turks and Khitans. Kansu was vulnerable to raids by Tibetans. These raids were driven off with increasing difficulty.

The army successfully mutinied in Hsu.

Moslem Empire Arab fractions led by the Caliph tried to free the Caliphate

---

*Indeed, "Normandy" was taken by "norsemen"; and the Normans took England in 1066. The descendants of "Northmen" (Vikings) still hold Normandy.

**It is amusing to note that the Spanish Christians were so highly mobilized from a century of attack by the Moors (Moslems) that they could rebuff a highly expert first attack, whereas the Moors and Barbary pirates who had been dishing it out succumbed to the violent surprise.

from the Mamluk Turks. The Caliph was killed, and Mamluks triumphed and controlled the Empire for the next hundred years.**

This internal weakness laid the Empire open to attack, and the Byzantine fleet attacked and sacked Damietta, Egypt.

Japan No significant events were chronicled for this decade.

North Africa The Saracens continued raiding for treasure including Christian slaves as before, and continued their long campaign to capture the central valley of Sicily.

Morocco under the Idrisids enters a period of anarchy as Berbers, Kharijites and rival factions of the ruling family battle for control.

Spain The Moorish / Christian border war continued.

Spanish / Moorish pirates continue to raid coastal Mediterranean towns, especially in Sicily and Italy. The Moorish pirates raided Marseilles against the erstwhile powerful Franks.

Khazaria Same as the last decade.

Silla Civil war continued.

Tibet Tibetan bands entering China were rebuffed.

Eastern Turkestan took advantage of the dissolution of the central government and broke free with Uighur help.

Holy Roman Empire The fighting among the royal family had merged over to an ethnic struggle — primarily between Germans and Franks.* Typical of the crippling revolts was that of Aquitaine which offered to join Louis the German; but after much fighting, they stayed under Charles the Bold (of the Franks).

The Vikings continued to raid and despoil the land.

They mounted a campaign up the Elbo River and up the Seine — where they established a permanent base.

**This is the last half of the equation of bringing in foreign mercenaries to keep the government in power. They stay for dinner and eat the host. Time and again throughout history this occurs. There is absolutely no reason for it not to happen. The foreign mercenaries have no emotional or moral reasons not to seize control; and many positive reasons to do so. Foreign mercenaries are the ultimate danger to which a society can expose itself. They are more dangerous than volunteer armies; which in turn are far more dangerous to a society than a drafted army.

---

*This schism was very much like the Arab / Persian schism in the Moslem Empire; and like the great Egyptian conqueror the great conquerers are very virile men. They are persuaded to take to wife some chosen woman of each major ethnic group. It makes for an

Bulgars Except for one major defeat by the Serbs, the Bulgars continued as in the previous decade.

England The Vikings made their first permanent settlement in England on the island of Thanet. They plundered London and Canterbury and mounted a huge invasion of Mercia.

Wessex defeated the Vikings at Ockley, but it was a secondary target.

Vikings The Vikings began to feud among themselves along ethnic lines.

Denmark has a civil war.

The Danish and Norwegian Vikings fought over Ireland; and the Norwegians won and ejected the Danes. Thereafter, the Danes tried to take Kurland (Latvia) from the Swedes.

The intensity of raids up all the rivers of Northern Europe and France escalated.

The first settlement in England, proper, was the forerunner of Daneslaw.

857-866 A.D.

VERY WARM.

(NOTE that tree-rings imply that this was the warmest decade of the warm period.)

T'ang Empire The last of the Uighurs left Mongolia for the Tarim Basin — recently taken from Tibet. Its availability for settlement implies elimination of the previous occupants.*

Weakness invited disaster everywhere.

---

entertaining home life and leaves many heirs — which great conquerers are persuaded (easily?) to do.

Being very busy folk, conquerers have little time to spend with each of their many heirs.

So the Mothers raise the heirs *ethnically.*

Thus the *ethnic split of royal families,* once Papa has gone to his richly deserved eternal rest.

The residue of strong people is a *pot pourri* of troubles generated by their human weaknesses.

There have been no really great women conquerers. The homelife is not as satisfactory to the conquered ethnic groups; and pregnancy is a greater distraction than intercourse.

---

*This happened again and again throughout history: One people was eradicated and another took its place on some particular piece of land.

(1) Copts eliminated on the Nile (Hamites by Semites — both Caucasian);

(2) Ainus in Japan by Mongoloid Japanese;

(3) Capoids (a yellow people) by Negroids in Southern Africa; and

(4) Indians in North America by Caucasians.

A Nan Chao invasion of Tonkin was rebuffed; but the army was not relieved and faced an invasion by Laotians.

Another successful army mutiny occurred in Hsu.

An army of 40,000 rebels in Chekkiang was very difficult to put down.

Moslem Empire The Arab power-play to control the Caliphate which began in this 807-816 decade ended in fighting which included the murder of the Caliph Mutawakkil, and complete control of the Caliphate by the Turkish Mamluks; thus Arabs and Persians who fought along ethnic lines both lost to Turkish mercenaries.

The Byzantine border war continued. A major Byzantine invasion was defeated. Three years later, the Arab counter-invastion went into Anatolia. As the Arab army was returning home—burdened with loot—it was annihilated.

Byzantine Empire The above-related wars became a part of Byzantine activities along with an invasion of Byzantium by the Varangians—Swedish Vikings who had crossed through the Slavic area that would subsequently be called Russia; and ravaged the Black Sea coast to the Bosphorus.

This was part of a planned two-pronged Viking attack—one through Russia, the Black Sea; and closing in on Constantinople from the east; while the other prong went around the Iberian Peninsula, and through the Mediterranean to attack Constantinople from the West.

Both raided en route, and the western prong of the attack didn't make it.

Japan No significant events were chronicled.

North Africa The Western prong of the Viking attack on Constantinople attacked North Africa and looted the coastline around Cabo Tres Forcas. Captured Negros were later sold as curiosity items in Ireland.

The Saracens continued their piratical operations. During the decade, their conquest of Sicily reached Hanna (Enna).

Spain The war between Christian and Moslem Spaniards was interrupted by the raids by the Western Prong of the Viking attack on Constantinople which was led by Bjorn Ironside. The Vikings sacked Murcia and Gibraltar —among the Moslem sites; and Pamplona in the Christian nation of Navarre.

The Moors took advantage of the Viking disablement of Pamplona to seize it from Navarre immediately.

Silla and Tibet Civil war in both countries was causing complete social disintegration. Except for the general condition, the chronologies reveal very little or nothing. They are more vague than usual.

Khazaria An invasion by the Patzinaks drove the main allies of the Khazars — the Magyars — from the Don Valley westward. Removal of the Magyars geographically separated the Khazars from their other allies, the Volga Bulgars.

The Rus seized upon this Khazarian weakness to occupy land far into the Ukraine.

Russia This formative decade created the Russians. The Slavic people who lived in the northern convergence swamp areas which give rise to the upper reaches of the Volga, Dvina, Northern Dvina and Dnieper Rivers* were conquered by the Swedish Viking tribe known as the Varangians. The people were consolidated to a city called Novgorod. The Viking leader, Rurik, established a ruling house that lasted 700 years.

Tree-rings of the logs used for streets in Novgorod are still in place, and they date back to this time.

The Slavic name for these people was the *Rus*, later to become Russia. These people — under Rurik — conquered Kiev at this time.

The Rus under Rurik seized areas around the Baltic, in the Ukraine from the Khazars, and struck at Constantinople.

Holy Roman Empire The Vikings continued to raid and settle to occupy land, despite military and peasant resistance. The Chronicles record that entire areas were left unpopulated.

Following is a list of cities and areas that were raided in the Roman Empire during this one decade: the Seine River Valley, Angiers, Orleans, Tours, Toulouse, Angoulême, Limoges, Perigueux, Bordeaux, Pisa, Luna,

---

*Portages, and subsequently canals interconnected the Baltic / North Atlantic; the White Sea / Arctic; the Caspian Sea; and the Black Sea / Mediterranean / Atlantic in this North-eastern swamp area of Russia — an incredibly strategic location. This is the crossroads of the greatest land area on earth — Eurasia.

NOTE: To understand these activities and to place them in historical context, consider the two decades: 857-866 and 1944-1953. These may have been (and probably were) the warmest, mildest climate decades — the earlier being the warmer — in the last three or four thousand years. In both of these decades, the Russians boiled out west and south with enormous power; took territory, sacked and plundered, and slaughtered unmercifully. In both cases, conquest from the west stirred them up; but the warm growing seasons had enabled them to accumulate the capital required for the commitment to such an effort.

In the former case, as the climate settled back to its normal misery, the Rus subsided. It is reasonable to expect the climate to force them to subside this time. Enough misery and hunger slows a people down considerably.

Oiselle Saucourt, the Marne River Valley, the Balearic Islands, Narbonne and the Rhone River Valley were raided by the Vikings. These were Western and Northern European portions of the Empire.

The Bulgars raided regularly in the east, and the Magyars raided in the east once in this decade.

The Aquitaine rebellion ended; a civil war in the northern part of the Empire continued with a revolt in the German royal family; and there was a Frankish invasion of Italy.

England The Danish Viking brothers Ubbi, Ivar and Halfdan led a major invasion to avenge the execution of their father by the Northumbrian King. They captured and killed him by torture, and took all of Northumbria south of the Tyne.

Raids continued elsewhere.

Vikings Raids on: The Holy Roman Empire, Moorish and Christian Spain, Moslem North Africa, Northumbria, Pictland, Strathclyde, Russia, Khazaria, and Byzantium.

After the internecine Viking war between Norse and Danes, they were driven from North Ireland.

In the North, Norway was unified by Harald Haarfager (Fairhair).

They discovered Iceland.

867-876 A.D.
VERY WARM, BUT STARTING TO COOL.

T'ang Empire The invasion by Laotians was the "last straw" for the unrelieved Annam army, so they mutinied and returned home to Kiangsu. On the way, they pillaged and ravaged every city on the way. Once home, they joined in a widespread peasant revolt against the central government.

The country was falling into a state of general anarchy.

Bandit gangs ransacked Honan, and freely roamed along the Great Canal committing acts of piracy and paralyzing trade.

Rebellions occurred in Kuang-hsi, P'ang Hsun and Hsu. A drought in Shantung and Honan triggered famine and a massive revolt.

Wang Hsien organized the peasants and mutineers into a great army, and led the revolt which in 14 years, according to records, cost more than 36,000,000 lives.

With the Uighur mainstay of the T'ang army gone, the government resorted to recruiting foreign nomads (Huns and Shato Turks) to fight its own people. The Shato Turks ultimately were destined to rule all of China.

Moslem Empire The Caliphate under the "bodyguard" Mamluks lost the ability to rule.

Ya'gub and Amr al-Saffir led a revolt against the hereditary governors — the Tahirids — and defeated them. They then attacked the capital, Baghdad, to try to force the Caliph to grant them hereditary rulership of Persia and Transoxania.

The weakness of the government was shown by a Negro slave revolt in southern Iraq, which it took 12 years to put down.

Byzantium gained territory at the expense of the weakened Moslem Empire.

Byzantium A coup started a decade of expansion against the Moslem Empire. The expansion was in two areas: Anatolia and, in alliance with the Franks, in Italy against the North African Saracens.

Malta was lost with the massacre of a Byzantine garrison.

Japan According to the chronicles, the event of this decade was government organized public prayer to meet the massive piracy along their coastlines by Koreans.

Silla and Tibet Their long civil wars continued.

North Africa The Saracen pirates extended their raiding throughout the Mediterranean Sea, and triggered the Franks, Italians and Byzantines to join forces to drive them out of Italy.* The Saracens lost territory — Bari in particular — but beat off the Byzantine attack to take back Sicilian territory.

Spain Border war between Christian and Moslem forces continued.

Khazaria The Khazars continued to be attacked by Vikings (Rus) from the north and Pechenegs from the east.

Holy Roman Empire The Chronicles became confusing during this decade; but this general situation emerged:

Vikings continued to loot along coastlines and estuaries.

People abandoned cities and coastal settlements and moved inland.

The Dynastic struggle for power continued, with Charles the Bald invading Italy and forcing the Pope to crown him Holy Roman Emperor.

Moravia's try for independence failed.

The Magyars continued small scale raids in the east as did the Saracens

---

*Throughout history, people who conquer and hold territory with organized armed forces have behaved as though privateers and pirates were immoral.

in the south.*

England The Viking brothers Ubbi, Ivar and Halfdan finished their English campaign in Mercia where they captured and killed the King by torture, and killed his heir. Mercia then became the foundation of Daneslaw.

Another campaign conquered East Anglia and King Edmund was beheaded. (He was subsequently declared to be a saint.) East Anglia became a part of Daneslaw.

The Vikings invaded Wessex and won numerous victories. They could not overcome the resistance which was led by Aetheired, and finally declared a five-year truce.

Vikings Raids were continued in Eastern, Northern and Western Europe, and throughout the British Isles.

The Norwegians began to settle in Iceland; the Orkney, Shetland, Hebrides and Faeroe Islands and in Scotland. This wave of emigrants was fleeing from the reign of Harald Fairhair who consolidated his rule of Norway in 872.

877-886 A.D.
STILL COOLER.

T'ang Empire The Peasant Rebellion that began in 873 reached its climax. The original leader Wang Hsien was killed and replaced by Huang Chao.

Plague drove them northwards.

They recrossed the river, looted numerous provinces, and captured both capitols** of China; drove out the Imperial Court; and declared Huang Chao emperor.

A two-year siege retook Chang'an and Huang Chao committed suicide.

The rebellion continued elsewhere with different leaders, working onward to its final count of 36,000,000 dead.

Side effects were numerous. There were 18 recorded coups and mutinies in provincial capitols; and the Khitan horde established an eight-tribe empire that grew at the expense of border territory.

The Shato Turks mutinied at the beginning of the decade; then after

---

*The peripheral raiding of the mighty Holy Roman Empire is reminiscent of a quotation by Ben Gurion of Israel: "The United Nations has no teeth, but it can gum you to death." the Arab / Norse / Magyar / Bulgar pirates and raiders could win any battle; but avoided war because they would probably have lost it.

** Anyang and Chang'an, the ceremonial and the political capitols.

being defeated, consolidated to become the strongest force fighting for the T'ang Emperor.

As the Peasant Revolt wound down, the Imperial Court was dominated by the Chinese General Chu Wen—a former rebel. The Shato Turks set up almost independent overlordship in the northeastern provinces, and battled the Chinese for control of the Emperor. This struggle was to last for a decade.

Moslem Empire The central government continued to be almost completely ineffective and in the thrall of the Mamluks.

The Negro slave revolt in southern Iraq was finally subdued; but the Saffarid conquest of all of Persia continued. The most significant event of the decade was the breakaway to virtual independence of Egypt under hereditary control of the Tulunids (Turks). Ahmed ibn Tulun extended the borders of Egypt to the Euphrates; and when the Baghdad government encouraged Syria to revolt, he beat down the revolt and forced Baghdad to "permanently" grant dominion over the land to Egypt and the Tulunid Dynasty.

All conflicts between Byzantium and the Moslem Empire resulted in Byzantine victories.

Another symptom of Moslem Empire weakness was the successful breakaway to independence by Tabaristan under a descendant of Mohammed.

Byzantine Empire The Byzantines extended their naval power. In addition to battling the Moslem Empire, they fought the North African Saracens, and reduced piracy in the Eastern Mediterranean.

They campaigned vigorously against the Moslems in Sicily and Italy; but although they were unsuccessful in stopping the conquest of Sicily, they stalled it for decades; and they reversed the Moslem conquest of Southern Italy.

Byzantines in Sicily began to emigrate to Italy.

North Africa Anarchy continued in Morocco. In the Aghlabid region, piracy continued, as Saracens spread their control of Sicily in Syracuse; but lost territory in Southern Italy to the Byzantines.

Tulunid Egypt attacked the Aghlabid territory, but was beaten off with difficulty.

Japan In the (877-886) decade, the Fujiwara clan became Kwampaku (regent), and the Yamato clan was relegated to the role of God Emperor with no power. The practice—which was to last for centuries—of retiring the Emperor to a monastery when he reached maturity, and replacing him with a child—began in this decade.

The Fujiwara Period began after they had gradually increased their power by marriage into the royal (Yamato) Clan. They took power official-ly in 877.

Silla and Tibet Civil wars continued.

Spain Christian and Moslem Spainards continued their border wars.

Khazaria The Khazars continued to fight the Varangians (Russians) on the north and the Pechenegs in the east.*

Holy Roman Empire From 877 to 881 there was general anarchy through-out the Empire.

Vikings began to hit the major centers of the Empire. They raided Sens, Hambury and Aachen—Charlemagne's old capitol. Lower Burgundy and Provence took advantage of the confusion to declare and secure their independence.

In 881 Charles the Fat invaded Italy and had the Pope crown him Holy Roman Emperor. When he was unable to rescue Paris from a long siege, Count Odo, who was the rescuer, was awarded the crown as King of the Western Franks.

The Normans (i.e., Norsemen or Norwegian Vikings) began to invade, and Frisia (now in the Netherlands) was given to Godfred the Dane in return for his forces protecting Frisia from further invasions. "Protection".

England Wessex bore the brunt of the Danish Viking attack during this decade; and the leader, Halfdan, was killed in a Danish / Irish-Norseman conflict. The attack continued, and after the Viking victory at Chippenham, all of Britain south of the Thames lay at the mercy of the Danes.

Five months later, a great victory at Edington by the native forces under Alfred the Great secured the independence of Wessex. Later Alfred took London from the Danes; who nevertheless continued to settle in Daneslaw.

Vikings The Vikings continued to spread. Though stopped in Wessex, they occupied Mercia, East Anglia, large portions of Northumbria, Scotland and its offshore islands, and Ireland. They acquired Frisia from the Holy

---

*This long, long war between the Russians, as they were establishing their identity and their place in the sun, with the Jewish Khazars probably established a very long-lasting tribal enmity of the Russians toward Jews.

Remember—these Jews were Asiatics—not Semitic Caucasians.

NOTE: A universal famine was reported for 879.

Roman Empire; and a relative of Rurik took Kiev and made it the captiol of the Rus Empire.

887-896 A.D.
FAIRLY COLD.

T'ang Empire Conditions continued to deteriorate.

The Khitan Empire (8 tribes) which was carved out of the northern border of the T'ang Empire continued to grow; as did also the influence of the Shato Turks who were led by Li-ke-yung, a former General of the T'ang court.

The most important development was the spread of his power by Chu Wen, who conquered neighboring provinces. For example, in 887, Chu Wen crushed a Bandit Gang of several thousand men — whom he then recruited to his campaign, and used them to crush Ch'ing and Yen.

He was heavily opposed by the Shato Turks.

At this time, a civil war in Western China and Szechwan was fought between provincial governors on one side, and palace eunuchs and their adopted sons on the other. The capitol was successfully invaded, and the government was forced to execute the eunuchs who had been running the bureaucracy for years. The end of the decade saw a provincial governor invading the capitol and forcing the Imperial court to flee to Hua.

Meanwhile, there were numerous coups and mutinies throughout the country.

Moslem Empire The Caliphate tried to regain some power. The Caliph campaigned against the Saffarid rulers of Persia; but the Caliph Al-Mu'tamid died and the *status quo* was restored.

The Caliphate backed a Syrian rebellion against Tulunid Egyptian control. Border fighting between Persians and Turks led to a Persian campaign westward to Taraz.

Byzantium Losses continue in Sicily; but territorial gains continue in Southern Italy. Sicilian Byzantines migrated from Sicily to Southern Italy.

The Bulgars declared war against Byzantium after having a civil war that installed a strong king. The Bulgars were almost defeated by the Magyars who were allies of Byzantium; but the Bulgars tricked the empire into abandoning their allies, and they won over Byzantium.

Japan By 890, there was complete anarchy. The records claim that the anarchy was quieted after a few months.

In 891, a power struggle between the Emperor and the Fujiwara Clan cost the Clan its power for 8 years.

Toward the end of the decade, the Japanese broke off official contact with China, and reasserted Japanese customs and institutions rather than copy China.

Silla The feudal lords and central governments so weakened each other that two enormous peasant revolts siezed territory. The "Red Trouser" revolt in 889 set up the Kingdom of Later Koguryo. The second revolt three years later took another part of Silla and set up the Kingdom of Later Paekche.

Tibet Same as last decade.

North Africa Tulunid Egypt had to contend with the Abbasid Caliphate of Baghdad-backed Syrian revolt. Morocco continued to have anarchy.

The Aghlabid Empire continued to prosper with its Saracens taking Sicily and raiding Italy — especially Northern Italy which was ruled by the Lombards.

Holy Roman Empire In 887, Charles the Fat was deposed, and the Empire was divided into East and West. (This was the end of the civil war which had followed Charles' consolidation of east and west.)

Within a year, Upper Burgundy declared independence.

King Armulf of the Eastern Empire was called to Italy several times by the Pope to help against the Italian magnates; and he himself was named a magnate.

Saracens raided further north. Vikings penetrated deeper into the Empire. Normans under Rollo roamed freely through Northern France. The Magyars fled westward and settled in the Middle Danube Valley, raiding neighboring areas on occasion. The Moravian Slavs both raided and fled from the Magyars, going north and southwest.

The Magyars aided the Empire against the Slavs.

Spain Same as last decade.

Khazaria Same as last decade.

England The Danes continued to settle in Daneslaw in the north, and raid Wessex; but Alfred the Great led Wessex to resist all conquest.

Vikings Harald Fairhair, having conquered and united all of Norway, followed the refugees and brought them all under his rule — in the Orkney, Hebrides and Shetland Islands, and the Isle of Man.

Viking settlement continued within the former boundaries of England,

Ireland, Scotland and the Holy Roman Empire.

They continued to expand in the Russian area.

897-906 A.D.

WARM BUT GETTING COOLER.

T'ang Empire The Dynasty ended in this decade. The Imperial Court was in Hua, having been forced to flee there by a governor of a province who had taken the capitol. The governor stripped the Emperor of his bodyguards and had his most loyal commanders executed. The Shato Turks led by Li K'o-yang, forced the governor to release the court and to restore the capitol.

General Chu Wan continued to increase his power. The palace eunuchs deposed the Emperor and offered the crown to the General. He restored the Emperor and killed all of the palace eunuchs. He thereafter (in 904) killed the Emperor; set up a puppet Emperor, and took the remainder of the court to his capitol in Honan.

He massacred the remainder of the imperial T'ang family; set himself up as Emperor, and established the Later Liang Dynasty.

The Shato Turks and Khitans continued to grow in the north.

The literates (who recorded the chronicles) concentrated on the north and events related to the throne. Other sources show that at this time, segments of Southern China had mutinied, revolted, and in some cases became independent kingdoms.

Moslem Empire The Caliphate had a resurgence of power in this decade. The Caliph intervened in the Syrian revolt against Tulunid Egypt; won, and retook both Syria and Egypt into the Empire.

The Carmathian sect tried to take Syria; and did take land further south in the Arabian Peninsula and along the Persian Gulf.

Persia had a civil war between the governors of Transoxania — the Samanids and the Persian Saffarid Dynasty.

Byzantium The last Byzantine settlement in Sicily — Taormina, was overwhelmed by the Moors.

The Bulgars, who had been making the Byzantines pay tribute, were invaded by the Magyars, and were driven out of Transylvania and Pannonia; thus relieving Byzantium.

The Saracen Corsairs (pirates) of Tripoli under Leo raided Thessalonia, and took 20,000 Byzantine civilians into slavery.

Japan The power struggle between the Imperial Yamato Clan and the

Fujiwara Clan ended with the Fujiwara's regaining power; although they did not officially regain the regency for another thirty years.

The court had so little power that they could not collect enough revenue to pay the Imperial Guards in Hsien. The mutiny because of no pay turned the Imperial Guards to bandits, and they looted the countryside causing anarchy.

Spain The border conflict between Christians and Moors continued; and the Christians captured Zamora during this decade.

Silla The two kingdoms established by peasant revolts in the previous decade became stable as the Kingdoms of Later Korguryo and Later Paekche in this decade.

North Africa Anarchy in Morocco decreased enough for court records to begin again.

Their neighbor, the Aghlabids of Tunisia, Tripoli and Algeria had to battle the Fatimid Shi'ites in a religiously motivated civil war.

The Tulunids of Egypt first had a Syrian rebellion which was then joined by the Abbasid Empire Caliphate. Egypt was beaten and reincorporated into the Empire.

The Saracen Corsairs completed the conquest of Sicily from the Byzantines, then formed a navy under Leo which raided and looted at will. The Saracens took the Balearic Islands from the Franks.

Holy Roman Empire Civil strife continued. The Italian King Louis III (of Burgundy) was overthrown by Berengarius (great-grandson of Charlemagne). The latter blinded the former and set himself up as a rival King and held the throne until the year before his death — 923.

The Saracens took the Balearic Islands.

The Vikings (Normans) under Rollo continued ravaging northern France.

The Magyars completed the conquest of Hungary, scattered the Slavs; and invaded the Empire, plundering Northern Italy and Bavaria.

England Vikings continued to settle Daneslaw. Norwegian Vikings began to settle the western coast. Only Wessex resisted successfully, despite the Danish-Viking-backed civil war in which Aethelwold tried to exercise his claim to the throne. Edward, son of Alfred the Great, won the war and kept the throne. He later beat a Danish invasion of the Thames valley.

The Danes destroyed the Kentish army as they withdrew.

Vikings The Swedes invaded Denmark and seized power. Despite internal troubles, the Vikings continued to expand their conquests in the British

Isles; the Holy Roman Empire; Islands in the North Sea and in the North Atlantic from Iceland to the Hebrides; the Baltic area and in Russia.

907-916 A.D.
WARM.

China The new Later Liang Empire—Emperor Chu Wen—could not be quieted. Chu Wen was killed by one of his bastard sons who was, in turn, killed by the legitimate heir.

At least five governors took the opportunity to declare their provinces independent.

Numerous other rebellions flourished during this decade, and both the Shato Turks and the Khitans expanded their holdings and power. They fought each other and came to terms.

Moslem Empire The Carmathian Sect grew in power. (The Carmathians were a Shi'ite Sect who, by careful steps, taught their followers to cease to be Moslem; thence to be completely liberal in beliefs. They disappeared about 1050 A.D.) During this decade, they took more of the Arabian Peninsula.

Persia continued its civil war. The Samanids, governors of Transoxania, defeated the Saffarids and became the rulers of Persia. Within three years, the ruler and his uncle were in a civil war that was to last for nine years.

Byzantium This decade was especially violent; war with the Saracens continued in Sicily and Italy. Naval war against the Saracen Corsairs of Tripoli (the fleet of Leo) was engaged.

The Vikings (Swedish Varangians/Rus) invaded from the North with 80,000 men. They besieged Constantinople. The Vikings were defeated, and the Empire made a trading treaty with them.

The Bulgars recovered from the Magyar attack, and attacked the Empire, which allied itself with the Serbs and Pechenegs, and fought to keep the Bulgars out of the lower Balkans.

Japan No event of particular interest, although the culture was evolving toward feudalism with peasants and Samurai attaching themselves to strong overlords.

Silla Continued civil war, but no special events.

Spain The Christian/Moslem border war continued, but no outstanding events occurred.

North Africa The Fatimid Shi'ites dominated this decade. The civil war that they fought against the Aghlabid Dynasty of Tunisia, Tripoli and Eastern Algeria was successfully concluded, and the religious leader became the Caliph of the area.

These Fatimid* forces attacked Egypt, but the Abbasids rebuffed them.

Piracy continued to be a successful part of the Saracen economy as the Corsairs ranged the Mediterranean. Piracy provided a critical additional capital in the form of slaves and concentrated wealth substances.

The war with Byzantium for Sicily and Southern Italy ended in this decade; with the Saracens completing the conquest of the former, and losing the latter.

Holy Roman Empire The Magyar and German forces fought and the Magyars won.

The Vikings under Rollo continued to ravage Northern France until 911, when Rollo was offered the Duchy of Normandy in return for ceasing raids elsewhere. He accepted, and a major Viking settlement of the Normandy area resulted.

Shortly after 911, a seven-year period of anarchy occurred.

England This was a mixed decade in England; but on balance, the English came out ahead.

Wessex under Edward and Mercia under Aetheired conquered Daneslaw, and took it back from the Danish settlers.

While the Danish Vikings were losing, however, the Norwegian Viking settlers on the western English coast plundered the Welsh kingdom of Guelph and a neighboring Saxon area; and kidnapped a bishop.

Vikings Lost Daneslaw, but continued to raid and settle in Ireland, Scotland and England. They acquired Normandy which became a major Viking settlement.

In Russia, they consolidated their position enough to attack Constantinople in 907 with 80,000 men; were beaten, and signed a trading treaty (Varangians and Byzantines).

917-926 A.D.

VERY WARM.

This decade was the last in the period reviewed for this study. The

---

*Fatima, the daughter of Mohammed married Ali, who became Caliph. Many Moslems believed that this lineage inherited the right to rule. Mohammedanism was / is very political; indeed, as the Shah recently learned, his secular government could not stand against the lethal mix of Shi'ite Moslem religion and fanatic politics.

theory was that after the high tidal force of December 23, 796, the effect of the resultant climatic change would have been sufficiently diluted as to be of less than first magnitude within 13 decades. The chronology includes the eight decades leading up to the high tidal force, and thirteen thereafter.

China The Later Liang Dynasty was overthrown by Li Ssu-yuan and the Shato Turks in 923. Three years later he was killed by his adopted brother. Within the year, another coup put a third Turk on the throne.

The Khitans to the north expanded, and took the Kingdom of Parhae (see decade 717-726) (i.e., Manchuria). Several Khitan / Chinese battles occurred as the confederation of 8 tribes tried to take more of Northern China.

Governors throughout the empire mutinied, and the Imperial armies mutinied and became huge, roving bandit gangs.

Moslem Empire The recent surge of Caliphate strength began to wane.

The Carmathian Sect increased its control in the Arabian Peninsula, including control of Basra.

Egypt was in chaos.

Persia was in a family civil war.

During the latter part of the decade, a Shi'ite rebellion arose in Persia, and would in later decades control Persia, Baghdad and the entire Caliphate.

Byzantium War raged on land and sea.

The twenty-year war against Leo and the Saracen Corsairs ended with victory by the Byzantine navy in 924. The defeat of Tripoli did not influence piracy by the North African Saracens.

The eleven-year Byzantine / Bulgar war was ended with Bulgaria seizing Macedonia, Thessaly and Albania. The Bulgars then went on to conquer and devastate Serbia as a sequel to the Byzantine-Serbian war alliance against the Bulgars. A great famine in Byzantium followed 927.

The Pechenegs also had been allies of the Byzantines, and they came out of the war in possession of Wallachia which they had taken from the Bulgars.

Japan During the decade, there were no recorded dramatic happenings; but a description written in 927 said that the country was in a most disturbed state. Rebellion threatened in the provinces; bandits were everywhere; the capital was so weak that robbers were entering the Imperial Palace.

North Africa The Fatimid Shi'ite Sect absorbed al-Maghrib (Morocco and Western Algeria) into their Empire of Central North Africa. They attempted to sieze Egypt; but were rebuffed by the Abbasids.

Egypt sank into total chaos, and the Abbasids were forced, after a dozen years, to relinquish it to a hereditary, semi-independent governor, the Turkish Ikshidites.

Piracy based in North Africa. The land was in chaos. Leo and his Saracen Corsairs were defeated in Tripoli, but Sicily continued to be exploited and piracy continued unabated in the rest of the Mediterranean.

Korea Korea was, at this point in history, divided into three countries: Silla, Later Paekche and Later Koguryo. The King of the latter was killed by his First Minister who changed the Kingdom to Koryo.

Paekche attacked Silla, looted its capitol and killed the King. Silla allied itself with Koryo — which in the next decade was to control all of Korea.

The flood of refugees from Parhae (Manchuria) entered Korea to escape the conquest of the Khitans and their nomadic allies.

Spain In retaliation for the aggression of Leon, the Moors campaigned and won against Leon, Navarre and Castille. The Moors forced surrender terms against all of the Kingdoms; but were not strong enough to absorb them.

Holy Roman Empire A major period of anarchy ended in 918. Later, the East and West Kingdoms had major civil wars. Further, the two kingdoms warred over possession of the Duchy of Lorraine.

During this war, Vikings were recruited to settle in Normandy. These Normans continued to raid Brittany, Aquitaine, Auvergne, Loire, Fauguembergue, and the Somme River Valley.

While the above went on in the West, the Magyars were raiding Italy, Bavaria, Swabia, Alsace, Lorraine, Champagne, Franconia, Pavia, Loire,

---

(*NOTE:* The growth of the Christian population — with three Kingdoms — stood them in sharp contrast to the tiny population in 720 — only 200 years before. The experience of gaining strength and ultimately winning by the Roman Catholic precept of large families marks the minds and beliefs of both the Catholics and Spanish forever. History has taught them that problems **can be solved WITH EXTREME FERTILITY**. Their knowledge of such **solutions in the past** will make it essentially impossible for "population planners" to persuade them that fertility will cause **problems in the future**.

It took some 500 years more; but the very Catholic Majesties Ferdinand and Isabella, with a large population, finally crushed the Moors in 1492.

The Spanish Catholic and the Chinese use their demographic time bomb to win. Together, they totaled 1,065,000,000 speakers in 1978. The Spanish speakers exceed those who speak Hindi; in fact, only Chinese, English and Russian exceed the Spanish speakers; and the latter will pass the Russian speakers within one or two decades.)

Venetia, Lombardy, Provence, Septimania and the Rhone Valley. They forced the Germans to pay tribute.

England Daneslaw surrendered to Edward the Elder of Wessex and Aethelred of Mercia, after a thirteen-year campaign. The Norwegian Vikings from Ireland seized York.

Vikings The Danes lost Daneslaw in England; were stalemated in the attempt to expand in Ireland; but exerted growing power in the Holy Roman Empire and in Russia.

In addition to the events of the preceding chronology, two other classes of events are covered in Tables I and II—Migrations and Famines respectively.

The events are coordinated with the summary of climate as shown in Chapter VI, Section A.1.

These plus the decadal maps in **Figure 51**, 717-926 A.D. (Literate Areas through 717-926), respectively; constitute an unprecedentedly thorough review of the period from 717 through 926 in the Northern Hemisphere- at 30° N latitude northward.

TABLE I.

MIGRATIONS – (∼30° + N) – EASTERN HEMISPHERE – 717 - 926 A.D.

(This table is inserted because the information is so hard to get. Information covering 1813 A.D. forward is easy; thus not published.)

647-720 A.D.	Japanese (from ∼35° N - 136° E to 38° N - 141° E)
663-757 A.D.	Tū Yü Hun from Chaing-hai to Ho-hei (From 33° - 38° N, 95° - 100° E to 33° - 40° N, 100° - 110° E)
696-c.720 A.D.	Khitan and Mongols - Yingchow to Northern Manchuria (Parhae) (from 41° N - 122° E to 39° - 48° N, 125° - 138° E)
700-800 A.D.	Irish hermits to Faroe Islands (from 51°30′ - 53°30′ N - 5°40′ - 10°30′ W to 63° -64° N - -7° W)
8th Century	Frisians to North Frisian Islands (from 53°0′ - 50° N - 4°40′ - 8° E to 54°30′ - 55°30′ N - 8°20′ - 55′ E)

717   Tungas, Arabs and Tibetans converge on Kashgaria
                     (to 39° N - 76° E)

717-732   Moors cross Pyrenees to Riviera and Rhone River Valley
                     (from south of 43° N to 43° - 44°30′ N - 0°30′ - 4°40′ E)

c.738   Qasite (Northern Arab) tribes to the Hawf of Egypt -
                     ordered by Caliph Hashim
                     (from 20° - 30° N - 37° - 45° E to 26° - 31° N - 35° - 30° E)

743-759   Moors go from Septimania, France, to south of the
                     Pyrenees
                     (from 43° - 44°30′ N - 0°30′ - 4°40′ E to below 43° N)

745   Khitans migrated westward
                     (from 42° N - 120° E to 40° N - 115° E)

c.745   Uighurs expanded throughout Northern Mongolia
                     (from 39° - 46° N - 100° - 110° E to 39° - 55° N - 75° -
                     110° E)

c.751 A.D.   Khitans from southern Manchuria to North China plains
                     (from 40° N - 117° E to 39° N - 112° E)

755 A.D.   T'ang (Chinese) court and army from Ch'ang An to
                     Szechwan
                     (from 34° N - 109° E to 31° N - 104° E)

756 A.D.   Arab mercenaries (4-10,000) sent by Caliph to China to
                     help T'ang against An Lu Shan revolution (10,000,000
                     descendants)
                     (from 44°30′ N - 33°30′ E to 31° N - 104° E)

758+ A.D.   Slavs leave Thrace (defeat by Byzantines) migrate to Asia
                     (from 40°30′ - 42° N - 24° - 28° E)

c.780 on A.D.   Norse settlements in Shetland and Orkney Islands
                     (from 58° - 65° N - 9° - 12° E to 58°30′ - 61° N - 0°50′ -
                     3°30′ W)

c. 790 to
   1000 A.D.   Swedes to East Baltic
                     (from 56°15′ - 62° N - 12° - 19° E to 56° - 59° N - 21° -
                     26° E)

795 A.D.   Japan resettled both Japanese settlers and Ainus in the
                     extreme south of Japan
                     (from 38° - 41° N - 140° - 142° E to 31° - 34° N - 130° -
                     132° E)

c.795 A.D.	Irish priests to Iceland (from 51°30′ - 53°30′ N - 5°40′ - 10°30′ W to 64° - 67° N - 16° - 24° W)
797 A.D.	Japan - 9,000 settlers from eastern provinces resettled in Iji in Mutsu (from 36° - 38° N - 140° - 141° E to 38° - 41° N - 141° - 142° E)
8th Century (exact time unknown)	Frisians moved to North Frisian Islands driven by Franks (1st Settlers) (from 50° - 53° N - 4°40′ - 8° E to 54°30′ - 55°30′ N - 8°20′ - 8°55′ E)
800 A.D. and later	Norse settlement of Faeroe Islands (from 58° - 65° N - 9° - 12° E to 63° - 64° N - 7° W)
804 A.D.	Saxony (Germany) — Entire settlements of Nordabingians uprooted (from 51° - 54° N - 7° - 11° E to ?)
817-826 A.D.	Moorish refugees from Cordova (rebellion crushed by Omayyads) flee to and conquer Crete and make it a pirate base (from 37°55′ N - 4°45′ W to 35° N - 23°30′ - 26°15′ E)
830-1072 A.D.	Moslems from Aghlabid Empire (Tunisia, Tripolitania, and Eastern Algeria) immigrate to Sicily and South Italy (from 29° - 38° N - 5° - 18° E to 36°35′ - 40° N - 12°30′ - 17° E)
830 A.D.	Two tribes from Arabia replaced in Egypt the Copts who had been killed in a rebellion (from somewhere within 12° - 30° N - 35° - 55° E to 22° - 32° N - 30° - 34° E)
835 A.D.	17,000 to 27,000 Gypsies — probably North India — arrive in Basra (to 30° - 32°30′ N - 46°15′ - 48°30′ E)
835 A.D.	Gypsies deported to Byzantine Anatolia (from 30° - 32°30′ N - 46°15′ - 48°30′ E to 34° - 36° N - 38° - 41° E)
c. 835 to 12th Century	Vikings resettle in Scotland (from 58° - 65° N - 9° - 12° E to 55° - 58°50′ N - 1°30′ - 6° W)

836+ A.D.   Thousands of Turkish mercenaries—Transoxania to Baghdad "Mamluk bodyguard for Caliph" City of Samarra built for Turks
(from 37° - 44° N - 60° - 70° E to 33°20' N - 44°30' E)

c.839 A.D.   Bulgars gradually expand into upper Macedonia and Serbia
(from 42° - 49° N - 17° - 30° E to 39° - 45° N - 17° - 24° E)

840-890 A.D.   Vikings settle in Frisia
(from 55° - 65° N - 7° - 14° E to 52° - 54° N - 4° - 9° E)

840-1103 A.D.   Norwegian Vikings settle in Ireland
(from 58° - 65° N - 9° - 12° E to 51°30' - 53°30' N - 5°40' - 10°30' W)

c.840 A.D.   Gypsies migrated from Asia Minor (Anatolia) to Thrace and the rest of Europe
(from 38° - 41° N - 34° - 36° E to 40°30' - 42° N - 25° - 28° E)

843-846 A.D.   Uighurs flee from Mongolia around Orkhon to Tarim Basin around Kuča
(from 45° - 50° N - 97° - 107° E to 35° - 42° N - 77° - 87° E)

843 A.D.   First Viking settlement on the Loire River
(from 55° - 65° N - 7° - 14° E to 52° - 54° N - 4° - 9° E)

851 A.D.   First Viking settlement in England (Island of Thanet)
(from 54° - 58° N - 8° - 19° E to 51°15' N - 1°20' E)

853 A.D.   Viking settlement of Sheppy Island at mouth of Thames
(from 54° - 58° N - 8° - 19° E to 51°30' N - 0° - 50' E)

862-896 A.D.   Magyars leave Don Basin; go through Moldaira (889); and finally settle in the Middle Danube Basin (now called Hungary) (895) (Magyars were fleeing from Pechenegs.)
(from 47° - 57° N - 30° - 44° E to 45° - 52° N - 14° - 28° E)

865-890 A.D.   Norwegian Vikings to Orkney, Shetland, Hebrides, and Faeroe Islands and Scotland fleeing Harald Fairhair's rule in Norway
(from 58° - 65° N - 9° - 12° E to 57° - 64° N - 1° - 6° E)

c.865 to 11th Century   Vikings (Varangian Swedes) settle in Russia
(from 56°15' - 62° N - 12° - 19°30' E to 45° - 60° N - 28° - 39° E)

866-872 A.D.   Rest of Uighur people moved to the Tarim Basin — from Monguha (Orkham) to Turfan, Bisbalyq and Kansu
(from 45° - 50° N - 97° - 107° E to 35° - 42° N - 77° - 87° E)

870-930 A.D.   Norwegian Vikings settle Iceland (No Irish were there.)
(from 58° - 64° N - 5° - 12° E to 64° - 67° N - 16° - 24° W)

876 A.D. - 10th Century   Danish and Norwegian Vikings settle in Daneslaw, England
(from 54° - 58° N - 8° - 19° E to 51°30' - 54° N - 1°40' - 3° W)

878-c.965 A.D.   Byzantines migrate from Sicily (which was being conquered by Moslems) to South Italy
(from 36°35' - 38°15' N - 12°30' - 15°30' E to 37°50' - 41°15' N - 15°30' - 18°30' E)

881 A.D.   Imperial T'ang Court and inhabitants of the capital flee from Ch'ang An to Chêng Tu, Szechwan
(from 34° N - 109° E to 31° N - 104° E)

883 A.D.   (NOTE: A two-year seige retook Ch'ang An, and the migration reversed.)

896-906 A.D.   Slavs leave Middle Danube Valley and flee Southwest and North
(from 45° - 52° N - 14° - 28° E to: scattered)

896 A.D.   Imperial T'ang Court fled from Ch'ang An to Hua
(from 34° N - 109° E to 34°20' N - 109°40' E)

c.900 A.D.   Bulgars flee Transylvania and Pannonia (from Magyars)
(from 44° - 48° N - 19° - 26° E to South of 44° N)

900-950 A.D.   Norwegian Vikings settle West Coast of England.
(from 58° - 65° N - 9° - 12° E to 53° - 55°15' N - 2°30' - 3°30' W)

911-1000 A.D.   Scandinavian Vikings (Northmen) actively recruited to settle on the North Coast of France, hence Normandy
(from 55° - 65° N - 7° - 14° E to 47° - 51° N - 5° W - 4° E)

917 A.D.   Patzinaks invade (i.e., migrate into) Wallachia
(from East of 30°30' E to 45°20' - 48° N - 27° - 30°30' E)

926 A.D.   West Welsh banished to West of Tamar (from Devon to Cornwall)
(from 50°15' - 51°15' N - 2°50' - 4°15' W to 49°55' - 50°55' N - 4°15' - 5°45' W)

TABLE II.

FAMINES — (~ 30 + ° N) — EASTERN HEMISPHERE — 717-926 A.D.
(Very hard to get data.)

720-819 A.D.	42 Drought-related famines in China[10] *
739 A.D.	British Isles[11]
779 A.D.	"Famine swept Charlemagne's Lands" (Drought) — France
780 A.D.	Italy — Lombards sold or volunteered slavery — extreme toll
786 A.D.	Germany — "A hunger year"; and food-stocks failed in Saxonland
791-792 A.D.	A great famine — peasants driven to cannibalism — have eaten members of own family (Carolingian Europe — France)[12] (Drought)
803 A.D.	China
818 A.D.	Japan — "A succession of bad harvests"
823 A.D.	British Isles[11]
820-919 A.D.	38 Drought- and Locust-related famines in China[10]
840 A.D.	Fukien, China[102]
850 A.D.	Germany
860 A.D.	China (Chekiang)
862 A.D.	Shantung, China[102]
867 A.D.	Kiev, Russia ("Severe"; people died)
869 A.D.	China (Shantung)
870 A.D.	China — successive years of famine.
873 A.D.	From Spain to Germany — locusts[102]
879 A.D.	Universal Famine[1]
882-3 A.D.	China (Pien and Sung) famines
908-1126	49 flood-related in China[10]
915 A.D.	Wheat rust famine in Spain[108]
917-8 A.D.	Kashmir (India)[10]
920-1019	94 Drought-related famines in China[10]
927 A.D.	Great famine in Byzantium

---

*The huge Bibliography on famines is not included.

B. Chronology — 1814 to 1979 A.D.

Introduction

Records abound.

The area of interest: 30° North Latitude northward, especially in the Eastern Hemisphere.

The areas will be designated in the chronology:

IBERIAN PENINSULA
NORTHERN EUROPE (England, Germany, Scandinavia, Low Countries)
MEDITERRANEAN AREA
   SOUTHERN EUROPE (Italy, France)
   BALKANS
   NORTH AFRICA
MIDDLE EAST
EASTERN EMPIRE
RUSSIA
SOUTH ASIA
CHINA
FAR EAST
NORTH AMERICA

Borders crawl around like an amoeba as pressures move from one site to another. The will to kill one's neighbor in order to acquire his substance grows in different times and places; and an attacker has a huge advantage, especially during the period of surprise.

Europe had been racked with the French revolution, and the example it set; then the Napoleonic Wars swept across Europe and even into Egypt. Casualties were extraordinarily high as modern weapons — rifles with bayonettes, artillery, etc. — came into intensive use. The slaughter was enormous, though the percentages killed did not differ significantly from previous, less populous times.

Piracy raged throughout the Mediterranean Sea, the Persian Gulf, the China Sea, the Western Pacific, and the Atlantic. The methods of pirates, freebooters and some men in uniform varied but slightly.

Indian Wars raged in North America as the Natives fought the encroaching Caucasians. A second invasion of Spanish Mexico (Texas) had occurred in 1812-13, and San Antonio was captured and several Mexican armies were destroyed. The invading army was finally overpowered.

Slave trade flourished with some areas of Black Africa being almost "hunted-out" for people to take as slaves. Almost everybody got into the act.

This extraordinarily violent time led into the period of our chronology.

1814-1823 A.D.
BRUTALLY COLD. GLACIAL MAXIMUM.

Iberian Peninsula With the defeat of Napoleonic forces, Spain regained her independence and her Bourbon monarch Ferdinand VII in March 1814. Ferdinand's attempt to rule absolutely-conservatively antagonized Spanish liberals and the growing independent mood of Spain's colonies. The colonies had previously refused to recognize Spanish control when Spain was ruled by the Bonapartes and the Bourbon's attitude exacerbated the existing revolts and triggered off new ones. This caused both a loss of Spanish income and an expensive campaign of Spanish reconquest. The campaign triggered mutinies and revolt and eventual imprisonment of the monarchy. France, in 1823 with the backing of the Congress of Vienna, restored Ferdinand; but by this time, Mexico, Central America and all of South America excepting Peru and Bolivia were free.

Portugal at the end of the Napoleonic War was in the curious position of having its monarchs in Brazil*, and being ruled by a British-appointed regency. An uprising in 1820 overthrew the regency and a year later forced the monarch Juan VI to return and consent to a constitutional monarchy. Brazil, resentful of reinstated Portuguese domination, declared independence, costing Portugal a source of income. A civil war then started in Portugal in favor of absolutism.

Northern Europe In the early part of this decade all of Northern Europe was immersed in the Napoleonic Wars, which ultimately ended on June 22, 1815, with the second abdication of Napoleon. In the resulting treaties and congresses, the Allies determined the fates of most of the countries in Europe. Denmark lost Norway to Sweden and Pomerania to Prussia. Sweden acquired Norway, which was allowed to retain a separate constitution, but lost Finland to Russia. Holland and the former Austrian Netherlands were united into one kingdom and had most of the former Dutch colonies returned to them. Switzerland was restored. The thirty-nine states and principalities were bound together in a Confederacy largely under Austrian dominance. Purssia was given large new territories, as compensation for territories lost previously in the wars. Finally, Great Britain was rewarded for its part in the wars by being allowed to retain Malta, Heligoland and some of the Dutch and French Colonies.

All of Northern Europe remained in this mold for the rest of the decade, despite growing nationalistic and liberal restlessness. A period of severe

---

*This is the only example of a European nation being subject to an American monarch.

economic depression swept Northern Europe, in association with extremely cold weather.

Southern Europe France was defeated by the rest of Europe in 1814 and, following the return of Napoleon, again in 1815. French territory was occupied by foreign troops until 1818, when France finally paid off its indemnity. The allies established a constitutional monarch, Louis XVIII, in 1814, who remained largely powerless while alternately reactionary and moderate parliaments ran the country for the rest of the decade.

Italy also suffered after Napoleon's defeat. In place of France, Austria now dominated Italy which was once again divided into nine kingdoms. These kingdoms were dominated by reactionary, absolutist, and sometimes violent governments which tried to crush the growing Italian nationalism. Two liberal revolts, one in Naples and the other in the Piedmont, arose and were crushed.

The Balkans The Balkans, dominated by the Ottoman Empire, were extremely restless during this decade. The Serbs, who had revolted in the previous decade, revolted again in 1815, and were granted limited self-rule under Milosh Obremovich. After leading the revolt, he was made hereditary prince of Serbia. In 1821, Greece, Wallachia, Morea, and Moldavia revolted. The Moldavian and Morean revolts were quickly crushed, but the Greek revolt continued. Russia tried to intervene, although Austria restrained it. By the end of the decade the Greeks had won the advantage.

North Africa The ascendancy of Mohammed Ali in Egypt and many pirate states everywhere else, constituted the major themes of North Africa during this decade.

Mohammed Ali, a former Ottoman, was appointed governor of Egypt; and showed a growing degree of independence which was influential in increasing Egypt's power. He introduced western technology and administration to his territory, and became the strongest military power in the Empire. After suppressing an army mutiny and a religious uprising in Syria and Arabia, he turned his army to the successful conquest of the Sudan. In 1823 he established Khartoum and intervened against the Greeks in return for the governorship of Crete.

The rest of North Africa was organized into numerous pirate states. It had reached such a state of piratical aggressiveness that first America and then the Dutch and British bombarded Algiers. Thereafter Algeria, Tunisia and Tripoli refrained from attacking American ships, and put an end to Christian slavery. Piracy of non-American shipping continued.

Middle East The Middle East was dominated by two powers during this decade; the Ottoman Empire and Persia. The Ottoman Empire at this time was occupied in crushing dissent. In Anatolia, the sultan displaced the derebeys. Meanwhile, Serbia, Moldavia, Morea, Wallachia and Greece revolted and Egypt showed a growing independence. From 1821 to 1823, Persia invaded Turkey in pursuit of rebellious tribes from Azerbaijan; but the war was uneventful.

Persia was undergoing a period of rapid growth of foreign — especially British — influence. In 1814, Persia formed an exclusive defensive treaty with England. During the decade, Persia attempted two invasions — one in Afghanistan and one in Turkey. Both proved unsuccessful.

Eastern Europe Thousands of Eastern Europeans were involved in fighting in the Napoleonic Wars, although by 1814 none of the actual battles were in Eastern Europe. Following the Wars, the peace settlements divided all of Eastern Europe between Russia and the Hapsburg Emperors.

Russia was allocated the Grand Duchy of Warsaw, which became a Polish kingdom with the Tsar as its sovereign. Poland was given a liberal constitution and was allowed to keep a separate Diet, language, army and institutions. After 1820 however, the Tsar refused to summon the Diet and ignored the constitution when ruling the country.

The Hapsburg Empire was also under autocratic rule. Francis I let Metternich run his foreign affairs; but aided by secret police, spies, and censorship, ran the Empire himself. The Hungarian Diet was ignored and the Empire was ruled in an autocratic manner.

Russia Like the rest of Eastern Europe, Russians fought in the Napoleonic Wars but by 1814 had none of the battles within their own territories. Previous expansion had spread Russia as far east as Alaska. Georgia had a growing interest in Central Asia. The Tsar, despite a liberal constitution, in practice ruled in a more and more reactionary and absolute fashion. Liberal secret organizations grew.

Central Asia Central Asia during the 1814-1823 decade was a group of largely illiterate tribes. The only area of seeming unification, Afghanistan, was destroyed in 1818 by a tribal revolt, drove the ruler, Mohammed Shah, to Herat and left the rest of the country to be divided up among his opponents into separate Khanates. Kashmir was taken from Afghanistan by Ranjit Singh during this decade of chaos.

South Asia British control of India was growing. By 1818, British soldiers had subdued all but Nepal, the Sikh state, and Afghanistan. During this decade the Gurkha were subdued, but the Sikh state was still expanding.

China During this decade, China was under the rule of the Manchus. The Empire was peaceful and the only real problem the Chinese faced was to resist the growing pressure by Europeans, especially the British, to open to large amounts of trade.

North America North America entered the decade swept by war. Mexico was struggling for independence from Spain, and the U.S. and Canada were attacking each other in the later phase of the War of 1812. This War, sparked by British interference with U.S. naval and shipping traffic, led to mutual American-Canadian border raids and British destruction of the U.S. capital. The New England states threatened to secede before peace was finally declared on December 24, 1814. Later in the decade, the U.S. and Canadian border was drawn firmly as far as Oregon.

Following the Treaty of Ghent, Canada remained basically peaceful but the U.S. remained aggressive — a not-unexpected correlate of their relatively smaller and larger populations. In 1815, Americans attacked Algiers and forced the North African pirates to "respect" (i.e., refrain from attacking) American shipping. Likewise, following the efforts of the British during the War of 1812 to exacerbate Indian-American relations, the U.S. fought two Indian Wars, against the Creeks and the Seminoles. Escaped slaves and hostile Indians used Florida as a refuge. To alleviate the problems, the U.S. forced Spain to cede Florida.

Mexico had an even more violent decade. The War of Independence had started by 1810 and had tapered off by 1815 with the execution of Morelos, its leader. A British- and American-backed invasion in 1817 also failed. Ironically Mexico gained its independence under General Iturbide, a pro-Spanish leader who had defeated Morelos. Spain's reactionary policy after Ferdinand VII returned to power antagonized the powerful creole class in Mexico and led to Iturbide declaring independence and himself as Emperor Agustin I in 1822. A year later a revolt led by Santa Anna deposed him.

1824-1833 A.D.
EXTREMELY COLD. GLACIERS IN BRIEF RETREAT.

Iberian Peninsula Spain had a quiet decade. By 1825 Spain had lost its last South American colony. Its king, Ferdinand VII, was involved in an orgy of reactionary repression as he tried to assure the succession of his daughter Isabella. (Isabella became Queen upon her father's death in 1833.)

Portugal also had an infant girl as Queen. On the death of King John his son Pedro refused to leave Brazil in order to take the Portuguese throne. Instead he appointed his daughter, Maria II, as Queen, and made his brother, Miguel, her regent. Miguel immediately tried to depose Maria but was stopped by England. When England withdrew two years later, Miguel drove Maria out of the country. Pedro abdicated the Brazilian throne and formed an alliance with France and England, to fight for his daughter's restoration. The Miguelito Wars continued for the rest of the decade.

Northern Europe This was a decade of social restlessness and parliamentary reform internally and minor foreign involvements externally for Great Britain. Internally many "rotten" and "pocket" boroughs were dissolved and 143 Parliamentary seats redistributed. Externally England had to suppress the Irish Tithe War, (i.e., Irish violence resisting enforced tithing to the Episcopal Church); and bombarded the Algerian pirates in alliance with other countries. England forced Turkey to recognize Greek independence and helped Pedro of Brazil to restore his daughter to the throne against the efforts of her uncle Miguel, the regent.

In Germany a similar internal restlessness led to the overthrow of the monarchs of three of the states in the Confederacy (Brunswick, Saxony and Hesse-Cassel). A new constitution in the Hapsburg* was also overthrown. This rise of German liberal nationalism finally led to an unsuccessful attempt to seize Frankfurt, and led to major repression by Metternich. Belgium, like Germany, was swept by a wave of nationalism; and in 1830 revolted against Dutch rule and declared its independence. After much fighting, a conference of nations met to arrange peace terms. It was unable to arrange terms that both sides would agree to by the end of the decade.

Only the Scandinavian countries had a peaceful decade. Denmark got its first representative bodies, while the Union of Sweden and Norway endured a chaotic conflict between their reactionary king and their more liberal Diets.

Southern Europe This was a restless decade for Southern Europe. After enduring Charles X's growing reactionary rule, Paris revolted and made

---

*The "Hapsburg Lands" was the name that history gives to the dominion of Francis — son of Leopold II, Grand-Duke of Tuscany, afterwards Emperor, and of his wife Marie Louisa, daughter of Charles III of Spain. (Francis, as Francis II, was the last Roman Emperor, and as Francis I, the first Emperor of Austria.) The dominions of the house of Austria included the Low Countries, parts of Germany and Italy, Hungary, Bohemia and, of course, Austria. After the Napoleonic Wars, Francis I's dominions were more compact, but more extensive.

Louis Phillippe King of France. When Louis Phillippe proved moderate, radical unrest and violence continued throughout France. This unrest climaxed in the great revolts of Paris and Lyons which were severely repressed.

Italy's national fervor was inspired by the Paris revolt, and unsuccessful revolts arose in Moderna, Parma, the Papal States, and Piedmont. Austrian and other reactionary monarchs successfully put down all revolts, but were unable to keep the drive for a unified Italy from growing.

Balkans During most of this decade the Balkans were swept up in the Greek War of Independence. Greece had driven the Turks out but then fell into civil war as factions fought among themselves. The Turks and their Egyptian allies took advantage of this dissention and recaptured Crete and the entire Greek peninsula. This roused Russian, English and French sympathy and aid. These three sent naval aid, and Russia also invaded across the Danube and seized Adrianople. These events led to a peace treaty and Turkish recognition of Greek independence, and an extension of Russia's border to the southern mouth of the Danube River.

Greece got a Bavarian king, but the Balkans still had not seen its last conflict of the decade. In 1832 Egypt invaded Anatolia and defeated Turkey. Russia intervened and sent its navy to the Bosporus. Russia then forced the two to agree to peace terms.

North Africa This decade saw the growth of power of two nations in North Africa: Egypt and France. Egypt, dragged into the Greek War of Independence, gained control of Crete. Subsequently, when Turkey refused to reward Egypt for its help by giving it control of Syria, Egypt declared war. By 1833, Egypt gained its objective — all Syria and Adana.

Meanwhile North African piracy provoked retaliation. First Great Britain bombarded Algiers and later, when piracy continued, France invaded. The French took Algiers and a few other coastal towns, then halted in their expansion.

Middle East Both major powers in the Middle East — Turkey and Persia — were badly injured during this decade and both found themselves unable to cope with the growing power of Russia. The Ottoman Empire lost control of Greece and Syria during this decade, in both cases yielding to Russian pressures. Only the destruction of the inefficient and frequently disloyal Janissary army strengthened Turkish power.

Likewise Persia found itself at war with Russia and lost control of Erivan and Tabriz, and the Caucasus territories.

China China found itself resisting foreigners. Moslems unsuccessfully tried to take Kasgar from Western China. Meanwhile there was increasing pressure from England for China to allow trade, especially the opium trade.

North America North America was fairly peaceful during this decade. There was no major conflict in Canada and except for the 1832 Black Hawk Indian War, most conflicts in the U.S. were political in nature. White, male suffrage spread throughout the states and the federal government chose to locate its Southeastern Indians, including the Cherokees, west of the Mississippi. Despite strong feelings, there was little violence over the issues.

Mexico, following the overthrow of Emperor Agustin I, set up a federal republic. After the term of Guadalupe Victoria general disorder grew. Spain tried to take advantage of this disorder by seizing Tampico but was driven out. The decade ends with the election of Santa Anna as president.

Texas, a colony within the state of Coahuila, began to have trouble over primarily ethnic differences. The abortive Republic of Fredonia failed in its bid for independence in 1826; then severe repression began in 1830. The first skirmish of this revolution was fought at Anahuac in 1832.

Eastern Europe The part of Eastern Europe under Hapsburg control was fairly peaceful, although forces of nationalism and liberalism underwent severe repression by Austria. The same could not be said of Poland, under Russian control. Inspired by the 1830 Paris revolution, Poland revolted and declared its independence of Russia, and union with Lithuania. The revolt was severely crushed by Russia and the Polish constitution was abrogated. This began the forced Russification of Poland.

Russia In 1825, with the death of Tsar Alexander and the crowning of Nicholas I, a pro-constitutional-monarchy revolution arose and was crushed. The Polish revolution a few years later was similarly crushed. Externally Russia attacked her Moslem neighbors, the Ottoman Empire and Persia, and gained territory from both.

South Asia A pro-Moslem, anti-British wave swept the Punjab and Northern India but the British East India Company was successful in suppressing revolt. Meanwhile in Afghanistan, Dost Mohammed was in the process of unifying the chaos-ridden country.

1834-1843 A.D.
VERY COLD. GLACIAL READVANCE.

Iberian Peninsula Both Spain and Portugal suffered identical misfortunes in infant Queens. In both countries, the Queens' uncles tried unsuccessfully to take control of the throne and were crushed by the intervention of France and England. The Miguelito Wars of Portugal had started in the last decade and ended in 1834 while the Carlist War of Spain lasted until 1840. Spain, however, continued to have problems as General Baldomoro Spartero attacked the young Queen's regency and eventually ruled in her name. In 1843 he was finally overthrown.

Northern Europe Northern Europe was quiet this decade. Little happened in Belgium and the Netherlands, which drifted apart with only minor, as opposed to major, battles. Likewise Scandinavia was undergoing a period of quiet, except for minor reform movements, and reestablishing the Icelandic Assembly in 1843. In the German Confederacy, the nationalist movement had been silenced temporarily in the last decade and did not rise to challenge the Metternich system in this decade.

In England there was Chartist agitation and liberal reform. England also intervened externally in Portuguese, Spanish, Afghan, and Egyptian affairs, and fought the Opium War with China. The latter opened Hong Kong and five Chinese ports to British trade.

Southern Europe France's radical movement climaxed in 1834 with the suppression of two great revolts in Lyons and Paris. France was swept up in rapid industrial development and most of its aggressiveness was expressed in the suppression of the Miguelito and Carlist rebellions of the Iberian Peninsula and subjugating Algeria.

Meanwhile Italy endured numerous abortive nationalist uprisings, but conditions remained the same.

Balkans The Balkans were marked by brigandage, internal dissention and, in a few states, like Roumania, economic expansion. In Serbia the internal strife drove out Prince Michael.

North Africa This was a period of extreme turmoil for North Africa. Throughout the decade, there was a continuing conflict between the French and the native chiefs of Algeria led by dey Abk-el Kader. The French lost throughout most of the decade but by 1841 Abd-el-Kader had retreated to Algeria.

The eastern half of North Africa was swept up in conflict with the Ottoman Empire. The Empire conquered Tripolitania in 1836. In 1839, a forcible attempt by the Empire to take Syria from Egypt led to war. After Egypt captured the Turkish navy and declared independence, France, England and Austria intervened and (despite initial French sympathy for Egypt) forced Egypt to yield Crete, Syria and the Turkish Navy in return for the hereditary rule of Egypt being granted to Mohammed Ali.

Middle East Both of the major Middle Eastern empires (Ottoman and Persian) were unsuccessfully aggressive and found themselves under increasing British influence. Persia, backed by Russia, invaded Afghanistan but was forced by Britain to withdraw. After initially invading Tripolitania successfully, the Ottoman Empire attempted to take Syria from Egypt. When this attempt ended disastrously, the British, French and Austrians intervened and forced Egypt to yield Syria, Crete and the Turkish naval fleet back to the Empire.

Eastern Europe There were no dramatic events during this decade — only increasing agitation for liberalization and reform. Poland was increasingly Russified and oppressed; but Hungary managed to get the Austrian Empire to allow it to use Magyar rather than Latin as the official language.

Russia Russia was increasingly bureaucratic and stressed orthodoxy, autocracy, and nationalism. This program resulted in increased internal restlessness and external growth. Russia began the conquest of the Khanate of Khiva (Kazakh, Uzbek, and Turkoman SSR) and, working with the British, had increasing influence over the Ottoman Empire. It also aided Persia in its invasion of Afghanistan.

South Asia England and the British East India Company grew increasingly concerned with the growing influence of Persia and Russia. This led to the Anglo-Afghan War, where Dost Mohammed, who had become Amir of Afghanistan in 1839, was deposed and replaced by Shah Shuja. This action created enormous anti-British sentiment in Afghanistan and eventually Shah Shuja and the British envoys were murdered and the British garrison massacred. Dost Mohammed returned to his throne.

China The unsuccessful resistance of China to British opium trade dominated this decade. When China finally began punishing British opium merchants, England retaliated with the Opium War. China lost and was forced to cede Hong Kong and open five ports to English trade.

North America The American states were restless during this decade. The United States was growing rapidly with whatever violence was necessary to achieve it, and all of its neighbors suffered accordingly. The "Five Civilized Tribes" were deported westward and their lands were occupied despite their resistance in the Cherokee War of Removal and the Second Seminole War. (The Seminoles escaped by hiding in the Florida Swamps.) Other Americans settled in Texas where they ultimately revolted against the

Mexican government and declared their independence. Even Canadian-American relations were strained and fighting took place in Aroostook County until a treaty settled the international boundary.

Internally there was a move toward universal male suffrage. This spread throughout the country and when it was blocked in Rhode Island, the Dorr rebellion broke out.

Canada, for different reasons, was going through equally difficult times. This was the decade that the British Parliament passed the Union Act that united Upper and Lower Canada in 1840. Both Upper and Lower Canada had had previous rebellions against the British-appointed governors and Upper Houses. The 1837 Papineau's Rebellion in Lower Canada was especially violent, but the government suppressed the revolt and the leaders fled to the U.S. The U.S. continued to support the rebels, and financially backed several unsuccessful invasions.

Mexico faced less internal and more external crises. In 1836 Texas, largely settled by Americans, won its independence from Mexico. At about this time, the Mayas in the entire Yucatan area won *de facto* autonomy which they managed to retain for about 12 years. Later in 1838 a French expedition occupied Vera Cruz and withdrew only when Mexico agreed to pay indemnities. Enough civil strife resulted from these actions that Santa Anna assumed dictatorial powers.

1844-1853 A.D.
GLACIERS AT MAXIMUM.

Iberian Peninsula Queen Cristina reentered Spain but until 1851 General Ramon Narváez ruled the country. In 1852 he officially became dictator. Portugal's Queen was in more control of the government, but her government had unstable ministers and chronic insurrection.

Northern Europe Of Northern Europe, only Sweden avoided major constitutional change during this decade. Denmark, the Netherlands, Belgium, and England yielded to unrest before it broke into actual revolution and liberalized their laws and constitutions. Germany, however, was inspired by the February Revolution of 1848, and the uprisings which were distracting Austria broke into active revolt in Berlin. Uprisings throughout Germany demanded unification into one country under King Fredrick William of Prussia. However, these ambitions were crushed by Austria in 1850 and the old German Confederation was reestablished. All the liberal reforms established in the past 2 years were revoked.

Neither England nor Denmark were successful in staying out of wars, however. Denmark warred with Prussia over the duchies of Schleswig and Holstein, which both claimed, and eventually both had to rule jointly. England found itself dragged into the bloody Crimean War, as well as intervening in the Schleswig-Holstein revolution. Britain also battled the Sikhs of the Punjab.

Southern Europe Southern Europe was swept by violence and revolution. Paris started the violence with the February Revolution and forced Louis Phillippe to abdicate. He was replaced by a republic, which, since it wasn't radical enough to satisfy the Paris mobs, found itself crushing repeated insurrection. In reaction, the country elected Louis Napoleon as President, and later approved by plebescite the *coup d'etat* by which he became Emperor.

Italy was equally strife-torn. Revolution broke out in Sicily, Tuscany, Piedmont, Milan, Venice, and the Papal States, and by 1848, coalesced into the Italian War of Independence. France intervened on behalf of the Pope and by 1849 the Austrians were able to crush the entire revolt. The rebel leader Garibaldi escaped and despite the defeat, the dream of unifying Italy continued.

Balkans The growing claim of foreign countries such as France, Britain and Russia, to meddle in Balkan affairs led to multiple crises and ultimately to the Crimean War. Catching liberalism from these foreign influences, both Greece and Wallachia had rebellions demanding liberal constitutions. The rebellion in Roumania led to Russian intervention and suppression. As Russian influence grew, Russia tried to pressure the Turks to grant it protectorate rights over the Orthodox churches by seizing the Danubian Provinces. This led the Ottoman Empire, backed by England, to declare war.

North Africa The death of Mohammed Ali and the assassination of his grandson, Abbas I, led to a more submissive Egyptian attitude toward the Ottoman Empire. Meanwhile, in North Western Africa, the French defeated Morocco and forced Abd el-Kader to surrender. This completed their conquest of Algeria.

Middle East Both empires of the Middle East suffered from Russian aggression. In Persia the Russians began to conquer the Syr Darya valley. In the Ottoman Empire Russia meddled increasingly in the Balkans and finally, when it seized the Danubian Provinces in 1853, it triggered the Crimean War.

Eastern Europe Severe economic depression swept Eastern Europe and by

1848 the Hapsburg Dominions were swept up in revolution. Hungary started the movement which rapidly spread to Vienna Croatia, Czechoslovakia, Moravia, Dalmatia, Lombardy, Galacia and Transylvania. The Imperial family fled from Vienna to Innsbruck and yielded to the demands of constitutionalists. A turning point came when the Princess Windischgratz was accidently shot in Prague. Her vengeful husband crushed Prague in return, then spread his conquests to Vienna and Hungary. Other generals recaptured Italy and aided Windischgratz in reestablishing federal control. The Imperial family returned and the Emperor abdicated in favor of his nephew Francis Joseph I. The reconquered territory was bureaucratically subdivided and systematically Germanized.

Poland, under control of Russia, went through more thorough-going oppression when news of the numerous Western rebellions reached the Tsar's government.

Russia The Tsar's government continued to champion nationalism, orthodoxy and autocracy internally while expanding at the expense of its eastern and southern neighbors. By 1850 Russia had finished its conquest of the Khivan Khanate and started conquering the Syr Darya valley of Persia. Its control of Siberia expanded and Russians had settled for the first time on the mouth of the Amur. To the Southwest Russia intervened, and helped Austria crush the Hungarian revolt; then intervened in the Balkans. When it seized the Danubian Provinces, its belligerence triggered the Crimean War. The end of the decade found Russia battling Turkey while British and French troops prepared to storm the Black Sea.

South Asia The British East India Company was rapidly expanding its control over India. According to the doctrine of Capse, the Company seized any state that had no heirs to the ruling family. Sind was annexed, and following the First and Second Anglo-Sikh Wars, so was the Punjab. Only in Afghanistan had the British successfully been driven out and the native Amir Dost Mohammed spent the decade regaining control.

China The weakness of China's Imperial government was revealed in the humiliating treaties it was forced to sign after the granting of special trading rights, and ceding cities to foreigners. The discontent of the people, mixing with the new doctrine entering the country, finally sparked the mystically led T'ai P'ing Rebellion in 1850*. Huge bands of bandits, led

---

*The T'ai P'ing Rebellion was led by two schoolmasters. One of these, Hung Hsiu-Ch'uan, had a long delirium and visions. ....he had seen God and his own Elder Brother, Jesus Christ, for whom as the Heavenly Younger Brother he must now save mankind from the devil.

by Nien Fei, took advantage of the war to plunder Anhuei, North Kiangsu, Shantung and Shansi.

Eastern Asia Japan was forced by America to open its ports to foreign trade in 1857, following initial contact in 1853. Korea remained basically isolated.

North America Many Indian wars were fought in the northwestern quadrant of the United States.

Relations improved between Canada and the U.S. but to the south the U.S. and Mexico finally declared war. Both warring sides had real grievances, but American annexation of Texas proved to be the trigger. War was declared in 1846. By 1848 the U.S. had captured all Mexican territory north of the Rio Grande and stormed Mexico City. In the 1848 Treaty of Guadalupe-Hidalgo, Mexico yielded all territory north of the Rio Grande to the U.S. The Mexicans settled quickly with the U.S., then shifted Mexican troops to the Yucatan to crush the Mayan autonomy.

By contrast Canada was comparatively peaceful. Indeed, as it underwent severe economic depression there was even a short-lived movement for annexation to the U.S.

1854-1863 A.D.
GLACIERS RETREATING RAPIDLY. EARLY WINE HARVESTS (WARM, DRY SUMMERS).

Iberian Peninsula There was a revolution in Spain in 1854 which drove the Queen Mother Cristina out of the country, and began a period of turmoil for Spain ending only in 1858 when O'Donnell became head of the government. From then on, Spain had only moderate civil strife internally and could begin a policy of expansion externally. The Spanish Ceuta in Africa was expanded and Spain gained some rights to the Moroccan coast of Ifni. Santo Domingo in the Caribbean was annexed during this time and Spain also joined France and England in an invasion of Mexico.

By contrast Portugal was beginning one of its more peaceful periods as the Liberal and Conservative factions of its Cortez began a quarter century of rotating in and out of power.

Northern Europe This was a decade of internal peace and external expansion for all of Northern Europe. In Scandinavia, the Netherlands, Belgium and Great Britain there was, in general, economic prosperity and liberal reform (the reform was most limited in Prussia.)

England used this period of internal peace to finish the Crimean War; war with Persia and China; crush the Sepoy mutiny; and support a French invasion of Mexico. When India's Great Mutiny was crushed, the British government took direct control of India from the British East India Company.

Germany also enjoyed a large peaceful era with many of its more restrictive governmental measures repealed. Bismarck entered the Prussian government as minister-president in 1862 and under his guidance Prussia began to aim at unifying Germany. When Denmark violated the joint-rule agreement and tried to annex the duchy of Schleswig-Holstein, the German Confederation voted to send troops into Holstein. The situation had not yet been amplified into war by the end of the decade.

Southern Europe For both France and Italy, this was a triumphant decade. France, under Louis Napoleon, returned to its previous status as a major military power. Internal prosperity and peace was coupled with external aggressiveness. During this decade France, in alliance with Turkey, Piedmont, and England defeated Russia in the Crimean War, expanded its African territory, successfully aided Italian independence and invaded Mexico.

Italy, led by Piedmont, began its successful struggle to unify and renounce Austrian domination. Louis Napoleon and Cavour, the Prime Minister of Piedmont, met secretly and agreed to fight against Austria. In 1859 both sides went to war, which ended with Piedmont gaining Lombardy, Austria retaining Venetia and France gaining Savoy and Nice. Following this war, the representative assemblies of Parma, Modena, Tuscany and Romagna ousted their rulers and voted for union with Piedmont. Plebescites confirmed this union. At the same time, Cavour backed the adventurer Garibaldi in a successful expedition against the Kingdom of the Two Sicilies. Piedmont then intervened in an uprising of the Papal States and annihilated the Papal forces. By September 10 the two armies met, Garibaldi from the south and Piedmont from the north. A month later Sicily, Naples, the Marches, and Umbria voted by plebiscite to join Piedmont. On March 17, 1861, the Kingdom of Italy was proclaimed by the first Italian Parliament. Five months later Cavour died. The decade ended with the Italian government having to battle the former hero Garibaldi to restrain him from invading and freeing Rome.

The Balkans This was a decade of growing Balkan discontent with Turkish domination. The decade began with the Ottoman Empire being completely distracted by the Crimean War. Greece took advantage of the distraction when it invaded Thessaly and Epirus. Turkey's allies aided it in retaining its territory, however, and Greece was forced by France and England to back down. At the same time, Austria took the Danubian Principalities from Russia and occupied them until the end of the war, when it returned them to Turkey. At the end of the war, Turkey granted Christian subjects security of life, religion, and property; and Russia renounced its claims to protect Christians in the Empire and Principalities. The Principalities were allowed to elect a prince and unify into the nation of Roumania, and Serbia was put under the collective guarantee of all powers.

Following the Wars, both Greece and Serbia had revolutions that drove out their Monarchs. Serbia then encouraged Bulgaria to revolt and Montenegro directly supported the revolution in Herzegovina. This latter led to a Turkish-Montenegrin War which forced Montenegro to recognize Turkish supremacy.

North Africa In North Africa, European powers expanded their control. Spain challenged Morocco successfully and expanded the Spanish Ceuta at Morocco's expense. France increased its holdings in Southern Algeria. Egypt, which underwent a peaceful decade, allowed Western commercial expansion.

Middle East This was a time of growing internal dissention, religious rebellion and European intervention for the two Middle Eastern Empires. The decade began with the Ottoman Empire's involvement in the Crimean War; and its dependence on England and France for protection from Russia; and upon Austria to keep its restless subject states. In return, the Ottoman Empire was forced to make enormous internal reforms abolishing torture and granting rights to Christian subjects. Following the war Turkey had to crush a rebellion of Herzegovina, backed by Montenegro. At approximately the same time it had to cope with an insurrection in Syria and fighting between Moslem Druses and Christians. France intervened and settled the dispute and Lebanon was founded and given a special constitution.

Persia also faced aggression from Russia, which was absorbing the Syr Darya Valley. It faced European intervention when England declared war on it over its seizure of Herat and other Afghanistani territory. England defeated Persia, and forced it to evacuate Afghanistan. Moreover, it also forced religious unrest as it battled the new mystical sect of Babiam (later Bahaism), first executing the founder and later expelling the numerous followers into Turkey.

Eastern Europe Eastern European subject people gained more autonomy during this decade. The prolonged mobilization of Austria's army during the Crimean War crippled its treasury. Another war between Austria and France in alliance with the Piedmont led Austria to lose its control over Italy. In a desperate financial plight, Austria tried to appease its subject peoples with two new constitutions which granted subject people the right to send representatives to a Diet, while reserving most of the power in Germanic hands. Only Hungary resisted these changes and consequently was ruled autocratically.

Russia also granted more autonomy to its subject people. Poland, however, demanded complete independence and in 1863, Poland revolted when Russia tried to suppress the widespread disorder by drafting discontents into the army. The rebellion spread to Lithuania and White Russia.

Russia Russia endured a decade of tremendous violence despite an able ruler who expanded Russian territory and freedom. After a crippling siege of its Black Sea ports during the Crimean War, Russia came to terms with the allies and gave up its claims to the Balkans. It turned eastward instead, and by 1860 forced China to yield the left bank of the Amur River and the Ussuri Region.

During this time the Tsar Alexander II emancipated the serfs and gave non-Russians more autonomy. The Poles, Lithuanians, and White Russians responded by revolting.

South Asia Britain consolidated its control of South Asia in this decade. The decade began with an Afghanistani-British treaty against Persia and a short war against Persia as a result of its seizure of Herat. England won and Afghanistan reclaimed Herat. The British East India Company continued to expand at the expense of native states.

The turning point was the 1857 Sepoy Mutiny. The Sepoy troops, insulted and enraged by their new grease-coated cartridges, and backed by native princes, turned against their British officers. In perspective it must be realized that the majority of India's Sepoys did not join the revolt and the British losses were small. However, the atrocities committed against English women and children and the savagery of the British reconquest poisoned British-Indian relations for the next hundred years.

This was a fatal blow to the British East India Company. It yielded control of India to the British crown which now ruled India directly. The British government overhauled the administration of India, made major reforms, started a vast system of public works and granted protection to native states.

In 1863 Dost Mohammed of Afghanistan died and a civil war resulted.

China Every province in China was in a state of revolt in this decade.

The preoccupation of China with the immensely destructive T'ai P'ing Rebellion almost destroyed the Manchu Dynasty. During this decade, the rebels seized Shanghai and sacked Nanking, Kiangsu, Chekiang, Soochow and Anking.

Subject people and foreigners took advantage of this preoccupation. The bandit bands of Nien Fei seized control of Anhuei, North Kiangsu, Shantung and Shansi; the Panthay Muslims of Yunnan created an independent state, and the Miao tribesmen revolted in Kweichow. Russia seized more Far Eastern territory for Siberia. England and France used the Lorcha Arrow incident to initiate the Second Opium War. Canton and Peking were seized and the Imperial Summer Palace was burned. In the end, China was forced to surrender. It yielded land to Russia, eleven ports to Britain and France, permission for legations to be in Peking, trade and Christian missions to be stationed in the interior, and legalization of opium. In return, the British (led by Fredrick Ward and "Chinese" Gordon) aided in the suppression of the T'ai P'ing Rebellion and Nien Fei.

Far East Korea remained isolated but Japan finally yielded to American pressure to open to trade, and was torn by civil strife as foreign trade and influence grew.

North America Canada drifted through a peaceful decade but the United States and Mexico were torn by civil war.

In the United States the growing sectional and anti-slavery sentiment exploded into violence. First the 1854-58 war for "Bleeding Kansas" pitted pro- and anti-slavery forces against each other for control of the Kansas state constitution. When Abraham Lincoln, a man known for his opposition to expanding slavery, was elected President, eleven states seceded from the Union and formed the Confederate States of America. War began in 1861 as the United States opposed the secession. For two years neither side was the clear victor but in 1863 the Union victories almost simultaneously at Vicksburg and Gettysburg turned the tide against the Confederacy. Complicating this conflict was a major Sioux uprising in Minnesota, which with the involvement of federal troops elsewhere, proved difficult to subdue.*

Mexico underwent even more trauma. Santa Anna was ousted from power in 1855 and the liberal reforms of Juarez triggered a three-year

---

*The U.S. was involved in this decade in separate fights externally in Japan, China, Fiji, Nicaragua, Honduras, and internally in several Indian Wars, a slave revolt, slave-related uprisings, and finally, the Civil War.

civil war that wrecked Mexico's finances. When Juarez suspended payments of foreign debts owed to Britain, France, and Spain they invaded to "protect their interest". The U.S. was busy with its own internal troubles so Louis Napoleon proposed creating a Catholic Empire under France to begin to resist American expansion. French troops seized Mexico City and placed Maximilian of Austria on the throne.

1864-1873 A.D.
GETTING WARMER.

Iberian Peninsula The contrast between Portuguese peacefulness and Spanish turbulence was especially marked in this decade. Portugal continued to have a Cortez that systematically rotated power between its two parties. Spain, on the other hand, had an absolute monarch, Queen Isabella, who allowed strong men to rule in her stead. This triggered an insurrection in 1866 and a full-scale civil war in 1868, and the Queen, whose immorality and corruption shocked her subjects, was exiled and deposed. A new monarch, Amadeo, Duke of Aosta, was given the throne but after two years of isolation, he resigned and the First Spanish Republic was declared. This immediately provoked uprisings in favor of crowning the queen's uncle as monarch.

Spain was also involved with an unsuccessful war against Chile, Peru, Bolivia and Ecuador during this decade.

Northern Europe This was a decade of rising nationalism in Northern Europe. Even the normally peaceful Scandinavian countries were disturbed, Sweden by the growing nationalism of Norway, and Denmark by a war with Germany which stripped it of Schleswig-Holstein, two provinces with heavy German populations.

England also was troubled by nationalism as restlessness mounted in Ireland. The Fenian Brotherhood, founded in the United States, financed rebellion. Events peaked in 1867. An unsuccessful uprising caused Parliament to pass the Irish Land Reform Act. This was one of many reforms which was passed in the era. British foreign expansion slowed during this decade, being confined to a war with Bhutan.

The Netherlands and Belgium were dwarfed in this period between the expanding demands of growing Germany and France. Indeed the Netherlands ended up yielding some of its African colonies to Britain, and Luxembourg to Germany.

Germany, however, was especially awash in nationalism, and used it to finally unite the Confederation into an Empire. Germany fought two wars of aggression, the first against Denmark for Schleswig-Holstein and the second against Austria for control of Northern Germany. The growth of Germany antagonized its neighbor, France, and led ultimately to the 1870-1871 Franco-Prussian War. Prussia triumphed and public opinion demanded the union of all German states under Prussia. The German Empire was founded in 1871.

Southern Europe Nationalism also swept Southern Europe, but in France this led to disaster. France, relying on Austria and Italy for support, vigorously opposed German expansion. Time and time again, the wills of the two emperors clashed and this ultimately led to the Franco-Prussian War. Louis Napoleon was crushed at Sudan. The Germans invaded France and put Paris under siege. After over 4 months without aid, Paris surrendered. The Empire had been dissolved and the Third Republic established.

A peace treaty was negotiated by the new government, but embittered Paris arose to resist the treaty and the new government. It formed a Commune and was crushed by the remainder of France.

Italy finished its unification at this time. Although it lost every battle it fought against Austria in the Seven Weeks' War of 1866, Italy's ally, Prussia, soundly defeated Austria. As a result of secret negotiations between Austria and France, Austria rewarded France for its neutrality by giving it Venetia, which France, during the peace negotiations turned over to Italy. This left only Rome, protected by Papal and French troops outside of the Kingdom of Italy. When the 1870 Franco-Prussian War exploded, France withdrew its troops from Rome and within a month, Italy seized it. Rome became the new capital of Italy and in the 1871 Law of Guarantees, defined the relations between the government and the Papacy. The Pope did not accept the law and thereafter posed as the prisoner of the Vatican. The Church had not affiliated with either of the three great movements of the 19th century — Italian national liberty, the socialist movement, and the modern scientific movement. It remained stiff; and excommunicated any ruler of Italy; thereby cutting itself off from Italy, and losing a historic chance to help shape the new consolidated nation.*

Balkans This was a fairly peaceful decade for the Balkans. Except for an unsuccessful revolt in Crete, which attempted to unite with Greece, and a few assassinations and bloodless coups, little happened.

---

*This Vatican policy may have been the most self-defeating policy ever carried out by any sovereignty.

North Africa North Africa came more under European financial control as both the Bey of Tunis and Khedive of Egypt borrowed more and more money. Egypt, during this decade, opened the Suez Canal and — led by British officers — conquered the regions of the Upper Nile.

Middle East Except for the military suppression of the island of Crete when it tried to revolt from the Ottoman Empire, this was a completely peaceful decade for the Middle East. Both Persia and the Turks reorganized their empires extensively, the Ottoman Empire going heavily into debt in the process.

Eastern Europe Eastern Europe was torn by war during this decade. In the beginning of the decade, Austria united with Prussia against Denmark on the Schleswig-Holstein question, and after a short war Prussia received Schleswig, and Holstein went to Austria. When Prussian troops invaded Holstein two years later, it led to the Seven Weeks' War. Most German states fought Austria as did its subject territories. When Austria lost, it lost control of all of the Northern German states and Venetia. This obvious sign of weakness caused increased restlessness of the subject states. The Empire reorganized the government. In Hungary the Magyars dominated all subject people, whereas in Austria, the German people were dominant. Both Austria and Hungary were subject to the Hapsburg Crown.

The Eastern European countries under Russian control, which had revolted when they had misinterpreted Russian liberalism as weakness, were humiliated during this decade. Revolt in Lithuania, Poland and White Russia was severely crushed. All autonomy in these provinces was abolished, Russian language was made obligatory in schools and the Catholic Church was persecuted.

Russia This decade began with Russia battling to suppress revolt in Eastern Europe. Thereafter, Russia crushed its European subject states but continued to reform and liberalize its government elsewhere. It sold Alaska to the United States; but gained territory elsewhere by advancing into Central Asia, the Ili Valley of China, and beginning its conquest of the Khanates of Kokand, Bokhara, and Khiva.

South Asia In South Asia, the tension between the two super-powers, Russia and Britain, intensified. Afghanistan concluded seven years of civil war with Sher Ali in control. He turned to Russia for support, which antagonized England.

The English government was consolidating its control of India. In 1865 it conquered Bhutan, ending a long-standing border conflict. Its growth sparked both Hindu and Moslem reform movements and intimidated Afghanistan.

China China spent most of this decade mopping up the various rebellions which had started during the last decade. In 1864 Nanking, the last headquarters of the T'ai P'ing rebels, was captured by Imperial and British troops. These same forces put down the Nien Fei rebels in 1868 and the Pathay Moslem troops in 1873. Only the independence of the Miao tribesmen continued.

Despite the displeasure of the Chinese people, Western missionaries increased in number, and their influence grew.

Far East The growing domination of the West created turmoil for both Korea and Japan. Korea systematically persecuted Christians and executed French missionaries, while resisting armed French, American and German military expeditions. At the end of the decade it still remained closed to trade.

In Japan pro- (Edo) and anti- (Cho shu) foreign forces battled for control of the Imperial throne. Finally the Emperor Mutsuhito took direct control of the government, abandoning the seven-hundred-year-old system of Shogun control. The pro-Tokugawa (Shogun) forces were defeated at the battle of Veno, and the Imperial capital was moved to Edo which was then renamed Tokyo. Under the leadership of Mutsuhito, the Meiji Emperor, Japan peacefully accepted modernization and change. Feudalism and fiefdoms were dissolved by Imperial edict, and western institutions including industrialization were adopted. This was an **extremely** important transition of power in Japan.

North America North America was torn by violence and Civil War. Even the usually peaceful country of Canada, with its tremendous surge of growth, had a western rebellion. During this decade, Canada bought the Northwest territories from the Hudson Bay Company, Prince Edward Island and British Columbia joined the Dominion, and Manitoba was elevated into a province. Manitoba's capital, Fort Gary (which was renamed Winnipeg) was the center of the Riel Rebellion. A group of discontented half-breeds* was led by Louis Riel, who protested the government survey policy. The rebellion was quelled. Besides this rebellion, Canada was plagued with Fenian raids across its border, as Irish Americans attempted to pressure England to favor Ireland more.

---

*Métis — persons of mixed blood — typically, in Canada, half-European (any race) and half-Indian (any tribe). These people were effectively excluded from both cultures.

To the south the United States was still immersed in the Civil War. The Union invaded the South, capturing Atlanta and Richmond, and forced the Confederacy to surrender in 1865. The government initiated the Reconstruction Act, placing the South under military rule, while promoting the rights of Negro ex-slaves. A period of cruel military occupation followed.

This was a period of expansion and Indian Warfare. The United States bought Alaska from Russia and, with the aid of the Prussian Emperor, successfully concluded its northwest border dispute with Canada, largely in favor of the U.S. Meanwhile the expansion of settlers westward disrupted the Plains Indians causing Cheyennes, Arapahoes, Apaches, Comanches, Kiowas and Plains Sioux to go on the warpath. All were ruthlessly suppressed, (the Sand Creek massacre was especially notorious) and numerous tribes were removed from their homelands and resettled. In addition, the U.S. fought pirates in Mexico, and fought a retaliatory battle in Korea.

The end of the United States Civil War had a profound effect on Mexico. The U.S. reasserted the Monroe Doctrine and France withdrew its support from Maximilian, who had been place on the Mexican throne by them. Juarez overthrew Maximilian and executed him in 1867. The liberal government of Juarez antagonized conservatives and after the death of Juarez, civil war broke out in Mexico.

1874-1883 A.D.
MODERATELY WARM.

Iberian Peninsula Although this decade began with Spain amidst the Carlist War, it was the beginning of a period of peace for the Iberian Peninsula. The First Spanish Republic originally found itself battling forces in favor of crowning Don Carlos, the former Queen's uncle, as monarch. Finally, in disgust, a group of generals overthrew the Republic and formed a conservatively-oriented constitutional monarchy under King Alfonso XII, son of the former Queen. The Carlist forces were defeated in 1876 and almost two decades of peace followed.

Portugal, continued as before, peacefully rotating conservative and liberal governments.

Northern Europe Despite a severe agricultural depression, this was basically a period of internal peace and external expansion and colonialism. Only England was troubled internally, when Irish terrorists began a campaign of bombing and assassinations from 1882 to 1883. This relative internal peacefulness, however, was frequently balanced by external acts of aggression. England found itself involved increasingly with debt-ridden Egypt, until finally it owned the Suez Canal and occupied Cairo and founded a pro-British government.* Likewise its Imperial policies pulled it into a war with the Zulus, Basutos and Kaffirs of South Africa, the Second Ashanti War of West Africa, and a war with Afghanistan. Both Belgium and Germany began forming colonial empires in Africa during this decade.

Southern Europe Like Northern Europe, Southern Europe experienced internal peace, with all conflicts being settled "constitutionally". All military action was external as a result of expansionist policies.

Both Italy and France competed for control of Tunisia, whose Bey was heavily in debt to both countries.* The French ended the competition by ultimately seizing Tunisia by force. Later in the decade they had to quell rebellions both in Tunisia and Algeria. At the same time the French began to expand northward from their West African colonies and militarily protect their financial interest in Egypt. At the same time they fought an unofficial war with China for control of Formosa and Indo-China.

Italy's only successful colonization was Eritrea.

Balkans Bulgaria started a massive rebellion in 1876 (following an abortive uprising in 1875) which swept up the entire Balkan peninsula. After the rebellion was savagely suppressed, Serbia, Montenegro, Crete and eventually Greece, (following an uprising in Thessaly) declared war on the Ottoman Empire. Russia, promoting a policy of Pan Slavism, attempted to mediate a truce after Serbia was defeated. When Turkey refused to accept Russian mediation, Russia declared war on the Empire and invaded Roumania. England, fearing Russian dominance of the Straits, intervened, and ultimately the Treaty of Berlin was agreed upon by Prussia, Russia, Austria, Britain, France, Italy and Turkey. Greece was given Thessaly and Epirus, Serbia, Roumania and Montenegro were made completely independent, a small Bulgarian principality was established north of Macedonia, Crete was given self-government, and Russia was granted control of Bessarabia. Thereafter, the Balkans remained quiet except for an unsuccessful revolt in Serbia.

North Africa North Africa lost much of its remaining independence to Europe this decade, and this loss of independence led to numerous uprisings. France's military seizure of Tunis led to uprisings in Tunis and

---

*Note that again and again and again, European powers have taken small "Third World" countries who defaulted on their debts.

Algeria. Likewise Egypt, which accepted British aid in its conquest of the Upper Nile, the Red Sea coast, and Darfur, and in its interior wars against Sudanese slave traders and Ethiopia, came increasingly under British supervision because of its enormous debts. There were four revolts of Egyptian or Circassian military officers against the government during this decade, and the resistance to increasing Western influence finally resulted in widespread anti-European rioting in Alexandria. England intervened and bombed Alexandria, defeated the Egyptian forces and set up a new prowestern government under the Khedive. While this was occupying Lower Egypt, the Sudan was being swept by a religious movement led by the Mahdi* Mohammed Ahmed, and British and Egyptian forces were being slaughtered.

Middle East The Middle East continued to reflect the growing antagonism of England and Russia. The Ottoman Empire found itself vivisected by this conflict. First Russia intervened in the Turkish suppression of the massive Balkan revolts; then Britain stepped in and reduced Russia's acquisition of Turkish territory to Bessarabia and the Trans-Caucasus territories of Ardahan, Kars, Batum and Bayazid. At the same time Britain intervened to keep the sultan from executing the members of the first Turkish Parliament. Later France stepped in and removed Tunis from the Empire, followed by England's 1882 occupation of Egypt which had also belonged to the Empire.

Persia became a victim of the British-Russian competition for control of Asia. The British-Persian Reuter Concession which would have had Britain economically help Persian development, fell through and Russia began to increase its dominance of Persia. The Persian army was trained by Russia and Russia's conquest of Turkmenistan brought it closer to Persia's borders.

Eastern Europe In general this was a time of internal peace and external expansion for European empires. Austria-Hungary remained at peace during the Russian-Turkish War and received Bosnia and Herzegovina as a reward for doing so. This led to the only serious internal trouble, as Germans and Magyars in the provinces revolted from the addition of more Slavs to the Empire. Aside from this disturbance, which was terminated within a year, Austria went through a period of increased minority rights.

---

*Among Mohammedans, the "Mahdi" is the last Imam — the leader of the faithful. Anyone who leads under this title is extraordinarily dangerous.

Russia was also growing and it was a peaceful time for their subject territories. However after the assassination of the Tsar, and the assumption of power by his son Alexander III, discrimination against and Russification of Eastern Europe became even more harsh. Roman Catholics and Protestants were severely persecuted and the pogroms against Jews began.

Russia Russia, as mentioned before, was internally peaceful and expanding rapidly. It went through a period of liberal reform which ended abruptly with the assassination of Tsar Alexander II and was reversed by his son. During this time Russia gained Bessarabia, Kars, Ardahan, Batum, and Bayazid from Turkey, southern Sakhalin from Japan, and the Central Asian lands of Kokand, Bokhara and Khiva. It had given up claim to the Kurile Islands but as the decade was ending was gaining control of Turkmenistan.

South Asia South Asia, like so much of the world, was torn by the British-Russian rivalry for power. While little new happened for India, aside from Victoria being crowned Empress of India, the rivalry centered in Afghanistan. Afghanistan's Civil War finally ended in 1878 with Sher Ali Khan, a pro-Russian in control. When Sher Ali signed a treaty of mutual support with Russia and refused to accept a British mission, Britain declared war. England won, Sher Ali was killed and his son was forced to accept British control of the Khyber Pass. A native outbreak against foreigners sparked British retaliation, Yakub was ousted and his cousin Abd-ar-Rahman put on the throne. For the rest of the decade Abd-ar-Rahman went through a balancing act between the two super-powers.

China Aside from subduing the Miaos, Tungans, and Kasgaria, the last of the minorities that broke away during the T'ai P'ing Revolt, this was a period of Chinese humiliation. England forced China to open ten more ports to trade while Russia forced it to pay money in return for the Ili Valley that Russia had seized previously. Money was also paid off against a Japanese expedition against Formosa, but by 1883 Formosa had become a source of war between China and France.

Far East Japan, under the Meiji Emperor, was Westernizing and industrializing rapidly. Some of these reform policies aroused resentment, however, and when the government attempted to abolish the Samurai (warrior) class, the Satsuma Rebellion broke out. The newly-recruited army of commoners crushed the rebellion. Imitating the west, Japan launched on a policy of expansion and opened Korea for trade.

Korea allowed itself to be opened for trade during this decade. In return for official recognition of Korean independence by Japan, Korea allowed a resident Japanese to be stationed in Seoul and trade in three ports. Trade treaties were also signed with America and England during this decade.

North America This was a period of peaceful growth and expansion for Canada, but war for its southern neighbors. The Indian Wars of the United States, like the wars of Northern Europe were expensive. Internally, reconstruction ended and the economy boomed. As immigration swelled, Americans surged west, displacing Indian tribes and causing a number of wars. The Cheyennes, Plains Sioux, Nez Perce, Bannock, Piute, Apache and Sheepeater Indians fought desperately against encroachment and all were defeated. This was the decade of Custer's massacre and Chief Joseph's attempt to escape with his tribe to what he visualized as the freedom of Canada.

Mexico concluded its liberal-conservative Civil War with the victory of conservatives under Porfirio Diaz. Under Diaz, Mexico grew economically while social discontent of *mestizos* and Indians mounted.

1884-1893 A.D.
WARM.

Iberian Peninsula Spain and Portugal began the now familiar pattern of internal peace and external aggression. There were occasional disturbances by anarchists and radicals but no major outbreaks. Externally the Spanish defeated the Moroccan Berbers while absorbing Rio de Oro and Spanish Guinea in West Africa. Meanwhile Portugal expanded its African claims from Mozambique to Angola. This led to tension between England and Portugal which was finally resolved by giving Portugal the two coasts while Britain claimed a large interior strip and financed Portugal's development of its colonies. During the same decade Portugal took Macao from China.

Northern Europe Once again Northern Europe was at peace internally and expanding outwardly. For Scandinavia, especially Sweden, this involved massive emigration to North America. For Britain, Belgium, and Germany this meant colonization in Africa and, for England, in Asia. Belgium's King Leopold promoted the conquest and colonization of the Congo, which he gave the Belgian State the right to annex in ten years in return for enough financing to exploit. Germany also was colonizing Africa, taking Togoland, the Camerouns, and East Africa immediately south of Lake Victoria.

Britain was especially active in this period despite the initial setback of the massacre in Khartoum of its Anglo-Egyptian forces led by General "Chinese" Gordon. During the decade Britain took Somaliland, East Africa, Nigeria, Zanzibar and, led by Cecil Rhodes, the British colony of South Africa spread northward. In Asia, Britain took Northern Burma, North Borneo, Port Hamilton of Korea and Sarawak. In the growing process Britain was involved in the Third Burma War, the Siamese Conflict, the Third Ashanti War, and serious confrontation with France, Portugal, Germany and Russia.

Southern Europe Southern Europe also was going through a prosperous period of internal peace and colonial expansion. The only internal troubles were a series of anarchist "outrages" (bombings and assassinations) and the Massacre of Fourmies when troops fired on a Labor demonstration, all of which happened in 1893.

Italy had acquired part of Somaliland by negotiation in 1886, and continued its African expansion with an unsuccessful attempt to seize Ethiopia. Johannes, Emperor of Ethiopia, defeated the Italians, but Italy expanded its territory after Johannes' death.

France was even more active in both Africa and Asia. In Africa, France expanded from the North Mouth of the Congo River to Lake Chad and, in West Africa, took French Guinea, the Ivory Coast and spread along the Niger River north of Timbuktu. This involved wars with the Ashanti, the Mandingo and Dahomey. In Asia the undeclared war with China led to France relinquishing any title to Formosa in return for China's recognition of French claims to Tonkin and Annam (French Indo-China). France expanded inland taking Laos and precipitating the Siamese Crisis with England.

Balkans As Turkish power over the Balkans faded, the area became the battleground for Russian and Austrian control. The major event in the Balkans during this decade was the revolt of Eastern Roumelia from Turkey in favor of union with Bulgaria. Turkey did not protest; but Serbia, who feared later Bulgarian growth at its expense, did. The Serbo-Burlgarian War resulted. Bulgaria won, to Russia's dismay; so Russian agents kidnapped the victorious Bulgarian ruler. He abdicated and there was a severe threat of direct Russian intervention at this point. Only the power of Austria backed by Britain kept Russia from invading. Bulgaria elected a new prince and survived the rest of the decade with only a small amount of political turmoil and assassinations.

Except for a severe agrarian revolution in Roumania, most of the events of this decade reflected the Austro-Russian conflict. Roumania allied with Austria, while Greece was kept from seizing Turkish territory during the turmoil of the Serbo-Bulgarian war by Austrian-British intervention and blockading. Crete again rose up in revolt and Turkey was allowed to subdue it and tighten its political control over it.

North Africa Europe continued to dominate North Africa. Egypt was forced by England to abandon its control of the Sudan, despite the massacre in Khartoum of General "Chinese" Gordon by the Mahdi Mohammed Ahmed. An outbreak in Morocco against Spain was severely subdued.

Middle East In the power wars of the Middle East, definite areas of control were being established. Britain was interested in preserving the Ottoman Empire. Although she allowed East Roumelia to break away, she and Austria prevented Russia or Greece from exploiting Turkish weakness.

Russia, which completed its conquest of Turkmenistan by capturing Merv in 1885, now was on the Persian border and increasingly dominated Northern Persia.*

Eastern Europe There was peace throughout this decade although in both Russia and Austria-Hungary, there were growing nationalistic movements by subject peoples. Russia severely repressed these movements and increased its Russification program—even to formerly autonomous Finland. In Austria, the government was unable to resolve the problems that these movements represented; but it at least kept the restlessness from breaking out in revolt.

Russia Russia was becoming increasingly in debt to France as it tried to finance a simultaneous program of territorial growth and industrialization. The industrialization created a large new class of dissidents, especially after the great famine of 1891-92. The expansion was more successful but was bringing it into an ever-growing number of confrontations with other great powers. In the Balkans Russian expansion was frustrated for the decade by Austria and Britain. Expansion in Asia led to severe tension with England. Turkmenistan and Merv were conquered and Russia dominated Persia. However Afghanistan was under British

---

*This dominance became so complete that by 1921 they had put a native Persian officer in the Cossacks in charge of Persia. By 1925, this Cossack officer, Reza Khan, had become Shah. The Reza "Pahlavi" Dynasty was to be forced out by the late 1970's.

control, with Britain determining its foreign policy. Russia and Afghanistan had a border clash at Penjdeh and Britain moved its navy within striking distance of Vladisvostok. The crisis was taken into negotiation. In Korea, an attempted Russian takeover was blocked by Britain.

South Asia Except for the Penjdeh incident, South Asia, now totally under British dominance, was peaceful. The Afghan-Indian border was agreed upon. Any attempt by Russia to expand into this part of the world was blocked.

China China steadily weakened during this period. It yielded total control of Indochina to European powers—yielding Annam, Tonkin and Laos to France; Upper Burma to Britain; and Macao to Portugal.

Far East Japan continued to model itself after the west and to blossom economically. It attempted to control Korea; a move which was resisted by China which still claimed Korea as part of its hegemony. This brought both sides in conflict and close to large-scale war; but a treaty finally got both powers to withdraw their troops.

Russia later attempted to gain control of Korea; but this move was blocked by the arrival of British ships in Port Hamilton, where the British remained until 1887.

North America Except for a growing restlessness among pro-labor forces and liberals this was a relatively peaceful time for all the governments of North America. All three countries experienced expanding economies and populations and both Canada and the U.S. experienced conflict (continuing Indian Wars) as a result of their expanding populations displacing existing inhabitants in their westward drive.

In Canada there was the Northwest Rebellion (*Metis* and Indians [primarily Crees]) led by Louis Riel, who had led a previous unsuccessful revolt in Winnipeg. The revolt was crushed and Riel hanged. Likewise in the U.S., expansion caused Indians, especially Apaches and some Sioux, to revolt. By 1886 all Indian tribes had been removed to Indian Territory or reservations. Then in 1889, Indian Territory was opened to White settlement and a year later reorganized into Oklahoma territory. Meanwhile in Hawaii, American settlers overthrew native rule and applied to join the U.S.

1894-1903 A.D.
WARM.

The high tide of 23 December 1893 had come and gone. As the tidal force rose, the Northern Hemisphere was purged of most of the volcanoes which were anywhere near ready to erupt.

As of the high tidal force, the earth changed its rate of rotation and a period of extreme earthquake hazard began. These crustal insults completed the purge of Northern Hemisphere volcanoes.* Thus began the increasingly warm period centering around 1939 — the warmest period since the 800's.

Iberian Peninsula Both Spain and Portugal maintained internal peace despite rising anarchist attacks and sporadic strikes and revolts. Externally, both empires were decaying.

This decay was most dramatic in Spain where the Spanish-American War stripped it of most of its non-African colonies. The three-year long Cuban Insurrection aroused U.S. sympathy and when the U.S.S. Maine blew up, America declared war. Spain lost and yielded up Cuba, Guam, the Philippines, and Puerto Rico.

Portugal's decline was not as dramatic, but her colonies were also revolting. Both Angola and Mozambique had wide-scale uprisings. Portugal went bankrupt and had to use these two African colonies as collateral on loans from England and Germany.

Northern Europe Northern Europe's pattern of internal peace and continued colonial expansion was leading to a growing number of international confrontations. By the end of the decade the great powers of Germany and Britain were definitely antagonistic toward each other.

Germany, England, and Belgium were still expanding. Belgium spread its Congo territories eastward to the Upper Nile. Germany got the Chinese port of Kiaochow and a number of Pacific Islands. Great Britain, however, grew the most.** In order to block an attempted French move to connect French Somaliland with West Africa, Britain reconquered the Sudan. There was similar expansion in British East Africa where Uganda was absorbed and dramatic northward expansion in South Africa and the newly-

---

*The great volcanoes in the early part of the century were: 1902, 1902, 1907, 1912

23 Dec. 1893 = 1893.978 + 8.85 = 1902.828

1902.828 + (8.85 / 2) = 1907.253

1893.978 + 18.03 = 1912.008

** It is interesting to note that in August 1898, England and Germany signed a treaty for the subsequent partition of Portugal's African colonies, if Portugal was forced to release them. Does the treaty still hold? The U.S. still holds a part of Samoa which was partitioned by a treaty signed by England, Germany and the U.S. on November 14, 1899 — the following year.

named territory of Rhodesia. This eventually led to the Boer War with the original Dutch settlers of Transvaal. By the time the war ended both the Orange Free State and Transvaal had been absorbed. The only non-African expansion of Britain was much more of the territory of the Kowloon Peninsula, and many islands next to Hong Kong.**

The Powers now encountered a growing number of "native" uprisings against colonial control. Holland had to subdue Sumatra and Belgium battled Batetela's rebellion in Upper Congo. Germany played a major role in subduing the Boxer Revolt of China. But Britain, with the largest Empire, faced the most colonial wars.* Besides the bloody Boer War and the Fourth Ashanti War, Britain had to subdue revolts in Nyasaland, Zanzibar, Rhodesia, two uprisings in Northern India, and an Ashanti Rebellion. At the same time there were international crises with France and Germany over African expansion, and with Russia over Asia.

Southern Europe Both Italy and France were troubled by anarchist attacks and labor strikes; Italy further endured bread riots which in some cases became violent, and France endured the nation-splitting Dreyfus Affair. But throughout these troubles the governments continued to function and there was little actual loss of life. Both countries continued to concentrate the majority of their aggressive efforts on colonization.

**Britain obtained these territories on a 99-year lease in 1898.

---

*Wright ("A Study of War") concluded:

"Probably at least 10 per cent of deaths in modern civilization can be attributed directly or indirectly to war."

This includes civilian casualties, which probably represents three times as great a rate as direct war deaths; which, in 20th century Europe, has increased from 2 to about 3 percent.

Wright quotes Dumas who has figures that 80 to 90 percent of all army losses during the Napoleonic period were from disease. During World War I, 30 percent of Russian army losses, and 26 percent of American army losses were from disease. Famines and disease also take a huge toll in war areas.

(Other figures for U.S. Army disease deaths / total active military deaths are:

Mexican war	88%
Civil War	66%
Spanish-American War	84%
World War I	26%)

Deaths in the active military service per 1000 in the total population:

Centuries	17th	18th	19th	20th
France	11	27	30	63
England	15	14	6	48

France consolidated its hold on the Sahara, seizing strategic oases from the Atlantic shore to the Nile. This led to the Fashoda Crisis with England, which was in the process of reclaiming the Sudan, and forced France to give up all claim to the Nile. Also in Africa, France gained control of Dahomey and after two wars, broke the power of the Modingos. By 1896 France had seized Madagascar. In Asia France won another port and numerous concessions from the Chinese.

Italy was less fortunate. Its attempt to seize Ethiopia was humiliatingly defeated and it was forced by Ethiopia to confine itself to Eritrea. Italy yielded to France most of its claims to Tunis. Even China frustrated Italy's claim to a trading port. The twentieth century has seen Italy in a severe state of weakness — as did the ninth century.

Balkans The Balkans remained troubled as small nations warred with each other and were manipulated by Russia, Austria and Britain. The Ottoman Empire was crippled by European powers in its attempts to deal with its former Christian subject states, and the Balkan countries exploited this weakness in attempts to tear even more territory, Macedonia in particular, from the Empire.

A Cretan insurrection led to war with Greece. Greece was the aggressor, blockading Crete and invading Macedonia; but when it was defeated, the European Powers protected it from Turkish retaliation. Eventually they even gave it control of Crete. Macedonia later revolted, after almost a decade of raids from Bulgaria, Serbia and Greece, and again Austria and Russia intervened and set terms. The King of Serbia and his wife were hacked to death in an assassination plot backed by Russia. An international commission set itself up to control Greece's finances when it defaulted on loans. Before the decade was over the great powers were casually discussing the advisability of dissecting the Ottoman Empire and the Balkans into zones of power.

North Africa North Africa was casually being divided by treaties into European territorial zones. Italy was to be granted a free hand with Tripoli, France already controlled Tunisia and Algeria and was granted the right to strip increasing amounts of territory from Morocco, which was going through a period of anarchy. Egypt was compelled by Britain to reconquer the Sudan that it had been forced to abandon only a decade before. Now, however, control of the Sudan was seen as a strategic maneuver to block French colonial expansion, so Anglo-Egyptian forces spent over two years battling the Dervishes* for control of the Upper Nile.   (see page 242 for footnote.)

Middle East Both the Ottoman and Persian empires found themselves in danger of being divided between the great powers. When the Ottoman Empire began massacring Christian Armenians, who were demonstrating for independence within Anatolia, the Europeans planned to seize Constantinople. Only French reluctance to go to war halted the invasion. This constant threat of intervention prevented Turkey from controlling the Balkans, or even halting the growth of Ibn Saud in the Arabian Peninsula.

Persia found itself dominated in the north by Russia and along the Gulf by Britain; and bound to both by huge debts.

Eastern Europe Although the governments remained in control and there was comparatively little loss of life, Eastern Europe was troubled by terrorism and nationalism. Austria-Hungary experienced widespread disorders, especially among the Czechs. Russia suppressed its dissidents enough to prevent outright demonstrations, but terrorism was widespread.

Russia Russia's government continued its conservative oppressive policies, maintaining a restless peace within, while expanding externally. It finally settled its boundary with Afghanistan and continued to dominate northern Persia. It made most of its gains against a weakened China, seizing the Liaotung Peninsula and Port Arthur* and occupying Manchuria. It gained greater influence in Mongolia and Tibet and, after the Korean king took refuge in the Russian legation, became the dominant power in Korea.

Southern Asia Russia settled its border dispute with Afghanistan by terms of a treaty which set the border along the Pamirs; and no longer disputed British control of South Asia. Except for a Chitral rebellion and a Trak frontier war against rebellious Afridi tribesmen invading the Khyber pass, (the Tirah Expedition), there was little to disturb or to threaten British rule.

---

*The Dervishes — some thirty-two orders — constitute the only ecclesiastical organizations that Islam has ever had. The *zikr* is the main devotional exercise of all orders of Dervishes; and the Mawlawis, or "Dancing Dervishes", sound a monotonous chant accompanied by a slow whirling movement around the floor, with eyes closed and arms extended. The dance continues until they fall into a cataleptic state. Thus "Whirling Dervishes".

They are ascetic and ideologically pure; they are formidable opponents, indeed.

---

*Port Arthur (Chinese: Lu-shun or Lü-shun-kow; Japanese: Ryo. jun) on the Liao-tung Peninsula which extends into the Yellow Sea, dividing Korea Bay from the Gulf of Chihli (Po Hai). This very important warm water port was the terminus (near Darien — [Rus.: Dalny; Jap.: Talienwan: Chin.: Lü-ta]) of the Manchurian Railway which connected Europe to the Pacific. It was (is) an extraordinary fortress.

China The decade began with the Sino-Japanese War when China resisted the Japanese attempt to take control of the Korean government. Japan won easily. China was forced to open up 4 more ports, and give Japan Formosa and the Pescadores Islands. Only the intervention of the European powers kept Japan from taking more. The Europeans expected to be rewarded for their help. In the next five years the Europeans scrambled for concessions with Britain taking Kowloon (by lease), France took Dwang-chowan Bay, Russia took the Liaotung Peninsula and Germany took Kiaochow Bay.

The defeat by Japan humiliated China and awakened the majority of educated Chinese to their plight. The Emperor launched a reform program; but when the Manchu upper class felt threatened by these reforms, his mother imprisoned him and cancelled the reforms. Instead the court chose to rely on the Boxers, a mystical anti-foreign movement. The Boxers began persecuting Christians and killing foreigners, and the court hoped they would drive out all foreigners. Foreigners, especially missionaries, were executed throughout China, and the foreign legations at Peking underwent a fifty-five day siege. Only the uniting of the legations into an inter-national defense force and the support of one of the court factions led by Jung-tu allowed the legations to survive until an international rescue force arrived. *

The court fled and eventually had to sign a humiliating protocol and pay indemnities.** Russia kept Manchuria, which it had seized during the Boxer rebellion. Long-awaited governmental reforms finally began.

Far East Japan began this decade triumphing in the Sino-Japanese War and getting money, Formosa and the Pescadores Islands from China. Japan now began to perceive itself as a western style power. It had the powerful queen of Korea murdered and reorganized the government. It participated in the international relief expeditions during the Boxer Rebellion. As its power and sense of importance grew, it found itself in ever-increasing conflict with Russia.

Korea was the main area of Russo-Japanese conflict. When the Japanese seized control of the king and the Chinese tried to intervene, the Sino-Japanese War resulted. As part of Japan's victory, Korea was forced to form an alliance with Japan, and Japan took control of its government.

---

*The Allies were: Japanese, Russians, British, United States, French, Germans, Austrians and Italians. Chinese Christians were also under attack and fought on the Allied side.

**The indemnity payments to the U.S. were returned to support education of the Chinese. This was the beginning of the U.S. policy of helping rather than hurting former enemies.

When Japan manipulated a faction into assassinating the Queen, the King fled to the Russian legation for refuge. This was the beginning of the Russian / Japanese struggle for control. After a year at the legation and almost total Russian control, the King returned to the palace and both countries struggled for influence. When the Russians failed to leave Manchuria and continued to penetrate northern Korea, Japanese-Russian relations reached a crisis point.

North America All three North American countries boomed during this decade. Mexico and Canada remained peaceful except for occasional radical disturbances.

The United States ended its Indian conflicts (Wounded Knee — 1898) with complete subjugation of the Indian peoples; but continued its expansion policies. Hawaii was annexed in 1898. The United States victory in the Spanish-American War gave it control of Cuba,* the Phillippines, Guam and Puerto Rico, although it chose to grant Cuba independence. When the Philippines tried to gain their independence, the U.S. fought a three-year war to crush it. In Latin America, the United States manipulated the Panama revolution so it could purchase the Canal Zone. The U.S. forced England to accept arbitration in the British Guiana — Venezuela boundary dispute.

1904-1913 A.D.
WARMER.

Iberian Peninsula Spain and Portugal ended their expansion during this decade and fell prey to internal unrest. In Spain there was an attempt to increase their control of Morocco, but the military draft sparked massive rioting and a massive general strike by Catalonia. Anti-clerical movements led to massacres of priests and monks and burning of churches. When Conservatives were in power, radicals and labor rioted, and when Liberals were in power they were so harsh to the Church that the army and Church demonstrated.

Portugal was undergoing even more turmoil. Angola revolted and Mozambique was allowed to set up its own government. Internally the revolts led to the assassination of the King and Crown Prince, and four years later drove out King Manuel II. A republic was declared and it attacked the Church and expelled religious orders. A general strike paralyzed the country in 1912 and radical revolt filled the country.

---

*Cuba was given its independence in continuation of U.S. policy. The Panama Canal Treaty and purchase gave independence and funding to Panama.

North Europe* Except for occasional labor strikes or anarchist attacks, Northern Europe again experienced a decade of interior peace. Even succession did not provoke war. Norway broke its union with Sweden amid a peaceful plebiscite. Ireland was in the process of being granted home rule by England's Parliament by the end of the decade. No issue seemed so major that it threatened the peace of Western Europe.

There was a pattern to outward aggression appearing in this decade. Actual expansion was slowing to a standstill. Germany, Belgium and the Scandinavians took no new territory. The Netherlands replaced their former indirect rule with direct rule over Bali. Even England held its colonializing activity down to the establishment of control of British Malaya, absorbed the Ashanti kingdom into the Gold Coast and seized South West Persia. Instead of activity expanding, however, most of this decade was spent drawing up treaties, where each great power recognized the others' territorial possessions, all agreed on borders of power (i.e., zones of influence), and each tried to halt any more expansion by the others. The drive to expand was dying, but the fear of rival growth was increasing.

One of the causes for this lack of enthusiasm was the ever-increasing difficulty of holding on to what one owned. The Netherlands forced a series of insurrections in Indonesia, while Germany had major revolts in all three of its African Colonies. Belgium lost some of its Congo territory and its right to exclusive trade. England found itself suppressing outbreaks in Egypt, Ethiopia, and Nigeria.

Southern Europe Both countries continued to expand despite increasingly serious internal disruption by labor strikes. However serious these strikes and demonstrations were, they did not stop the governments from functioning and took a relatively small number of human lives.

Italy had a war with Turkey at this time. Turkey lost and Italy won temporary control of the Dodecanese Islands and the right to control Libya and Tripoli. The major powers, apprehensive at the expansion of a newcomer constantly tried to mediate in the war.

France expanded in Africa, taking Mauritania and Wadni (Northern Chad) and, in a treaty, a small amount of West African coastlines. Morocco was in chaos, and clearly ripe for conquest, but it is interesting to note that before it occupied Morocco, France first carefully drew up

---

*This decade marked the end of the Christian Conquest of the World. The military triumph of Christians over all others had been almost total. Such lands as were not conquered could easily have been (Inner China), excepting only Japan and Thailand. These both fell later.

agreements with Spain. When Germany objected to the move, France appeased it with economic concessions in Morocco in return for recognition of its political control.

Balkans As one of the few areas in the world not clearly divided up into "zones of influence", the Balkans were a constant source of apprehension for the great powers. When Austria took advantage of the weakness of Turkey to annex Bosnia and Herzegovina, it antagonized Russia and the small Balkan states, and created a crisis which none of the great powers were able to adequately settle. In the confusion of this crisis, Bulgaria declared complete independence and Crete proclaimed union with Greece.

The helplessness of the great powers to settle the issue increased the drive of the Balkan states to seize Turkish territory before someone else did. Greece, Montenegro, Bulgaria and Serbia declared war on Turkey, in an attempt to seize more Turkish territory. Both Austria and Russia felt that their interests were being threatened and almost went to war. Britain hastily intervened and persuaded all parties to negotiate a treaty. When the treaty, in accord with Austria's desires, blocked Serbia's access to a coast and gave Bulgaria more territory than anyone else, it provoked a new Balkan War against Bulgaria. Roumania, Serbia, Greece and Turkey allied against Bulgaria which foolishly struck the first blow against Serbia and Greece. Meanwhile Serbia tried to take over Albania, which still belonged to Turkey. Bulgaria gave much of its previous gains up to Serbia and Greece and yielded territory to Roumania while Greece and Serbia were forced by Austria to back down from Albania; an ultimatum that cost Serbia a coastline. Russia was concerned at Austria's increasing control of the Balkans; and so it committed itself to back the Balkan states if they should again come in conflict with Austria.

Serbia's drive for a coastline and its fury at Austria for blocking this drive, guaranteed a potential explosion. Germany's backing of Austria and Russia's heavy commitment to back Serbia guaranteed a World War.

North Africa North Africa came totally under European control at this time. Morocco, which was the only North African territory not claimed by a European power created two major crises when its internal anarchy made it ripe for taking. After vigorous negotiation, it was agreed that Spain should own the Mediterranean coast while France owned the Atlantic coast and the interior and Germany gained economic concessions. All powers solemnly guaranteed the "integrity and independence" of Morocco, then France bombarded Casablanca and seized the country.

Likewise Italy signed several solemn agreements with France before invading Libya and wrenching it from the Turks.

Egypt, under British "protection" gained territory, including the Sinai Peninsula. Despite these gains there was a widespread anti-foreign movement that occasionally broke into violence.

Middle East The Middle Eastern empires were swept by civil war which Europeans were quick to take advantage of. Persia, for example, had a revolution against the Shah in 1905. This led to a Russian invasion of the north and British militia guarding the oil fields in the South West. By 1909 the Shah's son, a minor, was put on the throne and the government attempted financial reforms. Russia intervened and Persia remained dominated by Russia.

The Ottoman Empire's situation was even more complex. Its weakness invited exploitation, so Austria and the Balkans seized most of its European territories and Italy seized Tripoli, its last North African territory. Armenians within Anatolia demonstrated for independence and Turkish reactions and massacres brought threats of intervention by the great powers. Finally, when the Empire was about to cede Adrianople, the last European territory outside of Constantinople, to Europeans, rebellion broke out. The decade ends with the Empire swept by war and revolution. Ibn Saud was taking large portions of the Arabian Peninsula. The Young Turks were perpetrating widespread acts of terrorism. The only positive note was that Turkey still retained Adrianople.

Eastern Europe Eastern Europe under Russia and Austria-Hungary grew increasingly violent in its demands for recognition. The governments of both empires, however, were more concerned with developments in the Balkans.

Russia Russia began this decade with the Russo-Japanese War which its aggressive policy in the Far East and its contemptuous treatment of the Japanese had provoked. The Japanese annihilated all Russian opposition and forced Russia to yield Southern Sakhalin Island, the Liaotung Peninsula and all claim to Korea. The Russian government was humiliated and discredited and near-revolution resulted. There were strikes, mutinies, and widespread bloody outbreaks against the Tsar. The Tsar yielded to pressure by granting Russia a constitution with civil liberties, the franchise, and a legislative Duma. As soon as the revolutionary movement had faded, the Tsar published the Fundamental Laws which crippled the powers of the Duma, and allowed the Tsar to continue as an autocrat. Gradually the franchise was more and more restricted.

South Asia Russia officially, in a treaty, recognized British control of South Asia. Now that British control was officially recognized, it noted an increasing number of demonstrations in India against its policies.

China China's increasing weakness in its relations with Europe and Japan finally provoked the 1911 Chinese Revolution. The last Manchu Emperor was deposed*, and a Republic was declared. Yüan Shih-k'ai became president, which provoked an unsuccessful "Second Revolution". Yüan gained in power by purging the parliament of opposition party members.

Despite the new type of government, China still continued to lose territory. In 1913, it recognized the autonomy of Outer Mongolia.

Far East Japan emerged as a world power after its decisive victory over Russia in the Russo-Japanese War. After gaining more and more control over Korea's government, it finally formally annexed Korea in 1910. These actions provoked a Korean War of Independence which took Japan years to suppress. The demands of the campaign, plus the prestige gained by their victory, led to an increased role of the military in the government, especially after the death of the Meiji emperor.

North America Both Canada and the United States retained internal peace. The United States was increasingly overbearing in its relations with Latin America, this attitude provoked by the fear that its neighbors' financial carelessness would lead to European takeovers. It had forcefully prevented such a takeover in Santo Domingo in the last decade and had to do the same for Nicaragua and Honduras in the 1904-1913 decade. Action in the former country included a marine invasion.**

The policies of Diaz in Mexico had brought stability and material

---

*Emperor P'u-yi born in 1906, acceded to the throne in 1908, abdicated in 1912. The Nanking authorities agreed that the emperor was to retain his title for life and to receive a large pension. The Manchu was briefly restored in World War I. Later, after the Japanese had destroyed Chinese rule in Manchuria, they organized it into a New State called Manchoukuo, and recalled Emperor P'u-yi — now called Emperor Kuang-hsü — in 1934. Japan lost the war; so the Emperor lost his throne; but finally died — still Emperor in title, but with no domain, in 1967.

** It should be noted here that the United States initiated an unprecedented foreign policy in this decade. Completely unlike other countries, the U.S. in 1908 forgave the indemnities from China for the Boxer Rebellion (1899-1900); and authorized China to turn over all of the indemnity money for education of the Chinese. This policy of rehabilitation rather than despoilation of the *enemy* led to eventual independence of the Philippines, famine relief in Russia after the U.S. invaded (1918-1920 during the "Allied Intervention" 1918-1922); forgiving most World War I indemnities; the Marshall Plan in post-World War II days; and many other such contributions. (In 1848, after Mexico was conquered, some of it was

prosperity; but to the detriment of the lower classes who sank into peonage. This led to the Mexican Revolution which finally overthrew Diaz in 1911. The Revolution led to widespread anarchy. Madero, who overthrew Diaz, was himself overthrown by Huerta. Massive numbers of Mexicans fled north into the U.S. (some two million never returned to Mexico; while a million were killed by the Mexican revolution).

1914-1923 A.D.

WARMER. GLACIERS IN TREMENDOUS RETREAT.

Iberian Peninsula Although the Iberian countries played little or no part in World War I, they suffered turmoil. Socialists and anarchists demonstrated throughout Spain, and Catalonia demanded autonomy. Morocco had constant native uprisings. Spain attempted to subdue these uprisings and was defeated with over 12,000 soldiers killed. The defeat discredited the government and led to demonstrations and a mutiny in Barcelona. The decade ended with a coup by General Rivera —who, with the King's approval, proclaimed martial law and persecuted the liberals.

Portugal had an even more chaotic time. Portugal's small participation on the side of the Allies led to the government being overthrown by pro-German militia, then by pro-British forces. By 1917, Portuguese were fighting on the Western Front—which triggered another pro-German coup. General Pães was assassinated, and by the end of World War I, a democratic regime was reestablished. Portugal's reward for its part in the war was German Southwest Africa. However, its democratic government was unstable with a new cabinet every four months on average. Insurrections and coups abounded.

Northern Europe Nineteen-fourteen was the year that World War I was declared and basically marks the end of European expansion. Although some Northern European powers grew after this period, it was almost never into new territory, but instead involved seizing territory from another European power.

---

purchased, and the remainder released. Cuba was freed in 1898.)

The United States has been more generous in this century, quantitatively, than everyone else all added together, throughout the history of the world. The world's response has brought this period of generosity essentially to a close. Too bad for the world!

It obviously has no grasp at all of the other facet of the U.S. personality—which is more dangerous than the mind can grasp. For example, given severe irritation; the U.S. is quite capable of a first strike on a considerable number of countries simultaneously, with every weapon in its arsenal and with absolutely devastating effect. The world had best treat the U.S. gently for a long while yet.

The Scandinavian countries were the exception to this rule. While the rest of Europe went to war, they remained neutral. During the wars they had to accept various Allied restrictions on their trade due to the blockade; and it was during this time that Denmark chose to sell the Danish West Indies (Virgin Islands) to the United States. Immediately following the War's close, Denmark granted Iceland its independence, although the two sovereignties continued to share the same monarch and act jointly in foreign affairs. In the War settlements that followed, Denmark was granted northern Schleswig and Norway was given this almost-deserted Arctic island of Spitsbergen. The countries continued to experience peaceful democratic regimes. Various Danish fishermen settled along Greenland's coast and in 1921 Denmark declared its sovereignty over Greenland.

England was in the process of solving the Irish question by their passage of the Home Rule Bill when World War I intervened and postponed its enactment. On August 4, 1914, because of its commitments with France, and using Germany's invasion of Belgium as its basis—Great Britain declared war on Germany. In the next fourteen months Great Britain declared war on Germany's allies: Austria, Turkey and Bulgaria.

The war for Great Britain cost 3,000,000 casualties of which almost 1,000,000 died. On the home front, there was light bombing and there were extensive submarine raids on shipping. On the foreign front, the British forces fought successfully on the Western Front, in the Balkans, in Persia, and throughout Arabia and Mesopotamia. It also maintained a successful blockade against Germany. As a consequence for its victory, Britain took control or partial control of all of Germany's African colonies; and Mesopotamia, Cyprus and Palestine from Turkey.

Immediately after the war Britain found itself fighting in Ireland. Ireland seized the time of Britain's greatest peril and distraction, and rebelled in 1916 against continued British rule and successfully opposed conscription. As soon as the war was over, the Sinn Fein party declared Irish independence and fighting between Irish and British (Black and Tans) became intense until the Government of Ireland Act—which set up separate elections in Northern Ireland and Southern Ireland. Eventually, Southern Ireland became the Irish Free State, a British Dominion, while Northern Ireland retained its former status. The decade ended with the Republican Society fighting an assassination campaign in opposition to the established government of the Irish Free State, over the questions of Ireland's dominion status.

The Irish question was just symptomatic of the British post-war Problem. There was social unrest, a major coal strike and a slump in the economy with massive unemployment. The Dominions became restless and England granted them the right to make treaties with foreign powers. Egypt had a major insurrection and after subduing it, Great Britain granted it independence. A similar revolt swept Iraq, and India experienced anti-British terrorism.

The Low Countries suffered tremendously from the war, the Netherlands from trade interference and Belgium from the German invasion and subsequently being a part of the Western Front. As compensation Belgium was given Eupen, Malmedy and Moresnet, and a mandate over part of German East Africa. Both increased suffrage and enjoyed economic growth after the war. Belgium acted closely with France in its foreign policy and joined France in the invasion of the Ruhr.

Germany was the most obvious victim of this tumultuous decade. The process of Russian mobilization to aid Serbia involved mobilization along the German border, which sparked a German declaration of war. Anticipating France's attack in response to its alliance with Russia, Germany then declared war on France and attacked through Belgium. Before the war was over, Germany found itself fighting 23 different countries, as well as the British Dominions. Germans fought on both the Eastern and Western front, in Persia, the Balkans and in their colonies all over the world. The submarine warfare in the Atlantic sparked American intervention. Despite initial victories against Roumania and Russia, the crumbling of the Allies and the late entrance of the Americans along the Western Front guaranteed German defeat. Mutiny swept the northwestern German forces, revolution broke out in Munich and William II abdicated, ending the empire. The treaty of Versailles, which stripped Germany of her colonies and her military, and saddled her with an impossible war debt, was signed on 28 June and ratified on 7 July 1919. Germany had to grant Polish independence and lost Alsace-Lorraine to France, and the Saar and the Rhineland to Allied control.

The harshness of the treaty guaranteed unrest in Germany's new republic. Spartacists, extreme leftists who favored a Communist regime, revolted all over the country while pro-monarchist forces had an uprising in Berlin. Strikes swept the country and various ministries of the government resigned rather than accept the terms of the treaty. Meanwhile France and Belgium seized the Ruhr, because of default on their debts, and the Rhineland, encouraged by France, proclaimed a republic. One of the many uprisings, the Beer Hall Putsch, introduced Adolf Hitler and the National Socialists.

Southern Europe Both France and Italy suffered enormous losses in World War I and disillusionment afterwards. France was attacked by Germany and during most of the war fighting was on French soil. Moreover the French had to fight in the Balkans and Turkey. The property damage was enormous. Over a million soldiers, representing a huge percentage of France's young men, were killed. Although France received Alsace-Lorraine and mandates in German-owned colonies of the Camarouns and Togoland, and the former Turkish territory of Syria, it still felt inadequately compensated and vengeful towards Germany, whom it blamed for the entire war.

After the war France experienced internal peace. It concentrated on getting revenge on Germany. It occupied the Saar and the Rhineland, shipping coal and machinery back to France. The Rhineland was encouraged to become an independent republic, which would separate it permanently from Germany. After Germany had defaulted on the debt, France and Belgium occupied the Ruhr.

Italy, which had originally been neutral, eventually joined the Allies and attacked Austria-Hungary. It did poorly, fighting two years with a gain of only ten miles, then falling back dramatically following the battle of Caporetto. Its only advance was the seizure of Albania which was in a state of anarchy and unable to defend itself. This disappointing performance led to the Allies giving far less than it had originally been promised. Italy gained only Eastern Galacia, the Trentino, Southern Tyrol, Trieste and Istria, but no Dalmatia. What made this small gain of land even more disappointing was that Libya had taken advantage of Italy's involvement in the war and had driven the Italians from all but two cities. Italy now faced a long and expensive campaign to regain its colony.

Like France, Italy tried to make up for its losses by attacking others. In 1919, Italian forces landed in Turkey to claim southwestern Anatolia and seized the city of Fiume on the Dalmatian coast. Both adventures went badly and Italy had to abandon its territory. It also had to evacuate Albania and agree to yield the Dodecanese Islands to Greece.

These defeats and the general disillusionment with the government led to widespread Fascist and Communist riots. As Fascism grew more powerful, a band of Fascists re-captured Fiume. After this, Fascism began to militantly capture cities throughout Italy, the fighting extending to every major Italian city. Finally in 1922 the Fascists marched on Rome, forcing the government to resign. Mussolini was made dictator for a year. During this year Mussolini expedited the recapture of Libya and attempted to seize Corfu from Greece. The Corfu incident was a fiasco, and the Libya campaign was arduous; but before his term as dictator was over Mussolini guaranteed his party control of the Parliament.

The Balkans World War I started in the Balkans and spread outward. The Serbians resented the interference of Austria in Balkan affairs and agents of one of their societies, The Union of Death, assassinated the Archduke Francis Ferdinand, heir to Austria's throne. This led to an Austrian declaration of war on Serbia, which in turn dragged in Serbia's ally, Russia. This began the complex series of international alliances pulling country after country into the conflict.

Curiously it took a while for most Balkan states to join the war since most of them were still exhausted from the Second Balkan War of a year before. Bulgaria, who was courted by both sides, finally joined on the side of the Central Powers in 1915; and with Austria and Germany defeated the Serbian army and drove it out of the country to the island of Corfu. Roumania, persuaded by Russia, joined the Allies and was defeated within a year. The next year Greece, under extreme pressure from an Allied blockade, joined the Allies. In 1918, an alliance of Italians, Serbs, Greeks, British and French attacked and defeated Bulgaria, allowing Roumania to recover from invasion and re-enter the war. Almost simultaneously Turkey capitulated and World War I was over for the Balkans.

Serbia was the biggest winner, although the loss of 22% of its prewar population killed, and a like number injured, was a pyrrhic victory. The Allies encouraged Serbia's union with Croatia, Slovania and Montenegro into the country of Yugoslavia. The rest of the decade was spent in consolidating the kingdom despite the opposition of Croatian and other groups. Yugoslavia allied with Czechoslovakia and Roumania to form the Little Entente.

Roumania was the other major gainer from the war. Hungary yielded Transylvania, Banat and part of the Hungarian plain. It invaded Hungary in 1919 and seized Budapest in order to insure that it would receive the promised territory. Immediately afterwards it had to fight a short war with Russia in order to guarantee its promised possession of Bessarabia. The decade ended with internal reform of the government to make it more democratic. Roumania formed the Little Entente with Czechoslovakia and Yugoslavia.

Greece had more difficulty in obtaining its promised reward of Smyrna, the Dodecanese, Imbros, Tenedos and eastern Thrace. In 1919, acting as agent for the allies, Greece invaded Turkey, which was undergoing a revolution against the Ottoman dynasty. The war in Anatolia went poorly and the new government of Turkey negotiated the Treaty of Lausanne which granted Greece all the Turkish Islands except Imbros and Tenedos and retained possession of all Anatolian cities and eastern Thrace. Then Italy refused to turn the Dodecanese Islands over to Greece. Confusion resulted as a massive resettlement program began as Turks and Greeks moved out of each others' territories. The decade ended with Italy trying to exploit the confusion by seizing Corfu and failing miserably.

Albania neither gained nor lost in the war. During the war it had been occupied by Italy but by the end of the decade it had driven out the last Italian forces.

Bulgaria, as a member of the Central Powers suffered greatly. Having already lost massive amounts of territory in the Second Balkan War, it lost still more territory in Serbia including Aegean ports. As Thrace and Macedonian territory was given to Greece and Yugoslavia, thousands of refugees fled to Bulgaria. As the Greeks and Yugoslavians forced nationalization on their minorities, even more fled to Bulgaria. These refugees were a source of turmoil as they used Bulgaria as a base for terrorist attacks on its neighbors. The decade ended with a coup aided by these refugees, and Bulgaria in a state of tension with its neighbors.

North Africa Most of North Africa tried to take advantage of European preoccupation in World War I. Both Egypt and Libya had major insurrections. Egypt, which had been made a British Protectorate in 1914, had its rebellion immediately crushed, but subsequent British investigation led to Egyptian independence. Libya, which initially seemed more successful as it drove the Italians out of all but two cities, found itself facing a major Italian campaign by 1922. After the war the anti-European policies continued as bands led by Raisli and Abd-el-Krim successfully battled Spanish forces in Morocco.

Middle East The Middle East underwent a tumultuous decade with the Ottoman Empire finally dissolving under the pressure of European powers and its own militant minorities.

The Turks had a longstanding grudge against Russia, which had led to an alliance with Germany. When the war began, Turkey remained neutral until August, then it bombarded Russia's Black Sea ports. Soon it found itself fighting on a multitude of fronts. A Russian campaign across the Caucasus, British attacks first up from the Persian Gulf through Mesopotamia, then in 1916 in through Palestine, and a combined Anglo-French assault on the Dardanelles. Moreover its minorities were restless and revolted. Armenians revolted ineffectually (and were later punished with a massacre of at least a million); but the Arabs led by Thomas E. Lawrence broke completely free. By October 1918, the Turkish forces collapsed and the government agreed to the Armistice of Madros. The victorious Allies landed Greek and Italian forces in Anatolia and occupied Constantinople. The French made Syria a protectorate and Britain seized Palestine, Transjordan and Mesopotamia. The Arab Peninsula became completely independent.

When the Allies finally presented the Turkish government the Treaty of Sevres, a peace treaty that proposed even more dismembering of the Empire, the Turkish Nationalists, led by Mustapha Kemal Rasha revolted. While the Ottoman government meekly signed the treaty, the Nationalists fought against the Greek armies already in Turkey and negotiated agreements with other Allies. France and Italy were bought off with economic concessions while Russia was allowed to absorb most of the Armenians in the Armenian Soviet Socialist Republic. The Greeks were finally defeated and a new peace treaty, the Treaty of Lausanne, which allowed Turkey to retain Eastern Thrace, Constantinople and the intact Anatolia, was signed. The decade ended with the overthrow of the Sultanate and the declaration of the Republic of Turkey led by Mustapha Kemal (who took the name, Kemal Ataturk).

The French had difficulty holding Syria, which had been promised them. The Arabs revolted and the French had to depose their King Faisal. As the decade ended France was dividing up Syria into several small autonomous states.

English authorities also had tremendous difficulty. Iraq had two major insurrections; one of Arabs and the other of Kurds. Moreover King Faisal, of French-held Syria, fled into Iraq and was elected King of Iraq by a plebiscite. Palestine was even more troublesome, though not yet as violent. The Balfour Declaration stated that Palestine was to be established as a homeland for the Jewish People and Transjordania was to remain Moslem Arab. Jews began to settle and anti-Jewish riots had started before the decade was over.

The Arabian Peninsula was independent of Turkish control after World War I. However, the British had recognized two separate rulers — Sharif Hussein of Hajiz and Ibn Saud of Nejd; and the concessions made to them conflicted. This caused a war as both rulers fought for control of the Arabian Peninsula.

The Persian Empire had declared neutrality, but was too weak to enforce it. As it had in the past, it found itself a battleground of

European powers. First the Turks and Russians used Persia as a battle-ground. Then the Germans arrived and dominated for a year. The Russians displaced them, while the British seized control of Southern Persia. When Russia withdrew from Persia, due to its Bolshevik Revolution, the Empire fell into anarchy.

After the war the British and Russians made Persia their battleground. The British opposed Bolshevik Russia and took over Persia to prevent the Bolshevism. However the war between the Red and White forces of Russia did overlap into Persia. Eventually the British withdrew from northern Persia and 3000 Cossacks marched on Tehran led by Reza Khan and took over the government. He concluded a peace treaty with Bolshevik Russia and subdued Azerbaijan and a revolt in Gilan.

Eastern Europe Eastern Europe was where the Russian Empire battled Germany and Austria-Hungary, and all three were fragmented as a result of the War. Russia, due to its alliances with Serbia and France, did the initial mobilization that magnified the Serbo-Austrian conflict into a World War. Russia attacked both Austria and Germany. Despite initial success of Russia against Austria, the combined German / Austrian forces devastated the Russians, demoralizing the army which ultimately led to the Russian Revolution. Russia surrendered, and Germany formed the Polish state from their territory. Other Eastern European peoples chose the chaos of the Bolshevik Revolution and the humiliation of Russia as an opportune moment to escape Russian control*; thus Finland, the Ukraine, Latvia, Estonia, and Lithuania were established. The Treaty of Brest-Litovsk in 1918 formalized these separations. The Central Powers then proceded to sweep the Ukraine and Finland clear of Bolshevism.

Nineteen-eighteen was the beginning of the end for Austria-Hungary. Minorities of the empire had fought for the Allies demanding recognition of their national rights. As a result, the Allies insisted that Austria-Hungary be divided into Austria, Hungary, Yugoslavia and Czechoslovakia, and give territory to the already existing nations of Roumania, Italy and Poland. Moreover the Allies officially recognized the independence of the countries created by the Treaty of Brest-Litovsk.

This section will cover only countries that include portions of Austria-Hungary since most of the countries made entirely from Russian territory

---

*Russia got off to a bad start in the twentieth century with the humiliating defeats of the Russo-Japanese War and World War I. Then the government lost in very bloody revolutions (1905, 1918 and about 1922).

had to spend most of the decade struggling to confirm their independence. The Austro-Hungarian countries, however, were secure in their independence, since the old Empire was too crippled to attempt a reconquest. Instead, all of these countries began a series of wars to determine their national boundaries.

Hungary was probably the most warlike of the new nations. Hungary initially had become a republic and had initiated a series of land reforms when its government resigned to protest the territorial assignments of the Allies. A new government reformed under Bela Kun* and marched on Czechoslovakia in an attempt to seize Slovakia. Fearing attack on its newly acquired territory of Transylvania, Roumania attacked Hungary and seized its capital. At the same time a pro-monarchical counter-revolution swept the country and drove out Bela Kun. The Roumanians occupied the country, looting for the next six months until 1920, the same year Hungary signed the Treaty of Trianon recognizing its new limited borders. Even this didn't guarantee peace, since Hungary seized Austrian territory, endured a royal coup, and faced a threatened invasion from its neighbors in protest of monarchy, before the decade was over.

Poland had an almost equally violent history. Before World War I was even over, Poland was warring with the Ukraine over possession of Galacia. Immediately after the war Poland tried to expand to its 1772 boundaries. This involved occupying Posen, former German territory and brought it into conflict with Russia when it tried to take the Ukraine; and Lithuania when it successfully took Vilna. This resulted in constant turbulence as the new minorities resented their absorption by Poland.

Comparatively, Austria and Czechoslovakia were peaceful, since their only conflict was with Hungary over border territories. Czechoslovakia, made of some of the richest territory of the old Austro-Hungarian Empire, was fairly progressive and prosperous. By contrast, Austria, an industrial center now separated by tariff barriers from its raw materials and markets, went through an economic depression. It tried to unite with Germany but was forbidden by the Allies from doing so.

Russia Russia's disastrous defeats in World War I sparked mutinies and a coup forcing the Tsar to abdicate; and a provisional government took over. The provisional government granted the independence and autonomy of Poland, Estonia and Finland; and made widespread civil reform; but by continuing the war, insured its own downfall. The Bolshevik Revolution of November 6, 1917, overthrew the government, instituted Communist

---

*A Bolshevik who carried out a successful coup.

reforms of the economy and withdrew from the war. In the process it granted independence to its former territories of Estonia, Poland, Lithuania, Latvia, Trancaucasia, Moldavia, the Republic of Don, the Ukraine and Finland.

The new policies of the Soviet economy sparked a counter-revolution. The entire country was in a Civil War between Reds and Whites backed by the Allies. There were roughly six campaigns in the overall chaos, including one against the Cossacks, and four against newly independent republics. These four campaigns met with varying success: The Baltic-White Russian campaign reabsorbed White Russia, but had to concede independence to Estonia, Lithuania, Latvia and Finland; the Ukrainian campaign reabsorbed the Ukraine; the Southern Campaign reabsorbed Georgia, Armenia, and Azerbaijan; and the Eastern Campaign destroyed the autonomous Siberian Government and the Far Eastern Republic. Moreover the Allies, Britain, France and America invaded Murmansk and Archangel and set up a puppet government which was destroyed after the Allies left. Japan, Poland, Germany, Austria, Czechoslovakia as well as Britain, France and America, backed these independent countries.

The pressure of all these campaigns destroyed the Russian economy. Famine swept the country, bringing mutiny, and peasant uprisings and Red Terrorism to suppress it. Some 3,000,000 died in the famine and another 3,000,000 died in the fighting.

The former territories of Russia suffered enormously. Finland not only battled Russia for its independence, but underwent its own Red-White Civil War with the Whites winning. Estonia withstood two Russian assaults. Latvia was invaded not only by Russia, but also by Germany; while Lithuania was invaded by Russia, Germany and Poland.

South Asia The preoccupation of the European powers with World War I and the conscription it put on India sparked widespread unrest throughout South Asia. Afghanistan started a holy war against India but after a few invasions were thrown back negotiated a peace.

Meanwhile, in India an anti-British movement was sweeping the country. Millions were dying of influenza (approximately 18,000,000). The British attempted to terrorize the populace, and fired into a crowd (the Amritsar Massacre) killing 379 people; and sparked even more agitation. There was an uprising of Sikhs in the Punjab and a rising of Moplahs.

China While barely being involved in World War I, China was as troubled as the rest of the world. China declared war on Germany and Austria-Hungary and sent labor battalions to Europe, Africa and the

Middle East. In return it cancelled its Boxer indemnity to Germany and Austria-Hungary, and regained control of Tientsin and Hankow. Other German rights, however, were seized by Japan when it took the German-held Tsingtao and gave China the 21 Demands. Moreover Japan demanded special rights in Manchuria and Mongolia.

The government of China was falling into anarchy at this time. Yüan Shih-kái had to back down from establishing a new dynasty, following a rebellion in Yünan; and his successor was overthrown by a coalition of Nuthera Governors. The Manchus were temporarily restored and overthrown once again. Finally, in 1920, a Civil War broke out between warlords that reduced China to anarchy. What national government there was, merely sent envoys abroad but was unable to influence internal events.

During this time the Soviets established the Mongolian Peoples Revolutionary Government in Outer Mongolia, thus severing Outer Mongolia from Chinese rule.

Far East Japan was a major military power in this decade. Drawn into World War I by its treaty with England, Japan gained control of all formerly German-owned islands in the Pacific. Moreover it attacked German possessions in China and presented China with the Twenty-One Demands, gaining many of Germany's previous concessions.*

After the war Japan was equally restless. Internally there was serious rioting over universal suffrage, and externally it was dragged by its treaty with England into invading Vladivostok and Siberia in an attempt to subdue Bolshevism. The troops eventually withdrew from Russia but

---

*Note the complexity of the situation:

China declaring and engaging in war against Germany and Austria-Hungary.

Japan declaring war against Germany and Austria-Hungary; but attacking those countries, holdings in China; and China itself — its ally.

Russia had fought Germany and Austria-Hungary; lost; signed a treaty. Subsequently, it was attacked by most of its allies who took more from it than its former enemies had.

Russia seized upon China's weakness and took Mongolia from China.

Russia was attacked by Roumania because Russia tried to take Bessarabia which had been promised to Roumania.

Greece had to fight Turkey again because a rebellion within the Ottoman Empire abrogated the treaty.

Italy seized the opportunity to try to wrest Corfu away from both Greece (to which it had been assigned) and Turkey — who was trying to avoid giving it up.

Ireland seized upon Great Britain's discomfort to break away.

It was like a death-struggle melée in a starving pack of wolves.

retained Northern Sakhalin.

Korea revolted for its independence and was severely repressed.

North America Although all of North America went to war, Mexico remained the most tumultuous of the three countries. The decade opened with Mexico still in its Revolution. Not only was there conflict over control of the central government, which began the decade under Huerta, but various sections of Mexico were held by Zapata, Villa, Obregon and Carranza. Armies marched on Mexico City and overthrew the government twice in 1915, once in 1920 and again in 1923. War swept throughout the provinces as different armies struggled to increase their borders.

Twice the turmoil led to international incidents. In 1914 the arrest of American Marines provoked the United States into seizing Vera Cruz. Later, when Pancho Villa's army invaded New Mexico in pursuit of Mexican refugees, the United States invaded Mexico in return. After almost a year of fruitlessly pursuing Villa, the American troops returned to their own country.

The United States then entered World War I. Although it was officially in the war for a year-and-a-half, it was in active fighting for only three months. After the War, the United States enjoyed both external and internal peace interrupted by only an occasional major strike.

Canada also entered World War I. Its casualties were comparatively light, but the conscription acts aroused French-Canadian wrath, and provoked rioting. After the war Canada enjoyed both internal and external peace.

(*ED. NOTE:* World War I was a new experience for the world. The cost was estimated to be: 65 million troops mobilized with 8 million killed and 21.2 million wounded: 6.6 million civilians died [with an additional 20 million deaths due to influenza pandemic arising from war conditions]. Thus, the total deaths were about 35 million. The cost was about $281 billion in money.)

1924-1933 A.D.

VERY WARM.

Iberian Peninsula The Iberian Peninsula was torn by internal revolt. Spain was filled with unrest under Rivera, and finally he ended his dictatorship. Later in 1920, Catalonia tried to revolt and three years later a military revolt swept Ciudad Real. Universities all over the country had to be closed as student unrest spread. Another meeting indicated even military support for a republic. Finally, Alfonso XIII left Spain in 1931 and was replaced by a liberal republic which, among its other acts, recognized the autonomy of Catalonia. This liberalism provoked an unsuccessful counter movement in Seville, radical unrest in all major cities where the liberal regime was felt to be too slow, and minority unrest by groups like the Basques who also demanded independence.

Portugal was also struggling to survive revolution. In 1925 they had a bloody but unsuccessful coup followed in the next year by a large successful military revolt. The government was destroyed, but the new leader found himself facing a "communist" revolt of intellectual reformers. These were crushed and the government evolved into a dictatorship.

External expansion was almost non-existant. Portugal gained 480 square miles in a trade with Belgium along the Congo-Angolan border. Spain found itself fighting with even greater frustration against the forces of Abd-el-Krim in Morocco until France aided in his suppression.

Northern Europe Northern Europe was hit by a crippling depression. Norway and Sweden probably survived best due to tremendous social programs designed by the government; in fact, Norway even managed to expand. It annexed both Bouvet and Peter Island and attempted to annex East Greenland; but backed down when the Permanent Court of International Justice ruled that Greenland belonged to Denmark.

Denmark and Finland experienced the depression with even more severity. In Denmark this led to unrest among the Germans of North Schleswig; and in Finland, fascists (lapua) revolted twice.

Belgium and the Netherlands had the increased difficulty of coping with a depression and problems in foreign territories. The Belgian Congo was quiet, but the Netherlands had to subdue a fierce Communist uprising in the East Indies in 1926-27.

England, like the Low Lands, had to cope with depression and restless colonies. The Labor government lost office, and revolts swept Palestine, India and China against British control. Meanwhile, they had to cope with the beginning of religious disturbances in Ireland. The disturbances were sparked by Ireland's economic woes in the depression.

Germany suffered perhaps worst of all. Its economy had already been crippled by the war debts and occupation of its industrial centers. It had begun to recover when the Rhineland separatist movement ended and the Saar was evacuated when the depression destroyed all recovery efforts. Unrest prevailed between Nazis and Communists, and ultimately to restore peace, Adolf Hitler, leader of the Nazis was made Chancellor.

Southern Europe Southern Europe experienced internal peace and used this time to reconquer colonies that had escaped their control during World War I or that were currently trying to escape their control. Italy campaigned against the Libyan tribesmen for eight years and reconquered them by 1930. France conquered the interior of French Morocco and allied itself with Spain to subdue Abd-el-Krim and his fellow Riffs. They also had to devote two years to subdue the Great Insurrection of Druses in Syria.

The worldwide depression hit both countries hard. The Italian Fascists tightened their control over the entire country while the French experienced a series of short-lived cabinets as a result of their financial difficulties. To compound the difficulties of France they had to cope with several severe outbreaks in the Tonkin area (French Indochina).

The Balkans The Balkans were, by comparison, incredibly peaceful this decade. The only international conflicts in the Balkans were between Greece and Bulgaria and between Albania and Italy. The Bulgarian-Greek incident was a border dispute that resulted in an invasion of Bulgaria, and was settled by the League of Nations. The Albanian incident was the appearance of the Italian fleet off the coastline which intimidated Albania's government into allowing Italian colonization and more Italian domination. A series of frontier incidents along the Albanian-Yugoslav border caused a rupture in Yugoslavian-Albanian relations. While these incidents might seem tumultuous in another part of the world, for the restless Balkans this was comparatively calm.

Internally, this was a time of short-lived governments and widespread friendship treaties with a multitude of countries. Albania was first a republic which later evolved into a monarchy, crowning its former president. Bulgaria was troubled by feuding factions of Macedonians and Communist terrorists. Several governments tried to pacify them with methods that varied from conciliatory to harsh. Greece became a republic, but experienced a rapid turnover of government. Roumania, a constitutional monarchy, had 3 monarchs during this decade as well as a number of cabinets. Yugoslavia, like the other Balkan countries, experienced international peace but had a rapid turnover of governments due to the pressure of its restless minorities.

North Africa North Africa attempted to free itself of European influence during this decade with varying degrees of success. Egypt, for example, had been declared independent in the last decade but had to spend most of the decade negotiating with Great Britain on the terms of this independence. The Sudan was to remain British territory and British soldiers were to be stationed along the Suez Canal. There were several disagreements over

Sudanese use of Nile water and over British-Egyptian terms. The decade ended with a new constitution and anti-missionary, anti-Christian riots.

While Algeria caused France little trouble, Morocco was a different story. The Riffians were led by Abd-el-Krim. After driving the Spanish to the coast of Morocco, the Riffians attacked France. Eventually, Spain and France had to unite to subdue Abd-el-Krim. However when the world economic slump hit North Africa, Morocco was plagued by drought, depression and locusts, and native unrest exploded. Once again France had to embark on a pacification campaign. Inland, Libya had rebelled from Italian control during World War I. It was reinstated after an eight-year campaign by Italy.

Middle East All portions of the Middle East endured major revolts. Some of these were minorities, like the Kurds, while others were Arabs revolting against European domination.

Syria, under French control, had a Great Druse Insurrection when the Druses* felt that the French favored Christians. The rebellion was crushed and a republic was declared. Moderates were elected in the first election. The Druses remain a very powerful, totally uncompromising, forceful people.

Iraq, Palestine, and Transjordania were British. Iraq and Transjordania, totally Moslem, were more peaceful. Transjordania was made an autonomous state under King Abdullea Ibn Hussein, with Britain retaining economic and military control. Iraq experienced two Kurdish uprisings and a migration of Christian Assyrians which the Moslems quickly killed.

The three independent Middle Eastern countries of Persia, Saudi Arabia, and Turkey also endured internal revolts. Persia had a coup that drove out the previous shah and began the Pahlavi dynasty. The dynasty established itself firmly but was troubled by a large Kurdish insurrection. Turkey came firmly under the control of Mustapha Kemal (who became Kemal Ataturk). It suffered two large unsuccessful Kurdish revolts and a Dervish revolt. Saudi Arabia, which began this decade with a war between the rulers of Hajiz and Nejd, was in 1926 proclaimed to belong solely to Ibn Saud of Nejd. In 1932 it was invaded by rebels from Transjordania and this provoked an insurrection in Nejd.

---

*The Druses are followers of the 11th Century A.D. Fatimid Caliph of Egypt — Al-hakim bi'amrillahi, the son of a Russian mother, self-proclaimed incarnation of Allah — who established a reign of terror at Cairo, then disappeared in 1021 A.D. The Druses participate fully in the religious practices of the people among whom they live, and have no ceremonies of their own.

Eastern Europe There was international peace in Eastern Europe during this decade. Although no countries went to war, all were hit by the 1930 depression and most experienced German agitation, Fascism and dictatorships.

Austria, Czechoslovakia, and Poland all had large German minorities that agitated for union with Germany. All of Austria, with its entirely German population, tried to form a customs union with Germany but Western powers halted the union and destroyed Austria's economy in the process. After the victory of the Nazis in Germany, anti-governmental riots and demonstrations mounted in Austria and terrorism spread. Czechoslovakia, which had complaints from all its minorities and was trying to grant them more self-government, had particular trouble with the Nazi agitation among the three million Germans along the border (Sudetenland). Poland under Pilsudski and the rule of the military junta also had difficulties with its Ukrainian and German minorities, but its German minority along the Polish Corridor was a particular source of friction. The corridor, which gave Poland access to the sea cut Germany into two pieces. This geographic separation was intolerable to the Germans.

The three Baltic nations of Lithuania, Latvia, and Estonia also had their German Problems, since originally most of the landed wealth and influence was in German hands. Social legislation broke up these huge estates and the resentment of the German minority served as a constant invitation to intervention. As a result, Lithuania and Latvia made non-aggression pacts with Russia; with Estonia, which experienced Communist uprisings, resisting. The three drew closer together.

Hungary had little to no German population. It had a conservative regime with close ties to Fascist Italy. By 1933, it was hit with widespread Nazi agitation.

Russia Russia began this decade with the death of Lenin and the three-year power struggle. Despite this struggle there was some progress. The Japanese were persuaded to withdraw from Northern Sakhalin. Also during this period, the constitution was revised and new republics were added to the federation. By the end of 1927, Stalin's forces had won control of the government.

With Stalin in charge, new socialist programs were initiated at considerable cost of human life. Millions (the Kulaks) were executed or exiled in the collectivization of Russian farms. Heavy industry was built. After four years of this program, a massive famine swept the country (1931-33; 3 million dead). This disaster should not be attributed to—or at least not solely to—politics. There was a disastrous drought.

The decade ended on a negative note. The Communist Party purged itself of one third of the membership. At the border of Outer Mongolia several dangerous incidents against the Japanese hinted at future conflict.

South Asia South Asia broke out into violence. In Afghanistan a revolt against the royal family overthrew the monarchy, and replaced it with a former bandit leader as dictator. Within the year he was executed. Mohammed Nadir Shah became ruler. He concentrated on modernizing Afghanistan and when he was assassinated his son became ruler.

Meanwhile, India was filled with turmoil. When the British Simon Commission toured India to study the situation, mass agitation took place. Later, from 1930 to 1933, Gandhi led two major civil disobedience campaigns. Peshawar revolted.

China This was the decade of Communist uprisings, and the governments attempted to regain Chinese control of Chinese territory. There was growing Japanese aggression. To understand the situation at this time, one should realize that by now China was more similar to Europe than to the U.S., Russia, or other large unified nations. China was composed of a collection of sovereignties, each with separate dialects and government. Different warlords had staked out claims to different sections of the countryside and ruled independently, quarreling over boundaries. Rivers like the Yang-tze were *de facto* international waters, flowing past borders rather than inside a national territory. The Chinese national government was rather like today's United Nations. It handled foreign affairs and occasionally intervened militarily in dangerous situations, but it actually had very little direct power over the Chinese people.

China was in a state of civil war. In 1924 the Kuomintong, which at that time admitted Communists and had Russian advisors, had a national congress and agreed to try to regain control of the countryside. The campaign against northern warlords began in 1926, but halted a year later due to Communist uprisings. The Communists killed six foreigners in Nanking, provoking an international force of 40,000 to protect Shanghai. At the same time Communists under Mao Tse-tung seized land in Fukien and Kiangsi. The Kuomintong separated itself from the Communists and Russians and established headquarters in Nanking. It established a temporary truce, then began war against the Communists that resulted in over a million deaths and lasted into the next decade.

Resentment against foreigners and "unequal treaties" was rising. Widespread boycotts of British and Japanese plus renegotiations of treaties between foreign powers and the Nanking government of Chiang K'ai-shek led to nine nations losing their extra-territorial privileges in China and all nations agreeing to eventually abolishing it. Britain gave up control of Werhaiwei, Hankow and Kiukiang and Russia gave up Tientsin and Hankow and the rest of the Boxer indemnity.

Japan on the other hand became more aggressive. Chiang K'ai-shek's first campaign against the northern warlords had been blocked by Japanese troops stationed in Tsinan to protect civilians. A second campaign in 1928 again found itself fighting Japanese. Peking was successfully seized by Chiang and the Chinese expressed annoyance at Japanese interference with a boycott on Japanese goods. Unpleasant incidents occurred and finally on September 18, 1931, the Japanese began the seizure of Manchuria. The war against the Communists and massive floods on the Yangtze preoccupied the Chinese government and prevented effective resistance. The Chinese reacted with more intensive boycotting which provoked a Japanese attack on Shanghai. When the Japanese troops marched south of the Great Wall, China evacuated Tientsin. Japan claimed protection over the "independent nation" of Manchukuo, formerly Manchuria.

Far East The Far East was dominated during this decade and the next by the growing power of Japan. Japan's population was growing at a huge rate and emigration was failing as a solution. (America had forbidden any more Japanese emigration by 1924.)* Industrialization and foreign trade became necessary for survival. When this foreign trade became threatened, the Japanese society turned to military expansion.

Japanese-Chinese relations were dominated by the theme of Japanese militarism. Japan protected its concessions with military actions which provoked the Chinese to retaliate with economic boycotts and small unpleasant incidents like the murder of Nakamura by Chinese officers in West Manchuria. This in turn provoked the Japanese into a more militant stance. Thus you have the Japanese intervention in Shantung, the Sino-Japanese clashes in Tsinan and ultimately the Mukden Incident (an explosion on a railroad) that led to the Japanese takeover of Manchuria. The invasion of Shanghai, Jahal and control of Hopei by the Japanese followed. As military action dominated Japanese policy, it began to dominate the Japanese home government.

---

*The Protestant majority of the U.S., as late as 1928, defeated the Roman Catholic Democrat Al Smith for President, because of the implicit fealty of a Catholic for the Pope — who is head of a sovereignty — the Vatican. This was true, even though the Vatican was not military. By way of analogy, consider the American 1940 perception of the Japanese, many of whom continued to be Shinto — which is Emperor worship; the Emperor being the Head of State of an aggressive military power.

North America This decade was one of internal unrest and international peace in North America. Both Canada and the United States started the decade with a governmental scandal, the Teapot Dome in the U.S., and a customs scandal that unseated Prime Minister King in Canada. Both countries then were hit severely by depression, the U.S.A. beginning in 1929 with the Stock Market Crash; Canada a year later. Massive unrest filled both countries and caused a political change in the government, from Liberal to Conservative in Canada and from Republican to Democrat in the United States. The new governments started massive programs to relieve unemployment and suffering.

Mexico was dominated by Plutarco Elias Calles during this decade. He was always either President or the power behind the presidency. He initiated agrarian and educational reform and broke the power of the Roman Catholic Church in Mexico, nationalizing its lands, closing its schools and deporting foreign nuns, monks and priests. This provoked two great insurrections both of which were successfully crushed. As the decade progressed a compromise was worked out with the Church and the government becoming more conservative.

1934-1943 A.D.
VERY WARM, BUT STARTING TO COOL.

Iberian Peninsula The Spanish Civil War completely dominated the peninsula during this decade. The liberal government of Spain had provoked radical revolts from groups impatient with its rate of change, and, by granting autonomy to Catalonia, had provoked unrest among hopeful nationalists in Asturias and among the Basques. Its anti-clerical policy, distribution of land, and social reforms finally brought a conservative backlash.

The backlash started among the troops stationed in Morocco led by General Francisco Franco and spread to every garrison town in Spain. Italy and Germany intervened on behalf of the Insurgents, who chose Franco as their head, and before the conflict was over, Italy had sent over 50,000 troops and Germany over 10,000. Russia aided the Loyalists which included the government, liberals, communists, and sectional separatists. (This included the Basques who were given home rule in 1936.) The Loyalists fought bitterly, but by 1939, with the capture of Madrid and Valencia, were defeated. A coup in Madrid resulted in a government which tried to negotiate a peace. This produced a communist uprising which it had to put down before trying once again to negotiate a truce. It was unsuccessful and by March 28 the war was over and

Franco controlled Spain. Exhausted with war, Spain remained neutral during World War II. Spain lost a million dead in the revolution.

Portugal began this decade with a conservative dictatorship and an unsuccessful communist uprising. This made the government extremely sympathetic to the conservative Insurgents of Spain. It not only aided them but allowed its territory to be a highway for munitions from Germany and elsewhere. Tied by traditional bonds to Britain and philosophical bonds to Germany, Portugal refused to enter World War II and stayed neutral.

The neutrality of the Iberian Peninsula could not entirely keep them from being involved. Both countries found their trade heavily restricted. Meanwhile the Spanish Falangists sent a volunteer division to fight against Russia, and the Portuguese found their colony of Timor occupied first by the Japanese, then by the Australians and Dutch, while the Azores became a British naval base.

Northern Europe The growing power of Nazi Germany and World War II dominated Northern Europe. The new Nazi government was solving its economic woes by military growth and rejection of the Versailles Treaty which had been crippling Germany since World War I. It reabsorbed (unofficially in the case of Danzig which behaved like part of Germany) the Rhineland and the Saar provinces which the treaty had taken from it. Its military was tested during the Spanish Civil War and found worthy.

The next step was invading Austria which had previously tried to unite with Germany, but had been forbidden to do so. Next was the destruction of Czechoslovakia, absorbing first Sudetenland, then Moravia and Bohemia. Again, despite international conferences and warnings, there was no resistance.

A society whose economy is based upon its military must eventually use it. This came about in 1939 when Germany demanded the right to reabsorb the Polish Corridor which the Versailles Treaty had taken from it. Poland resisted all demands; so on September 1, after concluding a pact with Russia, Germany invaded. Poland's allies, France and England, declared war.

Germany's military exploded into action. Before the year was out, Poland was conquered and divided with Russia. In the next year Denmark, Belgium, Luxembourg, and France were conquered and Britain was attacked. Italy, Japan, Roumania and Hungary allied themselves with Germany. In the next year it gained two new allies—Bulgaria and Finland—and conquered Yugoslavia, Lithuania, Latvia, Estonia, and Greece. The Russian campaign began, the Western Ukraine was seized and Moscow and

Leningrad were beseiged. Campaigns began in North Africa in defense of their Italian ally.

The next two years were the turning point. American forces arrived and the Axis powers were driven out of North Africa. After spectacular gains in Russia, taking territory from Leningrad to Stalingrad, the Germans began to lose; withdrawing from all of the Ukraine to the Dnieper by the end of the decade. Fascist Italy collapsed and Germans had to pour in to defend it.

Besides this external violence, Nazi Germany was filled with government-controlled internal violence. Even before German expansion, the Nazis persecuted Jews, executed the mentally unsound, and bloodily purged itself of the S.A.* As expansion began, millions were enslaved and recruited for a labor-starved Germany. Others were driven from their land to give Germans more living room (Lebensraum). Still other "inferior races" of Jews, Slavs and Gypsies were systematically exterminated. The conquered territories teemed with partisan resistance and bloody revenge was necessary.

All of Northern Europe was affected by this great struggle. Even Sweden, officially neutral, had to allow the Germans to march through it. Denmark was seized in 1940, as was Norway. Norway, a leader in polar exploration before the war, (it had claimed over a million miles of Antarctic territory in 1939) put up resistance and was aided by British troops. Finland, on the other hand, found itself trapped between Russia and Germany, and it was Russia that attacked first. Russia demanded the right to establish air and naval bases. When Finland refused, Russia attacked. After heavy casualties, Finland yielded, giving up the Karelian Ismus and over 16,000 square miles (some 10% of all Finnish territory). Thus when Germany attacked Russia, it found eager allies among the Finns.

The Low Countries were casualties in the German invasion of France. All were conquered in 1940 and used as an invasion route to France. The

---

*The S.A. (storm troopers) were led by the able, but extremist, Ernst Roehm; the radical Gregor Strasser; Erich Klausener, a prominent Catholic leader. These men had aimed at incorporating the storm troops into the army. Hitler had formed the S.S. (defense corps), an elite, highly-educated, extremely lethal and fanatically devoted to the Nazi ideology.

When Hindenberg died (2 August) and Hitler succeeded to power and styled himself the "Fuhrer"; he had carried out his part of the 11 April, 1934, pact he had made on the Deutschland with the German Army Commander General von Fritsch and the Navy Commander Admiral Raeder. In return for their support of his succession of Hindenberg, he had the S.S. murder the entire leadership of the S.A. (some 400 to 1,000 men) on 30 June, 1934, "the night of the long knives."

The meek have not inherited the earth.

Netherlands suffered additionally by having its Pacific territories conquered by Germany's ally, Japan.

Before the war, Britain found itself coping with its troublesome Arab territories and trying to limit Axis expansion through the League of Nations and international conferences. The Palestinian territory was especially bothersome as the British found themselves having to quell anti-Jewish riots. A mandate that would have separated the territory into Jewish and Arab land was proposed, but further Arab demonstrations postponed it. Several towns were seized by Arab extremists and British troops had to retrieve them.

British attempts to limit Axis aggression were uniformly unsuccessful and climaxed at Munich. As it became obvious that these tactics would not work, Britain concentrated on forming protective alliances. Egyptian relations were smoothed by withdrawing all troops except for 10,000 soldiers stationed along the Suez Canal, and yielding the Sudan to Egyptian control. Alliances between Britain, Russia, and France were attempted, and a mutual assistance treaty with Poland showed an end to appeasement.

England declared war when Poland was attacked. By 1940 it found itself driven from the continent and under heavy bombardment. Its African colony of Somaliland was taken by Fascist Italy. In the next year its colonies of Hong Kong and Malaya were taken by Japan, and its Pacific fleet was attacked.

England, however, did not remain long on the defensive. Aided by the Commonwealth nations, the Free French, American, and underground movements throughout Europe, England again took the offensive. Airstrikes and naval blockades of Germany began immediately. Campaigns against Italian-held territory in North Africa and Dakar began in 1940 and by 1943 had successfully driven all Axis powers from North Africa. Iraq and Syria, both of which showed Axis sympathies were invaded and conquered. Almost 60,000 soldiers were sent to Greece to aid its successful resistance against Italy and Germany. Allied with the U.S., British forces invaded first Sicily, then Southern Italy. Iran was successfully pressured into cooperating with the British war effort. In the Far East, after losing Burma, the Allied forces successfully defeated an attempted Japanese invasion of Australia or the New Hebrides at the Battle of the Coral Sea. British, Australian, and New Zealand forces joined the United States in an island campaign against Japan.

Ireland, protected from German aggression by its geographical location behind England, could afford the luxury of complete neutrality. Its sympathies, however, for the Axis, made it extremely offensive.

Southern Europe Both major Southern European countries were extremely active militarily before World War II. France had to deal with two major colonial uprisings, one in Morocco, the other in Syria. It came close to warring with Turkey to insure the establishment of the Republic of Hatay which two years later, anxious for Turkish neutrality in case of a World War, it allowed Turkey to absorb. Italy was even more aggressive, seizing Ethiopia and Albania and intervening heavily in favor of Franco in the Spanish Civil War. Italy furthermore had been the one country to oppose Hitler and had prevented Germany from taking any action in Austria in 1934 when a Nazi coup aborted.

When England and France declared war on Germany in 1939, Italy, which had concluded agreements with all three countries remained neutral. After Germany had invaded the Low Countries and France and forced the British to retreat at Dunkirk, Italy chose sides and declared war on Britain and France. Italy invaded Southern France while Germany invaded the north and France was forced to surrender. Three-fifths of France came directly under German control while the rest was under the puppet government of Petain.

Over 140,000 French had escaped at Dunkirk and they were joined by General Charles de Gaulle to form the Free French. These worked side-by-side with the British throughout the war.

Surrendering to Germany did not guarantee peace for Vichy France. All of France was filled with an active underground and Germany dealt out harch reprisals and executed or enslaved thousands. French Indo-China was occupied by Japan. Even its former allies preyed upon it, the British destroying its navy rather than allowing it to be used by the Germans. The British and Free French seized Syria, Americans and British captured French North Africa and West Africa, a move that precipitated German seizure of Vichy France.

Italy was a weak and dangerous ally. Time and time again it diverted the German military from its plans. After invading France and aiding Germany in its air strikes against Britain, Italy launched a campaign against Greece. When Greece, with British aid, defeated Italy and invaded Italian-held Albania, Germany was forced to come to Italy's aid, delaying its Russian Campaign. Italy again started a campaign in Africa, taking British Somaliland and Egypt. In December 1940, however, the British attacked the Italians in Africa and after defeating them in East Africa faced the German-reinforced Italians in North Africa. Eventually the entire Axis was driven out of Africa, suffering enormous losses.

This was followed in 1943 by the Allied invasion of Sicily and Italy.

Mussolini was forced to resign and the new Italian government surrendered. Germany, once again, had to intervene and brought Mussolini back into power. Germans seized the country and blocked the Allied advance in Southern Italy.

Switzerland was the one country in Southern Europe allowed to remain neutral. Its threats to destroy all highways through its mountain passes made its conquest too costly for Germany to attempt.

Balkans Even before World War II the Balkans were internally restless. Albania was dominated by Italy, had a Moslem insurrection and was absorbed by Italy in 1939. Bulgaria had three coups. Greece experienced two coups and a revolt in Crete. Roumania endured a Fascist government, which the king then dismissed, and a major anti-Fascist campaign followed. Yugoslavia had its king assassinated, nearly went to war with Hungary and finally reorganized its government into a democratic federation that granted its Croat minority autonomy.

World War II, with the destruction of Czechoslovakia and the fall of France changed the international balance. Roumania had depended upon its alliances with France and Czechoslovakia to protect its claim to the land it had won from its neighbors in the Balkan Wars and World War I. Russia, Bulgaria, and Hungary immediately took advantage of this weakness to seize territory. Germany moved troops into Roumania in order to "protect" its oil fields from Russian control. Roumania and Bulgaria, seeing the inevitability of German domination, joined the Berlin-Rome-Tokyo pact. Yugoslavia's government attempted to do the same but was overthrown the day after the treaty was signed. Within a month Germany had invaded and conquered Yugoslavia.

Greece suffered a different fate. Italy demanded the use of Greek bases and when Greece refused, it was attacked. Britain immediately came to the aid of Greece and the Greeks wound up invading Albania, capturing almost 28,000 prisoners. Italy called upon Germany for aid and Greece was conquered, forcing the British to evacuate thousands of soldiers.

North Africa North Africa attempted to gain more independence from European control. There were violent anti-Jewish riots in Algeria and an unsuccessful rebellion in French Morocco. The rebellion of the military in Spanish Morocco spread and started the Spanish Civil War. Egypt used political pressure to get Britain to withdraw its forces from the Sudan and all of Egypt except the Suez Canal.

All chances of independence in this decade ended with World War II. Italy was imperialistic and tried to take Egypt. The British began a surprise

drive and not only defended Egypt but invaded Libya. Germany intervened and drove the British back to El Alamein. Almost simultaneously,
the British began a westward sweep from Egypt, and the Anglo-American
forces under Eisenhower seized French Morocco and Algeria from Vichy
France and swept East. The Axis was caught in the pincer movement
and trapped in Tunisia. Finally it had to abandon its North African
campaign to the Allies.

Middle East The countries not under European power spent this decade
insuring they would not be dragged into a European war while the countries
under European domination struggled to gain freedom.

Syria was forced to agree to a treaty that gave France extensive control
over its financial, military and foreign affairs in exchange for independence.
Rioting broke out against the treaty but it was ratified anyway. Minority
groups objected to the treaty. The Kurds revolted demanding independence
and were crushed. The Turks of Alexandretta revolted for independence
and were granted a separate republic of Hatay.

Palestine, under Britain, was also filled with Arab rioting. Britains studied
the situation and recommended a division into three parts, one under Jewish
control, one under British, and the third under Arab. This provoked
Arab resistance, and finally pitched Jewish-Arab battles. The British were
forced to delay the mandate and sent over 25,000 troops to Palestine.
Bombing shook Jerusalem, Haifa and Jaffa. Palestine was swept into an
undeclared war. The British finally called a Jewish-Arab conference and
agreed to grant Palestine independence in ten years.

The independent Middle Eastern states started to form protective
alliances. Iraq, which experienced revolts and a coup, allied itself with
Turkey, Iran and Afghanistan, an Oriental entente. Saudi Arabia which
had successfully defeated Yemen after numerous border incidents, was
prevented from seizing Yemen by a British peace settlement, and formed
alliances with Iraq and Egypt.

World War II was not as traumatic on the Middle East as it was on
the rest of the world. Syria and Lebanon were invaded by the British
and Free French, and by 1943 both were given independence. Iraq, which
originally invited German aid was occupied by the British and soon it declared war on the Axis. Iran had its Shah forced to abdicate by British
and Soviet forces; and subsequently declared war on Germany. The
Palestinians aided the British. The other countries, Turkey, Saudi Arabia,
and Yemen remained neutral though friendly to the Allies.

Eastern Europe The countries of Eastern Europe were hopelessly trapped between two antagonistic giants, Communist Russia and Nazi Germany. All were either absorbed or forced to join the Berlin-Rome-Tokyo alliance.

Austria was the first to be destroyed. Dollfuss had just assumed dictatorial powers when he was assassinated in a Nazi coup. The coup was aborted and German aid was prevented by a strong Italian and Yugoslavian stance. A new dictator, Schuschnigg, formed an alliance with Germany. Nazi-inspired disorder spread throughout the countryside and caused a plebiscite. However, before the plebiscite could be carried out, the Germans invaded. They destroyed all opposition to unification then held the plebiscite and announced its approval of their action.

Czechoslovakia was next. It foresaw its danger and formed protective alliances with Russia, France, Austria, Yugoslavia, Hungary and Roumania. The Germans of the Sudetenland were a restive minority and finally in September of 1938 Hitler demanded that they be allowed to join Germany. An international conference was held and all of Czechoslovakia's allies abandoned it. It was allowed to be dismembered with Sudete being taken by Germany and Slovakia and Ruthenia becoming independent. Early in the next year Germany absorbed the rest of Czechoslovakia, the provinces of Bohemia and Moravia and Northern Slovakia. Hungary absorbed Southern Slovakia and Ruthenia.

Poland was next. Like Austria and Czechoslovakia it had a large German population, and it tried to protect itself with treaties with both Russia and Germany. The government abandoned democracy and attempted to "Polonize" its population. This led to massive peasant strikes and Ukrainian unrest. It took advantage of international unrest to force demands on Lithuania and seize part of Czechoslovakia. Friction continued with Germany over the Polish Corridor and Germany, making an agreement with Russia, attacked and divided the country, starting World War II in the process.

The Baltic nations seeing their potential fate, formed the Baltic Pact. They formed non-aggression pacts with Germany even though Germany forced Lithuania to yield Memel. After the seizure of Poland, Russia prepared for possible attack by seizing all three nations. When Germany attacked Russia it absorbed the three Baltic nations in the process.

Hungary was the only nation that remained unabsorbed. It had a large restless German and Nazi element. After it became obvious that alliances with other nations would not protect it, it assumed Nazi-like policies. It absorbed portions of Czechoslovakia when it was dismembered and seized sections of Roumania when it was weakened by the fall of its ally, France. In 1940 it joined the Berlin-Rome-Tokyo Axis and aided Germany in its attack on Russia.

Russia Russia was acutely aware of the potential danger of the Axis. It found itself fighting Japan in Eastern Siberia and Manchuria. It formed numerous alliances, the most important being with its neighbors and with France, and began a major rearmament program. Massive purges cleaned party and government, leaving in mostly young people who could not remember pre-Bolshevik days. Finally the Czechoslovakian crisis came and Russia announced that it would protect Czechoslovakia if France did. When France chose appeasement, Russia concentrated on strengthening its own position in case it too was abandoned.

It concluded a trade agreement with Germany and together they divided Poland. Then, not trusting in treaties, it absorbed the Balkan states in order to use them for naval and air stations. An attempt to do the same with Finland resulted in the bloody three-month Russo-Finnish War. Russia won and took over 16,000 square miles and the right to establish its bases.

The attack it had been preparing for came in June 1941. Russia's harsh policy toward its neighbors backfired. The Finns aided Germany and the conquered territories of the Soviet, the Baltic states, White Russia, and the Ukraine did not effectively aid Russia in resisting invasion. (Indeed, Ukrainians greeted the Germans with flowers). During the warm weather Germany laid siege to Leningrad and Moscow, and seized the Ukraine west of the Dnieper.

Winter came and revealed the one Russian advantage - its deadly climate. The Germans were not equipped to handle the cold and fought poorly under its influence. The U.S. arranged a lend-lease program and the Russians made some small gains.

The German summer drive of 1942 was devastatingly effective. Germans seized the Ukraine and Northern Caucasus and controlled from Stalingrad to Leningrad. By November they reached their farthest line of advance. Winter came again and with it came a Russian offensive. The Germans lost Stalingrad and were driven back. When warm weather came again it was the Russians who took the offensive and the Germans were driven back to the Dnieper.

South Asia Southern Asia was restless before the war but experienced little effect of the actual World War. Afghanistan had an unsuccessful religious revolt in 1938. During the war it remained neutral, but as a gesture of friendship to the Allies asked citizens of the Axis to leave.

India had spent the pre-war years striving for independence while a greater and greater rift grew between Hindu and Moslem. During the war

India declared war on Germany. In return England promised autonomy after the war. Disturbances spread throughout the country as leaders demanded immediate autonomy and the decade ended with the British reorganizing the country to give Indians more of a say in the government.

China China spent this decade battling Japan. The Japanese unsuccessfully encouraged the five northern provinces to secede in an attempt to weaken China in order to make it easier to control. Instead the national government became stronger. Chiang K'ai-shek subdued Kwangtung and Kwang si. Meanwhile, the communists in Fukien and Kiang si were dislodged and took the Long March to Shensi. Once there they called for an end to Chinese fighting Chinese and a united battle against the Japanese. A Communist literally had to kidnap Chiang K'ai-shek to get him to assume the lead in a united Chinese defense against Japan. In July 1937, Japan began a campaign absorbing Northern China and in August a drive up the Yangtse began. The Chinese were short of supplies and lost steadily, forcing the capital to move inland to Chung King. However, resistance did not die. A pattern had emerged by 1943. Japan could control the city and transportation centers, but the countryside lay in the hands of the Chinese guerrillas.

Far East Japan's aggressiveness dominated the Far East as completely as Germany's aggressiveness dominated Europe. During most of the early part of this decade, Japan concentrated on trying to control China. After trying, unsuccessfully, to manipulate the Northern Chinese provinces into secession, Japan became more direct and in 1937 invaded China. As it succeeded in the cities where it consistently won, the majority of the Chinese remained undefeated and continued resistance.

The events in Europe left the European colonies in Asia ripe for the taking. Japan seized French Indo-China. When it did, the U.S. objected and placed an embargo on the sale of goods to Japan. This was hitting in Japan's most sensitive spot, its economy, and guaranteed war.

War came on December 7, 1941, when the Japanese launched a surprise attack on Pearl Harbor. Simultaneously, attacks were mounted on the Philippines, Hong Kong, and Malaya; all territories the Japanese felt that an uninjured U.S. would defend. Before the year was over Wake Island, Guam, and Hong Kong had surrendered. In the next year Japan successfully conquered the Philippines, Dutch Indonesia, Burma, Malaya and Singapore.

But 1942 was also a turning point. The battle of the Coral Sea halted a Japanese invasion of either the New Hebrides or Australia. A second sea battle at Midway crippled the all-important carrier fleet. Meanwhile, Americans landing in the Solomon Islands were giving the Japanese their first defeats on land.

While all this was going on, over a million Japanese troops were still battling in China, and Russian-Japanese conflicts at the Manchuria-Mongolia border diverted still more men.

North America The three North American nations experienced internal and external peace until World War II. There was some tension when Mexico confiscated all American and British oil companies and their lands without compensation, especially when Mexico proposed to sell this oil to the Axis, but eventually an agreement was reached on the issue.

Like so many other nations, the North American nations tried to protect themselves with treaties and agreements. Pan-American conferences agreed that hostilities were to stay away from Western Hemisphere nations: Canada and the United States made mutual defense treaties.

Canada was the only North American nation to go to war in 1939. As a member of the Commonwealth it fought alongside the British. In 1941 it declared war on Japan.

The United States, while officially neutral became more and more involved. It supplied the Allies with the Lend-Lease Act. It strengthened the defense of the Carribbean and established bases on British-American territory. After the Pan-American conference decreed that no American territory should change hands as a result of the war in Europe, the United States assumed protection over Greenland and Dutch Guiana. The Selective Service Act registered men for the draft and the defense budget was enlarged. After the Japanese attack on Pearl Harbor, the United States officially went to war. Four days after the attack, Italy and Germany, Japan's allies, declared war.

The United States fought a two-front war. The Japanese, within the first six months, seized the American territories of Guam, Wake Island, some of the Aleutians, and the Philippines. After the two major sea battles, the Battle of the Coral Sea and the Battle of Midway, the Japanese expansion was halted. Americans began to land on the Solomon Islands in 1942, and they and the Allies, especially Australians and New Zealanders, began the long slow island hopping campaign towards Japan.

Most American effort, though, was directed toward the European war. Americans fought with the British and Commonwealth nations in the North African and Italian Campaigns.

Mexico elected a new president and its relations with the United States improved. The two countries established a mutual defense treaty and on May 22, 1942, Mexico declared war on the Axis nations. Mexico actually saw little conflict, but some of its tankers were sunk and a unit of its air force operated in the Italian Campaign.

1944-1953
COOLING RAPIDLY FROM THE WARMEST
DECADE IN 1100 YEARS.

Iberian Peninsula Both Iberian Peninsula nations had been neutral during the World War, although Portugal had favored the Allies while Spain had favored the Axis. When the war was over both were initially excluded from the United Nations. Spain endured years of international pressure against its government. Finally pressure eased off and it allowed the United States to establish bases, shortly before receiving a Marshall Plan payment. In 1951 Spain endured a tremendous strike.

Portugal re-established a democracy and had the Azores returned to it by the United States. It joined NATO, although Russia kept it out of the United Nations. In 1948 Portugal extended for another ten years a friendship treaty with Spain.

Northern Europe Northern Europe spent this decade finishing World War II and suffering its after-affects in a weakened condition.

Germany suffered most as the aggressor who started the war. As the decade began, Germany found itself fighting a two-front war, in Italy and Russia. In 1944 the Anglo-American forces invaded at Normandy and opened a third front. Although the Italian front held until April of 1945, the other two yielded and soon the fighting was in Germany itself. When Berlin was beseiged by the Russians, Hitler committed suicide and his successor, Admiral Doenitz, surrendered. Germany was then divided into French, British, Russian, and American zones of occupation, and the Allied Control Council took control of the government. Berlin was also subdivided and the former Nazi leaders were put on trial. Germans throughout Eastern Europe were returned and resettled in Germany.

By 1946 Americans began to avocate more lenient treatment of Germany. While Britain and later France agreed to allow their occupation zones to reform into a single nation, Russia strongly disagreed and ultimately walked out of the Allied Control Council. It then cut off all rail transportation to Berlin. The Western powers used an airlift and by 1949 allowed their zones to unite into one — West Germany.

Gradually, the Western powers eased their economic restrictions on

Germany. The Saar remained autonomous and gradually Germany, with the help of the Marshall Plan recovered.

Eastern Germany, the Russian occupation zone, became a separate country under a Communist government. When the government lifted a ban on protests there was massive rioting. Russia intervened and with tanks crushed the riots, but reforms followed.

Britain was the winner but it too was crippled. Its economy was severely dislocated and, despite a dramatic program of socialization which tried to improve conditions, austerity and rationing continued.

The United States sent aid under the Marshall Plan and conditions gradually improved.

While Britain was preoccupied with its own affairs, its colonies took advantage of its weakness. Its Arab territories were especially restless, both Iraq and Egypt having widespread anti-British riots. In 1947 Britain, after trying vainly to quell the Jewish-Arab riots ended its Palestinian mandate. In 1951 Iran forced Britain to evacuate Abaden. The next year British troops had to fight against Egypt and two years after that it finally yielded control of the Suez Canal.

Other colonies were restless. British India gained its independence and immediately (with 5 million killed in the process) split into India and Pakistan in 1947, the same year Nigeria gained a new constitution. The following year the British had to send troops to attempt to subdue the bloody Mau Mau rebellion in Kenya. It also allowed Burma's independence.

The Low Countries had been a major battlefield and like most of Northern Europe had devastated economies. Holland remained internally peaceful but was too weak to keep its colony of Indonesia from gaining sovereignty in 1949. Belgium retained its colonies, but suffered internal violence and demonstrations over the question of whether King Leopold III should be allowed to return from exile, since his cooperation with the occupying German forces during the war had made him un-popular. Both countries spent most of this decade recovering from the war with the aid of the Marshall Plan.

The Scandinavian countries were the least devastated by war, although during the war Denmark lost control of Iceland—a loss it officially recognized in 1950. After the war Denmark, Sweden, and Norway became increasingly socialistic.

Finland was the exception. Due to the bitterness left by the Russo-Finnish War, Finland had aided Germany's attack on Russia. When they lost, they were charged reparations and territorial concessions to Russia, but their leaders were treated leniently, much to Russia's outrage. As

Russia's direct control waned, Social Democrats rose to governmental power despite strikes and demonstrations by Communists.

Ireland continued to be odd man out. It refused to join NATO as long as the island was divided, but a plebiscite showed that the majority of Northern Irish favored the division.

Southern Europe The decade began with the successful capture of Italy and France from German control. Both countries were in a war-torn condition and while they were trying to recover they lost their colonies.

Internally France had a rapid turnover of governments, poor harvests, and Communist-inspired strikes and violence. This left them in poor condition to deal with the riots and insurrections in their colonies of Madagascar, Morocco, Algeria, Tunisia, and Indo-China. Two of their territories, Lebanon and Syria had become independent during the war and after an attempt to recapture them France acknowledged their independence. In Indo-China both Laos and Cambodia were given limited independence.

Since Italy had been one of the aggressors in the war, it was stripped of its colonies and few border cities near France. It had executed Mussolini in 1945 and a year later its monarch went into exile and it became a republic. Despite Communist unrest, Christian Democrats dominated and Italy began to be regarded as a potential ally. It joined NATO and by 1950 had become so trusted, it was granted a mandate over Somaliland, one of its former colonies.

Balkans The Balkans had been conquered or dominated by the Axis and the Allies released them in 1944. The pattern of their release determined their subsequent government and history. Those released by Russia became Communist. Only Greece, not released by Russia, developed a non-communist government.

Bulgaria and Roumania had been pressured into allying with the Axis. The Russians occupied the countries, forced the governments to organize along Communist lines, and pressured the monarchs to abdicate. The war-torn Communist resistance forces became the new governments. Purges against the opposition followed as the new governments and economies were organized. In the early 1950's more purges followed, but these were of former resistance leaders and Communists whose ideology was judged incorrect.

Yugoslavia had a similar history, with the exception that it had been conquered, not allied with the Axis. Its Communist resistance, led by Tito, to German occupation had had popular support. The Yugoslav resistance movement led by Machailovich was wiped out by the Communists under Tito, who became the Communist dictator and, while closely associating with Russia, insisted on doing what he felt was best for Yugoslavia. This growing policy difference led to Yugoslavia being expelled from the Cominform and all relations with its Communist neighbors broken. Subsequently, Yugoslavia made economic agreements with Western powers, such as the United States. It cooperated with Greece, Turkey and Austria and in 1953 was in the process of negotiating with the former two when Russia backed down on the expulsion issue and requested formal relations. Both Yugoslavia and Bulgaria participated in the 1948 Greek-Communist War; and at the last kidnapped many thousands of Greek children.

Albania's history was different during the war, since it had been captured by Italy, not Germany. It was not freed until 1945, but thereafter, its history followed a pattern similar to Bulgaria and Roumania.

Greece was conquered by the Germans and freed by the British. It immediately sunk into civil war between pro-British and leftist factions attempting to control the government. A truce was signed in 1945, but the new government, supported by Britain, was extremely unstable and a year later a major civil war of Communists supported by its Balkan neighbors broke out. Yugoslavia's expulsion from the Cominform led to it closing its border as a refuge for guerrillas, and this plus American aid led to the Greek government's defeat of the Communists. However, the government continued to be unstable until the 1952 election of Premier Papagos.

North Africa North Africa had been a major battleground in the previous decade, and it spent this decade asserting its desire to be free of European domination. All three French territories of Morocco, Algeria, and Tunisia had massive bloody rioting and revolt, but continued to stay under French control.

Libya was more fortunate. As a former Italian colony it was allowed to become free of Italian domination after the defeat of the Axis. In 1949 the United Nations granted Libya independence. It became a monarchy under King Idris I.

Egypt, as the only independent North African country at the beginning of the war, had tried to remain neutral. Instead, it had been a major battleground. It reacted by demanding the removal of all British troops from its territory, and the sole ownership of the British-Egyptian-owned Sudan. Furthermore, it showed its hostility to Europe by invading Palestine, to aid the Arabs against the Israelis. In 1951 the Egyptians withdrew their alliance with Britain and in return Britain asserted the right of the

Sudan to, if it chose, become independent. Following the plebiscite, held the following year, the Sudan became independent, and Egypt lost control of land it had held since 1898. This same year massive anti-British riots forced a cruiser to fire on Port Said and British troops had to fire on Egyptian guerrillas trying to seize the Canal. King Farouk (a Turk descended from Ottoman Empire days) was deposed by a military junta in the following year. This was tremendously significant because it would be a period of Egyptian self-rule for the first time in 2300 years.

Middle East The Middle Eastern colonies won their independence from Europe during this decade and immediately were immersed in the Palestinian question.

Jewish and American pressure caused England to abandon its former plans for settling the Palestinian problem and try to determine a new solution. When all attempts to satisfy both Jews and Arabs proved impossible, Britain withdrew leaving the issue unsettled. On the same day, May 14, 1948, Palestine officially became Israel, a Jewish state. The Arab League opposed this and for the next year Israel had to fight to survive. Armistices were arranged in 1949, but border incidents continued until 1951.

Both Lebanon and Jordan, which had gained their independence from England through peaceful means in 1946, found themselves dragged into the Israeli issue. Jordan had absorbed the eastern, Arab portion of Palestine and in return aided them in their fight against Israel. The decade ended with the crowning of King Hussein (a Hashimite).

The Arab-Israeli War was one of only two fought by Syria and Lebanon. The French tried to retake these two countries as soon as World War II was over; but agreed to evacuate in 1946. Syria experienced five coups after attaining independence; whereas Lebanon experienced a fairly stable government except for one large general strike. Both, however, as neighbors of Israel, had border conflicts during the Arab-Israeli War and Syrian border incidents continued until 1951.

Both Iraq and Iran had been technically independent countries at the beginning of World War II; but British intervention had forced them to change to pro-Allied governments. Iraq responded to this pressure by forming alliances with Turkey and Jordan after the war, then terminating all alliances with Britain. The Iraqis rioted against British or American presence in their country, finally provoking the government to declare martial law.

Iran also struck back against Britain. The deposed Shah had been replaced by his son Mohammed Reza Pahlavi* who joined the Allies. Immediately after the war the Shah asked all British, Soviet and American troop to withdraw. At first the Soviets refused to leave, backing a Communist rebellion in Azerbaijan. Granting some autonomy and many reforms to the Azerbaijans and a Soviet-Iranian oil company, the Shah, with full backing of the U.N., finally persuaded the Russians to withdraw. The Shah's forces moved into Azerbaijan the day after the Russians left, and executed all of the Communists. After settling a rebellion in Fars, the government struck. Both the Russian and British oil fields were nationalized without remuneration. The British were forced to abandon Abadan and all diplomatic relations with them were severed.

A larger rebellion was brewing. When Premier Mossadegh resigned and was replaced by a western-oriented candidate, violent rioting resulted and Mossadegh returned. He was granted dictatorial powers. After being forced to turn over his estates to Mossadegh, the Shah abdicated in 1953 but returned after Mossadegh was convicted of treason. The United States had refused to grant any aid until the British were remunerated, (although it had been given an enormous grant when the Shah returned); so the decade ended with British-Iranian negotiations.

Eastern Europe Eastern Europe was freed from German occupation by Russia and as such, underwent a pattern of history similar to the Balkans. Poland, Czechoslovakia, and Hungary were pressured by the Russians into shaping their governments and economies along Soviet lines. Purges of non-Communist opposition followed. Boundary changes were commanded; Poland and Czechoslovakia giving territory to Russia while Hungary gave territory to Roumania and Czechoslovakia. Poland was allowed to move its boundary westward, at the expense of Germany. All three expelled Germans and attacked the Catholic Church. In the 1950's new purges began, this time of Communists who were believed to be "Titoist elements".

Only Austria, which had not been occupied solely by Russians, remained non-Communist. Austria was treated as a liberated country and given its 1937 boundaries, but, like Germany, was divided into four zones of occupation and ruled by the Allied Council. Russia claimed industrial establishments in their territories as German assets and delayed any final treaty and sovereignty for the entire decade.

The three Baltic nations, which had been absorbed by Russia before the war, remained incorporated in Russia, and unable to become independent.

---

*Now deceased after exile.

Russia Russia swept out from the east and conquered Eastern Europe and the northern Balkan countries in their pursuit of the Germans. Their war casualties had been tremendous (20,000,000 dead) and the countryside had been devastated, which left them in as vengeful a mood as France had been after World War I. Moreover, Russia was determined to protect its borders by surrounding itself with Communist neighbors. Thanks to the international postwar confusion, it was successful. All of the nations in Europe it occupied became Communist. After declaring war on Japan, Russia occupied Japanese territory and tried to insure that the Japanese arms in Manchuria got to the Communist Chinese who used them to gain control of all China. Outer Mongolia was granted independence, and that too became a Communist nation.

Internally, postwar Russia was peaceful, although a famine in 1946 left one million dead, and an unknown number were massacred for collaboration. In 1953 there was a renewal of purges that ended with the death of Stalin. The decade ended with Russia gaining the secret of the Atomic Bomb by espionage. (A curious historic note is that all of the spies were Jews — very curious, considering the Russian history of persecution.)

South Asia India gained its independence from Britain in return for aid during the war. After years of negotiating between Hindus and Moslems, it was decided to partition British India into Moslem Pakistan and Hindu India. Both countries became independent in 1947.

The partition of Pakistan and India was violent. The people migrated to the country of their religious preference. Millions moved and five million died in the process. Some areas, like Kashmir and Hyderabad, were areas of dispute. Pakistan and India warred for control of Kashmir until 1949, although incidents continued until 1951. Hyderabad, which resisted incorporation, was invaded by India.

India was filled with confusion during these early years. Gandhi was assassinated by one of his own Hindu followers, and Nehru became the first Prime Minister. India suffered from famine and had subsequent demonstrations. It decided to grant autonomy to Kashmir and Jammu; but the rest of the states had their rulers agree to merge their territories under the Dominion.

Pakistan, like India, suffered initial confusion, an assassination of their first Prime Minister, and a massive famine.

China The defeat of Japan by the Allies in 1945 caught China divided between the Nationalist and Communist forces. The Communists took advantage of the surrender to take North China and seize Japanese arms. Within a year of surrender the civil war renewed itself. America aided the Nationalists but they proved corrupt and refused to liberalize and aid was curtailed. Eventually, the Nationalists fled to Taiwan and in 1949, the People's Republic of China was proclaimed.

The Communists spent the rest of this decade subduing anti-Communists. They invaded Tibet and intervened on the side of North Korea. Internally, they concentrated on reconstruction and deflation.

Far East Japan endured three more months of war and two atomic bombs before it surrendered. United States' forces led by General Douglas MacArthur occupied the island. Under MacArthur, the imperialistic practices of the government were abolished and civil liberties established. War criminals were tried and the economic recovery was stimulated by large amounts of American aid. Eventually the American troops left, and Japan signed a treaty acknowledging the loss of overseas territory. These post-war years were internally peaceful despite a large number of strikes.

Korea, to some extent, suffered the fate of the Balkans, since the northern part was occupied by Russians and became Communist. Americans occupied the southern part which became a democracy. The United States withdrew in 1949 and a year later war broke out as North Korea invaded South Korea. The Security Council of the U.N. asked nations all over the world to aid South Korea. America contributed heavily and the U.S. and Korean forces drove the invaders back to their border. MacArthur, commanding the U.N. forces, crossed the border and was practically to Manchuria when China intervened. The war was ended by an armistice in 1951, although some action continued until 1953 when the armistice was signed by both sides, providing for a demilitarized zone between camps.

North America All three countries participated in the last two years of World War II, with the United States participating more heavily in the Pacific campaign. Since none of the three had been a field of battle, economic recovery was rapid and relatively painless.

Both Canada and the U.S. found Communist espionage in their governments and this, plus alarm at the Communist take-over in Eastern Europe, aroused growing anti-Communist sentiment. This helps explain why both countries willingly participated in the Korean War after the U.N. called for aid to South Korea. While Canada gave financial aid to England, the United States economically and financially aided Formosa and Western Europe, to help them resist Communist spread. The U.S.

gave its territory of the Philippines its independence.

Other events in North America were minor. All three countries were internally peaceful and, after Mexico compensated the U.S. for oil lands seized in the last decade, relations between the three countries were unusually harmonious.

1954-1963
RAPIDLY GETTING COOLER.

Iberian Peninsula Both Iberian nations remained under the rule of strong men, Franco in Spain, and Salazar in Portugal. This kept both countries internally peaceful, but externally, both were losing their empires. India seized three of Portugal's enclaves, and Dahomey seized Portuguese-held Ajuda. Spain lost its Moroccan protectorates. Restlessness spread to the remaining colonies and rebellion started in Angola while Spain made plans to grant independent to the Spanish Guinea.

Northern Europe The Northern European countries remained, on the whole, internally peaceful, but those countries with non-European colonies continued to lose them.

Britain, which had owned the largest colonial empire, lost the most. Its internal affairs were peaceful enough with only the Profumo scandal disturbing the government. It acquired the atomic bomb. Externally, however, this decade was a disaster.

It started poorly in 1956 when Egypt announced that it was nationalizing the Suez Canal. England and France backed an Israeli attack on the Canal Zone and demanded the right to occupy it. The U.N. condemned the action and England backed down, allowing Egypt to possess the canal. This was interpreted as a weakness that restless colonies were quick to take advantage of. In the next year Malaya and Ghana (a union of Gold Coast and Togoland) became independent, though both stayed part of the Commonwealth. Two years later Singapore and Cyprus gained independence. With the opening of the Sixties the rush for independence began. In 1960 Nigeria, in 1961 Kuwait, South Africa, Sierra Leone, and Tanganyika. Only Uganda broke free in 1962, but the decade ended with Britain granting independence to Kenya, Gambia, and Aden, as well as promising it to the Bahamas. Besides losing these colonies, Britain had to cope with the bloody Mau Mau revolts of 1952-56, and racial trouble in its East African colonies.

Both of the Low Countries lost colonies during this decade. Belgium granted independence to the Congo in 1960 and lost its mandate in

Burundi and Rwanda, in the following years. The Netherlands lost Surinam and the Netherland Antilles. Moreover, its relations with its former colony of Indonesia soured over its refusal to release the Netherlands New Guinea and the Union of the Netherlands and Indonesia was dissolved. Its citizens and their property suffered in Indonesia as a result.

Both had some internal trouble. The Netherlands government was unstable. Belgium, however, experienced riots and demonstrations over a dispute between Flemish and Waloons and their language. The government had to cope with the turmoil in the newly independent Congo and the danger to its citizens this turmoil represented.

Germany had no more territory to lose, so this decade was an improvement. East and West Germany were granted sovereignty as separate countries in 1954 and 1955, respectively. Russia tried to emphasize the difference between these two whenever possible. In 1961, Khrushchev of Russia declared they would rebuff any attempts by Western powers to cross East German territory in order to get to their zones in Berlin. When America sent troops to Berlin and insisted on its right of access, the East Germans, which had the year before restricted admittance of West Germans into East Germany, now closed its borders entirely. It began to build the Berlin wall and tried to forbid U.S. civilians to enter. This caused a confrontation between U.S. and Soviet tanks, as U.S. officials in civilian dress, crossed the border. All these tensions caused a mass flight of East Germans and Berliners to the West.

The Scandinavian countries and Ireland had no colonial territory to lose. All five enjoyed peaceful, relatively prosperous decades.

Southern Europe Southern Europe repeated the pattern seen elsewhere. France, a country with colonial territories, lost them. Italy, a country which had lost its territories in the previous decade, had a fairly peaceful time.

France found itself involved in two wars. The first fighting Vietnamese insurgents, a struggle that ended with the massive defeat of the French at Dienbienfu and granting independence to Indo-China in 1954.

This was the same year as the rebellion in Algeria took place. After seven years of fighting, threats of civil war spreading to France, and massive widespread acts of terrorism by the OAS, Algeria was finally given a plebescite on independence in 1962. Morocco and Tunisia, the other North African French territories, had already received their independence six years before.

The strain of these two conflicts was a huge burden on the French economy, a burden that the creation of the Common Market helped to relieve. After a number of cabinets, the government stabilized by forming the Fifth Republic, under de Gaulle. All territories were offered a vote on whether to become departments of France or autonomous members of the French community. All of its African territories voted in 1958 to become autonomous members of the French community except for Guinea, which became independent. Mali and Senegal fused into the completely independent Federation of Mali in 1959, and a year later, Cameroun, Central African Republic, Chad, Dahomey, Gabon, Ivory Coast, Madagascar, Mauritania, Republic of Congo, Togo, and Upper Volta also became completely independent.

Italy enjoyed a fairly peaceful decade. There was a rapid turn-over of governments and acts of terrorism by the German-speaking elements of Alto Adige, a territory Italy had seized from Austria as part of the World War I settlements.

Balkans The Balkans all enjoyed a peaceful decade. The Communist-controlled Balkan states, with the exception of Bulgaria, showed a growing independence of Russia. Yugoslavia made a twenty-year tripartite alliance with Turkey and Greece, which caused Russia to court Tito in an attempt to get him more in line with Soviet doctrine. Albania publically supported Communist China, not Russia and Roumania, after finally having Soviet occupation troops leave in 1958, called for neutralization of the Balkans.

Non-Communist Greece also enjoyed a peaceful decade.

North Africa North Africa had a turbulent decade but won complete independence from European control. Violence spread throughout the French colonies of Morocco, Tunisia and Algeria. France, after trying unsuccessfully to establish their candidate as monarch of Morocco finally granted independence in 1956. This was the same year Tunisia gained its independence. In the case of Morocco, the monarch ruled peacefully and pressured America, Spain and France to remove their bases. The decade ended with Morocco proposing to expand at the expense of its neighbors, especially Spanish-held territories. Tunisia on the other hand, had a coup overthrowing its ruler, and widespread fighting against both Algerian and French bases in its territories. France finally agreed to with-draw its bases, which were removed in 1956.

Algeria had an even bloodier struggle. In 1954 the Front de Liberation National revolted against France. France refused independence or to accept U.N. intervention in the struggle that followed. In 1958, the

Algiers Committee of Public Safety set itself up as a separate government. It had to fight not only France, but also an insurrection of French ultra-nationalists. In 1960, President de Gaulle of France visited Algeria to promote an "honorable" peace settlement, but Europeans in Algeria clashed with paratroops during the visit and Moslems were urged by President Abbas to work against the referendum. French troops staged an unsuccessful insurrection in 1961. The next year a massive general strike was held by Moslems. Acts of terrorism by the OAS attempted to block a peace settlement, but in 1962, after an all-out war against the OAS, Algerians voted overwhelmingly for independence and were formally recognized as a separate nation.

Independence did not bring peace. Within a year Algeria and Morocco had a border war.

Libya, which was completely independent, thanks to the defeat of Italy in World War II, had a peaceful decade. Egypt, however, despite its independence had conflicts with Europe. A treaty with England said that the British would evacuate the Canal Zone by 1956; but in 1956, in order to finance the construction of the Aswan Dam, Nasser nationalized the Canal. After months of international protests, Israeli forces, backed by Britain and France, invaded Egypt.

The European powers bombarded the Canal. Negative reaction to this action by the United States and Russia, forced the invaders to back down and return the Canal to Egypt. Israel, however, retained control of the Gaza strip until the next year.

In 1958 Syria united with Egypt to form the United Arab Republic. A month later they joined with Yemen to form the Federation of Yemen and United Arab States. Three years later a revolt of Syrian army officers forced Syria from the republic. This led Egypt to terminate its federation with Yemen, but in the next year aided Yemen's new government when it became involved in a civil war with its deposed imamate who was backed by Saudi Arabia.

The union with Syria was almost renewed in 1963, coupled with union with Iraq, but Egypt hesitated.

Middle East The small territories, (with the exception of Southern Yemen and Aden), won their independence while the larger independent countries experimented unsuccessfully with larger unions. As is typical among new countries, there were numerous border incidents.

Syria was an example. Having confirmed their independence in the previous decade, they experimented with union with Egypt in the United Arab Republic in 1958, and ended the union with a military revolt in 1961. The proposed re-union with the United Arab Republic in 1963 induced rioting, a revolution and a coup, and four changes in government. It experienced tension and border incidents with Turkey, twice had severe conflicts along its Israeli border. Besides these it had an army revolt in the beginning of the decade.

Iraq and Jordan formed an Arab Federation in 1958. However, an Iraqi coup assassinated King Faisal and replaced him with a general and broke up the federation as King Hussein of Jordan called on the British to help him resist being taken over. The British were called in three years later by Kuwait as it too found its sovereignty threatened by Iraq. In 1963 Iraq tried again to unify with Egypt and Syria, following a pro-Nasser coup. The union was eventually called off due to Syrian conditions and Iraq found itself involved in a war with its Kurds as they revolted against the new government.

Jordan had a restless decade, also. After its unfortunate attempt at federation with Iraq, Jordan found itself a refuge for Palestinians who used it as a base against Israel. Besides enduring numerous border incidents, its Premier was assassinated by a terrorist bomb.

Lebanon also had its troubles. The United Arab Republic incited riots against Lebanon's government. In desperation, Lebanon had to ask the United States and Britain for help. The rioting and attempted rebellion was successfully crushed as was a later coup in 1961.

Turkey, Saudi Arabia and Iran, as the three older, more stable, independent countries had difficulties with their neighbors. While internally Turkey experienced only a military coup which deposed of a government they claimed violated the Turkish constitution, and established elections which returned the government to civilian hands. However, in foreign affairs, there were numerous unpleasant incidents on the Turkish-Syrian border and the tension with Greece over Cyprus induced severe anti-Greek riots.

Saudi Arabia, likewise, was internally peaceful. Like Turkey, it had trouble with its neighbors, being dragged into backing one faction of the Yemen Civil War which led to conflict with the United Arab Republic.

Iran had trouble with its neighbor Russia, which attempted to dominate its foreign policy, while it in turn used its size to bring Bahrein under its jurisdiction.

Numerous small states, such as Bahrein, Kuwait, Cyprus, and Yemen gained their freedom from Britain. Each found itself in danger of being absorbed by a larger neighbor; Bahrein by Iran, Kuwait by Iraq, while Cyprus and Yemen found themselves footballs between larger rivals;

the former between Greece and Turkey, the latter between Saudi Arabia and Egypt.

Israel, as the only non-Arab country was as aggressive as its Arab neighbors. Backed by Britain and France, it attempted to take the Suez Canal, and only United Nations pressure was necessary to force it to yield up Egyptian territory it seized. It was under constant Palestinian harrassment and twice had major conflicts with its neighbor, Syria.

Eastern Europe Eastern Europe, with the exception of Austria, continued to be dominated by Russia. While Czechoslovakia remained docile, Hungary, in 1956, tried to revolt from Russian control. Rioting spread from Budapest throughout the countryside and in response the Hungarian government made major reforms and announced free elections. Russia's army then intervened with tanks and recaptured the countryside, abolishing all reforms and executing Premier Nagy.

Poland had been inspired by Hungary and the population rioted, attacking Russian troops. However, the government put the rioters on trial and opposed the anti-Russian movement. In return for this support, Poland was not attacked by Russia as Hungary had been, and instead signed a pact for equality in Soviet-Polish relations.

Austria began the decade by formally regaining its sovereignty in 1955. It had a democratic government and spent most of the decade peacefully except for demonstrations in the Austrian Tyrol against Italian mistreatment of Germans in South Tyrol.

Russia Russia underwent a power struggle following the death in the last decade of Stalin, and Khrushchev emerged as dictator. He denounced Stalin and expressed co-existence as the new goal of Russian foreign policy. This did not extend to liberalizing life for the average Russian, although five minority groups which had been exiled due to "disloyalty during World War II", now were rehabilitated. However, despite economic failures and a lack of political or economic freedoms, life inside Russia was peaceful throughout this decade.

Instead Russia found itself trying to control its satellite nations. It had to subdue the Hungarian and attempted Polish uprisings, and deal with the Berlin crisis and the U2 incident. In 1957 it launched its first satellite.

South Asia Although Soviet-allied Afghanistan and American-allied Pakistan remained peaceful during this decade, neutral India was decidedly belligerent. It had internal peace which allowed it to concentrate on confiscating all French and Portuguese territories in the Indian subcontinent. It protested that China was occupying Indian territory and several border incidents resulted. In 1962 Communist China invaded India. India asked for American aid and the U.S. immediately sent India transport planes with U.S. crews. On the same day China, which had been victorious up to now, called a cease-fire and withdrew to its previous borders. India got the point and recognized the border as official.

China Communist China was busy during this decade, expanding its communization of agriculture and expanding its control westward. In this expansion, China battled Tibet and according to some reports, practiced genocide on its people. It battled India to gain recognition of its border and forced Nepal to give up all extra-territorial rights on Tibet. During this time, its relations with Russia steadily worsened and a rift between the two Communist super-powers became obvious by the end of the decade.

To the east China met more opposition. When the decade began, China talked in terms of occupying Taiwan. However, the United States heavily backed Taiwan. China was allowed to the Tachen Islands in the Taiwan Strait, but when China bombarded Quemoy and Matsu, the U.S. 7th Fleet intervened. Although periodic bombardment continued, eastern expansion was halted.

Taiwan, occupied by nationalist Chinese, expanded mightily on the economic front, but gradually had to give up its dream of re-occupying the mainland.

Far East Japan, which had lost all territory, had a relatively quiet decade, with the only massive demonstrations occurring in 1962, to protest the ratification of a Japanese-American security committee. The Japanese-Russian peace treaty was finally settled in 1956 with Japan retaining two of the Kurile Islands, while Russia claimed the rest.

Korea had finished its conflict in the previous decade, and began this decade repatriating prisoners of war. Within four years the last of the Chinese Communists had withdrawn from North Korea. In 1960, there were massive demonstrations against the "rigged" election of President Syngman Rhee, which forced his resignation. The following year there was a military coup and a year later demonstrations protested General Park's withdrawal of elections.

North America Both Canada and Mexico experienced peaceful decades, both internally and externally, but the United States, which had overseas territories, had restless times.

Internally, there was a growing number of demonstrations in favor of extending full civil rights to Blacks. This began with the Supreme Court decision banning school segregation, grew with sit-in demonstrations and "freedom rides", to the march on Washington, in 1963, of 200,000 persons to pressure the passage of a civil rights bill. Only a month before the decade was over, the violence climaxed with the assassination of President Kennedy.

Externally, the United States was intervening militarily in anti-Communist activities. Troops handled the Berlin crisis and were threatened in Taiwan. Advisors were sent to aid South Vietnam, while 8,000 troops were landed in Lebanon. America's space race began this decade.

1964-1973
GETTING VERY COLD, VERY FAST.

Iberian Peninsula Spain renewed its claim to Gibralter, despite the 12,138 to 44 plebiscite vote to remain a British possession. Prince Juan Carlos was declared the eventual successor to Generalissimo Franco, dictator since the 1936-39 Civil War.

Portugal began to have a lot of problems with its colonial empire. The colonies got help from the Organization of African Unity, the Communists, and others, and mounted revolutionary movements. The Portuguese faced rebellion in Portugal against the Dictator Salazar; in Angola; Portuguese Guinea; Mozambique; Macao. Salazar died and was succeeded by Marcello Caetano.

Northern Europe Britain supported the Federation of Malaya against Indonesian encroachments, became evermore involved in the Irish-Catholic attacks in Ulster, and gave Malta its independence. That same year it withdrew from Arabia and Singapore, but did retain naval base privileges in Malta.

West Germany developed a slightly warmer relationship with East Germany.

Southern Europe France withdrew from NATO as it went through a decade of growing involvement in Africa. It intervened in Gabon, the Congo, the Central African Republic, and Chad. Meanwhile, they developed a nuclear capability; both fission and thermonuclear bombs, and a bomber delivery system.

Pope Paul VI, following the activist lead of Pope John XXIII, whose entire term was served in the previous decade, became a world traveller. He went to such diverse places as the Holy Land, New York, Istanbul, Uganda, Southeast Asia, the Philippines, Samoa, and Australia.

The Vatican began an aggressive campaign to regain some of its faded influence. Such issues as celibacy, birth control, political support of violent revolutions, or other political processes, and use of the vernacular, have been tearing the Church asunder. The stresses of the current era are the most severe since the Reformation.

Balkans Albania gained a degree of freedom by adhering to Communist China against the Soviet bloc, and succeeded in withdrawing from the Warsaw Pact. Not being contiguous with the Soviet Union probably saved it from invasion.

Greece had a rightist military coup, and dismissed the power of the crown. Ultimately, the monarchy was nullified.

Roumania achieved a partial withdrawal from the Soviet Bloc.

North Africa Morocco's King Hassan seized power for five years, with a declared "State of Emergency". In 1970, his absolute rule ended, but he retained a veto.

The last French troops left Algeria, and after a coup it became essentially socialist.

Egypt engaged in two wars with Israel, and Nasser attempted to federate with other Arab states, the Sudan and Libya as the United Arab Republic tried to expand. Nasser died in 1970 and Anwar Sadat became President.

The Suez Canal was closed for most of the decade by war damage.

Middle East The decade continued turbulent times in the Middle East. Two Arab / Israeli wars occurred in this decade, and Cyprus had escalation of fighting, but the threatened war between Turkey and Greece over Cyprus did not occur, as U.N. security forces helped suppress the fighting.

Syria fought Israel twice, and also helped the Palestinians against Jordan. The Syrian government was about average with its two coup d'etats.

Jordan's problem was unique. Forty percent of the entire population was Palestinian, and they fought a civil war with outside help to try to take Jordan away from the Jordanians. Only United States and Israeli intimidation prevented Syria from entering the conflict on the side of the Palestinians.

The royal family deposed King Saud of Saudi Arabia, and the royal family of Oman did the same for its Sultan. The Federation of Arab Emirates was established under the leadership of Qatar, and approved by the nine Persian Gulf countries which chose to participate.

The big influence in the Middle East was withdrawn with Britain's military, leaving the locals free to fight. Yemen broke into two warring factions — Southern Yemen being Communist.

OPEC, which was formed in 1960, saw its opportunity. Prince Yemani, the Saudi Arabian Minister of Petroleum Affairs said, "We are in a position to dictate prices, and we are going to be very rich."* Unlike others, he had concentrated on wealth, instead of using oil as a means of getting power.

Iraq was riddled with revolts. The Kurdish revolt, an attempted coup, a successful coup, execution of forty-four alleged plotters, another attempted coup, added to the pressures caused by active fighting with Iran.

Iran had a "white revolution". The Shah initiated "...agrarian land reform, distributing crown lands and estates to the landless peasants. The program established compulsory education, introduced women's suffrage, and provided for profit-sharing in industry. It cost the Shah the support of extreme right-wing groups, and in 1965 the Premier, Hassan Ali Mansur, was assassinated, and an attempt was made on the life of the Shah".*

People who preferred tyranny, especially clergy, opposed the Shah.

Eastern Europe Austria maintained its rigid neutrality.

Czechoslovakia had a liberalization movement under the leadership of Dubcek. It was invaded by Russia, Poland, East Germany, Hungary and Bulgaria, who re-imposed full-bore Communist rule.

Poland assisted in the invasion of Czechoslovakia, and also purged "Zionist" elements. Many Jews emigrated. Food riots in 1970 in Gdansk required military action to suppress them, killing over 200.

After East Germany recognized the Oder-Neisse line, (the Western Polish boundary), thus ceding 40,000 square miles of pre-war German lands, 50,000 ethnic Germans left their homes and went to Germany.

Repression of the Roman Catholic Church was eased and Poland was given a second Cardinal, Karol Wojtyla.

Russia Premier Krushchev was deposed peacefully, the reason was probably agriculture; inasmuch as he had reduced the military budget by $660 million and allocated a $46 billion expenditure to double agriculture in the next seven years. A total of 8.5 million tons of wheat were purchased by Russia, after a massive crop failure in 1963.

Following the fall of Krushchev, the industrial sphere was given more

---

*1974 - *The World Almanac*, p. 112.

---

*Quote from the 1975 *Information Please Almanac, Atlas and Yearbook*.

freedom of decision, profit-sharing was introduced, farmers were assured of a monthly wage and old-age pension. Expanded use of fertilizers and improved seeds was planned. Clearly, the Communists were in a major economic crisis, probably having to do with the volcanicity and 10% loss of sunlight which was their first whisper of the climatic change which was to come.

Communist planning couldn't replace sunlight. The feeling of insecurity jumped. Russia sided with the Arabs against the Jews in 1967. Czechoslovakia was invaded and occupied in 1968 and serious fighting with China broke out in 1969. In 1970, the Russians began arms limitation talks with the United States.

In 1972, a year of extreme cold winter, the Soviets had another extremely bad crop year. Spontaneous underground fires signalled drought of such severity as Russia had known only in its worst of times. (Mongol invasion, Crusades, etc.)

China China joined the superweapon club in 1964 when it detonated its atomic bomb. This was followed in 1970 by a hydrogen bomb, and in 1970 it launched its first satellite. Mao's "Cultural Revolution" killed millions.

Tibet had revolt after revolt to try to undo the 1950 conquest. The Dalai Lama charged the Chinese with committing genocide. Lin Piao replaced President Liu as Mao's heir apparent, but he was killed after he failed in the attempt to advance the timing, with a coup.

China demoted the United States from number 1 enemy and promoted Russia to that position.

Far East With defense furnished by the United States, (10% of Japan's GNP), Japanese had an economic boom. Industrial production went up a factor of three during the decade. The "Ugly Japanese" replaced the "Ugly American" in the eyes of the poorer people.

In South Korea, President Park, a general, had acquired his position as chairman of a military junta that took power in 1961 after President Syngman Rhee was forced to resign by a coalition of college students and others who charged election fraud and corruption. Park was reelected a second and third time in this decade. He proceeded to lead his country into the status of industrial might.

Korea gave the most help of any nation to the United States in Vietnam.

North America The United States got into and out of the Vietnam War in this decade, with Communism left in a state of severe disarray. Following the good crop weather of the 1960's, sharp deterioriation of weather began in 1972. The U.S. became the dominant world supplier of exportable food in this decade.

Liberal, racial and minority causes discredited themselves, and set up the entire movement of "government to advance social causes" to come crashing down on their heads in the following decade. This was a decade of extremes, and constituted the end of an era. At the end of the decade (1973) the power of the "forces of the left" was within eight months of forcing a conservative President, elected by 61% of the electorate, to resign. This was the high-water mark of political "Liberalism" spawned by 50 years of the warmest weather in 1100 years.

Mexico and Canada had a relatively peaceful decade, although Canada's Quebec separatists got going in the decade.

1974-MID-1981
THE CLIMATE IS GETTING MUCH COLDER, VERY RAPIDLY.

Iberian Peninsula Spain's Franco died of a heart attack on November 20, 1975, and Juan Carlos was proclaimed King two days later. He instituted a number of moderate reforms. The first steps toward Basque autonomy were taken, and Spain suffered severe economic problems.

Portugal had a military coup in 1974, and the return, by force, of the too-liberal government in 1975. Legislatures forced out a successor and set up a three-man junta.

Portugal granted independence to Guinea, Mozambique, and Angola, and Indonesia seized Timor. These events constituted the end of old-fashioned colonization in Europe. Only Communist Russia is still a great colonial power, and this in the sense that only China has found the word for — Hegemonism.

Northern Europe Great Britain, in a mood reminiscent of the Victorian era, elected a Conservative, woman Prime Minister — Margaret Thatcher. When Great Britain decides to bite the bullet, the world shudders.

Terrorism marked this decade for West Germany, and a gradual increase of economically severe times.

This decade saw an unseating of incumbents by Western powers. The Netherlands in 1973, and 1977; Denmark in 1973; Sweden in 1976; Great Britain in 1979; Belgium, France, West Berlin, and the United States in 1981. Only Norway and West Germany have not yet eliminated incumbents. This phenomenon signals very hard times, when the incumbents are the only "fall-guys" around. France's new Socialist government promises to nationalize industry, effectively ridding itself of foreign influence.

France is apparently reestablishing a pure French system suitable for the reacquisition of Empire.

Southern Europe France withdrew from its last possession in the African continent; but it interceded twice in the Congo (Zaire), Chad and Mauritania, and now has 12,000 troops distributed widely through Africa.

There may come a day, when either France or South Africa confronts Cuban troops, that either is capable of, and would be inclined to put an atomic bomb on Havana.

Italy has been plagued by three factors — widespread political terrorism, governmental instability, and economic hardship.

Two great changes occurred. In 1977 a new accord between Italy and the Roman Catholic Church replaced the Lateran Treaty of 1929. Italy no longer considers Roman Catholicism the state religion.

Secondly, the Italian Cardinals couldn't agree, so a Pole — Karol Cardinal Wojtyla — was elected Pope. He is the first non-Italian Pope since Adrian II of Utrecht in 1522.

The Pope was shot in an assassination attempt by a Turkish Moselm who accused the Pope of being a Crusader. It seems likely that the accusation is correct.

Malta seems about to fall to Libya, which is currently headed by Moamar Khadafi.

Balkans Greece voted (69% in favor) a referendum to substitute a republic for a monarchy in 1974. The military dictatorship collapsed in 1974, after bungling an attempt to seize Cyprus.

Turkey invaded Cyprus in 1974, and took about half the island for the Turkish community (20% of the population).

The entire Turkey / Greek / Cyprus War effectively removed these members of NATO. The United States was caught between them, and nothing good was going to come of a situation that had been going on for 700 years.

As the book goes to press, a Greek election has put in power a Socialist who is pledged to sever Greek ties with NATO.

Turkey has abolished all political parties in a pure military government which has undertaken to eliminate all rebellious elements.

North Africa Spain gave up the Spanish Sahara, and a struggle began between Morocco, Mauritania and the Communist Polisario (Spanish Sahara rebels) continues at this writing.

Morocco, in 1977, also sent troops to Zaire (Congo) and helped defeat an invasion from Communist-backed Angola. They helped Zaire against a second invasion in 1978. Algeria was on the side of the Polisarios.

Libya and Egypt had a very violent four-day war in 1977. Libya sent 2,000 troops to aid Uganda's President Idi Amin, who was losing to an invasion of Ugandan rebels and Tanzanian troops. Amin lost anyway, and Khadafi (Qaddafi) gave Amin refuge.

Khadafi's forces intervened in Chad, and he is now attempting to formalize a Libyan/Chaddian union; and, indeed, a union of Islamic North African States. He is undoubtedly the most dangerous man in the world today.

Middle East The U.S.-sponsored "Camp David Accord" made peace between Egypt and Israel (Sadat and Begin). They could judge each other well because Sadat had been a general, and had initiated the Yom Kippur War in 1973. Begin had been a terrorist and commanded the Jewish terrorist organization, Irgun Zvai Leumi.

Israel ended the period with an undeclared act of war on Iraq; namely, bombing a nuclear pile just outside Baghdad.

Egypt's Sadat was assassinated, and Air Force General Mubarak was elected to replace him.

Guerrilla warfare continued between Israel and the Palestine Liberation Organization.

Lebanon had a very bloody civil war between Christians and Moslems; and Syria entered as a peace-keeping force. Israel helps the Christians from time to time; but the Druses are the most militant Moslems. It is their stated intent to kill all Christians.

Iran overthrew the Shah and the clergy became wholly despotic. Iran began slipping back into the Dark Ages.* Iraq attacked, and they are at war, having destroyed much (of the oil fields near Abadan) that they fought to possess.

Islamic extremists are regaining control of the area.

Historically, the Moslems have become more aggressive than the Communists.

Eastern Europe Poland suffered food riots in 1976 (previous times of riots, 1956 and 1970). In 1980, the workers organized Solidarity—a union, and forced the government to recognize the right of workers to unionize. An invasion by the Soviet Union is threatened. The Polish Communist Party, Prime Ministry, and the Ministry of Defense have all been put into

---

*All of the modernizations achieved by the Shah have been rescinded, probably the most notable being that women have been returned to the shapeless black dress and mask.

the hands of General Wojciech Jaruzelski, the head of the Polish Army.

Poland defaulted on payments of a debt of almost $30 billion; and it was "rescheduled".

Roumania has maintained remarkable independence of the Soviet Union, being able to maintain ties with China, Albania, and Israel. Ceausescu visited the U.S. He became the only East European voice to protest the Soviet invasion of Afghanistan. Perhaps the only reason Roumania has escaped Soviet wrath is that it has never swerved from being a hard-nosed Communist tyranny.

Czechoslovakia's restored Communist government spent the decade sup-pressing its people.

Eastern European people have demonstrated that only the force of arms — especially Russian arms — keeps them suppressed; and even force of arms barely keeps them suppressed.

The area is ripe for an anti-Communist holocaust.

The trigger will be Soviet weakness.

Russia The most notable event in Russia (especially as distinct from the remaining 60% of the Soviet Union which the Russians hold in bondage) is that the Russian birth rate has gone so low that Russians (ethnics) are not being replaced. Their population is declining. This is the ultimate rebellion.

Likewise, Russian alcohol consumption has increased to 25% of their total personal disposable income. This pictures a people in an advanced state of demoralization.

The Soviet Union has had a series of crop failures — and has been forced to turn to its enemies for food, at the same time that its ability to suppress its neighbors has declined. Outright invasion and war in Afghanistan had to have been a last resort. It had three crop failures in a row — 1979, 1980 and 1981.

The Soviet Union is lashing about like a dying, mad dog.

Meanwhile, with the tidal-forces maxima going up since 1972, and in-creasing volcanicity, and the umbral/penumbral ratio going down since about 1932 (solar cooling), and with the magnetic field in its present position, the Soviet Union has lost its ability to feed itself and be a great nation.

As the weather continues to deteriorate, the Russian greatness has passed, and is headed for the nadir of 2010.

South Asia The underbelly of Asia is in turmoil. The authors estimate that the partition of the Indian Subcontinent had caused 7,000,000 dead by the beginning of this decade.

In 1974, India exploded a nuclear device. In 1975 it veered suddenly into dictatorship by the Congress Party under the leadership of Mrs. Gandhi. She decreed a state of emergency; got her rubber-stamp congress to extend it indefinitely; suspended civil rights; engaged in mass arrests; and did everything a good dictator should do except: she called for an election in 1977.

The electorate threw her and the Congress Party out.

Even out of power, Mrs. Gandhi discouraged her opponents, and helped them reach such a position that another election was called for in January 1980. She and the Congress Party swept the election.

She has not reverted to dictatorship, but everyone knows that she has no moral scruples, nor political impediments that would forbid it. Consequently, she is a very strong executive, which Indians apparently desire, because no one challenges the freedom of the election.

Pakistan continues under a dictator — General Zia.

It is developing, and will shortly have, an atomic bomb.

The election in 1977 put Bhutto into power, but General Zia seized the government, had Bhutto tried and convicted for murder, and executed.

Zia — with the backing of the Moslem league — is channeling weapons to the Afghan rebels to resist the Soviet invasion in Afghanistan.

Pakistan, like Iran and Libya, became a country run by Islamic law.

In southeast Asia, the Indo-China War* has drawn to a close, or at least a stalemate.

1947 through 1979: The Indo-China War

1945-54 The French Period - 430,000 dead
1954-65 The Geneva Period - 250,000 dead
1967-73 The United States Period - 4,000,000 dead
1973-75 The Cease-Fire Period - 2,500,000 dead
1975-81 The Vietnam Empire Period - 1,500,000 dead

Deaths by war including caused famine, civilian executions, as well as battlefield deaths totaled 8,300,000 deaths.

Such an experience is formative. The last two wars, the Vietnamese invasion of Cambodia and Chinese invasion of Vietnam, were Communist fighting Communist.

The seas around Indo-China are rampant with piracy (as is the

---

*This classification was presented by Dupuy and Dupuy — The Encyclopedia of Military History. Harper and Row: 1977.

Eastern Mediterranean, and to a lesser extent the Gulf of Mexico and the Caribbean). Boat people who try to escape the Indo-China area are robbed, raped, and murdered by pirates.

Thailand, the Philippines, Malaya, and even Australia have been flooded with refugees. It is an enormous problem. Thailand has had an election, a couple of coups, many skirmishes, and hundreds of thousands of refugees.

Burma's Communist insurgency continues as does Malaya's; but appears to not be gaining momentum.

Cambodia's losses were staggering (and are included in the Indo-China War estimate above). According to the *1981 Information Please Almanac*, "...in May 1980, a U.N. demographer said the normal increase from the last census, in 1969, would have brought the population to 8.9 million. UN relief agencies attempting to feed a starving nation calculated the current population as between 5 and 5.5 million making the number of deaths possible as high as 3.9 million." The authors used an estimate of only 2,560,000 in the Indo-China War. An estimate which may be much too low.

China This decade began with Chou En-lai having just restored Teng Hsiao-ping (pronounced Dung) to power, and promoting the Soviet Union to the position of number one enemy over the United States.

By the end of this period, Teng had removed the last revolutionary Communist from the Politburo, and China had cooperated with the U.S. in building two electronic spy monitoring stations on the Soviet border to gain intelligence on Soviet activities.

It was a spectacular period.

The Chinese are attempting to convert their military force from guerrillas to modern army.

In 1976, after Chou, Marshal Teh, and Mao died, Mao's wife Chiang Chang and three other Politburo members (the Gang of Four) were arrested. The generals methodically took over until, in 1981, Mao's successor (Hua) was forced to resign. China is now ruled entirely by "pragmatists" who place productivity above Communist ideology.

Great national disasters (earthquake with 550,000 dead in 1976) and severe climatic change spurred the political changes.

Far East Japan began an economic offensive which put it at great advantage over the other countries. As the only major nation in modern history whose defense is wholly borne by foreigners, the economic prowess of a society with low overhead is impressive.

The Japanese government has repeatedly promised its economic partners that it would reduce its trade surplus, which is injuring them. It has broken the promise each time.

Japan is playing a dangerous game — injuring its Allies, making false promises, yet having no defense. Japan should spend a little more time remembering what atomic bombs felt like, and start living up to its promises. Giants (U.S., Europe) who are in pain tend to spread it around.

South Korea's President Park was assassinated by the head of the Korean Central Intelligence Agency. This triggered an uprising which was harshly repressed. Meanwhile, South Korea was rapidly becoming an industrial giant.

North Korea continues as the most severely repressive Communist dictatorship. It became the first Communist country to default on international debts.

Its aggressive intent against the South has never faltered.

China (Taiwan) had recognition by the United States withdrawn by President Carter. It continues to be an industrial power, however, and the U.S. still guarantees its security.

The Philippines have been under the dictatorial ("emergency") rule of Marcos during this period. The Moro (Moslem) rebellion has cost tens of thousands of lives. The Moros continued the rebellion, (financed by Khadafi of Libya) and refused a settlement giving them autonomy over one-third of the entire Philippine country. The emergency — which is real — continues.

North America Canada is torn by separatist movements from Quebec, and the four Prairie Provinces. The issue of power of the Central Government versus the power of the Provinces is uppermost. It is unresolved; but the continued existence of Canada as a nation lies in the balance.

Mexico struck a bonanza of oil and gas, and is trying to use the resultant income for major development. Mexico backs Communist Insurgency in Central America.

The position taken by each one seems to be:

"What's mine is mine. What's yours is negotiable."*

The United States sank into bureaucratic tyranny in this period, with regulatory agencies disrupting every aspect of life. At the end of the period, an election swept people into office on the promise that they would, "...get the government off our backs."

Conservative columnists are saying, "...another revolution, bloodless

---

*A quote attributed to Dean Rusk when he was Secretary of State of the United States, when speaking of Communists.

but effective, might be an excellent move."**

There is a race which the government seems to be losing, between it restraining itself (which no government ever seems able to rationalize) or it being overthrown (perhaps by a Constitutional Convention). The majority of the population now lives on government largesse, at the expense of the minority who produce. The schism is between producers and non-producers, which includes all of the government except defense.

The U.S. government is in peril, because the people despise it, because it, "...has erected a multitude of New Offices, and sent hither swarms of Officers to harass our People and eat them out of their substance..." "...We have warned them from time to time of attempts by their legislature to extend an unwarrantable jurisdiction over us..."*

EPILOG

The climate is "going sour" just as it was when the Declaration of Independence was written. Institutions, in their efforts to survive, oppress their people, as institutions have always oppressed their people for the sake of the institution.

What history shows is that under such climatic stresses, people always explode and destroy their tormentors.

At the present, about one government falls somewhere in the world each week. It is not a "big deal".

**James J. Kilpatrick, Copyright, Universal Press Syndicate, 4 July, 1981.

---

*Quotes from the Declaration of Independence – then applied to Great Britain, now applicable to the United States Government.

Chapter IX

Discussion

The occurrence of historic tidal forces — and their relationship to climate via volcanic eruption, dust in the stratosphere, and effect on climate has been the reason for this study of history.

The pairs of tidal forces were: 23 December 796 and an almost equally high tide (at 30° N. Latitude) 18.03 years before (about 12 December 778); and on 23 December 1893 and an equally high tide at 30° N Latitude (about 3 January 1912).

The climate has been established as well as a search of the literature permitted.

A chronology of the eight decades preceding, and a number of decades following the high tidal forces, has been prepared and presented.

Climatically comparable decades are contained in the following **SUMMARY**. It is clear that geographical areas had enormous detail of history, and that the detail differed. This summary seeks out those important aspects that were similar. This obvious filtering of data is subject to criticism; but the synchrony of rising and falling of cultures under like climatic conditions seems well beyond the limits of chance.

Bitter cold, droughts, migrations and wars are unchallengably motivating forces on the behavior of societies, and there are undeniable periods of good climate in the entire Northern Hemisphere (the 1960's) and bad periods (1972-82). Famines are profound movers of societies.

Surplus food permits the cultural overhead called civilization to rise. Deficit food supply cancels the overhead, and civilizations collapse.

Always, it is the people and their food which determine history.

History is a series of job descriptions.

Hitler was a job description.

Kennedy was a job description.

Martin Luther King was a job description.

All were cut off in their prime. The requirement no longer existed.

Climate determines history — given that Man is present. You will search history in vain for a **major** effect of free will. Details, yes. Major effects, no.

Summary

There are two chronological periods detailed in Chapter VIII — 717-926 and 1813 to 1981.

The very beginning of both periods were unusual in that a traveller could have gone all the way from the Atlantic Ocean to the Pacific Ocean on land by passing through only two sovereignties: the Moslem Empire and the Chinese T'ang Empire in the first case; and the French and Russian Empires in the second case; a passage several degrees further north.

These were the only two times in all of history that this was so. (Hitler's Germany reached the Bay of Biscay — not the Atlantic.)

717 - 726	Very cold; getting colder	1814 - 1823
Byzantium in revolt — defeated Arab Moslem attacks.		Ottoman Empire in revolt — defeated Christian attacks.
Islam near end of extreme expansion.		Napoleonic Empire at end of extreme expansion.
French Riviera taken by Moslems; France invaded.		French Riviera taken by Austria; France invaded.
Extreme poverty in France. The King went abroad in an ox-cart driven by a ploughman.		Bad harvests and conservative reaction in Western Europe.
China relatively peaceful.		China relatively peaceful.

727 - 736	Still colder.	1824 - 1833
China being invaded and losing ground.		China being invaded and losing ground.

Greek revolt against Byzantines — crushed.

Greek revolt against Ottoman Turks — crushed.

England had internal wars among small kingdoms.

England fought Ireland in the Irish Tithes War.

Japan increased its expansion against the Caucasoid Ainus.

Japan became more militant in rejection of Caucasian advances.

Khazars (in the Caucasus — now USSR) attacked the Moslems and lost parts of Georgia and the Ukraine.

Russians attacked Moslem Ottomans and gained land in the Caucasus.

737 - 746   Very Cold.   1834 - 1843

End of Glacial Maximum.

Glaciers readvance.

China fought invaders and won.

China fought invaders and lost.

French began to drive the Moslems backward out of the Riviera.

France drove the Moslems back to Algeria.

Famine (739) in the British Isles.

Severe problems with peasants across Europe.

The Moslem world split apart.

Egypt's Governor was granted hereditary rule by Sultan Mohamud of the Ottoman Empire.

Lombardy continued expanding in Italy against the Byzantines.

Numerous nationalist uprisings in Italy.

Khazars in Caucasus fighting Moslems.

Russia fighting Moslems.

747 - 756   Very Cold.   1844 - 1853

Glaciers retreating.

Glaciers at maximum.

One of China's greatest Civil Wars. (An Lu Shan War — millions were killed)

One of China's greatest Civil Wars. (T'ai-P'ing Civil War — 20,000,000 were killed)

Tibet rebelled against the Chinese, and became independent in 755.

Tibet negotiated a treaty with invaders from Ladakh. The Chinese did not participate. During the 1850's and 60's the Chinese influence continued to decline.

Lombardy attacks Rome;
Franks invade Lombardy.

The European revolutions - 1848-'49,
immediately preceded by several
years of bad harvests.

Byzantium had the pro-icon
revolt; the Moslem Empire
is racked with revolt.

Romania rebelled against the
Ottomans.

The Second Frankish Dynasty
(Carolingian) replaced
the Merovingian.

The Second Empire (Napoleon III)
replaced the Second Republic.

767 - 776   Getting warmer.   1864 - 1873

China quieted down in a condition
of partial dismembership.
It was very weak after the
Civil War.

China finally put down the T'ai P'ing
Rebellion with the aid of Great
Britain. China was partially
dismembered.

Silla — one of three countries on
the Korean Peninsula — tried
to overthrow Chinese
authority.

Korea was given self-government
in domestic and foreign affairs
by the Chinese government.

The Byzantines quelled the
revolts of the Bulgars.

Bulgarian Revolutionary movement
began against the Ottoman Empire.

Charlemagne's France came up
against the Viking frontier
(Danes) in the war against
the Saxons. There were
several Viking Kingdoms.

France's preparation for war with
Germany (1867) after Napoleon III's
humiliation over Luxembourg
warned Germany. Bismarck united
several Principalities; and invaded
and conquered France after
Napoleon's defeat at Sudan.

The Moslem Empire was relatively
quiet.

The Moslem Area was relatively
quiet.

Japan set up its capitol in Heÿo
(Nara) in 710 — modelling
it on the Chinese capitol
Chiang-an; then moved it to
Nagaoka in 784; thence to
Heian (Kyoto) in 794. It
stayed there until 1868. The
move was involved in con-

Japan moves its capitol from Kyoto
to Edo (renamed Tokyo in
November 1868). The move was
involved in consolidation of
the Emperor's power (the Meiji
Restoration). These two times —
the 700's and 1868 were the
only two times it ever happened.

solidation of the Emperor's
power.

777 - 786	Getting Still Warmer	1874 - 1883

Japan's Emperor Kammu vigorously reestablished central author- ity to cope with Ainu aggression.	The Meiji Emperor (Japan) Mushuhito put down the Satsuma Rebellion and reestablished Imperial authority. An army — largely commoners — beat an army of samurai — to cope with foreign aggression.
In Spain — bloody war raged between Christians and Moslems.	In Spain, the Bloody Carlist Wars and a coup grew out of the problem of succession.
Byzantium was too weak to win.	The Ottoman Empire was too weak to win.
France's Carolingian Empire continued to expand. The French fought the Moors.	France continued to expand its Empire in North Africa. The French fought many groups of Moslems.
Vikings took the Shetland and Orkney Islands.	Germans and Belgians were setting up Colonial Empires in Africa.

787 - 796	Warm — Highest Tidal Time	1884 - 1893

The Popes had their second longest running average tenure at this time.	The Popes had their longest running tenure at this time.
China was extremely weak. There was widespread piracy.*	China was extremely weak. Piracy was very common. Two Great Famines.
Vikings began to raid the British Isles. France was expanding its Empire, and the Moors were	Germany, Russia, France, Britain and Belgium were busy expanding their Empires. Conquest for profit was

---

*There are different kinds of Pirates. Pirates are usually thought of as freebooters; but European pirates in 1500-1700 were licensed by their governments to prey on civilian shipping of enemy nations. They had to share their take with the crown.

Moslem pirates are usually official.

fighting to expand their Empire. Conquest for profit was highly moral.	again highly moral.
Europe — a Great Famine: Cannibalism: "...have eaten members of own family..."	Europe — The Great Famine in Russia (1891-2) led to political unrest. Major agricultural depression across Europe.

797 - 806	Getting Warmer	1894 - 1903

The Viking raids and power were rising. They raided with impunity. Charlemagne continued to expand his Empire.	Germany was on the relative ascendancy. She took two Portuguese colonies as collateral for loans. Britain and France were also expanding their Empires.
Byzantium was moribund.	The Ottoman Empire was moribund.
The Moslem Empire was breaking up.	The Moslem area was falling to conquest.
China's T'ang Empire continued to survive in a much diminished condition.	China's Manchu Dynasty was harassed and humiliated, and subjected to loss of territory and much of its sovereignty.
This was a decade of fierce Japanese fighting with the Ainus; but Japan began to sink toward feudalism.	The Japanese fought fiercely, but their successes were restrained in China by European Powers; and in Korea by Russia.

At this point of climatic history, the temperatures behaved differently. The 800's appeared to have two temperature surges, whereas the 1900's had only one. This resulted in two times that temperatures went up or down in the 800's but only one in the 1900's.

The following summary periods compare **Three** decades of like climate:

The above examples will suffice to convey the idea that similar climatic times produce similar human behavior. The careful reader will note that agricultural hard times (famines) frequently trigger all other kinds of troubles.

Some generalizations can be made about **Then** and **Now**; related to the **Then** that is climatically like **Now** (1980-2010): see page 313.

807 - 816	Peak warmth; but beginning to cool. 867 - 876	1934 - 1943
China was being attacked; could not win counter-attack. Revolts in several places.	China suffers a severe peasant revolt which its army joined. Severe famine.	China suffers a severe peasant revolt (Communist) which some of the army joined. Japan conquered much of China. There were other revolts.
Japan conquered the Ainus and applied "the final solution".	Japan's Chronicles record public prayer to meet the massive piracy along the coastline by Koreans.	Japan conquers much of China, fought Russia, and attacked the U.S. at Pearl Harbor.
Byzantium — Christians versus Moslems — also widespread war in the Balkans.	Byzantium — Christians versus Moslems. War reaching out into North Africa. Malta lost.	*Widespread Balkan Wars.* Mussolini's Christians took Moslem Albania; but lost it in the general fighting three years later. Turkey stayed neutral but was paid off with territory.
France's (Holy Roman Empire) growth ended in this decade. It gave up territory. Vikings attacked in the north.	France (Holy Roman Empire) was attacked by Vikings in the North. People abandoned cities and moved inland. The Empire was attacked by Magyars in the East and Saracens in the South.	France lost territory to Turkey, Japan, Britain and the U.S. It was attacked by Italy in the South and was conquered by a German attack in the North.
Britain was attacked	Britain was attacked by	Britain was attacked by

by Vikings and was beaten in battles, but not totally conquered.

817 - 826

Chinese Peasant Rebellion that began in 809 ended after 13 years. Other rebellions in Honan and Hopei crushed.

Japan – ghastly famine.

Western Europe – English famine in 823. Continued Viking Wars.

Russia (Rus or Varangian Vikings) first attacked the Jewish nation of Khazaria. Moslems had cowered Khazaria into paying tribute of children and corn annually from 731 to 861.

Vikings and was beaten in battles, but not totally conquered.

877 - 886

Chinese Peasant Rebellion that began in 873 wound-down with an estimated death toll of 10,000,000. Invaded by Turks. Great Famine; T'ang Dynasty overthrown.

Western Europe – "Universal Famine" –879. Viking raids everywhere.

Russians broke the Jewish Khazars. With the cry: "Pay nothing to the Khazars", they broke through. The Jews continued to war with the Moslems.

Germany and was beaten in battles, but not conquered.

Had been very warm; Cooling very rapidly.
1944 - 1953

China – World War II wound-down. Chinese estimate 10,000,000 dead. USSR invades and devastates Manchuria. Great Famine. Communists overthrow the Nationalists. (USSR estimated that Communists executed 20,000,000 between 1949 and May 1965)

(U.S. Senate estimated that Communists executed 35,000,000 by 1971.)

Western Europe – Netherlands famine. Germany at war everywhere.

Jews set up an independent Israel in 1948; fighting Moslems for land, and Great Britain for sovereignty. The Russians continue to repress the Jews.

1. **Then**
    a. Inability of peasant societies to cope.
    b. Reduction of farm lands and food.
   Now
    a. Third World (underdeveloped countries — peasant societies) has exhausted its credit.
    b. Deserts are expanding; famines and revolutions are sweeping the world.
2. **Then** — With spread of famines and food shortages, political unrest.
   Now — Every country that has had famine in the last ten years has had at least one government overthrown.
3. **Then** — Terrorism and piracy.
   Now — Every airport is guarded against terrorists. Terrorism and piracy are rampant. A multinational conference on piracy was held.
4. **Then** — Cities as target areas for terrorists — especially trade centers.
   Now — Squatters, hangers-on (i.e., camp-followers), underworld exploiters, urban terrorists and even nuclear blackmailers have begun the disintegration of cities.
5. **Then** — Flight from cities.
   Now — In the U.S., there is flight from all cities except those **growing in area** with low population density. Every city with a Black mayor is losing White population.
6. **Then** — Flight to or toward the South and Southwest in the area that is now the U.S.
   Now — A migration toward the South and Southwest is in full swing in the U.S.
7. **Then** — Inability of the large governments created during the warm period to cope.
   Now — Governments such as China and the Soviet Union, and the Bureaucracies in the U.S., Great Britain, France, etc. have lost contact with the people; and strong movements are afoot to return power to the people.
8. **Then** — Rise of strong local governments (feudalism, war lords, principalities, samurai, etc.).
   Now — Rise of call for States Rights; Provincial Separation; greater satellite independence in Poland, Czechoslovakia; put down of centralized Communist philosophy in China; denationalization in Britain; calls for Constitutional Convention in the U.S.

   Then gives us a foretaste of **Now** and the next 30 years.

Chapter X

Inferred Future Events
1980 - 2010 A.D.

The reader may disagree with or dislike the following projections; but he cannot accuse the authors of making them lightly.

For lack of a better organization, the projections are presented alphabetically.

The basis is an expectation of five good (ameliorated) years for food production (1983-1988); then a gradual sliding into colder and colder weather with any other relief occurring in the 1995-2000 year quinquenium.

The projection looks to 2010 A.D.

Afghanistan has become the battleground between Communists and Moslems. The dispersed targets, combined with extremely mountainous terrain diminish the effectiveness of modern mass weapons, especially the atomic bomb. The Moslems will at least stalemate the war.

War between Communists and either Moslems or Democracies works to the disadvantage of Communists in all non-mass-weapon encounters; because only a small percent of Communists are dedicated, whereas Moslems and Democracies have a large percent dedicated.

Argentina Food exports will drop after the crest of the high-tidal forces in 1986 has passed. Winter-kill of wheat will become commonplace by 2000.

Arizona Will become wetter than at any time in the last 1000 years.

Astrologers will be agitated by the Venus transits on June 8, 2004, and June 6, 2012, correlating with the Maya long count calendar, which equals 13.0.0.0.0 on December 24, 2012.

According to Yaqui Indian tradition, a Venus transit produces the appearance of a "visible tail" on the Sun, which some cultures consider an important omen. Thus, Cortez arrived on 4 March 1519, less than a year from a Venus transit (2 June 1518) on CeAcatl (1-Reed) on the 52-year Aztec Calendar. (The 52-year calendar is a "take-off" from the Maya Calendar.) They thought he was Quetzalcoatl returning (Quetzalcoatl was born on CeAcatl, 944, and sailed away on CeAcatl, 999, saying he would return on CeAcatl). Thus Mexico fell to the astrological belief in the 52-year calendar. If the Aztecs had not been deterred by their astrological beliefs, they might have won.

Australia The Southern sector with Mediterranean climate will narrow by one-third. Net rainfall will decline as the winters get cooler and the years get warmer.

The Northwestern quadrant will get increasing monsoons.

Black Africa is sinking into a Dark Age (no pun intended). It must improve to become attractive as the stuff of Empires.

Brazil will continue to be dominated by its 26-year weather cycle within 10-degrees Latitude of the equator. The current drought period (typically about 7 years) will end in about 1984.

Canada will cease to export grain because the climate will get too cold.

Cities will cease to be supported by their governments because they have ceased to be an asset to their societies. Automation makes remote factories feasible, and eliminates the virtue of having nearby masses of people.

Cities will be abandoned under continuous threat of nuclear attack – by terrorists as individuals or terrorist powers like Communists or fanatic Moslems. Afghanistan is a world laboratory to show how societies can cope with mass-weapon threats, including nuclear weapons.

The answer is apparently dispersal – abandonment of cities as Europeans did under pressure from Viking and Saracen raids in the ninth century.

Climate in the Northern Hemisphere.

Colder during the next 50 years, except for 1983-1988 and possibly 1995-2000.

Warmer and wetter along the East Coast of the U.S. and China, including off-shore Japan, and peninsular Korea.

Storm tracks will average further South: Canada drier, Arizona and New Mexico wetter. Northern Europe drier, Southern Europe wetter.

There will be frequent monsoon failures.

Winters will have fewer cold-spells; though the years will be cooler. Paralyzing cold weather will occur at high latitudes.

Communism in its present form will cease to exist. Absolute monarchy, feudal war-lords, and various sorts of dictatorships will take the place of it.

Decentralization of power as well as people will occur, inasmuch as any centralized power structure will become an attractive target. There are no means on Earth adequate to guarantee that the Capitol building will not be destroyed by nuclear terrorists. Decentralization is the only way to avoid being an attractive target.

The electromagnetic pulse of a nearby nuclear explosion would destroy all computers, for example. Thus, not only buildings, but all sophisticated electronics will be destroyed by atomic bombs.

Earthquakes and Volcanoes depend on rising and high tidal-forces triggering — will increase toward 2010.

Exceptional High Tidal-Forces: High Probability Triggering Potential Volcanoes and / or Earthquakes

Date	Latitude	Years Since Tidal-Force of Equal or Greater Magnitude*
1986	30° S	168
1990	30° N	36
1990	60° N	61
1992	20° N	18
1997	10° S	1170
2005	30° S	18
2008	30° N	96
2008	60° N	96
2010	10° N	53

Egypt has a 50% chance of having its High Aswan Dam removed by Israeli, Libyan, Saudi or Ethiopian atomic bombs. Both Egypt and Iraq are uniquely vulnerable.

---

*The probability of triggering some geological event increases with the time that stresses have had time to accumulate.

Europe — Eastern will break out of Russian control.

  Northern is losing the ability to feed itself, and must, perforce, turn to thoughts of Empire.

  Western will become much colder. This will decrease its food production and greatly increase its aggressiveness. Thus: thoughts of Empire.

Conditions will not become quite as severe as they were in the Little Ice Age.

Famine The famines that will sweep the Earth will nullify the birth rate that now furnishes 75,000,000 extra human mouths to feed every year. The world population will subside 10-25%.

Feudalism will sweep the Earth. Principalities, war lords, sub-divisions of sovereignties, whatever they are called (Provincial Separatism, States Rights, Patróns, Samurai, etc.) will have near-sovereignty in their own right. Centralized power will be reduced as its relevance to people's problems becomes more blatantly deficient.

Flexible People thrive most under the conditions of change that exceed the ability of inflexible people to adjust. The world has entered a period of change so rapid that survival will go to the flexible.

Food will become the major limiting factor in the Affairs of Men. As the climate becomes more debilitating to agriculture, food will dominate the World's concerns.

France will be deeply involved in retaking an Empire (a hegemony), though it probably won't be called an Empire.

Government facilities will become very diffuse as the possession of nuclear weapons proliferates.

Great Britain will regain its will and reestablish its hegemony when it panics because the French are doing it.

  The heavy-handedness of the Russians, Germans, Belgians, Dutch, Spanish, Portuguese and Chinese will militate against their reestablishment of Empires.

  The United States is sort of an Empire without a head, where the colonials run the store — it's not the same.

Iraq The Euphrates Dam will probably be bombed. The Iraqis are so offensive that no one may ever know who bombed them. Try Iran, Israel, the Communists and the Kurds as likely candidates.

Iran The destructive course will end up in the hands of a military man in time (like General Riza, the Cossack general who was put on the Peacock Throne in 1921). It is probable that Iran will break into smaller sovereignties.

Israel will probably be atom-bombed. Everybody can play and somebody probably will. The Jews have made a historical tactical blunder. They concentrated a fourth to a half of the World's entire Jewish population into the field of a single plane-load of hydrogen bombs just as the hydrogen bomb was invented.

The only answer for ethnic safety; Diaspora and possible syncretism.

Japan will get warmer and wetter for the next 30 years and more.

Unlike the other great nations, all of which will become less centralized; Japan, alone, will get more centralized because it alone, will be getting warmer and wetter. The result will be that Japan will lose some of its flexibility.

The East Coast of both the U.S. and China will give rise to the same tendency; but both the U.S. and China will be dominated by their more western people.

Korea will also be more centralized for the same reason, but does not have a big enough population to be a great power at this point in history.

Kondratieff Wave The long cycle economic wave appears to be geared to the same 45-year cycle as that recorded in Hudson Bay storms (work of Dr. Claude Hillaire-Marcel, *et al.*). It is probable that the economy does not drive itself; but is driven.

Libya is headed for a period of being the most aggressive nation on earth.

Atomic bombs will probably end this phase. So many people will have both bombs and a motive that someone will wipe Libya out — and the world may never know by whom.

Mexico — Northern will have increasing rainfall; **Southern**-most Mexico will have decreasing rainfall.

Mexico City Valley will suffer severe flooding. The lake has been through this flooding cycle before in the 1300's.

Middle East The countries of the area will not have peace.

Migrations will increase; possibly triggering genocidal wars.

Europeans against Asiatics and Africans.

Indians against Bengalis.

Americans against Mexicans.

South Africans against Bantus.

Australians against Asians.

Ongoing genocidal struggles:

Ethiopians against Falashas (Pogrom against Black Jews).

Vietnamese against Ethnic Chinese.

Africans against Europeans.

Money will lose much of its power to control. In very hard times — which will be near-universal — people revert to the sorts of exchange that could be called barter. Governments that use money for control, and money managers who exert control, will earn holocaust from people who produce goods and services — in country after country around the Northern Hemisphere. Money doesn't win battles. People do.

Atomic bombs will seek out power centers — money as long as it is relevant, then goods.

Northern High Plains States and Prairie Provinces will lose the ability to grow crops such as sunflower and spring wheat as the season shortens.

Oil will lose its financial power as other solutions to peoples' problems are made available. The largest conservation of energy will be smart machines which will economize compared to the brute-force solutions of the past.

Pacific Coastal states and British Columbia, except the area south of San Francisco, will gradually be drought-stricken. They will suffer great forest fires and the Columbia and Fraser Rivers will decline.

Papacy will remain unstable compared with the beginning of the Twentieth Century.

Peasant Societies will become increasingly unable to cope with even the most rudimentary needs — such as food.

Political Unrest will sweep the world. The Communists who try to capitalize on political unrest will prove to be totally incompetent to do so.

Population of the World will be in sharp decline by 2010.

Robots will become domestic slaves in Western countries because:

They will work without tiring;

They will not learn in the Master's absence things he doesn't want them to think about;

They will not have to be given Civil Rights;

They will not create future problems by reproducing in large numbers

and becoming social dependents; and
They won't marry the Master's Granddaughter.

Russia will lose control of the Soviet Union and, before 2010, will have had a major aggressive war with China. The puppet states will capitalize on any Russian preoccupation to gain full sovereign independence from Russian hegemony.

Russia has made so many enemies that no one will try to save her if they see her dying.

Slavery is being reinstituted and will again become widespread — especially in equatorial countries. Slavery keeps recurring in hard times when slaves are an asset. Masters must be hard people.

Socialism will essentially disappear. It is "good climate" politics; and there won't be any good climate anywhere to sustain it.

Social Evolution   There are widely disparate societies on earth, and one way of characterizing them is Humanistic versus Quantitative. To put it mildly, the computer and the manufacturing robots are forcing these societies apart.

During exceptional times in the past like the world will have in the coming climatic period, people have turned to slavery.

The Quantitative peoples will have high enough skills to go to Robotic slaves; but the Humanistic peoples will turn (are turning) to human slaves.

The cycle of history has been:
Winners go out and conquer losers;
And bring the losers home as servants or slaves;
To teach the children of the winners —
To be losers.
Robots will have no losing ethic to transmit to the children.

Survival in the face of robotics and slavery.
Slave owners gradually grow softer and weaker.
The owners of robotic slaves will face their perils; because they will be served so well they will forget how to survive without slaves.

The only societies with a high survival potential will be those who work as a matter of sacred principle (Work As a Sacred Principle — or WASP); so they will not forget how to survive.

A nearby nuclear blast would burn out many of a robot's circuits; so loss of robots would always be an eminent possibility. If people forget how to take care of themselves, and the robots fail, they will be in survival troubles.

Temperature in the Northern Hemisphere which has dropped about 1° C between 1940-80, will drop an additional 1.3-1.5° C by 2010 A.D. This makes Northern Mississippi (the State) about the same climate in 2010 as Toronto was in 1940. Crop-growing areas will have moved south by 700-750 miles from 1940-2010.

Trade Unionism will have essentially disappeared in the Western Nations by 2010. Only when ownership and proprietorship don't fight back does a mere employee have a say in the use of the property. Trade unionism and feudalism do not mix.

U.S. Regional Redevelopment - By 2010

Geographic Division	Economic Change	Population Change	Political Influence
New England	+	+	– –
Mid Atlantic	– – –	– –	– – –
East North Central	– –	–	– –
West North Central	–	–	–
South Atlantic	+	+	+
East South Central	+ +	+ +	+ +
West South Central	+ + +	+ + +	+ + +
Mountain	+ + +	+ +	+ +
Pacific	+	–	–

U.S. will either diminish or eliminate Federal power. Producer states will dominate or eliminate the union. Consumer states will yield or be expelled.

When the going gets rough, producers win or quit producing. Consumers have no rights in time of need.

"Civil rights" issues will fade away, and will be replaced with behavior based on the concept that: "Nobody owes anybody anything."

Vigilantism will continue to increase hugely, because the law not only has ceased to serve the needs of the producer – it has become his active enemy. The law has become the means of robbing the producer to supply the consumer who keeps the law-makers in power.

Volcanism will continue to increase sporadically. In the U.S., there will be major volcanism in the Cascade Range by 2010. Volcanism will continue to rise in the Northern Hemisphere into the next century, but diminish after 2000 in the Southern Hemisphere. (see **Earthquakes**)

Wars will move south in mean latitude within the Northern Hemisphere.

European wars will minimize.

There will be an increase in wars as people become desperate for food. Famines will typically be followed by revolutions and / or wars.

Water will be hugely redistributed for agriculture.

Welfare will disappear. Charity will reappear.

The above projections, the reader is reminded, are based on the following considerations:

1. Volcanism in the Northern Hemisphere will increase a very great deal.
2. The sun will cool off.
3. The position of the Magnetic field is such that its effects are aimed at highly populated land masses; consequently,
4. Food production will lag very severely.
5. Nuclear weapons will be widely available, and render numbers of people insignificant in the resolution of issues. (The Equalizer)
6. Robots of domestic servant intelligence level will become widely available.
7. The rate of change of human events will increase slightly; and even more changes will occur by 2010 as have occurred during an equal time just passed.
8. Hard times make hard people.

Appendix I

Civilization

Davidson (I-[1]) uses language which implies that the story of man is his "movement in the direction of civilization". Evidence accumulates through time.

One can infer from the evidence now available that neither extreme — the beast that was pre-man, or the zombie that is fully-civilized man — is the direction in which man is slowly moving.

Civilization after civilization has come into being, and descended into dust. This was not the character of **each** civilization — it is the character of **civilization per se**. Civilization fosters comfort, and form in lieu of substance, and the human spirit goes to sleep. When any dramatic climatic change occurs, a civilized society is too inflexible to cope, and it fails.

The society which copes most successfully is one in which there is little enough coordination to permit failure of parts without bringing disaster to the whole. It must have enough insecurity for its very young that most individuals are imprinted with enough self-confidence to function in unpredictable situations.

Sophisticated barbarian societies like the modern democracies have the greatest survival potential; and that potential diminishes with the degree of societal organization; which can be stated as the degree to which failure of individuals is forbidden by the whole society.

Woolley [2] writes:

"The very word 'civilization' by its etymology implies an urbanized society."

In 1979, the United States of America finds itself in the process of abandoning cities. Some 15% of its total population lives in mobile homes. The persistent tradition of migrating to areas with lower density populations continues at an accelerated pace with respect to the census category called White; and, curiously, the census category called Negro is migrating toward high density areas. All those who chose urban life must be regarded as more civilized.

The census category called Negro appears to be much more civilized than Whites — at least in the United States [2].

Every purchase for currency is form versus substance, with the sovereign power having control of the form, and through this form, exerting control of substance.

The threat level of sovereignty must be credible, or else the currency cannot be taken seriously. Thus Monaco uses the French franc and San Marino uses the Italian lira. Of what use is a threat by a sovereignty where an average person in the middle of it can run out of it in 2 to 10 minutes.

Attention to form may be found in any culture at any time, obviously; but the greater attention any society pays to form, the less attention it pays to substance. When enough attention is withdrawn from substance, a rude, crude, violent behavior can easily overwhelm the more orderly-behaved sector.

The French and Indians cut Braddock's army to pieces. Jackson's entrenched mixture of frontiersmen, French pirates and other irregulars had 8 killed and 13 wounded against 2,036 killed and wounded British veterans under Packingham at New Orleans. Both of these battles, and others too numerous to count made the case that parading into battle against hidden opposition was virtually suicide. Courage of the highest order, yes! Both Braddock and Packingham were killed, along with many of their men. Effective — no!

During desperate wars, the parades and brass-polishing tends to go away.

Toynbee pointed out that the flowering of the arts and literature is one symptom of a civilization in the final phase of decline. In their own right, art and literature are tools for presentation of form, itself; and of linguistically-transmitted concepts. And the beauty and joy of these forms go unchallengeable! But beauty does not win battles, and battles determine survivors. One may well be willing to die for beautiful culture. But that is a different matter.

As Patton told his troops: You don't win by dying for your country (culture); you win by getting the other s.o.b. to die for *his* country.

A final genetic judgment against Camelot occurs when its believers die.

One can — indeed must — enquire whether all of Man's greatest questions must be answered by combat. There is an extremely important reason to believe so!

Compare the two aspects of Man's performance — the mental and the physical.

The Nobel Prize Winner William Shockley did a careful study of creativity — as exemplified by the number of patents and the number of publications that each staff member had in a population of about 1000 technical staff-members. He found that he could plot the logarithm of either the number of patents or scientific articles as a straight line against standard deviations (i.e., "sigmas") of a normal (i.e., Gaussian) probability curve. Since this latter (the normal curve) is a standard descriptor of all complex biological characteristics, he showed that for each incremental sigma of this biological characteristic, there is an factorial increase of creativity.

An explanation by example of the above technical points would be as follows:

1. A discovery requires only one concept in the mind at any point in time.
2. The combination of red paint with a green wagon could be a creation which requires two concepts to be held in mind simultaneously.
3. As Shockley pointed out, the invention of the automobile "self-starter" required four novel ideas to be held in mind simultaneously.
4. The number of possible combinations of:

    1 item is 1;

    2 items is 3; A, B, or AB;

    3 items is 7; A, B, C, AB, AC, BC, ABC;

    4 items is 15; A, B, C, D, AB, AC, AD, BC, BD, CD, ABC, ABD, ACD, BCD, ABCD: etc.

Thus, with a small gain in memory and cognitive power, a huge gain in creativity occurs. Creativity can be applied to any field of mental endeavor — not only arts and letters, but also science and engineering — among a host of things.

Contrast the gain in mental productivity with the gain in physical productivity as the physical strength increases. A hod carrier can increase his load **linearly** with the linear increase of his strength.

Thus, per increment increase:

Of strength gives a linear increase of physical productivity; and

Of the mind gives a geometric increase of mental productivity.

Now, it has traditionally been true that the **gathering**, or even the **production** of food has depended upon physical strength much more than mental strength.

If mental powers can be made the only form of confrontation, then the individual with an edge in mental power has a factorial (higher than exponential or "geometrical") edge in competitive performance. Thus, the courts are heavy with solemn ceremony, and bursts of violence are severely restrained. The law insists upon calm debate that strictly adheres to its own rules. Bankers talk about loans and interest. If one takes out money some other way, it is called robbery.

If a person whose life is one of physical power confronts someone with mental power, he will inevitably lose if he permits the mentally-inclined person to limit the contest to mental rules. If, on the other hand, the physical person hits the mental person in the mouth every time the mental person tries to convey a mental point, the physical person will have transformed the confrontation from mental to physical. The tremendous advantage of the distracted thinker dissolves, and the physical person is no longer working with a huge disadvantage.

Civilizations develop forms of many sorts—artistic, literary, legal, medium-of-exchange, religious worship, grace, courtesy. A barbarian who copes regularly with the physical real world can win a clash of interests, because physical violence can distract a mental type from concentration on his artistic, literary, etc., efforts or pursuits.

Physical violence is physiologically compelling.

One can be assured that anyone who is not in the "form"—establishment —will resort to physical violence to vent extreme frustrations which the "mental elite" does not respond to. It is the only chance that the "underdog" has of getting attention, or ridding himself of his tormentors.

History confirms that physical violence has occurred repeatedly, apparently for that reason. Violence is substantive as compared with form. Uncontrolled violence merely destroys form. Organized violence wins over and replaces the previous cultural form.

The above rationale explains theoretically and quantitatively why all severe clashes-of-interest are, and by the nature of living things must be, resolved with violence.

It is, therefore, certain that future clashes-of-interest between "men of substance" and "men of ritual" (form, ceremony, etc.) will be resolved with violence.

Colin Renfrew [4] points out that "... most archaeologists were content to follow the very distinguished prehistorian Gordon Childe when he summed up the essential theme of European prehistory as the story of 'the irradiation of European barbarism by Oriental civilization'."

He continues:

"The new dating helps us to see that we have been underestimating those creative 'barbarians' of prehistoric Europe. It now seems that they were erecting monuments in stone, smelting copper, setting up observatories and doing other ingenious things without any help from the east Mediterranean. This is not to say that they were 'civilized' in the strict archaeological use of the term: they did not yet live in cities or keep elaborate written records. In this sense, they were indeed barbarians, but much more creative and productive ones than has been realized. They are not to be dismissed as uncouth yokels on the remote Atlantic fringe of Europe, far removed from the so-called 'hearthlands' of the civilized world."

Many other examples exist.

The Phaistos disc found in an Etruscan site points strongly to the first movable type originating — not with Gutenberg's Germany, nor Korea, nor China; but with a barbarian tribe in Anatolia [5] [6].

The 'heathen Indian' of America domesticated more kinds of plants than all the rest of the world added together. He apparently also invented the zero, the microlithic arrowhead, and basketry.

The wheel existed in the barbaric steppes of Asia long before it was brought to civilization by waves of barbaric conquerers. Domesticated animals are a product of barbarians.

The truth of the matter appears to be this:

Almost all great creative thoughts are by barbarians.

Civilizations are so stable that they discourage or forbid creative thought. They receive new ideas from barbarian conquerers only when they have no more power to resist conquest by them.

Civilization is the ultimate degradation of the spirit; where creativity is suppressed in the name of order, and incompetence is preserved in the name of humanitarianism.

The comforts and security of civilization are but one step removed from the painlessness and ultimate security of the grave.

Civilization is the whirlpool into which humanity empties its flotsam and jetsam on its passage to oblivion. All who are creative or strong or productive ultimately revolt against it.

DATA RELEVANT TO THE STANDING OF
THE U.S. IN FORM VS. SUBSTANCE

TYPICAL CHARACTERISTICS OF WAR IN THE SUCCESSIVE STAGES OF A CIVILIZATION*[1]

ASPECTS OF CIVILIZATION AND OF WAR		RISE		DECLINE	
		Heroic Age	Time of Troubles	Time of Stability	Time of Decline
Character of civilization	Dominant interest	Religion	Politics	Economics	Art [2]
	Typical political organizations	Warring states	Balance of power	Universal empire or federation	Universal church and political anarchy [3]
Character of war	Destructiveness of war	Moderate	Severe	Moderate	Severe [4]
	Commonest type of war	Imperial (inter-civilization)	Balance of power (interstate)	Civil (intrastate)	Defense (inter-civilization) [5]
Technique of war	Typical military strategy	Pounce	Charge	Maneuver	Attrition [6]
	Typical military organization	Chief, retainers, and militia	Citizen army	Professional army	Mercenary army, fortification, and mechanization [7]

Law of war	Internal law of war	Private internal violence forbidden (king's peace)	Private external violence regulated (letters of Marque)	Public internal violence regulated (constitutional guarantees)	Public external violence regulated (military discipline) (8)
	International law of war — Resort to war permissible	to protect natural rights	as an instrument of justice	as an instrument of authority	in self-defense or for police of civilization (9)
Function of war	Typical conception — War considered	natural solution of conflicts of interest	legitimate procedure to settle controversies (ultima ratio or trial by battle)	status which may properly be created by sovereign authority for reason of state	technique of government and politics to be used when expedient (10)
	Typical objectives	Expansion of civilization	Achievement of reforms	Preservation of order	Defense of civilization (11)
	Typical effects	Integration	Change	Stability	Disintegration

(1) from Quincy Wright, *A Study of War*. University of Chicago (1965) p. 678.

(2) Kennedy established the National Academy of the Arts. Art is now "official".

(3) The belief that to each according to his needs; from each according to his ability is espoused by the same anarchical school of thought that espouses rights; but never, never addresses the subject of duties. "Free lunch", some call it.

(4) We developed the atomic and hydrogen bombs. The Character of war has become severe.

(5) The Korean and Vietnam conflicts defended the U.S. side of civilization from the Communists.

(6) In neither war did we seek to take and hold land. Body counts, open firing areas, etc., were formalized attrition.

(7) We hired foreign mercenaries, and currently have a volunteer army. The McNamara line was a useless fortification; and mechanization exceeds manpower.

(8) Only the federal government can declare war. Only official parts of the government can regulate the manner in which wars are executed. Two wars in succession without a policy of winning shows a total elitist dominance of military discipline.

(9) The last two major periods of combat were police actions – against the godless Communists.

(10) In the United States, "government by crisis" has been the dominant method since World War II began.

(11) A quote from William T. Coleman, Jr., the Secretary of Transportation, is in the *U.S. News and World Report* of Nov. 17, 1975: Under the subheading "SOCIAL INTERESTS JUSTIFY SUBSIDIES":

Q. Why can't transportation become profitable if we're going to be spending more and more on it?

I'd say that freight can. I think that air can. I've described the rail-passenger dilemma. That leaves mass transit in the cities. I don't see how that can be profitable. But I think there are social interests in connection with urban mass transportation that justify subsidies.

Q. What do you mean by that?

A. One is the fact that you don't have a civilized country if you don't have major urban communities that can support the theater, support major hospitals, support major universities. support major banking institutions.

Once you recognize that, you then say that to preserve that city you have to have methods of getting people in and out in the most efficient way. You have to put in place a good urban mass-transportation system. And you have to operate that system in a way that will induce people to use it rather than to come in by automobile.

This defense of civilization seems peculiarly appropriate coming from the first Negro Cabinet Member. He was appointed by the first appointed President.

Altogether, he probably spoke for the attitudes of up to 10 or 15% of the people.

Bibliography

APPENDIX I

[1] Davidson, Basil (1964) *The African Past.* Little, Brown and Company: Boston, Toronto.

[2] Woolley, Sir Leonard (1963) *History of Mankind: Cultural and Scientific Development: Volume I, Part 2: The Beginnings of Civilization.* Copyrighted and Authorized by UNESCO. The New American Library: New York, Toronto.

[3] Browning, Iben (1978) Form versus Substance: or the games people play. *The Browning Newsletter* 2: 5.

[4] Renfrew, Colin (1973) *Before Civilization.* Penguin Books.

[5] Pope, Maurice (1975) *The Story of Archaeological Decipherment.* Charles Scribner's Sons: New York.

[6] Charles-Picard, Gilbert (Gen. Ed. 1972) Trans. by Anne Ward. *Larousse Encyclopedia of Archaeology.* Hamlyn: New York. page 252.

Appendix II

The Great Ideas of Mankind

	Years Ago	Population
	10 Million to 100,000	500,000

Family
Simple Tool
Speech
Fire
Conscious Volition
Clothing

800 Billion Man-Years per Idea

	100,000 to 10,000	3 Million

Domestication of Animals
Government for the Ruler
Games
Representational Pictures
Construction of Shelter
Domestication of Plants

45 Billion Man-Years per Idea

	Years Ago 10,000 to 1,000	Population 100 Million

Warfare
Money
Ritual
Representational Sculpture
Government for the People
Religion

15 Billion Man-Years per Idea

	1,000 to 100	500 Million

Art of Computation
Literacy
Anti-anthropocentrism
Government by and for the
   People
Music
Commerce

75 Billion Man-Years per Idea

	100 To Present	1,700,000,000

Mass Communication
Industry
Flight
Mass Education
Technology
Science

28 Billion Man-Years per Idea

Possible New Great Ideas

Enterprise - Individual or Communal
Organization - Civilization or Barbarian
Freedom or Security
Treatment - Medicine, Acupuncture, Psychomancy or Hospice
Ethics
Change

Many businesses have concerned themselves with obsolescence and **change**.

Many colloquia are given on the **management of change**.

Almost all laws are passed to **prevent change**.

Revolutions such as the one in Iran are fought to **prevent change** brought about by too liberal a government. An Absolute Ruler fostered change in excess of the tolerance of the religious figures.

Climatic changes produce social changes. Such social changes have racked societies before. Something new has now been added. The following shows that the pace of change has increased intrinsically — for reasons internal to the nature of Mankind.

The pressure of **climatic change** has exacerbated the trauma which was happening independently of climate.

Eric Hoffer — America's foremost primitive philosopher wrote a book entitled: *The Ordeal of Change*. Perhaps the following will help to explain it.

There are certain ideas which have gained almost universal acceptance across the mainstream of Mankind.

These ideas can be delineated as the ones which can be held independently of each other.

One can have a **family**, or not, independently of whether he is a **scientist**, or not. Such an individual might or might not have a **religion**, and play **music**. The idea is that these **ideas** are essentially independent of each other.

Long ago, when a new idea was introduced, whole tribal and/or linguistic groups could evolve and disappear before any new Great Idea arose.

A few generations ago, when New Ideas were coming at a faster rate, a little poem was very frequently quoted:

"Be not the first
On which the New is tried;
Nor yet the last
To lay the Old aside."

In recent times, New Ideas came every generation; and, coincidentally, people were living longer. The Old became obsolete, and lost the respect of the Young who were complying with the New Idea.

At present, several New Ideas are developing simultaneously; and the psyche which achieved its genetic basis long ago is torn asunder by bombardment with "New Ideas".

If one takes into account that only about 30 Great Ideas have occurred and been universally accepted in millions of years, it follows that perhaps no more than one in a thousand or a million New Ideas will turn out to be a Great Idea.

This concept can help in understanding the frenetic age that we live in.

A final introductory thought: All of the Great Organizations (sovereignties, religions, etc.) of the past have depended upon a small group gaining ascendancy over some aspect of a Great Idea. With New Ideas boiling onto the world scene, power is breaking up. A part of the psychic problem that some people have is the rapid disintegration of old traditions, establishments, etc.

The pace can **only increase**.

Group 1

FAMILY – The most fundamental idea in the species of Man (Homo sapiens) is Family.

Implicit in this explanation is the idea of **evolution**. This writer does not care to enter the battle between those who consider evolution the most **known** fact in all human knowledge; and those at the opposite end of the spectrum who believe in special Creation by a Supreme Being of Man as differentiated from all of the Beasts and other things. The position of this write-up is that a Supreme Being or random chance might have produced Man in this way; but the facts presented are as related by those who study physical evidence.

Three changes occurred in the species simultaneously, if, indeed, one can refer to events that occur within the same million years as "simultaneous."

The three events were:

People's brain size increased; this caused the head size at birth to increase; and

People stood upright; which decreased the size of the birth channel. The solution was a "premature" birth after a short gestation period. The nine-month gestation period of humans is grossly one-half the period of other like-weight animals; and whereas the gazelle, or deer is precocious (run with the herd within a few minutes of birth), the human baby is quite helpless for a few years.

Ik* children are put completely on their own at age three, and in a relatively benign climate. Some other children are on their own at five (a

---

*A tribe in Africa

small percent of the *gamenes* in Venezuela, for example); but most cultures wait longer to throw children on their own — especially in harsh climates.

Coincident with adoption of an upright posture was the utilization of simple tools (shaped stone); and the selective value of having a "tooth at the end of the arm" was spectacular. Animals who depend on biting put their heads (brains) in danger. Man with tool had the advantage.

Spears, bows and arrows, crossbows, guns, I.C.B.M.'s and lasers lengthen and strengthen Man's arm.

The freed hands cared for the baby.

The final aspect of change that made Family a viable idea was the increase **in sexual receptivity of the female**. Whereas periodic rutting of hoofed-animals fostered a herd-behavior; with herd-bulls, male-fighting, and the necessity of infant precocity because of lack of individual care; the almost continuous receptivity of the human female fosters small family groups with shared care of helpless infants.

Family is the central idea of Mankind.

FIRE — Only Mankind masters fire, and its mastery has fostered property rights (in order to keep the home-fires burning); augmented life expectancy (more digestible and antiseptic foods); and added to Man's intellectual prowess (light to extend his active day).

Wertime (*Amer. Sci.* 61: 670, [1973]) stated that anthropologists agree that Men have been using fire for light and heat for at least a million years. He also stated that cooking of food has been a "consistent art" for 100,000 years.

SIMPLE TOOL — As indicated under Family, above, having the hands free from walking, and a sharp rock (hammer) in the hand gave Man a tremendous advantage over biting animals.

Sticks as well as rocks could be wielded with desirable effect (as chimpanzees do today).

One site in the Olduvai Gorge where the Leakeys became the world's most famous archaeologists, featured an apparent production-line of stone axes. This "factory" dates back a half-million years.

Glynn Isaac of U.C. Berkeley said in 1973 that in four years of field work in Kenya, he had found nearly 600 tools used by man nearly 2.5 million years ago; and thousands of tools used by men existing 1.3 million years ago.

The skull of a child which dates back to 2.7 to 2.8 million years before the present shows that the child probably was killed with a stone axe.

Tentative conclusion: 1) Simple tools have been around a long time; and 2) People haven't changed much.

SPEECH—Recent experiments with chimpanzees has shown that they can and do formulate sentences—given a suitable medium such as meaning symbols (blocks) or a computer—with which to communicate. There has been no example as yet of a chimpanzee **inventing** the medium. Also, the medium does not include **speech**, apparently because of the physiological inability of chimpanzees to speak.

The parrot and the crow can speak—but appear to have no message.

Man had the ability to speak; invented speech as a medium of communication; had a message; and spends a significant fraction of his time transmitting and receiving messages. In addition, the sound "runs around in Man's head" and evokes a memory system which increases his total capacity.

Other means of conveying messages exist; but speech is Man's number one medium.

Although there is no hard proof that speech began in this first period at the dawn of humanity; the seeming inseparability between Man and Speech suggests that the one could not have occurred without the other.

CLOTHING—The fig-leaf seems an inadequate tale to explain clothing. Running through briers seems a better excuse.

Man was a lot smarter than the hermit crab—which has the perception that a shell is a great improvement over an unprotected and delectable body.

The other great apes use sticks as tools; but don't seem to have invented clothing. One has got to believe, it seems to the author, that the human brain that can set up a production line for stone axes can see the advantage and mechanism of clothing its body.

We select this time period for the introduction of clothing despite the lack of hard evidence.

CONSCIOUS VOLITION—One of the early differentiations between Man and the other great apes was his proclivity for planning ahead—or Conscious Volition in our terminology.

When man carried a stone axe around with him—it wasn't much of a plan; but it was an enormous improvement over nothing in case of a fight.

Given these six aspects of Dawn Man, he was off to a distinguished beginning.

Between 10 million and 100,000 years ago, the average population is estimated to have averaged about one-half million people. Their six great ideas cost mankind about 800 billion Man-years per idea.

Group 2

DOMESTICATION OF ANIMALS – The Australian Aboriginee obviously took the dog (from which the dingo evolved) to Australia – probably 20 to 50,000 years ago. *Canis familiaris* was present in North America – brought from Asia – by about 8400 B.C.

With all the evidence of slavery from the very earliest times, it would appear that Man domesticated Man (or at least tried to do so) as slaves from the very early times; but had to wait until means of confining his slave evolved to a workable level before it began to work.

Man as a domesticated animal hasn't been a great success. He keeps cutting his Master's throat and / or marrying his granddaughter.

Before 10,000 years before the present, it is possible that the cow was domesticated. Evidence shows that the cow was domesticated by or before the 5th millennium B.C. in Catal Huyuk (Turkey). The ability to plan ahead and to postpone until tomorrow the killing of what could have been killed today had to have preceded the domestication of animals.

Considering the cave art (35,000 years), calendar (an accurate calendar dated back to about 13,000 years ago in Spain, Man was organized to handle domesticated animals long before 10,000 years ago.

GOVERNMENT FOR THE RULER – It was a great discovery for Man that he could exploit a herd made up of families in a way analogous to a herd-bull's exploitation of his herd. The real difference is that the herd-bull's primary motivation is sexual exploitation, and his primary contribution is fighting.

Government for the Ruler made a subtle transformation from other species to Man. Sexual exploitation was not the **primary** motivation; and the Ruler can, in the case of humans, get the members of his tribe to fight in his stead. There were, oddly, advantages to both the Ruler and to the members.

GAMES – The "premature" human baby has both a very large, and highly undeveloped brain.

It s arms and legs are merely simulations of adult arms and legs.

Not only can humans not get up and run like their precocious hoofed cousins; but they are so uncoordinated that they could scratch their own eyes out, if their arms were long enough.

The simulated arms and legs learn by churning and moving – with motions geared to sound – so that coordination is gained before strength and size is acquired.

The entire idea of "play" with the concomitant organization of the activity became "games". Childhood lasts a very long time in the human species.

It is a truism that the greater the intelligence of a species—the longer is its "childhood". Snakes are not known to play; rabbits play very little; puppies play a lot and man almost never stops.

REPRESENTATIONAL PICTURES—General practice of representing ideas with art swept the world; and caves, cliffs and bones retain these images and give present people some idea of the world as perceived through the eyes of our remote ancestors.

CONSTRUCTION OF SHELTER—Not only did people live in caves; but also they made shelters of logs and other natural materials in the period of 100,000 to 10,000 years ago.

Such constructs are found in North America, the Middle East and other places.

DOMESTICATION OF PLANTS—Sometime around 9000 B.C., local food production began in Southwestern Asia.

From Nubia, one obtains evidence that grinding grain was a known technology—fully developed by 12,500 B.C. This left 4,500 years within the period up to 10,000 years ago for a fully developed technology to **raise** instead of just gather the grain.

David L. Greene (*Bio-Science* 20(5):278 [1970]) flatly stated that "Around 10,000 years ago in the Mideast, Man began to control the domestication of plants and animals."

SUMMARY OF GREAT IDEAS—GROUP TWO—From 100,000 years to 10,000 years ago, with an average of 3 million humans in the world population, there were 45 billion Man-years of life lived for each new great idea.

With the next group of Great Ideas, which occurred between 10,000 and 1,000 years ago, human life began to take on a very modern shape.

Group 3

WARFARE—The earliest battle of which a partial account exists is referred to (Eggenberger, *A Dictionary of Battles*. Crowell; 1967) as Megiddo I (Armageddon). It came complete with Kings, army groups, an attack, a rout, a seige, a walled city, an Egyptian Empire putting down a revolt in Northern Palestine. The same Egyptian King (Thutmose III) had 14 more successful campaigns in his 54-year reign.

This message is that warfare was a highly developed art by this period, and a way to settle inter-group issues. The Chinese, Egyptian, Greek, Roman, French, Moslem, Maya, Old Ghanan, Hunnish, Persian and many other Empires were established by warfare and ran their course during this period.

MONEY — A medium of exchange took the place of barter during the course of this period. Under large sovereignties, coercive power of the government forced subjects to accept the medium as though it reflected reality; even though it always tended to decay away from intrinsic barter value (silver, gold) to some highly debased sort of currency.

International trade has tended to keep currency "honest" with exchange rates; but is far from a perfect instrument.

Currency comes in four forms:

Constant;

$$V_1 = V_O;$$ (None of this around);

Inflating;

$$V_1 = V_O e^{kt};$$ (Western countries 1910-30);

Accelerating;

$$V_1 = V_O e^{k^1 t};$$ (Brazil 1910-65);

Indexed and / or exploding;

$$V_1 = V_O e^{k^{1^m} t};$$ (Germany, Post WW I; China, Post WW II)

where later value V_1 is dependent on the rate of change and time.

Governments try to control the purchasing power of currency, and fail. This delusion is one of the most persistent in all of history.

RITUAL — The greatest proponent of conscious ritual in all history was Confucious, although every religious leader stresses the ritual as a means of compliance with religious requirement.

Ethnicity is highly dependent upon ritual to establish ethnic identity. One is "comfortable" around people who have familiar rituals, and uncomfortable if rituals are strange.

Familiar rituals can help a person to go through times of trial and stress — as though at least some part of the uncomfortable situation is familiar — which implies an acceptable outcome.

REPRESENTATIONAL SCULPTURE — During this period, many cultures developed sculpture to as high a skill as it ever became. Mechanical means (lasers, grinding tools, acids, etc.) have been subsequently developed; but quality has never been improved.

GOVERNMENT FOR THE PEOPLE — Both the Persian and Roman states were at one time or another governed for the people. Normally, however, a government is run on behalf of the governing people.

One symptom of government for the people is no tax exemptions at all. If **anyone** is tax exempt, it is clear that the government is for that person or class of people. If any governmental discrimination exists, the government is not for the people — it is for the government which uses discrimination to achieve tenure.

RELIGION—When religion expanded conceptually so that a particular religion could be equally embraced by more than one ethnic group, it became a Great Idea.

Great religions that swept the world were mostly in the period under consideration: Hinduism, Judaism, Confucianism, Buddhism, Christianity, and Moslem. Near-great were Zoroastrianism, Sikh and Jain.

Schismatic religions seldom become wholly removed from the original religions.

The most radical religious perception may well have been Judaism with its perception of an intangible God—rendering the perceived God secure from physical capture.

The Protestant Christian perception that each person deals directly with God was a shattering concept. Such a perception severely threatens "middle-men".

During the last millenium, the great beliefs in the tens of millions of adherents have been Orthodox Christianity—schismatically separated from the Roman Church; Protestantism; possibly belief in Democracy; and certainly the Communist belief.

Certainly Communist violence to obtain adherents does not exceed the violence of the Crusades or Moslem expansion.

Ethnicity has become a sub-set of religion.

SUMMARY OF GREAT IDEAS—GROUP THREE—During the period from 10,000 to 1,000 years before the present, there was an average population of about 100 million people. The above six ideas, therefore, took some 15 billion Man-years of life per idea—the fastest rate Man has ever achieved.

Group 4

ART OF COMPUTATION—Computation was a very pragmatic way that many peoples used to achieve quantitative purposes.

In France some 34,000 years ago, Ice Age men scratched calendars on bones and stones. These calendars showed days (time with respect to the sun) and lunar phases (time with respect to the lunar month).

From 1900 to 1600 B.C., very sophisticated men built Stonehenge, an astronomical observatory of outstanding accuracy, on the Salisbury Plain in Wessex, Great Britain. These Beaker people had made a great computer, and with it could compute astronomical facts which could have been used to assist in planting, harvesting, and the like—for these were farmers.

Mathematical tables are found on clay tablets dating back to the third or second millenium B.C. Ancient Egyptians surveyed land and great architectural constructs precisely. Between 1000 B.C. and 830 A.D., the Mayas developed a precise knowledge of astronomy; but they **knew** it — they did not **compute** it.

But within the last thousand years, almost all peoples everywhere have fallen under the influence of a monetary economy and must use computation. The most primitive peoples must cope with trade values, because barter as a **sole** mechanism of exchange has virtually disappeared. The holdouts probably do not equal 0.1% of humanity, nor did they a century ago.

LITERACY — The use of writing at first was symbolic at the level of one character per idea. The representation of ideas by writing proceeded through simplified representation (cunieform); puns (the symbol for a mono-syllabic-named thing was then used on complex representations of terms which included the sound in the word — hieroglyphics); syllabics (Linear B) and alphabetic.

The systems which involved more than a thousand characters required that literacy be a profession.

Systems with between 64 and 1000 characters are simple enough that professionals can be literate.

With 64 or fewer letters, lay people can be literate.

ANTI-ANTHROPOCENTRISM — Man discovered that he was not at the center of the Universe — despite the fact that the name China means "Middle-Land" — or, the middle of the Universe.

No simple term expresses such an idea, thus the complex title used above.

The idea that a human is not the center of the universe is essential to any effort to think objectively about the world.

As an anonymous poet said:

"I exist", said the Man to the Universe.
"Even so", replied the Universe —
"I feel no sense of obligation."

GOVERNMENT BY AND FOR THE PEOPLE — The first succinct expression of this thought was by Abraham Lincoln, although the general idea was kicked around by Athens, the English Colonies, and Voltaire and his friends.

Of course, all of the citizens were entitled to participate equally in Athens; but only 3% of the population was citizens. The rest were slaves, foreigners, women and children. This was clearly an oligarchy.

The Founding Fathers gave the vote to adult / white / male / land-holding freemen. Lincoln and the Civil War expanded participation to eliminate color as a requirement.

Women were given the right to vote in the U.S.A. by the 19th Amendment; and 18-year-olds were enfranchised by the 26th Amendment.

Recent Supreme Court rulings permit discrimination against white-males; so the "deliberate" approach to government by and for the people has become a "deliberate" withdrawal from that principle.

Taxation without representation has become rampant (Washington, D.C., prisoners with income, "minor" wage earners, etc.); search without legal process (OSHA); punishment without due process (EPA fines); and, in general, the U.S., France, and others have never quite reached, and have since withdrawn, from the ideal expressed by the title.

Despite these doleful facts, every government has felt the necessity of claiming that it **does** consist of "government by and for the people". Even the Communists have elections (one candidate per office). It is an idea whose time has not come; but which everyone claims.

MUSIC — Every culture has its music, and to a degree — depending upon the musical training of the listener — conveys information about the culture.

The bandwidth of sound transmission of communications media determines what is conveyed to the listener of the cultural offerings.

Even the Ayatolla Khomeni of Iran is cognizant of music, although he has tried to ban it: Communist rulers constrain the variety of music offered to their subjects.

By 100 years ago, every culture felt compelled to develop and display its own music.

COMMERCE — Empires were founded for commerce. Instead of pure tribute which earlier Empires exacted from their subjects; later Empires have used commerce to exact a profit **in lieu of** tribute.

The cold, hard nature of tribute lacked subtlety, and caused people to revolt. The revolts were messy, and caused a lot of subjects to get wounded or killed, and thereby diminished the quantity of materials available from which to exact tribute.

The last great tributes were exacted by the Soviets from enemy and ally alike at the end of World War II.

Commerce has a subtlety which permits governments and businesses alike to scrape off a profit without excessive pain to the consumers; and has been used universally for two to three centuries.

SUMMARY OF GREAT IDEAS — GROUP FOUR — Between 1000 and 100

years ago, six Great Ideas were generated by the population which averaged 500 million. The resulting time required was 75 billion Man-years per idea.

Group 5

MASS COMMUNICATION — A spate of mass communications' means have spread across the scene in the last hundred years. Unlike previous times when great battles were fought after peace treaties were signed, almost everyone is bombarded with information today. The intensity of bombardment is a measure of the resources of the bombardier.

The duration of a particular kind of bombardment depends upon life cycles of humans and the rise or decline of credibility.

The kinds of media are the printed word in the form of scrolls, books, newspapers, magazines, signs, circulars, etc. These place a literacy requirement upon the public. Sound issues from criers, public address systems, radio, phonographs, and tape players; and both sight and sound from movies and television. One reason for the success of these media is that they — especially free TV — place such a small requirement upon the bombarded public.

The rising cacophony is certainly helping to shape the future of Mankind.

INDUSTRY — The beginnings of industry were to be found across Mankind's domain for the better part of a million years. Only since the introduction of mass production has industry become a Great Idea.

Given the close supervision of production lines, the naive beginner can quickly learn the few simple actions necessary for an incremental section of the production process.

The consequence of this philosophy is to diminish the significance of arts and crafts skills; and to flood the world with products. The result has been to raise the quality of life of people in general.

FLIGHT — Little is required to remind thoughtful people of the uniqueness and significance of flight.

The impact of flight has been enormous on almost every other facet of life — war, games, religion (example: The Pope's travels), government — everything.

MASS EDUCATION — The basic concept of education is the transmission of information from those who have it to those who do not.

Institutions have been playing a large role in the process — which thereby filters the information.

Apprenticing has been the traditional way to train beginners — formally or informally. This sort of training involves mostly learning by doing. Education is mostly involved in abstracting and discussing an activity, with a minimum of doing.

To apprentice is **to learn**. To acquire an education is **to learn about**.

Mass education **teaches the many about much**. But it is not **learned**; rather, it is **learned about**. This leads to a lot more talk than action— more form than substance.

The current economic and sociological disasters in western countries are due to laws made and backed by educated people who **know about**— **but do not know** the activities that make society work.

It will probably be shown in the fullness of time that Mass Education has been the most fruitless "garden path" that Mankind has ever walked down. It has been "the royal road to knowledge"; but having and using knowledge are as different from each other as are failure and success.

TECHNOLOGY — Technology has advanced steadily in the process of being an integral part of the development of Man.

The idea of **technologists** is much more recent.

World War I made it clear to most people that technology is essential to having a significant role in world affairs. Most societies are hostile to advanced technology, being humanistic in orientation. This hostility is shared in the affluent countries by the humanists—artists, social workers, civil rights activists, etc., as a rule with exceptions—some of which are notable exceptions.

Every sovereign state avails itself of technological advantages. Even the most inadequate sovereignties during famines accept and use food that is flown to them.

SCIENCE—World War II gave rise to radar, the atomic bomb, widespread aerial bombardment, long-range rockets, and altogether impressive performance of science in advancing the interests of sovereign powers.

Growth of productivity in "developed" countries has been shown to depend heavily upon both Science and Technology. Hostility to these two ideas fosters enduring poverty, shortened life expectancy, and other symptoms that accompany "humanistics".

Science has taken its place along with the other Great Ideas.

SUMMARY OF GREAT IDEAS—GROUP SIX—Six Great Ideas arose to the level of world acceptance during the last hundred years. The world had an average population of about 1.7 billion people during the period, hence some 28 billion Man-years per idea.

Inasmuch as the world population now exceeds 4 billion people, it takes only seven years to accumulate an extra 28 billion Man-years; so timing-wise, new ideas can come very fast these days.

There are **FUTURE POTENTIAL GREAT IDEAS**:

ENTERPRISE — Individual or Communal. Some ethics teach their adherents to avoid personal risk; so they must wait until other people have eliminated risk, then copy.

Communal societies are among those which do not take entreprenurial risks, although they seem well-adapted to taking risks along historically rewarding lines — such as military conquest.

ORGANIZATION — Civilization vs. Barbarian; or equivalently — Security vs. Freedom.

Given enough organization, a society can become highly-civilized, well-behaved (by extreme law enforcement), and very secure.

With little organization (democracy or less), people are free; but have very little security.

The world is very divided on this issue, though the majority opts for security at this point in history.

To have both security and freedom is impossible. They are opposites.

TREATMENT — Medicine, Psychomancy, Acupuncture, or Hospice.

Only a fraction of the world accepts medicine. Herbalism is one form.

Psychomancy includes prayer; "laying-on-of-hands"; shamanism; witch-doctoring, voudou; etc.

Acupuncture has become known in the Western World; but its efficacy is under severe dispute.

Hospices are special places to die, and must include the old being given a four-day supply of food and left in a remote place as a standard practice among certain Central African tribes. The conclusion is to be eaten by lions. Eskimo oldsters are given food and pushed out to sea on an ice-floe. The main idea of this concept is to permit the old and helpless to be seen last by their families with their dignity intact.

Certainly, medicine can keep some people alive beyond their point of dignity.

CHANGE FOR ITS OWN SAKE — This is occurring.

Appendix III

Climatic Influences Surrounding Tutankhamon

The greatest surge in Egyptology in recent centuries occurred as a sequel to two events—the translation of hieroglyphics by Jean-Francois Champollion in 1825 [1]; then the spectacular discovery of Tutankhamon's tomb by Howard Carter on 4 November 1922 [2].

The boy's tomb had been robbed, but the cemetary ghouls had been caught in the act, and much of their plunder had been returned; although the heavy golden vessels and much other magnificent work were evidently too great a temptation for the officials [2].

It was the good fortune of our times that two hundred years later, "...when the Empire was tottering, the architects of Rameses VI, excavating the tomb of this Pharaoh just above that of Tutankhamon, ordered the workmen to throw their waste limestone chips down the slopes below it, thus completely covering up the tomb of Tutankhamon [2].

To see where this boy fit into the scheme of things, consider the schedule of events. The climate dictated the dynastic tenures and changes in Egypt— not only in past historic times; but to this day. The following essay is quoted in its entirety from the *Browning Newsletter* 2 (7), © dated 21 August 1978.

348

Climate as a Forcing Function of History — The Case of Lower Egypt

In previous articles tidal forces via triggered volcanism, magnetic field via cloud cover, ozone, etc., and solar activity via the same routes have been explained as the sources of climate. Climate, it has been contended, shapes history.

This essay meets the challenge head-on, and gives a working case.

The history of Egypt has been studied perhaps as much as any subject on earth. The work on Egyptian archaeology has been absolutely phenomenal as to quantity and quality.

Let us simply examine it from the point of view of the driving forces.

The list of regimes which have ruled Egypt include both domestic and foreign dynasties, periods of colonial rule, time spent incorporated into someone else's empire, short rule under conquest, and now, self rule under a Republic. The list of regimes below is from standard sources, and while not every source agrees on dates, is at least very close:*

		B.C.
Dynasty I	-Domestic - 9 Kings	3110 - 2884
Dynasty II	-Domestic - (8-10) Kings**	2883 - 2665
Dynasty III	-Domestic - 4 Kings	2664 - 2615
Dynasty IV	-Domestic - (6-8) Kings**	2614 - 2502
Dynasty V	-Domestic - 9 Kings	2501 - 2342
Dynasty VI	-Domestic - 6 Kings	2341 - 2181
Dynasty VII	-Domestic - Interregnum***	2180 - 2175
Dynasty VIII	-Domestic - ⎰ 31 to 40 K. ⎱	2174 - 2155
Dynasty IX	-Domestic - ⎱ in 60 Yrs. ⎰	2154 - 2130

With the downfall of a central government, Egypt broke up into smaller units in this extraordinary confused period. At Heracleopolis the 9th and 10th dynasties ruled the north (Lower Egypt) while after a short interval the monarchs of Thebes (Under Egypt [the Sudan]) formed the 11th Dynasty in the south. In 2052, King Mentuhotep II in the south extinguished the Lower Egyptian Dynasty, and "reunited" the country.

---

*The lower Nile and the Delta are considered here. The Upper Nile (now partly the Sudan) is considered foreign here, since it had a different climatic driving force.

**Some Kings ruled simultaneously — thus more Kings than reigns.

***Some talk of 70 Kings in 70 days. Was it a committee, or did 70 get killed off at 1 a day? This began a 50-year Dark Age — drought, famine, rebellion, slaughter — every kind of bad happening.

Dynasty X - Domestic — 5 Kings - 2130 - 2052
Dynasty XI - Thebes   — 4 Kings (2134) - 2052 - 1999
(This included an interregnum.)

There was a disastrous drought from about 2002-1992 B.C. It was a short Dark Age.

Dynasty XII - Domestic - 8 Kings - 1991 - 1786.

Again Egypt broke up into pieces, with the 13th and 16th Dynasties ruling in Thebes, the 14th in the north at Xois, and the 15th Dynasty, the Hyksos***, later ruling part of the country from Thanis and finally all of the country before Sekenre and other princes of his family in Thebes ejected the Hyksos from Egypt (See Table 1).

Table 1. A confusing period in Egyptian history.

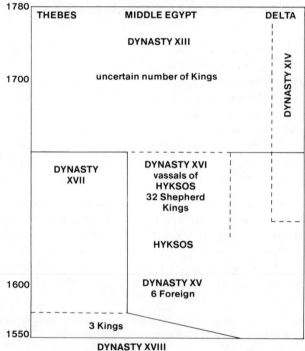

***Asiatic invaders finally conquered Egypt and imposed a harsh rule. They were Phoenicians and Israelites—the Shepherd Kings. They destroyed Egyptian Temples, and around 1600 B.C. were attempting to force the worship of one God—Set Sutekh. They were apparently attempting to kill all Egyptians, or Egyptian culture, or both.

Dynasties XIII and XVI	Thebes	1785 - 1647 B.C.
Dynasty XIV	Domestic	1785 - 1603 B.C.
Dynasty XV	Hyksos - 6 Kings	1678 - 1570 B.C.

(Note that the XVI Dynasty at no time ruled Lower (Delta)
Egypt.)

Dynasty XVIII	Domestic - 14 K&Q	1570 - 1304 B.C.
Dynasty XIX	Domestic - 8 Sovereigns	
	7 Kings	1304 - 1181 B.C.
Dynasty XX	Domestic - 10 Kings	1181 - 1075 B.C.

A Dark Age began with extreme drought in the eastern
Mediterranean Basin area.

Dynasty XXI	Domestic at Tanis - 7 Kings	1075 - 940 B.C.
Dynasty XXII	Foreign-Libyans - 9 Kings	940 - 730 B.C.
Dynasty XXIII	Thebes - 4 Reigns, 6 Kings	817 - 730 B.C.
Dynasty XXIV	Domestic - 2 Kings	730 - 715 B.C.
Dynasty XXV	Foreign-Ethiopian - 5 Kings #	751 - 656 B.C.
Dynasty XXVI	Foreign-Assyrian - 6 Kings	663 - 525 B.C.
Dynasty XXVII	Foreign-Persian - 5 Kings	525 - 404 B.C.
Dynasty XXVIII	Domestic - 1 King	404 - 398 B.C.
Dynasty XXIX	Domestic - 5 Kings	398 - 378 B.C.
Dynasty XXX	Domestic - 3 Kings	378 - 341 B.C.
Dynasty XXXI	Foreign-Persian - 3 Kings	341 - 333 B.C.
Greek Period	16 Reigns (Kings or Queen)	332 - 30 B.C.
Roman Period	Egypt was a colony	30 B.C. - 324 A.D.
Byzantine or Coptic Period		324 - 640 A.D.
Islamic Conquest	Rule from Mecca	642 - 661 A.D.
Umayyad Caliphate	Damascus - (Arabic)	661 - 750 A.D.
Abbasid Caliphate	Baghdad - (Persian)	750 - 868 A.D.
Tulumid Dynasty	Turkish	868 - 905 A.D.
Abbasid Caliphate	Baghdad - (Persian)	905 - 935 A.D.
Ikhshidids	Turkish	935 - 969 A.D.
Shi'ite Fatimids	Tunisian	969 - 1171 A.D.
Ayyubid (Sunnite) (Kurd-Saladin)		1171 - 1250 A.D.
Mamelukes (Bahri)		1250 - 1390 A.D.
Mamelukes (Burji)		1390 - 1517 A.D.
Ottoman Empire (Turks)		1517 - 1798 A.D.

Dark Age in the 1700's like 2190-39 B.C.

French Empire (Napoleon)		1798 - 1801 A.D.
Ottoman Empire (Turks-Albanian)		1805 - 1914 A.D.
British Empire		1914 - 1953 A.D.
Republic (UAR)		1953 -

Analysis of these data is straightforward. The most recent low tidal force date (considering the 179.33-year tidal force cycle) was 1972. On the average, $\frac{1}{4} \times 179.33 = 44.8325$ years on either side of such a low tidal force date gives:

$$1972 \pm 44.8325 = \begin{array}{c} 1927.1675 \\ \\ 2016.8325 \end{array}$$

between which dates the tidal forces were below average.

From 1837.5025 until 1927.1675, the forces would have been above average.

There have been 46 Dynastic Regimes established in the 5088 years of Egyptian history distributed as follows:

		Domestic	Foreign
Tidal			
Hi	4		11
Lo	17		14
Force			

The probability of this distribution occurring by chance is only one in thirteen — barely significant. Other force patterns act on invaders; so if one considers lower Egyptian Dynasties only, the odds of the establishment of 17 at low tidal force times, and only 4 when it is high is **less than one in a hundred — highly significant.** [†] Historically, the present must be reckoned as an extremely unstable time, and it will be a long, long 39 years before the stable times come. (This reference to stability is with respect to the 179-year cycle — and to pressures **within** Egypt).

The second factor which altered climate was magnetic field strength changes. Fairbridge (1977) checked the relationship of the magnetic field strength during the geomagnetic excursion (called the "Gothenburg") to a global climatic change that occurred simultaneously. The period was from 13,750 to 12,350 years before the present (as detected on the cores from Lake Erie).

Weakening of the magnetic field strength would permit more charged particles from space to penetrate the earth's magnetic "shield", and would result in high altitude atmospheric ionization, and increased cloudiness at all latitudes with warming at high latitudes and cooling at low latitudes as the consequence of the general cloudiness.

Bray's data shows that at the time, there was a moderate to major volcanic phase in New Zealand and Japan and a major southern South American volcanic wave.

[#] Although the Ethiopian Dynasty started in 751, it did not conquer Lower Egypt until 715 B.C.

[†] When tested against a null-hypothesis.

Every documented basin in Africa experienced minimum water levels in the 14th millennium B.P. (before the present), with the doubtful exception of Tibesti. Lake Victoria and probably Lake Albert ceased to overflow into the Nile. During this period of low flow, a great wedge of silt 40 meters thick built up as a great alluvial fan near the headwaters of the Nile.

Then the lakes went very high, and a period of flooding occurred with four times the present flow. The great river flow cut through the sediment to bedrock.

The probable cause of these events was as follows:

The decrease of ice loading on the continents at the end of the last Ice Age and uplifting as the result of isostasy caused a period of volcanism with its associated period of earthquakes. These, in turn, caused a disturbance of the earth's magnetic field. Fluid motions generated by earthquakes may have enough energy to be in equipartition with fields as large as 100 gauss.

In summary, earthquake disturbances may have lowered the magnetic intensity of the earth's field which diminished the flow of the Nile. ##

There is a proven ### magnetic field intensity cycle that has a westward precession in the northern latitudes. The rate of precession of this magnetic intensity is about 0.24° per year toward the westward. Other like measurements show a magnetic field intensity precessing westward at different rates: 0.18°, 0.2°, and the average of these is about 0.2067° per year. In addition, the magnetic pole is swept around by the polar precession cycle of one revolution in 25,800 years; and in the same westward direction. Adding these two frequencies:

$$\frac{1}{P} = \frac{1}{(360 \div 0.2067)} + \frac{1}{25,800}$$

$P = 1631.5$ years per period of the
magnetic field intensity beat at
any geographic point (such as Egypt).

(All of this information is heavily documented.)

The method of proof of magnetic field intensity at historic times is as follows:
1. Identify and date potsherds — as to time and place of manufacture.
2. Select the types which:
   a. Contain remnant magnetization from the original baking; and
   b. On which measurements of the remnant magnetization can be measured by reheating.
3. Measure the ratio of ancient and present-day earth magnetic fields by comparing the original and present field values before and after reheating.

Bucha *et al* (1969) showed that the archeomagnetic curves for Czechoslovakian and Central American pottery samples proved the westward drift. The curves shown are superimposed on the earth's geomagnetic moment curves derived from a multiplicity of sources #### (see **Figures 1** and **2**).

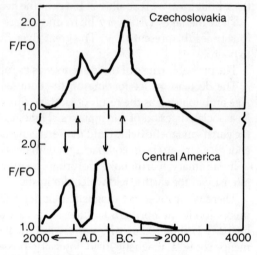

Figure 1. F/Fo is the ratio of earth magnetic field intensity at the test time to the field intensity at present (i.e., 1970).

The period of the geomagnetic moment apparently derives from the alignment variation period (i.e., precession period) of the earth's axis (25,000 years) and the period of variation of orbital ellipticity (hence earth proximity to the sun [92,000 years]).

$$\frac{1}{P_1} = \frac{1}{25,800} - \frac{1}{92,000}$$

$P_1 = 35,855$ years

This is the periodicity imposed on the earth's field as a consequence of its polar alignment with the sun's polarity, and also the average proximity to the sun (a cubic function — i.e., magnetic field influence varies as the cubic power of the distance.)

Tidal forces show a shorter period:

$$\frac{1}{T} = \frac{1}{12,900} + \frac{1}{92,000}$$

$T = 11,314$ — the tidal cycle at high latitudes.

The consequent period of geomagnetic moment is, in effect:

$$\frac{1}{G} = \frac{1}{T} + \frac{1}{P} \; ; G = 8,600 \text{ years.}$$

Refer to Figure 2.

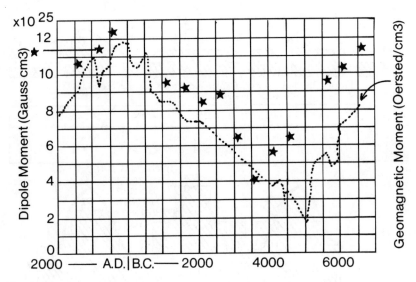

Figure 2.

Inasmuch as the Nile Delta is about 13° latitude eastward of Czechoslovakia, the high field intensity in Egypt would have occurred 55-60 years earlier. Thus, the phase of the high intensity wave would have corresponded quite accurately as shown in **Figure 3**, and drifted westward after that time.

The magnetic intensity at a site varies through time, and whichever way it moves, the ten-year mean temperature moves in the opposite sense. At the present date, the magnetic intensity is increasing at Helwan, Egypt; and the ten-year mean temperature is decreasing there.

Such a relationship was shown for 40 geographical locations by Wollin *et al* in 1973. This is rationally related to the Gothenberg event discussed before.

Comparing the increasing and decreasing field intensity (approximately 1600-year cycle) with the establishment of new dynasties in Egypt (see **Figure 3a**), and the same data smoothed (see **Figure 3b**), we can easily see that Egypt was less stable (i.e., had more dynasties when the intensity was high).

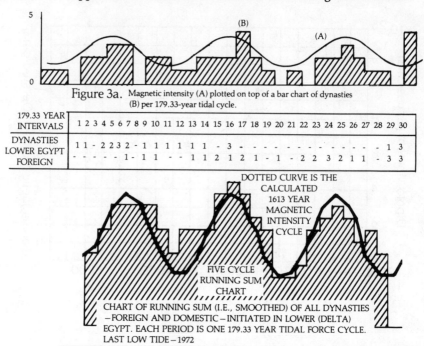

Figure 3a. Magnetic intensity (A) plotted on top of a bar chart of dynasties (B) per 179.33-year tidal cycle.

179.33 YEAR INTERVALS	1 2 3 4 5 6 7 8 9 10 11 12 13 14 15 16 17 18 19 20 21 22 23 24 25 26 27 28 29 30
DYNASTIES LOWER EGYPT	1 1 - 2 2 3 2 - 1 1 1 1 1 1 - 3 - - - - - - - - - - - - 1 3
FOREIGN	- - - - - 1 - 1 1 - - 1 1 2 1 2 1 - 1 - 2 2 3 2 1 1 - 3 3

DOTTED CURVE IS THE CALCULATED 1613 YEAR MAGNETIC INTENSITY CYCLE

FIVE CYCLE RUNNING SUM CHART

CHART OF RUNNING SUM (I.E., SMOOTHED) OF ALL DYNASTIES —FOREIGN AND DOMESTIC—INITIATED IN LOWER (DELTA) EGYPT. EACH PERIOD IS ONE 179.33 YEAR TIDAL FORCE CYCLE. LAST LOW TIDE—1972

BC / AD

3228 3048 2869 2690 2510 2331 2151 1972 1793 1614 1435 1255 1076 896 717 538 358 179 1 179 358 537 717 896 1075 1255 1434 1613 1792 1972 2151

Figure 3b. A five cycle (i.e., 5 x 179.33 = 900 years running sum of all dynasties founded in Lower Egypt—whether domestic or foreign. This smoothes the data which is seen listed above.

The relationship shown in **Figures 3a** and **3b** is obvious and large.

Another driving force periodicity has had its influence on Egyptian history, in addition to the two previously considered. Just as high and low tidal forces—almost certainly through climatic influence—were related to the establishment of dynasties, so the generally rising tidal forces had their influence. The tidal force in the higher latitudes increases with the alignment of the tilt of the earth's axis exactly in line with (either toward or away from) the line of closest approach of the earth to the sun; i.e., the perihelion.

Figure 4 shows the envelope of high tidal forces with each point on the curve being the highest force in any given 179-year period. The dotted curve shows the contribution made by the earth's precession.

Variations above and below the dotted curve have to do with eclipses, precession of the moon's orbit and alignment with the perihelion, etc. This variation, too, is cyclic.

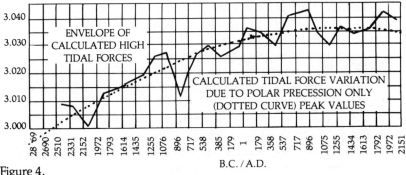

Figure 4.

Taking only the smooth precession tidal force, subtracting 3.000 from it (i.e., assuming a critical level of force as prerequisite to tidal triggering of volcanoes), and multiplying the remainder by the magnetic intensity curves shown in **Figures 3a** and **3b**, one obtains **Figure 5**. The bar graph in **Figure 5** shows dynastic data, and separates domestic from foreign established dynasties. A spectacular description of the occurrence of dynasties established by foreign invaders is thereby obtained.

Figure 5.

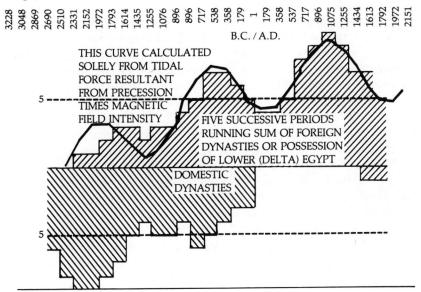

In summary, three physical forces have been found to describe dynastic history of Lower (Delta) Egypt to a surprising degree of accuracy. These are:

1. The 179.33-year tidal force beat;
2. The 1600-year westward precessing magnetic intensity field; and
3. The 20,100-year precession-induced high latitude tidal forces.

Perhaps as much as 90% of the long-term dynastic data of Lower Egypt is explained by these three forces.

The forces can be projected, and imply that Egypt has certainly not become a country with long-term political stability.

For a very long while to come, Egypt will be spending more time being ruled by foreigners than they will ruling themselves.

These calculations indicate that — at most — Man's effect on his history is much more tactical than strategic.

Barbara Bell [3] said:

"There can be little doubt that the climate of Egypt, with the normally dependable regularity in the seasonal flooding of the Nile, provided conditions uniquely suitable for the development of the concept of divine kingship. The predictability of natural conditions would readily inspire the people to believe any claims to magic powers and divinity that a king might make. [3]

The rise, decline and fall of the XVIII Dynasty (1570-1304 B.C.) was climate-related.

The Hyksos ("Shepherd Kings") who ruled Egypt during a confused time between about 1678 to 1570 B.C. (see Table I, this Appendix) were identified with the Israelites by Josephus (c. Apion. 1. 14). These Kings did not recognize the responsibility of the ruler for floods on the Nile. They did not, therefore, accept the traditional divine responsibility of the true Horus.

The times were severe with a minor Dark Age that corresponded to the Dark Age in the entire Mycenaean area. Only the Beaker people in England (Stonehenge) [4] and the Mayas were making great civilized constructs (dams, in the latter case) at the time.

The Nile had had great floods during the XII Dynasty [3] and had learned to thrive with them. Then the great floods ceased, and scarcity became relatively common. The Gods had deserted the people.

The significance of "Shepherd Kings" is that their God (in all probability Yahweh [i.e., Jehova]) was "the God of the Fields" — the "One God" — the "God of Abraham". Abraham, the Chaldean, was reputed to have lived in the period around 2000-1900 B.C. Thus Egyptians would have been exposed to the "One God" concept during the reign of the Hyksos.

It cannot be said to have been a pleasant experience, for tradition holds that the Hyksos were engaged in the systematic extirpation (extermination) of Egyptians when the latter overthrew the former.

A second, more pleasant exposure to the "One God" belief occurred over a hundred years later when Thutmes (Tutmosis) III extended the Empire by conquest. More than most rulers have done, he brought the ruling families of the Empire back to the capital, and had the children trained to serve the Empire's (i.e., Egypt's) needs and desires. Once more, and this time under much more favorable conditions, the Egyptians (or at least the "court") was subjected to a "One God" influence by the One God-worshipping royalty being trained and residing at the court.

It helps in understanding the times in which the One God was propounded by Aknaton to recognize the fact that Egypt in these times (the XVIII Dynasty, etc.) was mildly matriarchal (a basically warm-climate phenomenon). The line of inheritance of property—indeed, even the "crown"—passed only through women.

Women had enough power to destroy men—but not vice versa. It was in this context that Aknaton came upon the stage.

Tradition has it that Aknaton was hermaphroditic.

It is clear that he was pacifistic—apparently totally so; in any case, he and his court drank deeply from the cup of pacifism and mysticism; and consumed the vanishing substance of Empire while refusing to honor any violent step—however urgent—that would have prevented the Empire's death.

Aknaton was a co-ruler of Egypt at just the time that the "Ammon" (traditional Gods) influence was at the point of wielding great power. The priesthood was about to gain control over the throne.

How could a ruler best cope with this threat?

Establish a new religion and destroy the old, thereby eliminating the powers of the Priesthood!

And what new religion?

The Shepherd Kings had worshipped One God. They, of course, were overthrown. But at this very time, captive princes and princesses from the many lands of the Empire were being trained in the Imperial court. Among these were "Yahweh worshipping" Semites. The kids were well-behaved captives; so the One God was not a frightening concept.

Theirs was obviously a weak God, or His followers would not be captives—but the Sun was obviously above all. **That** was the One God of Aknaton. There could be no life without the Sun.

Small wonder that Amenhotep IV—the Great-Great-Grandson of

Thutmes III—chose the precept of One God (aton), and adopted the name Aknaton.

Small wonder that the Priests of Ammon (Amun) helped to overthrow the dynasty; and forced the boy-king—the son-in-law of the son-in-law of Aknaton—Tutankhaton to go back to the old capital and change his name to Tutankhamon. The boy never lived to his majority.

The struggle between Church and State continued.

The Priesthood was insatiably greedy. As a measure of the appetite of the priesthood when they had the situation under control about 200 years later: during the 31-year reign of Ramses III (1175 to 1144 B.C. [c]), according to Durant [6] p. 214; Ramses III gave to the priests:

32,000 kilograms of gold and one million kilograms of silver during his 31-year reign.

Cash flow (calculated [in U.S.A.] 11 / 20 / 79; Gold $389.00; Silver $16.23)

Gold, per year (1032.25 kg; 33,209.15 Troy oz.)	$12,918,359
Silver, per year (32,258.064 kg; 1,037,794 Troy oz.)	$16,843,396
Taxes from 169 towns in Egypt and Syria—calc. estimate	$21,125,000
Corn—185,000 sacks (Barley corn?)	$ 2,081,250
Cash flow—Per Annum	$52,960,000
Capital—	
Slaves—107,000 (calc. at $2500; av. 1979 prices)	$267,500,000
Cattle—500,000 (calc. at $500; av. 1979 prices)	$250,000,000
Land—750,000 acres (est. at $2500 / acre)	$1,875,000,000
(throw in structures)	
Total	$2,392,500,000
With no taxes, earnings should have been about 20% or:	$478,500,000
plus cash flow of	$ 52,963,000
Annual net	$531,468,000

The G.N.P. of the Egyptian Empire at that time can be guessed at about $200 per capita, population about 7,000,000; $1,400,000,000

The priesthood chewed up about 38% of the G.N.P.

Povertyville! It was enough to drive a king to outlawing the priesthood.

Finally, from 1150 to 1090 B.C.; the Priests, themselves, ruled Egypt; and were followed by a Dark Age.

For a brief moment, there was Camelot;* but as Camelot goes; so went Aknaton.

---

*The concept—Camelot—may be defined as:
Living up the profits of previous conquest and greatness, and doing nothing for the future.

Bibliography

APPENDIX III

[1] Pope, Maurice (1975) *The Story of Archaeological Decipherment*. Charles Scribner's Sons: New York.

[2] *Encyclopaedia Britannica* (1943) *Volume 22*: 634 — Tutankhamon. The University of Chicago.

[3] Bell, Barbara (1971) *op. cit.* I.B.: 9.

[4] Hawkins, Gerald S. (1965) *Stonehenge Decoded*. A Delta Book (Dell Publ. Co., Inc.): New York.

[5] Aharoni, Yohanan and Michael Avi-Yonah (1968) *The MacMillan Bible Atlas*. The MacMillan Company: New York.

[6] Durant, Will (1954) *The Story of Civilization*. I. Our Oriental Heritage. Simon and Schuster: New York.

Appendix IV

The Energy Budget and Mechanisms Available for Volcanic Modulation of Climate

Summary

In order for an Ice Age to be caused by volcanic dust veil, there must be a "...very direct..." mechanism and an adequate energy budget. Such a mechanism—tidal triggering of volcanoes (and earthquakes) is documented. Likewise, the energy budget is accounted for.

One mechanism must be detailed to achieve complete understanding of the process—namely, the transformation mechanism by which the energy budget is transformed to tectonic plate subduction, whence volcanoes are produced and complete the positive feedback cycle.

This essay addresses itself to the detailing of the missing transformation mechanism.

The Energy Budget and Mechanisms Available For Volcanic Modulation of Climate

Chappell [1] writes as follows: (Quote 1)

"...The overall conclusion is that mean rate of vulcanism may need to increase at least by 40% for glaciation to be initiated by dust veil effects within a period of a few thousand years."...

362

and: (Quote 2)

> "Vulcanism is concentrated along plate boundaries, especially sub-duction zones associated with major island areas and mountain chains..."

and: (Quote 3)

> "...The hypothetical variation in vulcanism thus requires that plate motion be modulated by energy inputs between 2×10^{18} and $> 10^{19}$ ergs / sec,..."

finally: (Quote 4)

> "...For there to be any connection between vulcanism and astronomi-cal motion, therefore, the mechanism must be very direct because there is little leeway in the energy budget. We seek a mechanism whereby ca. $\geq 10\%$ of the length of day variation energy periodically influences mean motion in the upper Mantle."

Responding to Quote 4 first:

1. A calculation of lunar-solar tidal stress at 60° North latitude was made. The envelope of highest tides is shown in **Figure 15**. In **Figure 1**, Appendix IV, the individual tidal forces (not the envelope) are plotted along with earthquake energy released.
2. Don L. Anderson [2] has shown that length of day variation coincided with a period of sharply-increased earthquake energy (see **Figure 15** in the "box").
3. Assembling **Figure 15** on a single time base shows that the great jump in earthquake energy, and change in Earth's rotation rate, coincide with the occurrence of the high tidal force in the northern hemisphere that occurred on 23.2 December 1893. This was — at 60°N., the highest vector sum high tidal force since 23.2 December 796 A.D. — 1097 years. (see **Figure 43A**)

   These two tidal forces were the highest in about 10,000 years.

   Judging from the fact that Anderson recorded an increased wobble after 1895, as well as increased earthquake energy, the tidal stress apparently insulted the Earth's crust.
4. Heaton (1975) [3] confirms tidal stress triggering:
   "Shallow oblique-slip and dip-slip earthquakes whose magnitude is greater than 5 appear to correlate with tidally-generated shear stresses which are sympathetic to failure."
   "...not...deeper than 30 km. ..."

2.A1

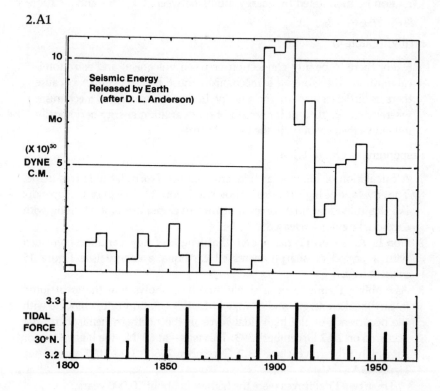

5. Johnston, M.J.S. and F.J. Mauk (1972) [4] showed that Earth tides have triggered Mt. Stromboli during this century; and Hamilton (II, Intro. [19] showed the phenomenon on a much broader scale in 1973.
6. Charlier [5] calculated orbital excentricity (sic) for a period from −300,000 to +100,000−using 1850.0 A.D. as the referent. Gow and Williamson [6] showed both vulcanism and low temperature at the time that Charlier's excentricity calculations indicated rising solar tides.
7. Hamilton and Seliga [7] show the relationship of temperature to vulcanism (see Sub-Appendix IV.B.)

Summarizing the response to Quote 4:
Tidal triggering of earthquakes is shown by the work at Cal. Tech., and the relationship of solar / lunar tidal stress, earthquakes and change of earth rotation is shown in **Figure 15**. Tidal triggering of volcanoes is shown by [4] and [7], and the relationship of volcanoes to temperature is shown in Sub-Appendix IV.B.

The qualitative relationships are therefore satisfied.

Responding now to Quote 3:

Flint [8] (p. 84-Table 4-E) shows the difference in volume of water tied up in ice is:

Today - 24.06 × 10^6 km³
Glacial Age - 71.36 × 10^6 km³
Water = (71.36 − 24.06) × 10^6 km³ = 47.3 × 10^6 cm³ = 4.73 × 10^{22} gm.

He points out that Antarctica and Greenland each gain only about 10% in ice because the ice "calves"−i.e., breaks off at the shore line. Thus, by examining the maps − **Figures 4 - 8** and **4 - 9** on pages 74 and 75 (in Flint's book) respectively, it can be conservatively estimated that the center of the differential ice mass is at about 60° latitude. (Closer and more detailed study [re: thickness] will undoubtedly show the mass at a higher latitude.)

Examination of a globe shows the ocean waters to have a mean latitude of ~ 35° latitude. (Detailed study will almost certainly show that the center of mass is at a lower latitude.)

The latitudes are, for purposes of this calculation, taken on the conservative side.

Mass transferred, Water to Ice = 4.73 × 10^{22} gm = m
Mean latitude of water removed = 35° lat.
Mean latitude of ice deposited = 60° lat.
Time of ice age cycle ≤ 100,000 years.
Velocity of a particle at the equator = .464 km / sec.

Velocity of a particle at 35° lat.

$$= (\cos 35) \times .464 = .380 \, \text{km/sec} = V_1 = .38 \times 10^5 \, \text{cm/sec}.$$

Velocity of a particle at 60° lat.

$$= (\cos 60°) \times .464 = .232 \, \text{km/sec}. = V_2 = .232 \times 10^5 \, \text{cm/sec}.$$

Kinetic energy per half-cycle (i.e., ice deposition)

$$= \tfrac{1}{2} m \, (V_1{}^2 - V_2{}^2) = \tfrac{1}{2} \times 4.73 \times 10^{22} \times .0906 \times 10^{10}$$
$$= 2.14 \times 10^{31} \, \text{ergs}$$

The full Ice Age cycle of ice deposition followed by ice melting is therefore:

K.E. Total $= 2 \times 2.14 \times 10^{31}$
$\qquad\qquad = 4.28 \times 10^{31} \, \text{ergs}$

The time of the cycle $\leq 100,000$ years

$$= 10^5 \times 365.2422 \times 24 \times 60 \times 60$$
$$= 3.15569 \times 10^{12} \, \text{seconds}$$

The available energy from the Ice Age water-ice cycle is, therefore:

$4.28 \times 10^{31} \, \text{ergs} / 3.15569 \times 10^{12} \, \text{sec}. = 1.3656 \times 10^{19} \, \text{ergs/sec}.$

Chappell's Quote 3 calls for between 2×10^{18} and 10^{19} ergs/sec. Thus, this process conservatively accounts for it.

There is not a steady ice deposition and melting — there is a lot of "backing-and-forthing", every episode of which contributes energy.

Summarizing the response to Quote 3:

The energy is very conservatively accounted for.

Responding now to Quotes 2 and 1:

Cailleux [9] (p. 84) estimates the thickness of the oceanic crust to be ≤ 7 km. and the mean sea water thicknesses 4.5 km. The oceanic crust density is 2.7 to 2.8 (*ibid.*, p. 92) — say 2.75.

When the water evaporates to transfer to continental ice caps, the "fluid" mantle (which has a viscosity $\sim 10^{23}$ times that of water [*ibid.*. p. 93]) flows out from under the "overloaded" continents, and floats up the "unloaded" ocean bottoms. With the density of the ocean bottoms about three times as great as the water they support, the ocean bottoms rise upward slowly about one-third as much as the thickness of the evaporated water that the oceans lost. This would have amounted to about:

Ocean bottom rise $= 130 / 2.75 = 47.3$ meters $= 4730$ cm.

through the process of "isotasy" — by which everything seeks its level.

The ocean bottom has at present, a radius calculable as follows:

Ocean Area $= 361.254 \times 10^6$ km^2 (12)
Ocean Volume $= 1.34 \times 10^9$ km^3
Ocean Depth $= 3.7119113$
                $= 371191.13$ cm
Radius to top of Ocean Crust $= 637,839,000 - 371191.13$ cm
                    $R_1 = 637,467,809$ cm
The isostatic lift $= 4730$ cm.,
Hence radius to the top of the Ocean Crust after isostasy:
  $R_2 = 637,467,809 + 4730$
     $= 637,472,539$ cm

When the oceans (which constitute 71% of the Earth's surface) rise 4730 cm, they expand (like an inflating balloon has an increasing surface area) by a total area of 5.09×10^{13} sq. cm. (5090 km^2).

The area of expansion divided by the length of subduction zones (given as 50,000 km by [1]) gives the centimeters which must be subducted upon subsequent melting.

Thus:

  $5.09 \times 10^{13} / 5 \times 10^9 = 10,800$ cm / cm length

This amount could be added to the normal ~ 5 cm / yr over a period of perhaps 3,000 to 5,000 years; i.e.,:

  $10,800 / 5000 \sim 2$ cm / yr.

during the period of melt, producing thereby a 40% modulation as called for in Quote 1.

The weight of the ice mass on Greenland and other places is causing the ice to flow radially outward with an enormous drag — which would tend to cause the area to "grow". Similarly, any continental mass which is being thrust outward by ice flow must have a tendency to grow and break up — as the islands off the northern coast of Canada may record.

Cailleux [9] estimates a population of 10,000 volcanoes, most of which Chappell [1] points out are along the subduction zones.

The mechanisms need detailed elucidation to show how the energy is used — vulcanism, earthquakes, heat, etc.

Bibliography

APPENDIX IV

[1] Chappell, J. (1973) Astronomical Theory of Climatic Change: Status and Problem. *Quaternary Research* 3: 221-236.

[2] Anderson, Don L. (1974) Earthquakes and the Rotation of the Earth. *Science* 186 : 49-50 (1974, 4 Oct.)

[3] Heaton, Thomas H. (1975) Tidal Triggering of Earthquakes. Contribution No. 2566, Division of Geol. and Planetary Sciences, Cal. Tech., Pasadena, Cal. 91125.

[4] Johnston, M.J.S. and F.J. Mauk (1972) Earth Tides and the Triggering of Eruptions from Mt. Stromboli, Italy. *Nature* 239 : 266-267 (29 Sept. 1972)

[5] Charlier, C.V.L. (1901) *Contributions to the Astronomical Theory of An Ice Age.*

[6] _____ (1972) Eruptions and Climate: Proof from an Icy Pudding. *New Scientist*: 17 Feb. 1972 : 367.

[7] Hamilton, Wayne L. and Thomas A. Seliga (1972) Atmospheric Turbidity and Surface Temperature on the Polar Ice Sheets. *Nature* 235 : 320-2 (11 Feb. 1972)

[8] Flint, Richard Foster (1971) *Glacial and Quaternary Geology.* John Wiley and Sons, Inc.: New York, London.

[9] Cailleux, André (1968) Trans. by J. Moody Stuart. *Anatomy of the Earth. World University Library.* McGraw Hill Book Co.: New York, Toronto.

[10] Milliman, John D. and K.O. Emery (1968) Sea Levels during the Past 35,000 Years. *Science* 162 : 1121-3 (6 Dec. 1968)

[11] Weast, Robert C. (Ed.) (1970) *Handbook of Chemistry and Physics.* The Chemical Rubber Co., 18901 Cranwood Pky., Cleveland, Ohio 44128.

SUB-APPENDIX IV. A. 1.

PEAK TIDES $\phi = -30°$

703	DEC	17.3	3.448
1110	DEC	20.3	3.448
871	DEC	19.8	3.447
1411	DEC	24.7	3.447
1579	DEC	28.1	3.447
1818	DEC	27.6	3.447
−5	DEC	9.0	3.446
13	DEC	19.3	3.446
296	DEC	12.4	3.446
1393	DEC	12.3	3.446
−412	DEC	5.0	3.445
−394	DEC	16.4	3.445
464	DEC	15.8	3.445
685	DEC	4.9	3.445
721	DEC	27.7	3.445
889	DEC	30.1	3.445
1128	DEC	30.6	3.445
1278	DEC	22.7	3.445
1561	DEC	16.8	3.445
1800	DEC	16.3	3.445
1986	DEC	31.1	3.445

PEAK TIDES $\phi = 0°$

−4257	SEP	24.3	3.467
−4425	SEP	20.9	3.465
−3912	SEP	21.2	3.465
−4089	SEP	28.7	3.464
−3868	SEP	15.8	3.464
−3337	SEP	29.5	3.464
−4195	SEP	29.3	3.463
−3700	SEP	20.3	3.463

PEAK TIDES $\phi = +30°$

796	DEC	23.2	3.452
1486	DEC	20.2	3.452
778	DEC	12.8	3.451
1203	DEC	27.2	3.451
−80	DEC	12.4	3.450
88	DEC	14.9	3.450
389	DEC	20.3	3.450
610	DEC	9.4	3.450
1017	DEC	12.3	3.450
1035	DEC	23.7	3.450
1185	DEC	15.8	3.450
1504	DEC	31.6	3.450
1893	DEC	23.2	3.450
1912	JAN	4.5	3.450

SUB-APPENDIX IV. A. 2.

PEAK TIDES $O = +60°$

796	DEC	23.2	3.042
1893	DEC	23.2	3.042
628	DEC	19.8	3.040
88	DEC	14.9	3.036
1318	DEC	16.8	3.036
1725	DEC	19.8	3.036
778	DEC	12.9	3.035
256	DEC	19.3	3.034
964	DEC	26.6	3.034
1486	DEC	20.2	3.034

Personal Communication from an Associate

B. 1.

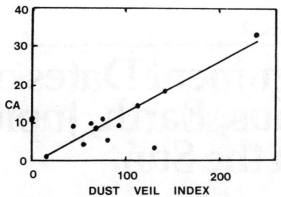

Since 1500, Calcium (CA) concentration
in Camp Century, Greenland ice cores
have correlated with the volcanic Dust
Veil Index.

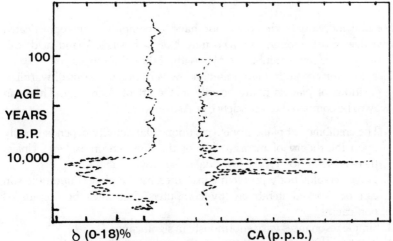

δ (O-18)%   CA (p.p.b.)

For near a 100,000-years, the change in Oxygen-18
concentration varied inversely with Calcium concentration in the ice core. Inasmuch as temperature of the world's atmosphere has been shown to
vary with change of oxygen-18; then it follows that
volcanic dust depresses temperature.
(from Hamilton and Seliga, *Nature* 235:320-2)

Appendix V

Alignment Dates of Venus, Earth, Jupiter and the Sun

For the individual who does not have a computer, or sophisticated knowledge of astronomy, but who may have a business (hand held) calculator, here are some numbers to play with, if the spirit moves you.

Please permit the authors to present a few very urgent words of warning. The positions of planets figure heavily in the art of Astrology. This is in no way to be compared to the science of Astronomy.

1. The credibility of planetary effects upon solar activity depends heavily upon the theory of metastability of the Sun's chromosphere. Unless there is metastability, the low tidal forces could do little.
2. The three-plus body problem constituted by the planets upon the sun can be worked iteratively by computers; but must be considered non-causal.
3. Simple resonances vary enormously in significance.
4. A total solution would show an **extremely** complex tidal force action on the sun.
5. A frequency analysis of the tidal-force envelope — which, alone, would contain the long-term frequencies — would show up completely unexpected interactive frequencies at amplitudes comparable to, or even larger than, simple resonant frequencies.
6. For beat frequencies to be real — i.e., to do work — something with

which the forces interact (example, chromosphere) must respond non-linearly. This, then, becomes another assumption piled on the assumed metastability of the chromosphere.*

It is far out scientific endeavour, indeed, to work with assumed characteristics of previously unproved assumptions.

The salient points are:

Jupiter produces its highest tidal force on the Sun when it is closest to the Sun (i.e., perihelion)—every round of its orbit in 11.862 years. Reference time at perihelion was 1928.1635196 A.D.

Earth and Venus line up with the Sun about every .799 years (alternately on the same or opposite sides of the Sun); and the Earth, Venus, and Sun lineup is at the same time that Jupiter is closest to the Sun and also in the same straight line once every 367.722 years.

Dates that all four line(d) up with Jupiter extremely near its orbital perihelion:

2117.9555 A.D.
1750.2335 A.D.

A period of 367.722 years, with a subsidiary basic periodicity of   71.180 years.

The period is 31 full periods of Jupiter, and 460 successive alignments of Venus and Earth with the Sun.

Start with the planets at Epoch 1925.000

Jupiter's position at Epoch	277° 6′ 16.69″ = 277.1046361°
Perihelion	13° 6′ 51.4″ = 13.1142778°
Sidereal Period	= 11.862 tropical years (of Earth)
Earth's position at Epoch	99° 38′ 33.06″ = 88.6425167°
Sidereal Period	= 365.246 solar days
Tropical Year	= 365.2422 solar days
Venus' position at Epoch	212° 10′ 10.23″ = 212.1695083°
Sidereal Period	= 224.701 solar days (of Earth)

Jupiter revolves about the Sun at the average rate of 0.0830928° / solar day;

Earth's rate = 0.9856371° / solar day; and

Venus' rate = 1.6021291° / solar day of Earth.

The above is where we novices get separated from the professionals;

---

*Some very competent astronomers have bumped our heads on this subject. Our earnest thanks to them.

because orbital ellipticity results in a variable rate of movement. Professionals will either laugh or wince at the multi-decimal precision with which the above calculation is done incorrectly.

Thus: Jupiter is at perihelion at 1928.1635196:

$$[(360 + 13.1142778) - 277.1046361]/0.0830928 = 1155.4509 \text{ days}$$
$$(1155.4509/365.2422) + 1925.000 = 1928.1635196 \text{ A.D.}$$

and this is the time of highest Jupiter tide on the Sun.

Venus and Earth aligned with the sun at 1926.0990551.
$$(360 + 99.6425167) + \times (.9856371) = 212.1695083 + \times (1/6021291)$$
$$\times = 247.436016/0.616492 = 401.42129$$
Venus-Earth-Sun alignment period (P) = 0.79939997 tropical years:
$$(1/P = 2/224.701 - 2/365.246);$$
(Okal and Anderson used P = .799).

Date (YEAR A.D.)	V-E alignments (from reference 1926.0990551)	Date (YEAR A.D.)	V-E alignments (from reference 1926.0990551)
1679.0615	−309.02351	1904.4395	−27.094245
1690.9235	−294.18521	1916.3015	−12.255863
1702.7855	−179.34674	1928.1635	2.582519
1714.6475	−264.50836	1940.0255	17.420901
1726.5095	−249.66998	1951.8875	32.259283
1738.3715	−234.83159	1963.7495	47.097665
1750.2335	−219.99321	1975.6115	61.936047
1762.0955	−205.15483	1987.4735	76.774429
1773.9575	−190.31645	1999.3355	91.612812
1785.8195	−175.47807	2011.1975	106.45119
1797.6815	−160.63968	2023.0595	121.28958
1809.5435	−145.80130	2034.9215	136.12796
1821.4055	−130.96292	2046.7835	150.96634
1833.2675	−116.12454	2058.6455	165.80472
1845.1295	−101.28616	2070.5075	180.64310
1856.9915	−86.447774	2082.3695	195.48149
1868.8535	−71.609393	2094.2315	210.31987
1880.7155	−56.771009	2106.0935	225.15825
1892.5775	−41.932627	2117.9555	235.99663

The 180-Year 'Wave' of Drought and Flood
That is Moving Westward Across North America

A climatic wave of drought followed by flood appears to sweep westward across the North American continent about every 800 years. At the latitude of the Colorado River Basin, the time required for the climatic wave to pass is about 180 years. The clearest description of this phenomenon was given by Schulman in 1958:

"Evidence is strong for the existence of a great 200-year wave in rainfall and runoff in the Colorado River Basin; the 1200's extraordinarily dry, the 1300's extraordinarily wet (more precisely, perhaps, 1215-1299 and 1300-1396). The droughts of the first interval and the floods of the second appear to have far exceeded in duration and intensity those recorded by modern gages."

The precipitation pattern in North America during the winter of 1976-1977, has the same structure described by Schulman; with the western U.S. and Canada drought-stricken, and eastern U.S. flooding. If this mean pattern now persists and moves westward slowly, then we should see the winter 1976-1977 pattern recurring again and again — each time about 0.225 degrees (about 11½ miles) per year farther west.

Question: Do you mean that the 180-year period of drought is beginning now 800 years after the last one was recorded?

Answer: Consider three points: First, the period of drought and flood was —all told—about 180 years, with about half each. That is what happened in the Colorado River Basin.

Second, Bryson showed that the Panhandle area of Texas and Oklahoma was occupied in that era by farming people who had abandoned the Iowa/Wisconsin/Minnesota area. The people had not arrived between 1180 and 1200 A.D., but **had** arrived by 1220 A.D. The western end of the Corn Belt changed to semi-arid climate, driving farmers out.

Third, the present period seems as severe as the period in the 1200's.

The present climatic fluctuation was best described by Schulman:

"Comparison of growth fluctuations in recent decades with those for the past several centuries suggests that in many areas of the West the interval since 1870 or so has been one of decidedly abnormal climate. The present climatic fluctuation has taken the form of a major drought in recent decades over much of the West; it is pronounced in the Colorado River Basin and particularly in southern Arizona. In the latter region the drought began in 1921, has been broken in very few years, and appears to be the most severe one since the late 1200's."

"The evidence is very strong that the present fluctuation represents, in terms of centuries-long dendroclimatic data, a major disturbance in the general circulation, at least over western North America."

This says that the next great drought is under way in the Colorado River Basin.

Q: So the wave is a relatively brief severe change which is followed by a long period with less change?

A: Yes.

Q: You are thinking of explaining this event in terms of variation of the magnetic field?

A: Yes. There is a mass of evidence from a great number of scientific papers concerning the earth's magnetic field that shows that the North magnetic pole, which is about 73° North latitude, is precessing westward around the north geographic pole. It probably goes around in about 1600 years.

The inclination of the magnetic field is sort of elliptically shaped, and lies across the arctic to one side of the north geographic pole. There is a zone of high intensity around the North magnetic pole northwest of Hudson's Bay, and another high intensity zone across the north geographic pole over eastern Siberia.

Since the magnetic pole precesses around the geographic pole every 1600 years, one end or the other of the magnetic field sweeps past any one geographic point every 800 years.

Q: What do you know about the mechanism?

A: We know more than we understand. There appears to be something about solar winds that causes a persistent high pressure ridge that lies on top of the high intensity magnetic field. This is not clearly understood, but several things could be at work. The solar winds do constitute the aurora; might nucleate high thin clouds which we know to occur; might produce ozone which we know to be concentrated over the magnetic high intensity field. We do know that the high intensity zone is over eastern Canada and the eastern U.S., and that the eastern U.S. has lost about 3 percent of its sunlight in the last 20 years.

Comment: The aurora has a large heating effect which would also play some part in the production and / or maintenance of the high atmospheric pressure ridge.

Response: Yes. If you will look at **Figures 1** and **2**, you will see the similarity of the high atmospheric pressure zone to the isoinclination lines of the earth's magnetic field.

Fig. 1 Earth's Magnetic Field   Fig. 2 Atmospheric Pressure

Q: The whole pattern rotates, does it?

A: Yes. In 1600 years.

Q: Is there a similarly-shaped field in the southern hemisphere?

A: No. This is a uniquely northern hemisphere pattern and phenomenon.

Q: What hard data do you have to show the actual rotation of this magnetic pattern, in addition to very short-term trends?

A: The best data that I know of is this plot from a paper by Ring and Webb in a 1975 NASA publication. It shows that the earth's magnetic inclination varies with about an 800-year period; which can be visualized as the rotation of an elliptical field. The temperature at a nearby point varied with the same 800-year period.

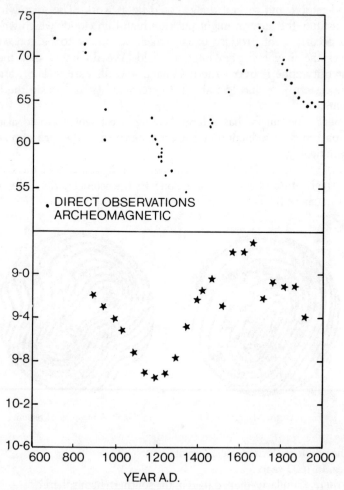

Fig. 3 Upper section: magnetic inclination at Paris since 700 A.D. (after Thellier, 1970). Lower section: average temperature in central England since 900 A.D. (after Lamb, 1966).

The fact that the pattern is moving from east to west is illustrated by the plot from Wollin *et al* (1973), which shows a magnetic field reversal occurring sequentially from Egypt, Sweden, Scotland and Greenland.

The plot is really not as simple to interpret as it might appear at first, because the observing stations are at different latitudes, and the field has a "twisted" configuration. (see **Figure 4**)

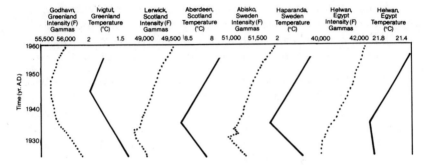

Fig. 4 Annual means of magnetic intensity (*F*) at individual observatories correlated with the 10-yr. means of air temperature from nearby weather stations. Opposite trends in intensity and climate can be observed for different parts of the northern hemisphere.

Q: The thing that bothers me is that the disturbance is only 180 years. Why does it occur in such a relatively short time and then stay steady for so long?

A: Probably because this datum is from the Colorado River Basin, which is so far south that it would be unaffected except when the magnetic field elliptical pattern is pointed almost at the basin.

Q: Do you have any data taken north or south of the Colorado River Basin?

A: Yes. North first. In Western Nebraska, there have been many droughts documented with tree-rings. The longest period between droughts was a 68-year period centering around 1348 which was the **same year** as the center of the wet period which was identified in the Colorado River Basin data.

Q: And south of the Colorado River Basin?

A: This is harder to convey.

In the Valley of Mexico, archeological studies show that areas under agriculture are typified by structures called *chinampas*, which were described in 1599 as follows:

> "...they make garden plots...carrying, in canoes, sod cut in the mainland, to heap it up in shallow waters, thus forming ridges from...(about 2.52 to 3.36 meters)...wide and raised...(about 0.42 meters)...above the water; a farm has many of these ridges, and the farmers circulate in their canoes between them to tend the crops." [from **de Vargos Machuca** (1519) via Armillas (1971)]

The water level was too high for such *chinampa* construction between A.D. 1 and A.D. 1200. Standing ponds spread and coalesced to form a large lagoon that completely filled the bottom of the basin. After this long delay, the *chinampas* were expanded during the 1200's by the Toltecs. This expansion could have occurred only if a period of relative drought reduced the lake so that it was shallow enough to be reclaimed.

The Aztecs were wanderers from about 1168 to 1319 after which they established their residence in Chapultepec. During the 1300's (when flooding was occurring in the Colorado Basin to the north) the Aztecs conquered the Valley of Mexico - being forced to abandon some battles, it is said, because they could not find the enemy in the snow. The weakening of the Toltecs is what would be expected of a farming society whose lands were flooded with the result that the agricultural base was wiped out.

> "The data conclusively show that the peak of *chinampa* expansion was attained during A.D. 1400 to 1600." [Armillas (1971)]

In brief, the Valley of Mexico was unusually dry in the 1200's when there was concurrent drought in Nebraska and the Colorado River Basin, and such sites as Mesa Verde and Chaco Canyon were abandoned. The Valley of Mexico was flooded in the 1300's when Nebraska was wet and the Colorado River Basin was flooded.

The great drought of the 1870-plus period which Schulman points out is coincident with droughts in Nebraska; and Lake Texcoco in the Valley of Mexico has actually gone dry. There is good reason to expect that the wet wave will follow.

If the wet wave comes and refills the lake, there are two additional matters of interest:

1. Mexico City has been built in the old lake bed, and
2. Underground water has been withdrawn to such an extent that the ground level has sunk 10 to 30 feet.

My thought is that among many other interesting climatic happenings that will accompany the wave of drought and flood, it is probable that some people now living will see the bulk of Mexico City 10 to 30 feet deep in water. Some fifteen million people now live in the city and its suburbs.

Iben Browning is an escaped South Texas cotton farmer, born in 1918 in Vanderbilt, Texas. He has stated, "I consider that going off to get an education, being a pilot, working in the horrible weapons business, and taking terrible risks of other sorts have all simply been excuses to get out of chopping cotton."

"Going off to get an education" included a B.S. from Southwest Texas State Teachers College in Physics, Mathematics, and Education; an M.A. from the University of Texas in Zoology (Physiology), Physics, and Bacteriology, and a Ph.D. in Zoology (Physiology), Genetics and Bacteriology.

Iben's additional education in a great variety of military and technical schools included such skills as learning to fly military aircraft and studying the effects of atomic weapons.

This has enabled him to hold 66 patents, publish approximately three dozen scientific papers, and write three books — including **Climate and the Affairs of Men** and **Robots on Your Doorstep (A Book About Thinking Machines)** — both co-authored with Nels Winkless III.

A sampling of fields in which Iben currently acts as a consultant to some major organizations include: bioengineering, computers, electronics, environmental systems and resources, information theory, microbics, microminiaturization, optics, space navigation and — of course — climate.

Evelyn M. Browning Garriss, daughter of Iben and Florence Browning, is a graduate of the University of California at Santa Barbara, with a B.A. in Anthropology and History. She has taught Anthropology, Archaeology, Civics, Economics, U.S. History, Russian History and Far Eastern Cultures for the past nine years.

She co-authored a publication, **Climate and Aggression,** and is currently working on her doctorate in Quantitative History at the University of New Mexico.